paddling washington

paddling
washington

Flatwater and Whitewater
Routes in Washington State
and the Inland Northwest

Rich Landers, Dan Hansen,
Verne Huser, and Doug North

THE MOUNTAINEERS BOOKS

THE MOUNTAINEERS BOOKS
is the nonprofit publishing arm of The Mountaineers Club, an organization founded in 1906 and dedicated to the exploration, preservation, and enjoyment of outdoor and wilderness areas.

1001 SW Klickitat Way, Suite 201, Seattle, WA 98134

First edition, 2008

Manufactured in the United States of America

Project Editor: Annabel Cassam
Copy Editor: Jane Crosen
Cover and Book Design: The Mountaineers Books
Layout: Mayumi Thompson
Cartographer: Blue Mammoth Design
All photos by the authors unless otherwise noted.

Cover photograph: © Veer.com
Frontispiece: *Autumn paddlers take a break upstream from the Rodeo Hole. (Kathy Spencer photo)*

Library of Congress Cataloging-in-Publication Data
Paddling Washington / by Rich Landers . . . [et al.]. — 1st ed.
    p. cm.
  Includes bibliographical references and index.
  ISBN 978-1-59485-056-1 (alk. paper)
  1. Canoes and canoeing—Northwest, Pacific—Guidebooks. 2. Kayaking—Northwest, Pacific—Guidebooks. 3. Canoes and canoeing—Washington (State)—Guidebooks. 4. Kayaking—Washington (State)—Guidebooks. 5. Canoes and canoeing—British Columbia—Guidebooks. 6. Kayaking—British Columbia—Guidebooks. 7. Northwest, Pacific—Guidebooks. 8. Washington (State)—Guidebooks. 9. British Columbia—Guidebooks. I. Landers, Rich, 1953-
GV776.N76P35 2007
917.9504—dc22
                                    2007038021

♻ Printed on recycled paper

contents

WESTERN WASHINGTON PADDLE ROUTES

North Puget Sound

South Puget Sound

Olympic Peninsula

Southwest Washington

NORTHERN CASCADES PADDLE ROUTES

INLAND NORTHWEST PADDLE ROUTES

Eastern Washington

12 "CHOICE" WHITEWATER RUNS FOR PADDLERS

APPENDICES

LEGEND

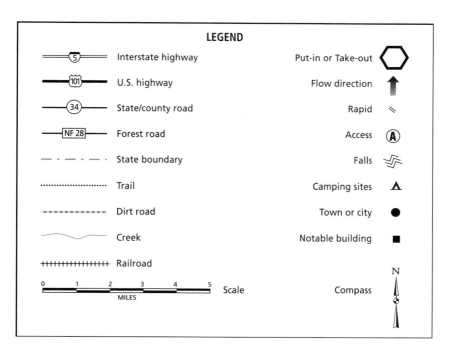

═══⟨5⟩═══	Interstate highway	Put-in or Take-out	⬡
──⟨101⟩──	U.S. highway	Flow direction	⬆
──⟨34⟩──	State/county road	Rapid	≋
─[NF 28]─	Forest road	Access	Ⓐ
— · — · — ·	State boundary	Falls	⟰
··············	Trail	Camping sites	⏶
▪▪▪▪▪▪▪▪▪▪	Dirt road	Town or city	●
～～～	Creek	Notable building	■
+++++++++++++	Railroad		

0 1 2 3 4 5 Scale
MILES

N
Compass

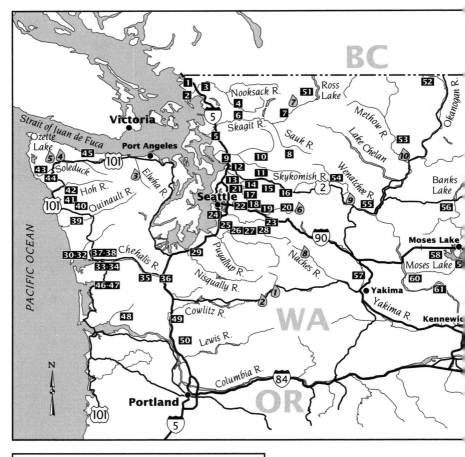

BC

Ross Lake
Nooksack R. 51 52
Okanogan R.
Methow R.
Strait of Juan de Fuca
Victoria
Skagit R.
Sauk R.
Lake Chelan 53
10
Ozette Lake
Port Angeles
Soleduck
Elwha R.
Hoh R.
Ouinault R.
Skykomish R. 54
Wenatchee R. 55
Banks Lake
Seattle
56
Chehalis R.
Puyallup R.
Naches R.
Nisqually R.
Moses Lake
Moses Lake
Yakima
Yakima R.
Kennewic
Cowlitz R.
WA
Lewis R.
Columbia R.
Portland
OR
PACIFIC OCEAN
N

MILES
0   100

28 Paddling Trip
11 Whitewater Trip

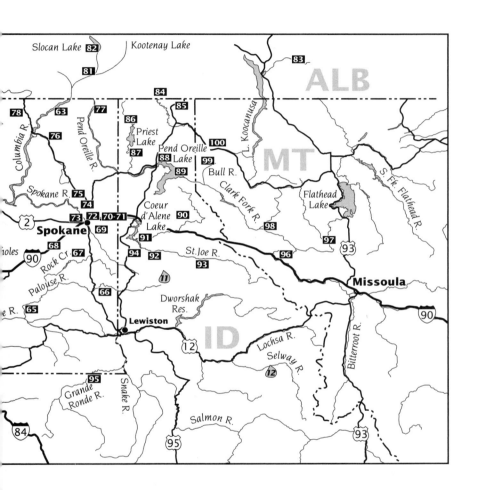

preface: 3 books in 1

Proposals that have surfaced in the State Legislature were only half-hearted, but Washington could indeed be cleanly divided into two distinct states: one comprised of the heavily populated, damp, and saltwater-influenced region west of the Cascades, the other encompassing the sparsely populated, drier, and more wide-open farm and ranch lands of eastern Washington and beyond to the mountains of Montana.

Similarly, rafters and paddlers see clear distinctions in the region's waters, depending on where the streams tumble out of the mountains or whether they flow into the Columbia River, into Puget Sound, or directly into the Pacific Ocean. The West Side streams tend to be more developed, often influenced in the lower reaches by tides and frequented by salmon and steelhead. The waters of eastern Washington and the rest of the Inland Northwest tend to be less developed and more inviting to campers and trout or smallmouth bass.

In addition, whitewater roars and rumbles down the mountains east and west of the Cascades, giving the region a third dimension to the paddler's eye.

Until this book was published, these distinctive waters were largely covered only in three separate guides published by The Mountaineers Books:

- *Paddle Routes of Western Washington,* by Verne Huser, who forgot more about paddling and poling techniques in his first forty years as a professional river guide than most paddlers will learn in a lifetime.
- *Paddle Routes of the Inland Northwest,* by Rich Landers and Dan Hansen, two Spokane outdoorsmen and journalists who apply a reporter's nose for detail to chronicling their many field adventures in eastern Washington, northern Idaho, and western Montana as well as southern British Columbia and northeastern Oregon.
- *Washington Whitewater,* by Doug North, a river-running veteran and Seattle judge who takes every whitewater river description as seriously as a life-or-death sentence. While *Washington Whitewater* is geared primarily to rafters, he has selected ten trips for this book that are appealing to skilled canoe paddlers. (Dan Hansen has added two additional whitewater trips from the Inland Northwest.)

The book you're holding in your hands compiles into one volume the best of these three reputable guides geared specifically for paddlers, plus the fruits of additional reconnaissance.

Washington's east and west sides hang together because regional diversity is good for a state's bottom line. This book has come together because exploring a wide range of waters is good for the river-runner's soul, not to mention the pulse rate of the flatwater enthusiast.

There's a wealth of water to cover here, so start paddling.

acknowledgments

For western Washington coverage, Verne Huser offers special thanks to Vicki Adams, Marcy Allen, Jim Ballou, Bob Berry, Vivian Blossom, Mike Bozanich, Charles Brennick, Brad Cameron, Kim Cooke, Tom and Debbie Cox, Kathy Dickson, John Evans, Paul Florek, Caycee Furluie, Mark Grabski, Heidi Hackler, Captain Kirk Hackler, Dan Henderson, Jonathon Hurd, Willa Huser, Paul and Kathy Jones, Stephanie Jones, Gary Korb, Chris Lewis, Pete McCleod, Amy and Jeff Margolis, Anna Matsche, Roger Michel, Herbie Meyer, Lee Moyer, Kelsey Mydske, Jennifer Owen, David Paola, Mark Parker, Gary Peterson, Robert Michael Pyle, Theo Pyle, Gary Ralstin, Don Rice, Tim Ricketts, Debbie Shaner, Ty Tice, Hiltrud Verdier, Michael Villella, Ginny and Terry Walker, and Victoria Walters.

For Inland Northwest coverage, Rich Landers and Dan Hansen offer thanks to members of the Spokane Canoe & Kayak Club, with special thanks to Brian Burns and Jean and Kevin Dragon; Brad and Debbie Summers, Doris Albert, Gerhardt Glaas, Jim Gillman, Bill Demchuk, and Gordon Silverthorne, as key contacts for British Columbia; plus additional home-waters expertise from Richard and Kathy Spencer, Dick Roberts, and Rick Gren.

For Washington whitewater coverage, Doug North offers special thanks to John Garren and Professor Joel M. Andress, and his geography students at Central Washington University.

Finally, the U.S. Geological Survey Water Resources staffers throughout the region, plus our friends and families, get a tip of the hat from all four authors.

introduction

The 120-some great paddling trips featured here are not the only routes to be found in the huge watersheds of Washington and the Inland Northwest. Washington alone is covered by more than 4700 square miles of water, and that leaves a lot of room for discovery. Consider these routes the authors' favorites, the ones that have passed muster with our most honest and ruthless critics—our friends and families.

Along the way we've learned that popular canoeing and kayaking waters can change from serene to wicked as quickly a raccoon surprised by a stray dog. That much you should know before you read another word of this book. This is a guide to a watery world with countless variables. You are the ultimate judge.

HOW TO USE THIS GUIDEBOOK

Don't take shortcuts! Read the introductory material in this book before focusing solely on the individual trip descriptions. Essential warnings, explanations, and information are presented in this introduction so they don't have to be repeated for multiple trips.

Individual trip descriptions follow a format that offers a wealth of information at a glance, a text full of details, and sources for further information. The twelve whitewater trips have added information topics.

Here's how the trips are described under the name of the designated water.

In the information block:

Location. Gives the general area of the trip or specific stretch of stream described.

Distance. Indicates length of trip in miles. As a navigation aid, most of the trip narratives and maps in this book refer to "river miles" (RM), which are measured from the river mouth.

Paddle time. Also known as "river time," paddle time indicates the average time you can expect to be on the water, minus time taken for stops. References to "several days" or "overnight" identify trips particularly suitable for camping.

Season. Suggests months the waters generally are free of ice or have sufficient water for paddling. Be aware that variables in weather and flows can make waters unsafe for paddlers for periods during the floating season. Each of the twelve featured whitewater trips also includes a graph that correlates recommended flow levels with the season.

Rating. Offers a general and subjective guide to the difficulty of the trip and the

Opposite: The bushwhacking required to float the Colville River was a factor authors considered in leaving the trip out of this book.

skills required, based on six classifications under the Safety Code of the American Whitewater Affiliation. See details on each classification below under "River and Water Classifications."

Hazards. Highlights some of the predictable dangers a paddler should be prepared to encounter.

Elevation (for whitewater trips). Shows the elevation at start and finish plus the average drop per mile (gradient), particularly useful in judging and comparing whitewater runs.

Shuttle. Indicates the traveling distance and conditions for getting vehicles to put-ins and take-outs if applicable.

Flow information. Lists the source for flow information; refer to Appendix B for the telephone number and/or website to get current streamflow data or lake/tidewater levels. For flowing streams, government gauging instruments generally measure river levels (flows) in cubic feet per second (cfs); for pool elevations on dammed lakes and tidewater, water levels are measured in feet, either from sea level or from a designated point on the river bed.

River gauge. Lists the official river gauge number if available. (Gauges are not installed on all rivers.)

Historic flows. Gives a summary of U.S. Geological Survey statistics on the minimum, maximum, and average flows in cubic feet per second (cfs) for this section of water. *(Note:* Canadian gauges record flows in cubic meters per second. To convert Canadian readings to cfs, multiply the metric flow by 35.)

Lake levels. Lake pool level information is substituted for flow information when applicable, measured in feet above sea level.

In the text:

Introduction. Highlights the trip.

Access. Details driving directions to the put-ins and take-outs. (Highways are abbreviated I for interstate, US for federal highway, SR for State Route, and FR for Forest Service Road.)

Paddle Route. The authors' on-the-water observations, including details about flows, landmarks, geology, historic events, flora and fauna, hazards, campsites, and options for shortening or lengthening the trip. Many trip descriptions refer to "river miles," which are measured from the river mouth. This information helps paddlers on tributaries determine how far they are, say, from the confluence with a main stem river. RMs are particularly useful to western Washington paddlers who can use the numbers to gauge how close they are to tidewater. RMs are less important to inland paddlers, and the waypoints are not even listed by the U.S. Geological Survey or Canadian ministries for many streams.

Maps. U.S. Geological Survey (USGS) topo maps, National Oceanic and Atmospheric Administration (NOAA) charts, and other useful maps specific to this trip.

Information. Helpful contacts that might include agencies, groups, and businesses offering current information. Refer to Appendix B for the telephone numbers and/or websites for these sources, listed in alphabetical order.

On the trip map:

The maps for each trip in this book are helpful in locating access points, reference points, notable river features, and some hazards. They are intended to enhance but not replace the information provided on USGS topo maps, NOAA charts (especially good for coastal areas), Canadian topos, or special maps such as those noted at the end of each trip description. The DeLorme *Atlas & Gazetteer* for states covered in this book are helpful for getting to access points on any of the trips. Similarly, the *Backroad Mapbook: Kootenays,* by Russell and Wesley Mussio (Mussio Ventures), is helpful for finding road access to waters in southeastern British Columbia. (*Note:* Especially in Western Washington access routes are constantly evolving because of development.)

Online and digital map sources, such as Google Earth and TopoUSA, are great tools for trip planning and mapping. Beware, however, that home printers tend to print on paper that's too small and with ink that smears when wet. Sources for maps are listed in Appendix D.

RIVER AND WATER CLASSIFICATIONS

Rafters, canoeists, and kayakers judge individual rapids and stretches of river according to the International Scale of River Difficulty outlined in the Safety Code of the American Whitewater Affiliation. Serious whitewater paddlers should study the entire text of the scale, which is available with other safety information on the American Whitewater website (see Appendix E).

Following is a summary of the scale of river difficulty plus classifications for other waters as used in this book:

Flatwater. Little to no current, no unavoidable obstructions. Wind and possibly other boats are the main variables to consider.

Tidal flatwater. Waters that include tidal influence, which means the water can flow in opposite directions with the incoming and outgoing tides, sometimes with powerful current. Wind and possibly other boats are other main variables to consider.

Class 1. Moving water with some riffles and small waves. Few or no obstructions. Correct course easy to find. *Note: Serious hazards may be present in some conditions.*

Class 2. Generally easy rapids for paddlers with intermediate or better technique with waves up to 3 feet, and wide, clear channels that are obvious without scouting. Skills to do some maneuvering are required.

Class 3. Rapids with high, irregular waves often capable of swamping an open canoe. Narrow passages that may be difficult to read, often requiring complex

Hangman Creek, minus 24 degrees, February 3, 1996

Hangman Creek, 47 degrees, February 7, 1996

Paddlers must be prepared to evaluate water conditions that can change quickly and unpredictably. To illustrate the point, check out these two photos, taken just four days apart on Hangman (Latah) Creek upstream from High Bridge Park. (Chris Kopczynski photos)

maneuvering. Requires scouting from shore, spray covers on canoes, and skills for maneuvering and catching powerful eddies.

Class 4. (Not suitable for open canoes.) Long, difficult rapids with constricted passages that often require precise maneuvering in very turbulent waters with strong hydraulics. Scouting from shore is necessary, and conditions make rescue difficult. Boaters in covered canoes and kayaks should have the ability to Eskimo roll. Lining may be necessary.

Class 5. Extremely difficult, long, and very violent rapids that should always be scouted from shore and tackled only by experts.

Class 6. Difficulties of Class 5 carried to the extreme of navigability and beyond the scope of this book.

Also in this book:

Tidal, open ocean. Saltwater routes that can be calm and easy flatwater at one moment, but always susceptible to strong tidal influence, rip-currents, high waves, wind, and ship traffic.

Defying Classification

Classifying waters, especially rapids, is subjective and variable in changing river conditions. One rapid can wash out and disappear in high water while another becomes fiercer in higher flows. Minor whitewater can become a major hazard if strainers or other new obstructions are added. There is no shame in portaging around a Class 2 rapid or obstruction if the paddler is uncomfortable running the stretch—in fact, only a fool would proceed with such reservations.

Whitewater is only one indication of a trip's difficulty. When selecting a trip, paddlers should carefully and honestly consider their ability, their familiarity with the water, and the quality of boats and safety equipment available to them. Remote trips must be judged more cautiously than those close to home and emergency assistance.

"Rule of 100." Trips should be judged one class level more difficult than normal if the water and air temperature added together is 100°F or colder. (Remember, too, that wet suits or dry suits are recommended in cold air or water temperatures.)

BASIC PADDLING SAFETY
Top Ten Elements

1. **Wear a life jacket at all times.** The number one cause of death on the nation's waterways is failure to wear a life jacket, aka personal flotation device (PFD). Good-quality modern life jackets (Coast Guard–approved Type III or V) are comfortable, fashionable, and effective when worn.

2. **Never boat a river beyond your ability.** Size up a river and the current conditions to your abilities, craft, load, and rescue scenario before you put in. Factor the power of the river's flow on that particular day into every decision. If just one rapid in a long stretch is beyond your skill level, you

must be able to safely line or portage around it. Otherwise, look for another trip until you've upgraded your skills. Also, consider enrolling in a paddling class taught by a local club, shop, or recreation agency.

3. **Never boat rivers flowing at dangerously high levels.** Heavy flows reduce the time to make important decisions and gain access to shoreline and safe eddies, while increasing river hydraulics to deadly forces.

4. **Be wary of hypothermia.** A wet suit or dry suit is mandatory equipment on most Washington whitewater rivers during prime river-running seasons, especially those flowing from ice or snowmelt. Flatwater paddlers must consider dry suits in some conditions or at least waterproof shells over fleece layers.

   The shock of being dumped into cold water can render you helpless immediately. Hypothermia can otherwise eliminate your ability to swim in as little as 3 minutes. Death can come in as little as 10 minutes when immersed in water colder than 40 degrees. Even if you never capsize, the splash of water from rapids or cool, damp weather can lead to hypothermia's chilling effects on muscle function and decision making.

   Tip: Bring a dry bag with, at the least, a spare dry top layer.

5. **Paddle with a trained, organized group.** The emphasis of this warning and the number of watercraft that should be involved increases with the risks and difficulty of the trip. Always go with at least one other boat (preferably at least three), and stay together. (For a list of paddling groups and contacts, see Appendix E.)

6. **Be wary of natural river hazards.** Sweepers and strainers are downed trees and brush in the river. Boaters forced into these obstacles can be snagged or pinned underwater by the force of the flow through the limbs and debris. Logjams can range from minor obstructions to death traps. Even slow-moving, shallow water can push distracted paddlers into troublesome snags or wrap a boat around an otherwise avoidable obstruction.

   Note: Every high-water event has the potential to reroute or decorate the river landscape.

7. **Be wary of man-made river hazards.** Dams, weirs, fences, and bridge abutments are examples of obstructions that can present serious danger. Certain weirs can cause deadly "keeper" hydraulics in a drop of as little as 2 feet. Unwary or unskilled boaters taking the wrong line can be quickly pinned along with their boats, possibly underwater, by the force of the flow against bridge abutments and other obstacles.

8. **Consider wearing a helmet.** A good idea in any river with rapids, wearing a helmet is mandatory in whitewater situations.

9. **If you capsize or get ejected from the craft.** Stay calm. Let your PFD keep you afloat. Keep your feet at the surface facing downstream and scull (as you would if sitting in an inner tube) as you work quickly toward safety, whether it's back into a boat or to shore and out of the grip of

In cool weather, even for short floats, paddlers should carry extra clothing in a dry bag.

hypothermia. Look downstream for obstacles such as logjams, rocks, sweepers, souse holes, or strong "keeper" eddies—and try to avoid them. Do not let yourself get pinned between a boat and an obstacle. Do not put your feet down on the bottom in current. If a foot becomes entrapped in rocks, the force of the current can bend you over and hold you underwater. Water temperature and river conditions dictate whether you stay with your boat, seek a rescue boat (see No. 5), or beat it to shore.

21

10. **Never use drugs or alcohol while paddling rivers or lakes.** Imbibe only at the end of the day, when travel in boats and vehicles is done.

ESSENTIAL BOATING EQUIPMENT

An in-depth discussion of boating craft and equipment is beyond the scope of this guidebook (see the checklists in Appendix A), but a few items are worth emphasizing. Always consider the need for bow and stern lines (painters), throw ropes, bailing pumps or buckets, spray skirts and covered canoe decks, extra paddles or oars, dry bags, and water filters. Everything that goes in or on a boat must be attached in a manner that will not entangle boaters should the boat capsize.

Whitewater rafts should have multiple chambers so flotation is maintained if one chamber is deflated.

Canoeists paddling Class 2 or higher waters should give attention to flotation bags that can be installed to displace water that comes into the boat while running rapids. A canoe filled with air is much more maneuverable than one filled with water. Also, a boat equipped with flotation bags is much easier to rescue and right, should it capsize.

THE TEN ESSENTIALS: A SYSTEMS APPROACH

Following is the revised version of the Ten Essentials that one should carry for safety and for emergencies, in watercraft or otherwise. The Ten Essentials have evolved from a list of individual items to a list of functional systems. The classic list has been expanded in the systems approach to include hydration and emergency shelter.

1. Navigation (map and compass)
2. Sun protection (sunglasses and sunscreen)
3. Insulation (extra clothing)
4. Illumination (headlamp or flashlight)
5. First-aid supplies
6. Fire (firestarter and matches/lighter)
7. Repair kit and tools (including knife)
8. Nutrition (extra food)
9. Hydration (extra water)
10. Emergency shelter
        —*The Mountaineers*

ESSENTIAL SKILLS

While virtually anybody can paddle a canoe, the ranks are considerably more exclusive when it comes to paddling efficiently, keeping a straight course, and turning with precision.

Teaching paddling techniques is beyond the scope of this book. Consider the following an introduction on the most basic techniques a paddler should know before tackling many of the trips described here. Knowing the basics of paddling proficiency will add to your range of trips and make paddling more fun while adding an extra margin of safety. Don't let ego get in the way of buying a good instruction manual or, better yet, taking lessons from a teacher or club (see Appendix E)—even if you once survived a summer-camp canoe trip. As one Spokane paddling instructor said, "I did a lot of canoe trips before I went to instructor school and found out how little I knew."

Different strokes work for different folks, but some strokes work better than others. Every tandem canoeist should learn these basic techniques and the subtle hand twists and body English that make them sing:

Power forward stroke. Bend and reach forward for a short stroke that includes slight torso rotation so your arms don't do all the work. Don't bring the paddle back too far behind your hip, or the paddle starts to drag and turn instead of applying strict forward propulsion.

Hut and switch. Tandem-canoe racers and power paddlers can improve efficiency by simultaneously snapping paddles to opposite sides every two to eight strokes (the rear paddler can call "hut" when needed) in order to maintain a straight course while both paddlers apply full forward power to each stroke.

Practice surfing waves (above) and catching eddies to develop paddling skills while having fun.

J stroke. Recreational paddlers, however, can enjoy a more leisurely paddling cadence and avoid switching sides if the stern paddler uses a J stroke—a slight twist and outward thrust of the paddle at the end of the stroke—to correct the course of the canoe.

Draw. A maneuvering stroke, the draw involves reaching the paddle out perpendicular to the boat and, keeping the paddle almost vertical, pulling water back toward the canoe.

Pry. The maneuvering counterpart of the draw, the pry involves jamming the paddle blade slightly under the canoe and parallel to the keel, and then pulling the top of the paddle back toward the boat, using the hull and gunwale of the canoe as a fulcrum to pry the paddle and push water away from the boat.

Sweep. Reach forward and pull the paddle blade in an arc away and then back toward the boat as it comes behind the paddler. Sweeping on the right side will turn the boat to the left while maintaining forward propulsion.

Backpaddle. A stroke that pushes the boat backward; very useful in maneuvering and midstream ferrying to avoid rocks, sweepers, and other downstream dangers.

Once proficient in these skills, press on to learn how to brace to avoid tipping (see Appendix G). Studying good paddling instruction and rescue manuals is recommended for advancing proficiency. The goal is to work up into more challenging water, gradually learning techniques and rescue skills for the moment in which all else fails. River rescue classes and workshops are frequently available in major cities and from many paddle clubs.

WASHINGTON WHITEWATER

The whitewater section of this book is for canoeists and kayakers of at least intermediate skills who already know the basics of maneuvering and controlling their boats in significant rapids. Whitewater junkies will want another book, since these are not the most difficult whitewater stretches in the region. Rafters might consider them relatively tame. Paddlers are more likely to consider them "choice."

Following are a few worthwhile observations and reminders.

Continuous action. Washington's whitewater rivers tend to be different than the pool-and-drop streams found in much of the country. Most of Washington's whitewater stretches are in U-shaped glacial valleys that have even gradients and continuous fast water that offers little opportunity to recover from an upset before the next rapid. The term "never a dull moment" may have originated on these waters.

Whitewater safety. All of the issues mentioned previously under "Basic Paddling Safety" apply to whitewater travel with more urgency and emphasis on every point. Whitewater paddlers should always go in organized groups of at least three boats. Each boat should hold paddlers trained in fast-water rescue.

WESTERN WASHINGTON

With its heavy rainfall, and numerous rivers that drain the well-watered land into the bordering salt waters, western Washington is a paradise for paddlers. The first people to thrive in this region made their living out of a canoe, just as the Native Americans of the Great Plains prospered on the horse.

The natives didn't have shuttles. They used muscle power to go up and down stream. They also used their heads, timing their travels up and down with the ebb and flood of the tides. Modern paddlers can use the same techniques even more effectively by using the precision of tide tables. Although good paddlers can propel boats with great power and precision, the old technique of standing and using a long pole to maneuver upstream or through technical waters is still a functional if not thriving art. Poling is especially pleasant for solo canoeists on the lower reaches of many western Washington streams and sloughs.

Yes, much of the Interstate-5 corridor is packed with people and buildings and streaked with pavement. But it's remarkable how quickly a paddler can melt away from the chaos. Often within a few strokes, the lush streamside vegetation will filter out the noise and sight of passing vehicles, leaving you in a natural world of birds, blackberries, and fish.

Fresh Water Meets the Salt

Estuaries—where freshwater rivers meet the salty sea—are the richest sources of life on the planet. Wildlife above and below the surface flourishes here where the tides stir, cleanse, and recycle the nutrients twice a day. In the estuaries, more than anywhere else on a western Washington river, boaters have an opportunity to feel the pulse of the Earth in its waters.

Tides can affect paddlers in estuaries and even miles upstream on rivers feeding into Washington's salt waters. Use tide tables to help time your paddling direction so you can "go with the flow" and avoid being stranded on mudflats. Remember, on most days there are two high tides and two low tides that vary in height from day to day.

The lower reaches of a few western Washington rivers continue to attract paddlers. Both the Lower Duwamish and the Lower Snohomish are popular evening outings for sea kayakers, but watch out for oceangoing vessels.

Endangered species designation for some wild salmon stocks has raised issues that can affect paddlers. Some tribes have sought to limit recreational boating in areas where it might affect the fishery or their fishing techniques. Woody debris might be fastened in clumps or across some rivers to provide salmon and steelhead habitat. This debris can be hazardous to boaters in some water levels, especially in cases where the logs are poorly anchored.

NORTHERN CASCADES

The Cascade Range, stretching 700 miles from southern British Columbia to northern California, is named for the abundant streams and waterfalls that tumble from impressive peaks and glaciers. These waters contribute to the delight of downstream paddlers in three states and a province, including Washington's Skagit and other mainland rivers flowing into Puget Sound. Five trips in this book, however, stack up as a tutorial on the unique qualities in the northern portion of this impressive divide between the wetness of the west side and the sunnier skies of the east side.

Out of the Wilderness

Archaeologists have documented 260 prehistoric sites, some dating older than 8500 years, in North Cascades National Park. But despite such a long association with humans, the region's terrain generally turned a stone-cold shoulder to development, leaving the opportunity to protect the spine of the northern Cascades in the largest and most rugged connection of parks and alpine wilderness areas in the lower forty-eight states. Glacier-fed Ross Lake extends 25 miles into the virgin fir and cedar forests of North Cascades National Park on the west side of the Cascades, while the Similkameen River originates in Manning Provincial Park and the Pasayten Wilderness before flowing through sagebrush flats to the Columbia River on the east side. The Pasayten also contributes to the Methow River, while the White River flows chalky with glacier till from the Glacier Peak Wilderness to bolster the Wenatchee River, which rages with spring melt from both the Glacier Peak and Alpine Lakes wilderness areas.

Lake Chelan is a waterway of major historical and recreational significance running 55 miles into the belly of the range where ferries and floatplanes service the isolated village of Stehekin and North Cascades National Park facilities. The lake, most of which is managed in the Lake Chelan National Recreation Area, offers numerous opportunities for sea kayaking, including fifteen boat-in campgrounds. Paddlers also may want to check out the options for boarding a ferry to rent kayaks at the Stehekin area or paying operators of the *Lady of the Lake* to haul sea kayaks up lake (see Appendix E for Lake Chelan Chamber of Commerce contact information and links to Stehekin and ferry schedules). Ultimately, the editors chose not to include a trip write-up for Lake Chelan in this guidebook. Excessive powerboating activity can make the Chelan end of the lake unpleasant for paddling in summer. Winds on this lake can be exceptionally treacherous because steep shorelines can thwart emergency pull-outs for miles. Regardless of whether you have the skills to tackle this lake, any paddler can appreciate its ruggedness as a virtue that keeps the northern Cascades a fixture in our wildest dreams.

INLAND NORTHWEST

The Inland Northwest ranges east from the Cascades to the mountains of western Montana, a phenomenal landscape that drains into the Columbia River. But even the mighty Columbia could not match the flooding forces that carved the landscape for much of this region. It's a story that has particular appeal to paddlers and others with a keen interest in flowing water.

Ice Age Floods

Glacial ice dammed the Clark Fork River about 15,000 years ago near the current site of Lake Pend Oreille. The massive natural dam built a pool up to 1800 feet deep and spreading into portions of western Montana. When the ice dams broke, centuries of accumulated water flushed out of the lake in about 48 hours, creating the most cataclysmic flood identified on Earth. The flow had ten times more water than the combined flow of all the rivers in the world today, with water rushing to depths of about 500 feet above present-day Spokane. Geologists believe similar floods occurred many times over the following centuries.

The estimated flow of the first flood was 400 million cubic feet per second (cfs). For comparison, the average peak runoff of the Spokane River is about 24,000 cfs. The flow of the ice age flood, rushing at about 65 miles per hour, combined with succeeding floods caused by more ice dams, scoured the eastern Washington landscape and left its mark for 550 miles to the Pacific Ocean. It is unclear whether humans occupied the region at that time, although it's fairly certain that no paddler caught and rode out the first wave.

The floods carved giant riverbeds. Some, such as the Spokane and Clark Fork rivers, continue to run as rivers. Others, such as the Grand Coulee, are simply chains of lakes. The central Washington area around Lake Lenore, including Dry Falls Lake, shows classic "channeled scabland" features created by the floods. At 3 miles wide and 417 feet deep, Dry Falls would have put Niagara Falls to shame. A few miles south of Soap Lake on SR 17, seemingly misplaced boulders stand out in fields of sagebrush. A normal river current constantly moves small sand grains and pebbles downstream. But the great floods were big enough to suspend huge boulders. Known as "erratics," these boulders were bounced downstream and deposited.

Designs in Rock

Artistic columns of basalt are scattered throughout the Columbia Basin of central Washington. The color ranges from coppery to coarse black. Basalt is cooled lava that flowed throughout this region as little as 6 million years ago. The molten rock seeped out of cracks in the earth, cooled, and then flowed some more. When the lava cooled and solidified, it shrank and cracked, forming horizontal layers and vertical columns that sometimes arch into elaborate designs.

Classic examples of this volcanic art can be enjoyed while paddling the Grand Ronde and Palouse rivers, and along Lakes Lenore, Hutchinson, Shiner, and many other waters in the Inland Northwest.

HISTORY IN A NAME

Elwha means "elk," a hint that the big creatures that inhabit the Elwah River valley were important to Native Americans. Stillaguamish means "river people," indicating the close association between a tribe and those moving waters. Just as in western Washington, the waters of the Inland Northwest have histories that range from colorful to dark. Something of their past is invariably reflected in their geographical names. Commonly the names stem from thousands of years of Native American heritage. More often, they derive from early white explorers, trappers, settlers, and missionaries.

William Clark, of the Lewis and Clark Expedition, is the namesake for the Clark Fork River. The region's French-Canadian influence is evident in names like Coeur d'Alene, which means "awl-" or "needle-hearted." The trappers apparently gave the name to the Indians for their shrewd trading practices, and it later was transferred to the lake, town, and river. "Pend Oreille" meant "hanging ears," although some historians say tribal members did not wear jewelry in their ears. Likewise, the Flathead Indians did not flatten the heads of their children, as some coastal Northwest tribes did.

Methow evolved through the white man's pronunciations of "Smeetheowe," an Indian tribe that ranged near the river. The tribe was chronicled as Smeetheowe by fur trader David Thompson in 1811. The word apparently means "sun," appropriate for the Methow Valley, which typically gets clear skies in the rain shadow of the North Cascades.

Priest Lake is derived from the influence around the 1840s of Jesuit missionaries. The Catholic influence also is obvious in the names St. Joe and St. Maries. Kootenai (spelled "Kootenay" in Canada) is from an Indian word meaning "water people."

Selway is derived from the Nez Perce word for "good canoeing." Similkameen meant "treacherous waters" to Native Americans. Slocan came from a Canadian Indian word meaning "pierce, strike on the head." It refers to the Indian practice of spearing kokanee salmon, which used to be plentiful in the region.

Spokane, according to most authorities, derives from a Salish Indian word meaning "sun people," the tribe that gathered to fish for salmon near the Spokane Falls. Walla Walla is an Indian term for "place of many waters."

Wenatchee is derived from Indian reference "We-na-tcha" or "We-na-tchi," meaning "river coming from the canyon." In 1805, Lewis and Clark used the word "Wahnahchee" in referring to this location. The name was used for the Indian tribe that lived in the valley and fished for the river's salmon.

While many places are named for Indians, most of the descriptive place names coined by the tribes have not survived, often for disappointing reasons. The river now known as the Little Spokane was called the "Salmon Trout River" (for steelhead, called salmon trout by Lewis and Clark), but downstream dams ended the salmon migrations. The Columbia was the "Big River" before an explorer from Boston named it for his ship. Hangman Creek is derived from the 1858 executions, in which U.S. soldiers hanged six to eight Indian leaders, including Chief Qualchan, along the creek.

RESPONSIBILITIES FOR ALL BOATERS

The following commonsense points on river rules and etiquette are emphasized here for those who may have forgotten their importance in assuring river access on public and private lands and maintaining friendly and healthy river conditions.

1. **Obtain required permits.** Various local, state, and federal agencies may require boaters to obtain permits—free or for a fee—in order to float or launch on certain waters. For example, even nonanglers are required to have a Washington Department of Fish and Wildlife Vehicle Access Permit in order to use sportsmen's access sites. These permits can be purchased on the agency's website or from fishing license dealers.

2. **Respect private property.** Get permission to put in or take out on private land, and certainly don't disturb anything such as livestock, crops, or equipment.

3. **Don't leave anything behind.** This applies to litter, equipment, and evidence of a fire. Pack it all out, and pick up trash left by others when you can.

4. **Use a stove or fire pan.** If you need to have a fire, use a fire pan to prevent charring the ground and make it easier to pack out ashes.

5. **Dispose of human waste and wastewater above the high-water mark.** The best alternative is to pack out all waste—mandatory on most heavily used rivers. Otherwise, bury human waste and wastewater from cooking or cleaning in the top 6 inches of soil beyond the reach of high water. But still pack out all toilet paper in sealing plastic bags.

6. **Respect the privacy of others.** Avoid stopping where others are stopped or camped.

7. **Respect wildlife.** Many animals and birds that nest and feed along rivers can be seriously disturbed by boaters, especially when people try to approach too close. Enjoy them quietly from a distance. Store food in hard-sided containers or by hanging bags off the ground to prevent critters from becoming campsite junkies.

CREATURES GALORE

The places paddlers play—stream corridors, wetlands, lakes, and estuaries—are wildlife magnets. The opportunities to observe wildlife from the quiet ride of a boat are unmatched, especially on the waters in this book.

A partial list of frequently sighted species in the Inland Northwest includes muskrats, beavers, turtles, great blue herons, and a variety of other birds. The truly lucky might spot bears, moose, raccoons, otters, bald eagles, or loons. Even on urban waters, such as the Spokane River, visitors can expect to see ospreys, hawks, geese, mergansers, and other waterfowl.

Western Washington waters harbor many of these same creatures, plus marine mammals and a remarkable bounty of shorebirds.

Wildlife watching may be the prime motivation to paddle some of the waters

in this book, such as a stretch of the Skagit River that's famous for attracting more than 500 wintering bald eagles; the Nisqually River Delta, a stop for more than 200 species of birds; or the Creston Valley Wildlife Area, a British Columbia hot spot for waterfowl. Angling could be the lure at many of these waters, such as when salmon are running in the Stillaguamish in western Washington, or the panfish are biting on Hutchison Lake in the Columbia Basin, or the cutthroats are rising for the caddis hatch on Idaho's St. Joe River. Be mindful of timing. Pink salmon flood into many western Washington streams during summer and fall, but only in odd-numbered years.

Bald eagle, a featured attraction along the Skagit River

Otter live along most undammed rivers in the Northwest.

Keep a camera handy in a waterproof case, since canoes and kayaks are excellent vehicles for approaching wildlife with little disturbance. Avoid getting too close, however, especially to nesting areas or to wild parents tending to their young. Interfering with feeding times can affect survival of young creatures. Also, predators have learned to follow human trails and activity to easy meals.

RIVERS NEED FRIENDS

With few exceptions, rivers throughout the Northwest, and the paddling activities they provide, are threatened in one way or another by development. Of the thousands of miles of streams in Washington alone, only 176 miles are officially protected under the National Wild and Scenic Rivers Act.

Plans to remove the dam on the Elwha River are among the rare examples of clarity in public thinking about the future of important waterways. For every plan to restore a stream to a natural free-flowing status, there are numerous proposals to foul our streams with new dams, increased water withdrawals, shoreline development, and other degradations.

Please unite with sportsmen and river conservation groups involved in maintaining water access, negotiating dam relicensing plans, and other critical issues.

See Appendix F for a list of notable river conservation groups. But pay attention locally, where area groups can have big impacts. Rafters and canoeists, bird-watchers and kayakers can find common ground with hunters and anglers, for example.

In an age of divisiveness, rivers connect us all.

A Final Word on Safety

Safety is an important concern in all outdoor activities. No guidebook can alert you to every hazard or anticipate the limitations of every reader. Therefore, the descriptions of roads, routes, and natural features in this book are not representations that a particular place or excursion will be safe for your party. When you follow any of the routes described in this book, you assume responsibility for your own safety. Under normal conditions, such excursions require the usual attention to traffic, road, and river conditions, weather, terrain, the capabilities of your party, and other factors. Keeping informed on current conditions and exercising common sense are the keys to a safe, enjoyable outing.

—The Mountaineers Books

Route Comparison Chart

TRIP	RATING					DURATION MILES
	TIDAL FLATWATER	FLATWATER	CLASS 1	CLASS 2	ABOVE CLASS 2	
WESTERN WASHINGTON						
NORTH PUGET SOUND						
1. Dakota Creek/California Creek	x					Up to 8
2. Lummi River	x					3
3. Nooksack River I				x		8, 18
4. SF Nooksack				x		8–13
5. Skagit River I	x			x		3–17
6. Skagit River II	x			x	x	5–60
7. Skagit River III				x		16
8. Sauk River				x	x	27
9. Stillaguamish River	x			x		16
10. NF Stillaguamish				x		18
11. SF Stillaguamish				x		11
SOUTH PUGET SOUND						
12. Snohomish River Sloughs	x					3–23
13. Snohomish River	x			x		8
14. Skykomish River I				x		4–12
15. Skykomish River II			x	x		9
16. Skykomish River III				x		9
17. Snoqualmie River I			x			25
18. Snoqualmie River II			x			11
19. Snoqualmie River III				x	x	4
20. Snoqualmie River IV			x	x		4
21. Sammamish River			x			2–13
22. Issaquah Creek			x			1–2
23. Cedar River				x		14
24. Duwamish River/Waterway	x			x		12
25. Green River I			x			7
26. Green River II			x	x		16
27. Green River III			x	x		7
28. Green River IV				x		3
29. Nisqually River Delta/McAlister Ck	x			x		8

OVERNIGHT OPTIONS	SHUTTLE NEEDED	BICYCLE-FRIENDLY	FEES/PERMITS	PREDOMINANTLY PUBLIC LANDS	SPECIAL FEATURES
					Birding, wildlife watching
	x		x		Mount Baker views, winter birding
	x		x		Mount Baker views, birding
					Sandy beaches
x	x		x		Winter birding, fishing
x	x		x		Wild & Scenic River, fishing
x	x		x	x	Wild & Scenic River, fishing, eagles
x	x		x	x	Wild & Scenic River, eagles, views
	x		x		Fishing, birding
	x	x	x	x	Fishing
	x		x		Fishing, good for paddling practice
			x		Birding
	x	x	x		Numerous islands
	x		x		Wildlife, swimming
	x		x		Fishing
	x				Fishing, swimming
	x		x		Bucolic scenery, fishing
x	x		x		Good for novices
x	x	x	x		Variety of water
x	x	x			Mount Si views, picnicking
	x	x	x		Options for short trips, wine, brews
			x		State park, fall salmon run
	x				Bucolic, semirural
	x		x		Seattle skyline, fishing
	x		x		Birding
	x		x		Suburban wildlife
	x		x		Local summer produce
	x		x		State park, fishing, yo-yo trips
	x		x	x	Wildlife refuge

TRIP	RATING					DURATION MILES
	TIDAL FLATWATER	FLATWATER	CLASS 1	CLASS 2	ABOVE CLASS 2	
OLYMPIC PENINSULA						
30. Hoquiam River: E & W Forks	x					5–9
31. Little Hoquiam River	x					3
32. Wishkah River	x					8
33. Chehalis River I/Sloughs	x					13
34. Chehalis River II			x	x		20
35. Chehalis River III/Lower Black River			x			9–18
36. Black River			x			12
37. Wynoochee River				x		6–16
38. Satsop River, E & W Fks				x		4–11
39. WF Humptulips River				x		7
40. Queets River				x	x	12
41. Clearwater River				x		12
42. Hoh River				x		7–20
43. Quillayute R/Lower Dickey R	x					6
44. Bogachiel River				x		7–15
45. Strait of Juan de Fuca	x					Up to 60
SOUTHWEST WASHINGTON						
46. Willapa River and Sloughs	x					10
47. Palix R/North R/Smith Ck	x					2–7
48. Grays River/Seal Slough	x			x		Up to 10
49. Cowlitz River			x	x		8–22
50. Lower Kalama River				x		8–10
NORTHERN CASCADES						
51. Ross Lake		x				Up to 50
52. Similkameen River			x	x		13
53. Methow River			x			10
54. White River		x				8
55. Wenatchee River			x	x	x	10
INLAND NORTHWEST						
EASTERN WASHINGTON						
56. Lake Lenore		x				Up to 9
57. Yakima River Canyon			x			9–19
58. Winchester Wasteway		x				19–25
59. Hutchinson and Shiner Lakes		x				Up to 3
60. Crab Creek			x	x		7–18
61. Columbia River I			x	x		15–33
62. Columbia River II		x				20

OVERNIGHT OPTIONS	SHUTTLE NEEDED	BICYCLE-FRIENDLY	FEES/PERMITS	PREDOMINANTLY PUBLIC LANDS	SPECIAL FEATURES
	x		x		Urban to rural
	x		x		Small, peaceful
	x		x		Small, intimate
	x		x		Urban and pristine stretches
x	x		x		Fishing
	x		x		Wooded areas to farmland
	x	x	x		Fall colors, remote feeling
	x		x		Pool and riffle, gravel bars
x	x		x		State park, intimate
x	x	x		x	Lush, pristine
x	x	x	x	x	Fast, challenging, wildlife watching
x	x				Densely vegetated, intimate
x	x	x	x		Meandering, braided, fishing
x	x		x	x	Rain forest
x	x		x		
x	x		x		Numerous access sites, endless options
	x		x		Rural river and saltwater bay
x			x		Wildlife watching, fishing
	x	x	x		Birding, history
x	x		x		Mountain views, fishing
	x		x		Clear and swift, fishing
x			x	x	National Recreation Area, cabins
x	x				Remote, arid, overlooked
	x				Wildlife watching, fishing
	x			x	Fall colors, state park
	x				Challenging variety
			x	x	Fishing, geology, no motors
	x		x	x	Desert river canyon
x	x		x	x	Spring bird migration, unique desert stream
				x	Wildlife refuge, fishing, no motors
x	x			x	Desert waterway, wildlife area
	x		x	x	National Monument, fishing, wildlife
x	x		x	x	National Recreation Area, beaches, fishing

| TRIP | RATING | | | | | DURATION MILES |
	TIDAL FLATWATER	FLATWATER	CLASS 1	CLASS 2	ABOVE CLASS 2	
EASTERN WASHINGTON (CONTINUED)						
63. Columbia River III				x		10–20
64. Walla Walla River		x				4
65. Palouse Falls		x		x		4–13
66. Palouse River			x			8–16
67. Bonnie Lake		x				2–11
68. Fishtrap Lake		x				1–8
69. Hangman Creek			x	x		5–11
70. Spokane River I			x			7
71. Spokane River II				x		8
72. Spokane River III			x			4
73. Spokane River IV		x				5–10
74. Little Spokane River			x			3–6
75. Horseshoe Lake		x				2–4
76. Little Pend Oreille Lakes		x				1–5
77. Pend Oreille River			x			12
78. Kettle River I			x			12
BRITISH COLUMBIA						
79. Kettle River II			x			4–30
80. Granby River			x	x		12
81. Slocan River			x	x		4–24
82. Slocan Lake		x				Up to 23
83. Elk River			x			7–17
84. Creston Valley Wildlife Area		x				Up to 19
NORTHERN IDAHO						
85. Moyie River			x	x		12
86. Upper Priest Lake		x				6–12
87. Priest River			x	x		15–25
88. Pack River		x	x			4–23
89. Clark Fork River Delta		x				Up to 7
90. Coeur d'Alene River I			x	x		9–14
91. Coeur d'Alene River II		x				Up to 16
92. St. Joe–Three Lakes		x				5–10
93. St. Joe River			x	x		17
94. St. Maries River			x			7
OREGON						
95. Grande Ronde River				x		7–19

OVERNIGHT OPTIONS	SHUTTLE NEEDED	BICYCLE-FRIENDLY	FEES/PERMITS	PREDOMINANTLY PUBLIC LANDS	SPECIAL FEATURES
X	X	X		X	Variety of water, fishing
	X	X	X	X	Wildlife watching
X			X	X	Waterfalls, fishing, flatwater option
	X				Best during runoff, basalt cliffs
X					Serpentine channel leads to lake, fishing
X			X	X	Wildlife watching, fishing
	X				Wildlife
	X	X			Fun family float except at runoff
	X	X			Play water, rapids, fishing
	X	X			Whitewater park proposed, fishing
	X				State park
	X				State park, birding, wildlife
			X		Waterfall, wildlife, fishing
X				X	Fishing
X	X				Waterfalls, cliff
X	X				Near National Recreation Area
X	X				Multiple trip-length options
X	X				Sandy beaches
	X				Sandy beaches
X	X		X	X	Provincial park, hiking, fishing
	X				Mountain views, fishing
	X				Birding, fishing
X	X				Mountain stream, fishing
X				X	3-mile thoroughfare, hiking trails
X	X			X	Scenic getaway, fall colors
	X				Wildlife watching
X				X	Wildlife watching, coves, islands
X	X	X		X	State park, fishing
X	X	X		X	Wildlife, fishing, boat-in camping
X	X			X	State park, fishing, "river in a lake"
X	X			X	Fishing
	X			X	Scenic forest bottomland, wetlands
X	X			X	Variety of water, easy to scout

TRIP	RATING					DURATION MILES
	TIDAL FLATWATER	FLATWATER	CLASS 1	CLASS 2	ABOVE CLASS 2	
MONTANA						
96. Clark Fork River			x	x	x	13–23
97. Flathead River			x			14–54
98. Thompson River				x	x	5–30
99. Bull River			x	x		6–14
100. Kootenai River				x		16

	RATING			DURATION MILES	OVERNIGHT OPTIONS
	GRADIENT FEET/MI	CLASS 2	ABOVE CLASS 2		
WHITEWATER RUNS					
1. Cowlitz River	25/mi	x		3, 8	x
2. Cispus River	23/mi	x		8	x
3. Elwha River	32/mi	x	x	4	x
4. Soleduck River I	23/mi	x	x	7	x
5. Soleduck River II	10/mi	x		7	x
6. Upper MF Snoqualmie R	24/mi	x	x	7	
7. Skagit River	13/mi		x	9	
8. Naches River	35/mi	x	x	6–26	x
9. Wenatchee River	28/mi		x	9	
10. Methow River	21/mi	x		10	
11. St. Maries River	26/mi		x	19	x
12. Selway River	15/mi	x	x	9–16	x

OVERNIGHT OPTIONS	SHUTTLE NEEDED	BICYCLE-FRIENDLY	FEES/PERMITS	PREDOMINANTLY PUBLIC LANDS	SPECIAL FEATURES
X	X			X	Fishing
X	X	X			Indian reservation, big river
X	X			X	Requires tight maneuvering
	X				Forest Service rental cabin
X	X			X	Fishing, fall colors

SHUTTLE NEEDED	BICYCLE-FRIENDLY	FEES/PERMITS	PREDOMINANTLY PUBLIC LANDS	SPECIAL FEATURES
X		X	X	Mount Rainier views
X			X	Options for bigger whitewater
X	X	X	X	Mountain views
X		X	X	Rain forest, more challenging water
X		X	X	Rain forest, easier water
X	X	X	X	Wilderness-like trip close to Seattle
X		X	X	Wildlife watching
X			X	Generally sunny, dry weather
X		X		Challenging water
X		X		Varied water, fishing
X			X	Long rapids in remote canyon
X			X	Good campsites, fishing

western washington paddle routes

1 Dakota Creek/California Creek

Location: Near Blaine, northwest of Bellingham
Distance: Up to 8 miles
Paddle time: 2 to 3 hours
Season: Year-round
Rating: Tidal flatwater
Hazards: Tides, wind on the saltwater
Shuttle: None
Flow information: Tidal
Maps: USGS Blaine; Whatcom County Department of Public Works Official Road Map of Western Whatcom County; NOAA Chart 18421
Information: Whatcom County Parks and Recreation Department and Semiahmoo Park

Both Dakota Creek and California Creek flow into Drayton Harbor just south of the U.S.–Canada border. The harbor created by Semiahmoo Spit is well protected for canoe and kayak paddling. Mudflats offer excellent bird-watching, and the harbor provides fine views of Mount Baker and nearby Canadian peaks. The creeks themselves allow access to amazing wildlife habitat for an urban setting. This is a quiet trip through a riverside community, a mix of majestic old homes and new condominiums that blend into the picturesque surroundings.

Access. The access is at Semiahmoo Park on the spit. From this put-in, paddlers can make a round-trip by water, 2 miles each way, to the mouth of either creek and back. The creek mouths are several hundred yards apart; at low tide a mudflat will force a detour of more than a mile between the two.

From I-5 about 3 miles south of the U.S.–Canada border, take Exit 274 and turn right toward Old SR 99 (Portal Way), then turn left (south) onto Blaine Road. Half a mile after crossing the bridge over Dakota Creek, turn right onto Drayton Harbor Road (almost immediately you will cross California Creek) and follow it westward along the southern edge of Drayton Harbor to Semiahmoo

Drive. Turn right to Semiahmoo Spit at Semiahmoo Park and launch onto the bay from the east side of the spit.

Paddle Route. The navigable portions of both creeks are tidal. A good way to explore them is by paddling (or poling) upstream with the incoming tide, then following the outgoing tide back to the harbor. The eastern portion of the harbor is shallow, a mudflat exposed at low tide—forcing paddlers who would explore both rivers in one day to detour out into the harbor at low tide, not an altogether unpleasant experience because of the bird life on the mudflats and the marine life in the water including migrating salmon during certain seasons. Bottom fish and crabs scurry among the eelgrass, and shorebirds—spotted sandpipers, dunlins, sanderlings, wandering tattlers—feed on the exposed mud.

Dakota Creek flows primarily with the tide, except during heavy rains, and the tidal flow is strong. The riverbed is virtually unnavigable at low tide. Lower reaches of the creek are developed. There is a shipyard near the mouth, then several bridges—Blaine Road, the Burlington Northern Railroad, Old 99, then the double spans of I-5—and finally homes set back from the creek. Within half a mile, the creek narrows, wilderness begins to encroach upon the stream, and the experience becomes more intimate.

California Creek's tidal basin at low tide has broad mudflats that attract feeding shorebirds.

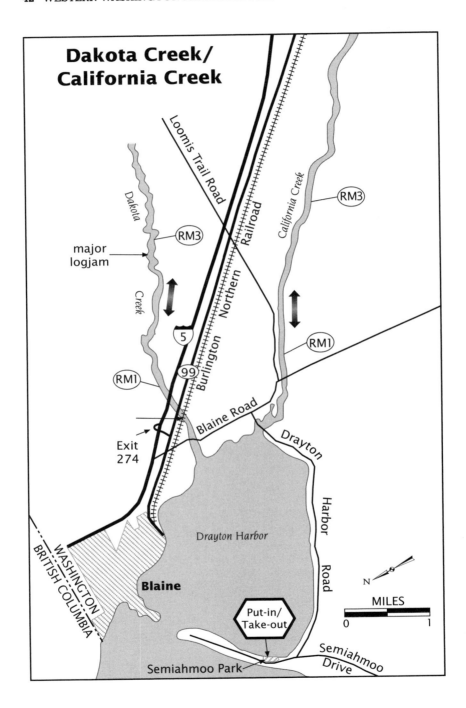

Dakota Creek/ California Creek

Barnacles encrust logs and dock pilings—even living trees—and there are raccoon tracks, deer in the flesh, great blue herons, and nesting Canada geese. Boreal birds abound. High grassy banks are resting spots for sunning geese. Blackberry bushes festooned with fresh fruit in late summer and early fall hang over the creek. Chamomile, which smells like pineapple and grows wild, can be picked for tea.

Forge up the creek for a mile or two or as far as the tide or fallen trees will allow, stop for lunch on one of the grassy banks, and let the tide turn. Then return to the harbor with the pull of the tide. Explore the other creek, or call it a day.

California Creek is broader than Dakota Creek in its lower reaches. Seals occasionally follow fish into California Creek's tidal basin just above the bridge at its mouth. Numerous waterfowl congregate here as well. Flanked by new condominiums that are soon left behind, the lower creek quickly gives way to more open country and occasional views of Mount Baker.

The creek curves, crossed by low bridges, flanked by Loomis Trail Road. Channelized in earlier days, it flows almost straight for a couple of miles. It is more open than Dakota Creek, more developed; but geese and gulls are here, as well as ducks and raptors. Deer and raccoons visit at dawn and dusk, and great blue herons are always nearby.

Although roads cross and parallel California Creek, paddling on its tidal waters offers an opportunity to get away from the work-a-day world. An early-morning run of either creek can be daybreaking glorious, and a late-afternoon trip may reward the paddler with a spectacular sunset. Keep in mind that at low tide, both creeks offer only muddy shores.

2 Lummi River

Location: Northwest of Bellingham
Distance: 3 miles
Paddle time: 1 to 2 hours
Season: Year-round
Rating: Tidal flatwater
Hazards: Low water, tides, man-made debris
Shuttle: None necessary
Flow information: Tidal
Maps: USGS Lummi Bay; Whatcom County Department of Public Works Official Road Map of Western Whatcom County; NOAA Charts 18423, 18424
Information: Lummi Indian Tribal Council

Marked "Red River" on some maps, Lummi River is a tidal high-water overflow channel of the lower Nooksack River. Channelized and diked, it may seem an unappealing river at first glance, but it makes an excellent birding trip—especially

The Lummi River can be paddled in either direction if tide charts are followed.

in the winter, when it has everything from swans and snowy owls to soaring raptors, a dozen species of ducks, and several kinds of geese. It offers views of distant mountains and refreshing winds off the Strait of Georgia.

Note: The Lummi River is on the Lummi Indian Reservation and permission to boat the river must be obtained from the Tribal Council (see Appendix B).

Access. Put-in and take-out points are continuous for most of the Lummi from North Red River Road and South Red River Road, which run along opposite sides of the river. It is possible to launch a lightweight boat almost anywhere along the runnable route, but the unpaved lower end of South Red River Road is badly choked with tall weeds in summer and early fall, making access difficult.

From I-5 north of Bellingham, take Slater Road (Exit 260) and travel west to Haxton Way. Turn left (south) on Haxton to North Red River Road, and turn right—or cross the Lummi River and turn right onto South Red River Road. (The two roads parallel the river.)

Paddle Route. The Lummi River, named for the Lummi Indian Tribe on whose lands the river flows for its runnable course, offers many fine views of Mount Baker and of the Canadian peaks to the north. It flows through open country, for the most part, with its upper reaches bordered by thickets. Wintering snow geese and trumpeter and whistling swans use the area, as do numerous raptorial species. It's a bird-watcher's paradise.

This can easily be a round-trip river; no shuttle is necessary if tide charts are consulted and followed. Launch near the junction of Haxton Way from either of the river-flanking roads and paddle southwestward past muskrat dens, nesting ducks, feeding pheasants, fishing great blue herons, peregrine falcons, and bald eagles. A model-airplane flying field lies on the left bank in the first mile; don't be surprised to see and hear a variety of miniature planes.

Some of the riverbank has been used as a dumping ground, creating unsightly areas especially along the upper reaches of this small river. But its tidal waters

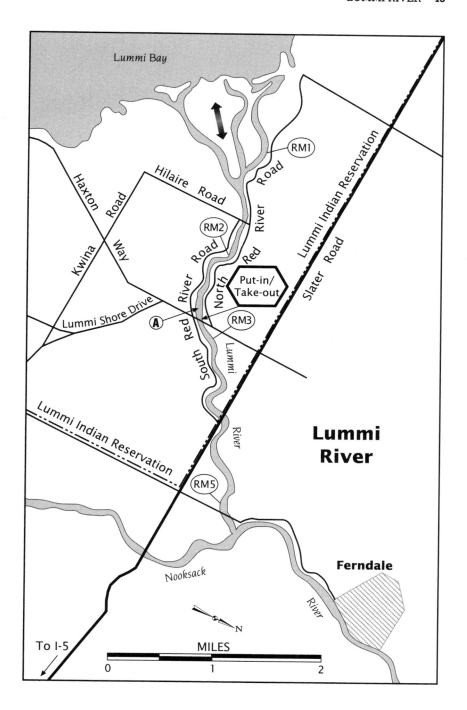

Lummi Bay

RM1

Haxton Road

Hilaire Road

Kwina Way

Red River Road

RM2

North Red River Road

Put-in/
Take-out

Lummi Shore Drive

A

RM3

South Red River Road

Lummi

Lummi Indian Reservation

River

RM5

Slater Road

Lummi
River

Lummi Indian Reservation

Ferndale

Nooksack

River

To I-5

N

MILES

0   1   2

are delightful, despite the fact that the river is diked. The Lummi delta attracts numerous species of bay ducks, waterfowl, and shorebirds. Bald eagles often vie for perching places among the pilings remaining from decaying developments along the shoreline.

Blackberries cover much of the dike, offering succulent snacks during late summer and early fall. While winter birding is ideal, spring migrants also stop along the Lummi. On windy days or when the tide is turning, the delta can be dangerous, but its many channels and small bays still offer relatively protected paddling.

3 Nooksack River

Location: Everson to Lynden
Distance: 8.5 miles to Lynden, 18 miles to Ferndale
Paddle time: 1.5 or 3 hours
Season: Year-round, except flood stage
Rating: Class 2
Hazards: Fast, cold water; logjams; sweepers
Shuttle: 8.1 miles to Lynden, 22 miles to Ferndale, pavement
Flow information: USGS Washington website
River gauge: 12210500 near Deming
Historic flows: Average 3339 cfs; maximum 53,200; minimum 430
Maps: USGS Lawrence, Suma, Lynden, Bertrand Creek, Ferndale; Whatcom County Department of Public Works Official Road Map of Western Whatcom County
Information: Whatcom County Parks and Recreation Department.

The Nooksack River below the confluence of its major forks is a cold, swift river that can be dangerous even to experienced paddlers. Coming off the glaciers on Mount Baker, the river is usually milky with glacial flour in summer and fall. Often clear in midwinter, it offers the finest views of Mount Baker of any river in this book. This segment flows through farmlands, where the aroma of berries, new-mown hay, silage, and manure mingle with the river smells of spawned-out salmon in late fall to fresh mountain snowmelt in spring. This 8.5-mile segment, which can be extended to Ferndale for an 18-mile trip, is part of the annual Ski to Sea Race, a multi-event competition from a headwater ski slope to the mouth of the river at Bellingham Bay.

Access. The best launch is at a small city park at the west edge of Everson, just east of the right-angle curve on Trap Line Road. From here downstream the river is fast, but broad enough to allow paddlers ample room to maneuver around and away from obstacles.

The best of several take-outs for paddle craft is a public fishing access at RM 15.1

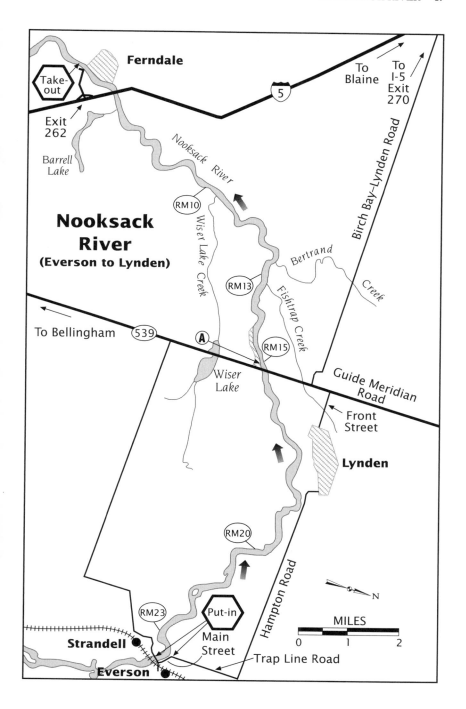

Ferndale

Take-out

Exit 262

Barrell Lake

To Blaine

To I-5 Exit 270

Nooksack River

Birch Bay-Lynden Road

RM10

Nooksack River
(Everson to Lynden)

Wiser Lake Creek

Bertrand Creek

RM13

Fishtrap Creek

To Bellingham   539

(A)

RM15

Guide Meridian Road

Wiser Lake

Front Street

Lynden

RM20

Hampton Road

N

RM23

Put-in

Main Street

Strandell

Trap Line Road

MILES

0   1   2

Everson

(Degrout) off Guide Meridian Road (SR 539) southwest of Lynden, although it has no boat ramp.

To reach this take-out, leave I-5 at Exit 256 and follow Guide Meridian Road (SR 539) north out of Bellingham to the public fishing access through a trail of blackberry vines immediately south of the river. Or, approaching from I-5 northwest of Bellingham, take Birch Bay–Lynden Road, Exit 270, and head several miles east. Turn right on SR 539 and drive 1.5 miles to the public fishing access.

For the launch site at Everson, take SR 539 north from this public fishing access to Front Street; turn right into Lynden and head east through town, taking Hampton Road toward Hampton. At Trap Line Road, turn right and follow it south to the river in a city park on Main Street at a sharp curve at the west edge of Everson.

For a take-out at Ferndale, use Ferndale Exit 262 off I-5 and head southwest. Just before reaching the Nooksack River bridge, turn left onto Hovander Drive, then turn right almost immediately into the public fishing access and boat ramp at RM 5.8, jointly funded by the Whatcom County Parks Department and the Washington Department of Fish and Wildlife.

Paddle Route. The main Nooksack flows fast and furious, a gray river in summer, even under blue skies. It gets a Class 2 difficulty rating primarily because mishaps on the cold, fast-flowing water of the main Nooksack may lead to serious

The Lower Nooksack River flows through a broad agricultural valley.

consequences. During winter and spring, when it contains less glacial flour, it has a lovely greenish hue. The speed of the current is remarkable—at moderate water levels, paddlers can average 7 mph without really trying.

The river meanders among gravel islands through agricultural land where head-high corn and fields of blueberries, raspberries, and strawberries line the bank. The smell of fresh-cut hay mingles with the odor of animal waste. A dairy barn appears, a farmhouse, a wall of close-set pilings to deflect the river. Wild blackberries grow along the riverbank, and foxgloves, tansy, and Queen Anne's lace enliven the shoreline with their voluntary blossoms.

Tractor sounds mingle with bird songs and the music of the river. Goldfinches (Washington's state bird), crows, song sparrows, red-winged blackbirds, red-tailed hawks, spotted sandpipers, robins, great blue herons, and several species of swallows populate the river in midsummer. Cottonwoods, willows, and alders make up the taller vegetation.

More barns and houses appear, and a few retaining walls of riprap and pilings protect the banks from erosion, especially at high water. There are logs and snags in the river (potential hazards), vast gravel bars, and good bird habitat. One canoeist finds the easy parts of the Nooksack "not scenic enough, but the birding potential is high." So is the potential for views of Mount Baker. The river environment, while not wilderness, offers much to enjoy, not the least of which is the fast-flowing current.

For parties wanting a longer run, the river is much the same to Ferndale, another 9.5 miles downstream.

4 South Fork Nooksack River

Location: Saxon to Van Zandt vicinity
Distance: 8, 11, or 13 miles
Paddle time: 3 to 4 hours
Season: Late spring, early summer
Rating: Class 2
Hazards: Logjams, sweepers, high water
Shuttle: 8.1 and 10.6 miles, pavement
Flow information: USGS Washington website
River gauge: 12210500 near Wickersham
Historic flows: Average 746 cfs; maximum 22,400; minimum 59
Maps: USGS Acme, Deming; Whatcom County Department of Public Works Official Road Map of Western Whatcom County
Information: Everybody's Store in Van Zandt

The Nooksack's South Fork, a perfect river for canoeing, roughly parallels SR 9. The spectacular tips of the Twin Sisters can be seen from the river, and while the

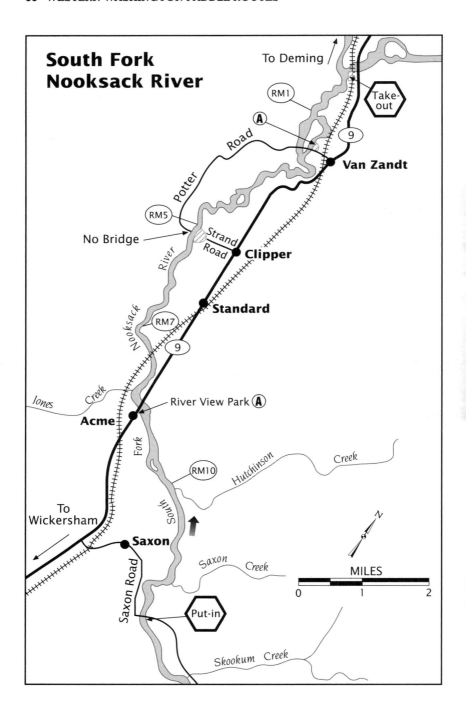

South Fork Nooksack River

To Deming

RM1

A

Potter Road

Take-out

9

Van Zandt

RM5

No Bridge

River

Strand Road

Clipper

Nooksack

RM7

Standard

9

Jones Creek

River View Park **A**

Acme

Fork

RM10

Hutchinson Creek

To Wickersham

Saxon

Saxon Road

South

Saxon Creek

Put-in

Skookum Creek

N

MILES

0   1   2

Logjams and low water levels can narrow the South Fork of the Nooksack River.

course of the river flows through farmlands, much of it is well wooded. There are riffles and mild rapids, temporary challenges to boaters, with few serious consequences except at high water. The South Fork is clear, the warmest of three Nooksack forks, and offers good practice for more challenging runs elsewhere. Inner tubes and other hand-paddled craft are forbidden here to protect the fishery.

Access. The best put-in is at a bridge on Saxon Road about 1.5 miles southeast of Saxon at a wading and picnic spot that is a summer favorite among local residents. The launch site is a sandy beach upstream from the bridge on river right.

To reach the put-in, turn east off SR 9 about 2 miles south of Acme, onto Saxon Road. Travel 2.1 miles (passing through Saxon) to a bridge across the South Fork, where the paving ends. There is limited roadside parking here. Park east of the bridge (the road is gravel) if possible and carry the craft down to the right (east) bank of the river immediately upstream of the bridge.

To reach any of the possible take-outs, return to SR 9 and head north through

Acme. The river flows beneath the highway just north of Acme and continues northward on the west side of the road for the remainder of this run. Take-outs include:

(1) River View Park in Acme, which lies on the river's left bank immediately upstream of and adjacent to the South Fork Nooksack (SR 9) bridge at RM 8. (2) Potter Road Bridge, reached by driving north to Van Zandt and turning left (west) onto Potter Road. With only roadside parking here and private property on both sides, it is best to arrange a shuttle pickup. (3) Confluence gravel bar, reached by paddling another 2 miles downstream to the river mouth, beneath the SR 9 bridge over the main Nooksack, to an iffy take-out on a huge gravel bar on the right bank near the mouth of the South Fork. Four-wheel drive usually is needed to negotiate the steep, rutted road. A long carry is still required, and the South Fork's right riverbank can be muddy and unstable in wet conditions and impossible in high water. The turnoff is on the west side of SR 9 (between the highway and the railroad tracks) about 200 yards south of the bridge across the main Nooksack.

Paddle Route. The South Fork is mellow and shallow in summer, clear and delightful on a warm sunny day. The river may flow through agricultural land, but the farms are unobtrusive, shielded by forest. These same forests no doubt contribute to the extensive debris in the river. There are logjams, sweepers, and snags—occasionally trees all the way across the river—that could be problems at higher, swifter water levels. In late summer the biggest problem is low water.

Boaters can expect to see ospreys, killdeer, kingfishers, spotted sandpipers, violet-green swallows, and beaver sign. Midsummer low water levels provide plenty of gravel bars and sandy beaches. At high water levels, it might not be as safe a run, and under overcast skies, not as delightful.

The South Fork flows over riffles, forming pools and tongues as it meanders slowly northwestward with a few swift chutes, for the first 4.5 miles to the SR 9 bridge just north of Acme. Nearby River View Park could eventually become a major river access point, but at the time this book was researched the park had no launch ramp; canoes and kayaks had to be carried to the river. The Twin Sisters peep over the eastern ridge a time or two in the next few miles.

Agricultural activities are more noticeable below Acme, but there is still plenty of forested riverbank, and the river continues to offer challenges in tight squeezes and a few sharp corners as timber debris litters the river.

Meandering through a couple of broad bends, the river slows perceptibly in the next few miles, forming more pools and becoming more open and more obviously agricultural. Downstream from the Potter Road bridge, the railroad tracks approach the river as it continues to bend broadly and become woodsier again until it reaches its confluence with the main Nooksack. Floaters who run the entire 13 miles to the mouth of the South Fork should beware that the main Nooksack is extremely swift here—a good Class 2 river. Be sure to beach on river right before reaching the confluence.

5 Skagit River I (Mouth)

Location: South of Mount Vernon
Distance: 3 to 17 miles
Paddle time: 2 to 5 hours, depending on tides
Season: Year-round, notably winter
Rating: Tidal flatwater (up to Class 2)
Hazards: Strong tides and currents, fog
Shuttle: None needed
Flow information: Tidal
Maps: USGS Utsalady, Conway; NOAA chart 18423
Information: AquaTrek, Blake's Skagit Resort and Marina, Skagit–Snoqualmie Wildlife Area, Northwest Source, Washington Department of Fish and Wildlife website for Wildlife Areas and Access Points

The mouth of the Skagit River divides into a North Fork (actually more of a west fork) and a South Fork. Either branch can be run, but the South Fork is more accessible. It also offers better access to Skagit Flats, where numerous migratory birds winter, including tens of thousands of snow geese. Bald eagles, trumpeter and whistling swans, and numerous ducks and geese are common winter visitors.

Blake's Landing launch area on the North Fork of the Skagit

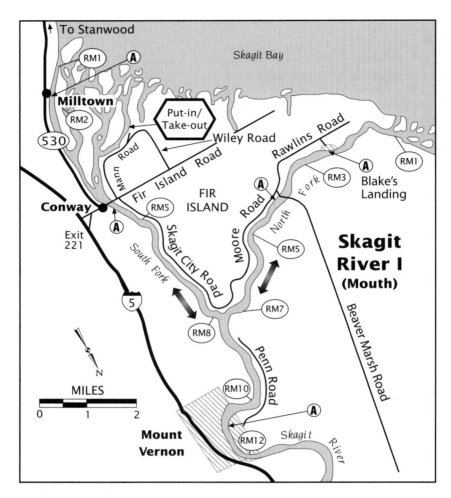

Year-round residents include great blue herons and great horned owls, as well as shorebirds and bay ducks. The tidal flats also offer interesting marine life.

Access. The best access to the lower South Fork is from the Skagit Wildlife Recreation Area on southern Fir Island, southwest of Conway off Mann Road. A boat ramp near a major parking area offers access to Freshwater Slough, the most direct route to the Skagit Flats.

From I-5, take Conway Exit 221 and head west through Conway. Before crossing the bridge over the South Fork, turn right, then immediately left to an access with a boat launch beneath the bridge. To reach the Skagit Wildlife Recreation Area access, cross the Skagit Bridge on Fir Island Road. Turn left almost immediately onto Mann Road, which follows the Skagit Dike south, then west to the Skagit

Wildlife Recreation Area. You can also continue west on Fir Island Road to Wylie Road and turn left (south) to the Skagit Wildlife Area. Parking is available left of the headquarters area; the boat ramp lies beyond (over the dike from) the parking area.

Other access points include:

(1) Milltown boat ramp on the Pioneer Highway (formerly SR 530) between Conway and Stanwood, a primitive access at RM 1.4; take I-5 Exit 221, go south 2.1 miles on Pioneer Highway, then right onto Milltown Road 150 feet. (2) Blake's Skagit Resort and Marina, the lowest launch site to the North Fork at RM 2.5 off Rawlins Road. (3) Public access on the south side of the North Fork at RM 4.2 off Moore Road. (4) Edgewater Park in Mount Vernon, from the west (right) bank at RM 11.2.

Paddle Route. At the Skagit Wildlife Recreation Area launch site, the river is deep and swift; a glacial green much of the year, the water cold and surprisingly clear. It is a salmon and steelhead river and gets heavy fishing pressure, but when the fishing season is closed and the migratory birds are on Skagit Flats, it is a boater's paradise, even in midwinter. Paddlers should check weather reports carefully; winter storms can seriously impact Skagit Bay, the saltwater body embracing the flats.

The lower South Fork is wooded for the first mile or so; saltwater intrusion seems not to adversely affect the alders and cottonwoods that, with a few conifers and assorted shrubbery, form most of the riverside vegetation. Great horned owls congregate in the taller trees along the river even during daylight hours; paddlers have seen as many as a dozen in the first mile downriver. As paddlers near the mouth of Freshwater Slough, the tall trees fade away and the highest vegetation may be the roots of dead stumps lying on the flats—as often as not they serve as perches for bald eagles or great blue herons. Tall grasses replace the trees for a few hundred yards, then even the grasses give way to pickle weed and other salt-tolerant species.

The pull of the tide accelerates the flow of the river current, which moves at several miles an hour. This flow enhances the downriver movement of paddle craft but, conversely, is extremely difficult to paddle against. It may be wise to carry a pole. The bottom is shallow and sandy or gravelly in most places, offering good purchase for poling against the current, should that become necessary. It is better to check the tide charts first.

Once out on the flats during the winter, paddlers may see the thousands of snow geese they have been hearing since launching. With thundering wings, the birds fly en masse, then settle down to a new feeding area, all the while making a deafening cacophony. As the tide ebbs, the water moves swiftly out. Paddlers should remain aware of the flow, lest they become stranded on the flats. Numerous tiny channels flow in dendritic patterns, draining the mudflats. Spending several hours stuck in the mud can be decidedly unpleasant, especially in midwinter.

Fog poses the possibility of becoming lost. A map and compass or GPS should be standard equipment for any saltwater venture by canoe. (On one trip to Skagit Flats, the author was totally fog-bound for more than an hour, but he and his partner kept their direction by compass and by the flow of water beneath the canoe. When the fog finally lifted, they were right where they'd planned to be.)

The numerous channels and branches of the Skagit Flats lend themselves to confusion. Select certain stumps and promontories as guideposts. For a first trip, it may be best to join an established group that includes people who have been out before.

When the tide turns, it takes a while for the current to begin flowing upstream with any force, but it will do so eventually, taking paddlers back to where they started—if they select the right channel. When the river is high, the upstream current created by the tide may not be as strong as desired.

A 17-mile loop trip around Fir Island requires reading tides carefully. After heading down the South Fork from the Conway boat ramp, paddlers can head northwest across the face of the flats, find a channel leading into the North Fork, and follow the North Fork upstream 7.3 miles to its confluence with the South Fork, then travel down the South Fork to the boat ramp beneath the bridge at Conway—all with careful consideration of the tides.

6 Skagit River II

Location: Rockport to Mount Vernon
Distance: Up to 60 miles, with shorter segments
Paddle time: 12 to 15 hours (at 4 to 5 mph)
Season: Year-round, except flood stage
Rating: Tidal, Class 1+/2+
Hazards: Logjams, woody debris anchored to enhance salmon habitat, snags and sweepers, cold and fast water, big river, high water
Shuttle: Approximately the same as river segment, pavement
Flow information: USGS Washington website
River gauge: 12181000 at Marblemount
Historic flows: Average 6033 cfs; maximum 64,800; minimum 620
Maps: USGS Rockport, Conway
Information: REI/Outdoor Recreation Information Center; Washington Department of Fish and Wildlife website for Wildlife Areas and Access Points

The lower aspects of this 60-mile-long stretch of the Skagit River may be developed, but it is such a big, fast-moving river, so wide and so open that it offers wonderful views of Mount Baker and the North Cascades. Its upper reaches are forested; much of it flows through agricultural lands between logged-over hillsides. The river is cool and clear, slightly green in color, and full of deep pools and shallow riffles, lined

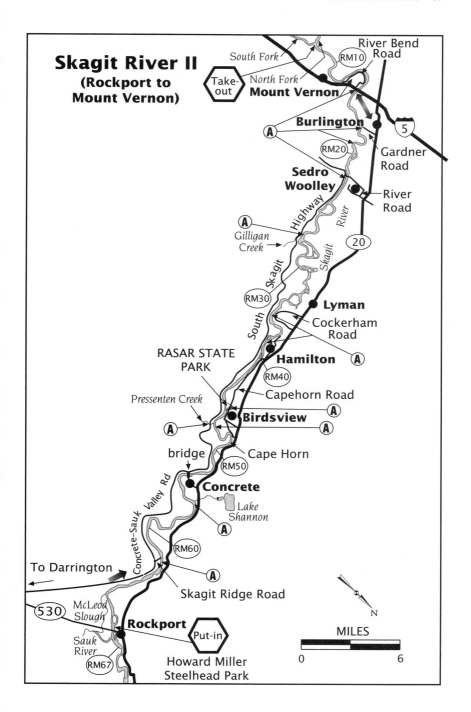

Skagit River II
(Rockport to
Mount Vernon)

South Fork

River Bend Road

RM10

Take-out

North Fork

Mount Vernon

Burlington

Ⓐ

RM20

5

Gardner Road

Sedro Woolley

River Road

Ⓐ

Highway

River

Gilligan Creek

Skagit

Skagit

20

RM30

South

Lyman

Cockerham Road

RASAR STATE PARK

Ⓐ

Hamilton Ⓐ

RM40

Pressenten Creek

Capehorn Road

Ⓐ

Ⓐ

Birdsview

Ⓐ

bridge

Cape Horn

RM50

Concrete

Lake Shannon

Ⓐ

Concrete-Sauk Valley Rd

RM60

To Darrington

Ⓐ

Skagit Ridge Road

530

McLeod Slough

Rockport

Put-in

N

Sauk River

RM67

Howard Miller Steelhead Park

MILES

0   6

Paddlers keep an eye out for bald eagles during winter anywhere on the Skagit River in the Rockport area. (Patrick Maxwell photo)

by gravel bars and marked by occasional islands. A favorite salmon and steelhead stream, the entire stretch has so many access points that no stretch is more than a few miles long. You could run the whole distance in two or three days.

Access. For north-bank accesses, follow SR 20 eastward through Burlington and take appropriate turnoffs to the river; for south-bank accesses, take the South Skagit Highway westward from Concrete and do the same. The only highway river crossing between Mount Vernon and Rockport is at Concrete.

The North Cascades Highway (SR 20) parallels the north side of the river and serves as a main stem for numerous spur roads to access the river. Among them: (1) Gardner Road at the east edge of Burlington; (2) River Road, which leads to Riverfront RV Park in Sedro Woolley; (3) Cockerham Road between Lyman and Hamilton; (4) Capehorn Road in Hamilton and again in Birdsview; (5) Rasar State Park (no boat ramp); (6) mouth of Baker River off South Everett Road at RM 56, an excellent access with limited parking; (7) John G. Young Landing off SR 20 just west of Sauk Store Road, limited parking; (8) and Howard Miller Steelhead Park at Rockport, the ultimate access point for this segment.

South-side access points are reached by crossing the bridge over the Skagit at Concrete to connect with the Concrete–Sauk Valley Road upstream or the South Skagit Highway downstream. A boat ramp offers access on the left bank at RM 62, from Skagit Ridge Road across from the Young Landing. Other south-bank accesses lie at the mouth of Pressenten Creek (RM 46), at RM 36, between RM 26 and 27, at RM 19, and off River Bend Road at RM 13 and 14.5.

Paddle Route. The Skagit is a big river, its upper reaches designated Wild and Scenic. At Rockport the river is normally clear except during heavy rains and at high water. A mile downstream, the Sauk River, also Wild and Scenic in its upper reaches, enters from the left, silting the river and causing a series of islands through which the Skagit braids its way downstream.

McLeod Slough, part of the Sauk Delta, enters the river where it turns sharply right to flow northwest for 2.5 miles before bending gradually left below a pair of islands and making another sharp right at RM 59.5. Major logjams have clogged the river here in some years.

At Concrete, the flow is boosted by reservoir-release water from Baker Lake and Lake Shannon on the Baker River. Five miles downstream, the Skagit bends sharply around Cape Horn, then straightens for a 5-mile run between Birdsview and Hamilton, a stretch that includes Raser State Park. The river flows more gently as it loses gradient. Woody debris, anchored by fisheries agencies for salmon habitat enhancement near Hamilton, creates hazards for paddlers.

Four miles below Hamilton, the river splits around a large island south of Lyman, meandering for the next 5 miles, braiding among more islands. At Gilligan Creek, which enters from the left, the river runs in a single channel for 2 miles before splitting around another large island near Sedro Woolley. The river has reached its tidal zone and paddlers will be bucking the tide if it's flooding, racing downstream if it's ebbing. On clear days, paddlers may catch glimpses of the San Juan Islands downstream at certain bends of the river. Development crowds in upon the river as it approaches Mount Vernon, where several Washington Department of Fish and Wildlife access points offer alternative landings.

7 Skagit River III

Location: Copper Creek to Rockport
Distance: 16 miles
Paddle time: 3 to 4 hours
Season: Year-round, notably winter
Rating: Class 2
Hazards: Sweepers, logjams, cold and swift water, minor rapids and chutes
Shuttle: 16 miles, pavement
Flow information: USGS Washington website
River gauge: 12178000 at Newhalem
Historic flows: Average 4395 cfs; maximum 63,500; minimum 54
Maps: USGS Marblemount, Rockport
Information: Mt. Baker–Snoqualmie National Forest, Mt. Baker Ranger Station in Sedro Woolley; Skagit River Bald Eagle Interpretive Center in Rockport; North Cascades National Park visitor information in Sedro Woolley; Washington Department of Fish and Wildlife website for Wildlife Areas and Access Points

Bald eagles, salmon, trout, and autumn colors are featured attractions to the paddle route on this portion of the Skagit River that's federally protected as Wild and

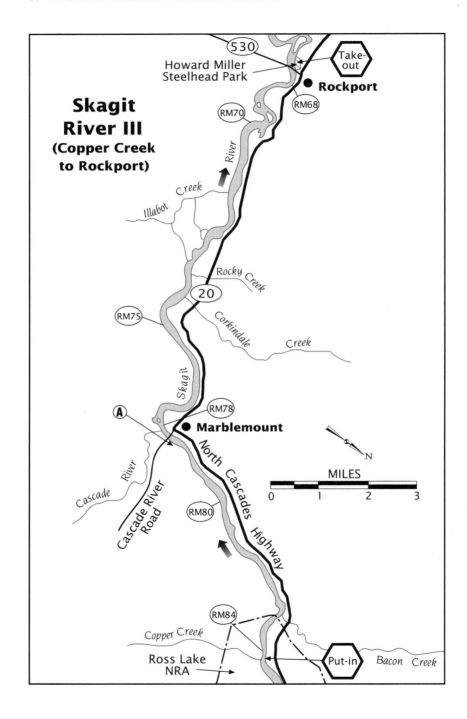

Scenic. The Skagit, clear and cold above Marblemount, has a greenish tint that gives it an almost pristine quality despite its reservoir-release origin. During the autumn of odd-numbered years, this stretch of river has an impressive pink salmon spawning run, especially visible at Bacon Creek, which enters on the right a mile below the launch site. The streamside vegetation offers some of the finest autumn colors in the North Cascades, and the fishing can be excellent, especially for sea-run cutthroat trout. SR 20 parallels much of the route, but its roadless portions offer solitude.

The segment below Marblemount is the famous eagle run, the stretch of river that has the greatest concentration of wintering bald eagles. The author has seen as many as 173 eagles on a single 2-hour trip. Much of the shoreline is in private ownership, but the best eagle habitat is owned and protected by The Nature Conservancy in the Skagit River Bald Eagle Natural Area. November through mid-March, boaters are requested to launch between 10 AM and noon; float quietly, minimizing movement and noise; and refrain from stopping between Marblemount and Rockport.

Access. A launch site opposite the mouth of Copper Creek, within the Ross Lake National Recreation Area, offers access to the upper segment of this run. A popular boating access on Cascade River Road beneath the bridge at the edge of Marblemount, a Forest Service facility, provides an alternate take-out or launch site. Other roadside accesses are possible along the North Cascades Highway (SR 20) between the put-in and the take-out. The usual take-out is at Howard Miller Steelhead Park in Rockport, at a well-used boat ramp.

To reach the take-out, drive SR 20 to Rockport. Immediately north of the SR 530 bridge across the Skagit, turn into Howard Miller Steelhead Park and drive west a hundred yards. The boat ramp is left of the road, on river right.

To reach the put-in, drive east on SR 20 about 6 miles from Marblemount toward Newhalem. After crossing the bridge over Bacon Creek, which flows into the Skagit within sight of the bridge, you will enter the Ross Lake National Recreation Area. Within half a mile (between mileposts 111 and 112), on a slight bend to the left, turn right on a dirt road that leads to a rough put-in ramp at the river.

To reach the Forest Service access beneath the bridge in Marblemount, turn onto the Cascade River Road and cross the Skagit River bridge (visible before SR 20 makes its turn to the north). Immediately beyond the bridge, turn right to the Marblemount Boat Launch beneath the bridge.

Paddle Route. The first mile of river is as peaceful and pristine as any, a favorite salmon-spawning stretch where vine maple and old man's beard offer colorful contrasts in the fall. At the end of the first mile, Bacon Creek comes in on the right, an important tributary for pink salmon spawning, where, in the fall of odd-numbered years, hundreds of fish may be seen working their way upstream.

Below the Bacon Creek delta, the river swings to the left (southwest) through a series of chutes, the only rapids on this stretch. The river broadens and shallows below this point, providing excellent spawning beds for the salmon, which can be seen in the clear water during the fall. An old cabin molders in the rain forest on the left bank.

The highway follows the river closely for the remainder of this short trip, but the wooded left bank resembles wilderness, and the bucolic setting conveys a peacefulness worth experiencing. The cozy homes along the right bank represent gentle and historic development that, for the most part, fits into the natural world of the Skagit.

From the popular launch site under the bridge at the east edge of Marblemount, the river flows gently south past the mouth of the Cascade River—another element of the National Wild and Scenic Rivers System. The Skagit turns west, forming a deep pool next to a modest cliff, then north, then west again in a big bend through Marblemount. It flows past the backyards of residences, through Studebaker Hole (named for the old car body, once used as riprap, that has lodged near the left bank), and over a little riffle as the river narrows to the left.

A Skagit River channel near Illabot Creek in the best eagle-viewing area

The road embraces the river for a mile, then drops away as the river flows beneath high-power cables carrying electricity to Seattle from the dams upstream. Beaver cuts appear near the powerline crossing, as tiny Corkindale Creek flows in from the right (north). The left bank, privately owned, is lined with cabins and weekend homes. Rocky Creek comes in from the right.

Immediately downstream, the "eagle run" begins as the river divides around an island. The usual route is to the right, but at higher water levels, the left-hand channel is possible, though it may have more logjams and sweepers than the main-flow right-hand route. In the next few miles the river splits and meanders, providing the eagles with daytime roosts and gravel bars for feeding on the spawned-out salmon that litter the shore in late fall and early winter.

The river approaches the road a time or two, then gathers itself together for a long, straight run (nearly 2 miles) below the mouth of Illabot Slough/Creek. It splits again, turns south through some choppy waves, then curves west once more before splitting into several channels (generally stay right) above Rockport. After the river flows beneath the SR 530 bridge, take out at a busy boat ramp on the right bank at Howard Miller Steelhead Park.

8 Sauk River

Location: Darrington to Skagit River
Distance: 26 to 27 miles
Paddle time: 5 to 6 hours
Season: Year-round, except at flood stage
Rating: Class 2/2+
Hazards: Sweepers, logjams, cold and fast water, big river
Shuttle: 26 to 28 miles, pavement
Flow information: USGS Washington website
River gauge: 12189500 near Darrington
Historic flows: Average 4332 cfs; maximum 106,000; minimum 572
Maps: USGS Darrington, Rockport, Finney Peak, Lake Shannon
Information: Mt. Baker–Snoqualmie National Forest, Darrington Ranger Station; Skagit River Bald Eagle Interpretive Center in Rockport; Washington Department of Fish and Wildlife website for Wildlife Areas and Access Points

As it flows into the Skagit, the Lower Sauk is part of the Skagit River Bald Eagle Natural Area. It is wooded but provides views of several spectacular peaks. Enhanced by a slough system that can be explored at various water levels, it is a good place for eagle watching in the winter. Fishing can be excellent at the mouth of the Sauk as it joins the Skagit. This short segment of the lower Sauk, coupled

Rock hazards upstream from Sauk Valley Road bridge

with the Skagit immediately below Rockport, is a seldom-paddled stretch offering a variety of river experiences that change with each flood.

The upper segment of the Sauk (Darrington to Sauk Park), part of the National Wild and Scenic Rivers System, offers fine views of the North Cascades, especially the peaks above Darrington. A challenging run for canoeists, it has several mild rapids and some interesting chutes, especially at low water. The current is swift, the water clear much of the year, but it turns milky with glacial flour from midsummer through early fall below the mouth of the Suiattle. SR 530, which approximately parallels the river, is largely unobtrusive and handy in case of trouble on the river.

Access. To reach take-out points on the Skagit and the lower Sauk, drive I-5 to Burlington and take the North Cascades Highway (SR 20) east to Concrete. Two accesses on opposite sides of the river a few miles upstream from Concrete offer take-out possibilities.

From Concrete, head east on SR 20 about 4 miles to a public fishing access with limited parking on river right (north bank) at John G. Young Landing (Skagit RM 62). For a take-out on the left (south) bank, cross the Skagit in Concrete and follow the Sauk Valley Road toward Darrington, turning left to a Public Fishing Access about 5 miles southeast of town on Skagit Ridge Road at RM 62 (across from the John G. Young Landing).

To reach the rough put-in at Sauk Park, return to the Sauk Valley Road and turn left (east and south) toward Darrington. When you reach Sauk Park, turn left into the main entrance and find a spot nearest the river for a steep carry-to-the-river launch.

To reach the upper put-in, drive to Darrington on SR 530. North of town, turn east onto Crawford Loop Road (immediately south of the town's major lumber mill) and travel toward the bridge over the Sauk. Just before reaching the bridge, turn left onto a paved road between the lumber mill and the bridge that offers a rough (often four-wheel-drive) boat ramp to the left bank beneath the bridge. This is a common take-out for whitewater trips on the upper Sauk and the only put-in for the upper part of this segment.

For any of the alternate take-outs, drive back to SR 530 and turn right, heading north. Six miles north of Darrington there is an access between SR 530 and the river, opposite the mouth of the Suiattle—a possible take-out for an 8-mile run. A mile beyond this point the road makes a right-angle turn and crosses the Sauk. Just before the bridge, turn left to the boat ramp and parking area on river left.

Other options: Since the Sauk meets the Skagit less than half a mile below Rockport, it is possible to take out at Howard Miller Steelhead Park in Rockport, but that means paddling or poling or lining up the Skagit. With SR 530 following the entire course of the Sauk in this segment (first on the west bank, then on the east), roadside launches suggest themselves at several points.

Paddle Route. From the lumber mill on the north edge of Darrington, the Sauk meanders northeast for 5 miles—dividing around small gravel islands where logjams may pile up, flowing strongly against cut banks where sweepers may overhang, mumbling over shallow bars where stumps and rocks may offer obstacles. Don't forget to look back upstream for the views of Whitehorse Mountain.

The right bank is low, offering views of peaks in the North Cascades and of the massive clear-cuts on Huckleberry Mountain in the Mt. Baker–Snoqualmie National Forest, geometric patterns that follow survey lines. Glacier Peak Wilderness lies just beyond; the wilderness can be seen from the river, beyond those unsightly clearcuts. At RM 16, the Sauk turns north, as Gravel Creek and then Prairie Creek enter from the right. The Sauk still weaves its way among gravel bars, against cut banks, and through timber debris. The views to the east improve as the ridge between the Sauk and the Suiattle descends. At RM 13, the Suiattle joins the Sauk.

A mile below the mouth of the Suiattle, the river flows under the SR 530 Sauk River bridge, then continues north, still swinging from side to side through its floodplain. At RM 9.6 (where there is a small rapid that at low water offers several chutes), the Sauk brushes the road (indeed, it washed out part of SR 530 at this point in the early 1980s) and parallels it closely to the RM 7 bridge that carries the Concrete–Sauk Valley Road across the Sauk. Large boulders in the river here create irregular currents. A small riffle lies just below the bridge as the river turns left and approaches the rough take-out on river left at Sauk Park. Sauk Mountain looms downstream as the peaks upstream diminish with distance and bends of the river.

The lower Sauk is a mellow river in this stretch, isolated from the roads and surrounded by tall timber. Beware: It is fast-flowing and may be decorated with

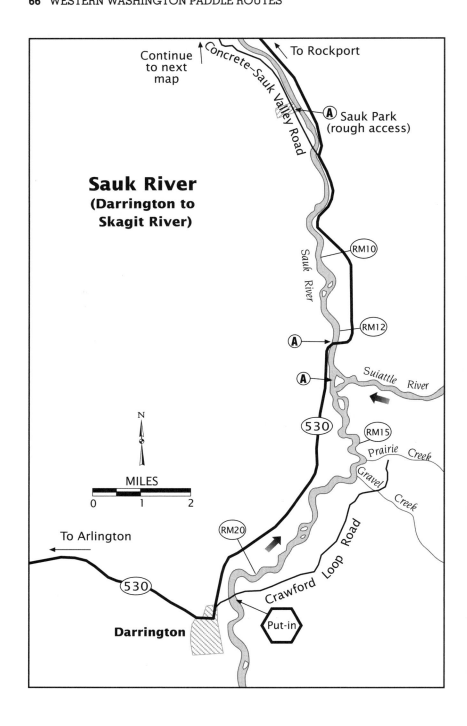

Continue to next map

To Rockport

Concrete–Sauk Valley Road

(A) Sauk Park (rough access)

Sauk River
(Darrington to Skagit River)

Sauk River

RM10

RM12

(A)

(A)

Suiattle River

530

RM15

Prairie Creek

Gravel Creek

Creek

N

MILES
0   1   2

To Arlington

RM20

Crawford Loop Road

530

Darrington

Put-in

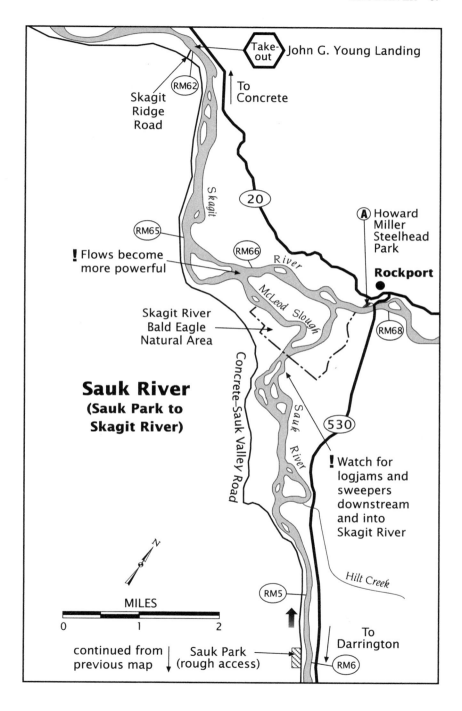

Take-out → John G. Young Landing

RM62

Skagit Ridge Road

To Concrete

Skagit

20

RM65

RM66

River

(A) Howard Miller Steelhead Park

Rockport

! Flows become more powerful

McLeod Slough

Skagit River Bald Eagle Natural Area

RM68

Sauk River
(Sauk Park to Skagit River)

Concrete-Sauk Valley Road

Sauk River

530

! Watch for logjams and sweepers downstream and into Skagit River

N

Hilt Creek

MILES

0   1   2

RM5

continued from previous map

Sauk Park (rough access)

To Darrington

RM6

sweepers and logjams as it nears the Skagit, depending on the debris left by the last high water. The views of nearby Sauk Mountain (5416 feet) and distant Mount Baker (10,775 feet) are worth the trip. The left bank is relatively low, rising to cutover timberland. The right bank is initially steep (except where Hilt Creek comes in at RM 3.3) as the Sauk approaches its delta by breaking through a portal between opposing ridges into the Skagit floodplain. The lower 3 miles of the Sauk are low-lying and marshy.

McLeod Slough branches off to the left, taking 2.2 miles to reach the Skagit at Sauk RM 0.9. The main channel reaches the Skagit at Skagit RM 67.3; McLeod Slough, at Skagit RM 65.9. The delta area changes from year to year as floodwaters alter its configuration, but at high water levels it offers some interesting exploration possibilities. The entire mouth, including McLeod Slough, is part of the Skagit River Bald Eagle Natural Area and includes a section of land owned by The Nature Conservancy.

The Skagit itself is a stately river—fast, deep, and powerful, the primary reason for the Class 2+ rating of this segment (otherwise it would be simply 2). There is a large island just below RM 66, where McLeod Slough enters the Skagit. It is easier to run on the left if reached from the Slough, but it can normally be run on either side. Between the lower end of the island (RM 65), an area commonly known as Mix Master Corner, and the take-out, several more small islands split the river. The lower ones, between RM 63.5 and the take-out, are usually run on the right, following the main flow.

9 Stillaguamish River

Location: Arlington to Hat Slough
Distance: 16 miles
Paddle time: 4 to 5 hours
Season: Year-round, best early spring through autumn
Rating: Tidal flatwater (up to Class 2)
Hazards: Logjams, sweepers, low dam, mild rapids
Shuttle: 14 miles, pavement
Flow information: Tidal
Maps: USGS Arlington, Stanwood; NOAA charts 18400, 18423; Bicycling in Snohomish County map from Ride Store in Lynnwood
Information: Snohomish County Tourism Bureau; Washington Department of Fish and Wildlife website for Wildlife Areas and Access Points

The Stillaguamish, which means "river people," is a favorite steelhead river flowing through farmlands between Arlington and Port Susan. The Stilly, as it is known in local jargon, is a mellow river, marred in a few places by human activity and barnyard

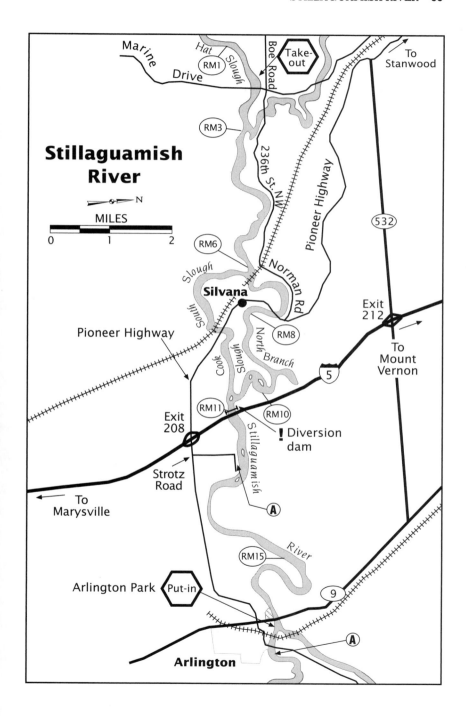

smells, but nevertheless full of wildlife including deer, beavers, nesting bald eagles, and plenty of other bird life. A low dam within view of the I-5 bridges suggests a portage. The lower few miles are tidal. This rural river is picturesque and pleasant, its bottom sandy, and its shoreline well vegetated and marked by a few high bluffs.

Access. To reach the take-out, take Exit 208 from I-5 and head west through Silvana passing low-lying farming country on Pioneer Highway (SR 530). Go about 4 miles and after crossing the bridge over the North Branch turn left onto Norman Road and follow it west. A low-overhead railroad underpass (10 feet 5 inches) may be a hazard to canoes on van-top carriers. If that would be a problem, use the alternative approach described below.

For an alternate route to the take-out, leave I-5 at Stanwood Exit 212 (SR 532) and head west toward Stanwood; then take Marine Drive south to 236th Street NW and turn right to the boat ramp take-out at Hat Slough just off Boe Road.

To reach the put-in just north of downtown Arlington, retrace the route to I-5, then head east on Pioneer Highway (SR 530). Turn left onto SR 9 and head north in Arlington; turn off SR 9 onto Burke Avenue and then drive to Arlington (Haller) Park at the end of N West Avenue. This access is on the left bank of the Stilly, east of SR 9 immediately below the confluence of the two forks that create the main river.

Another river access is on the left bank along the Dike Road west of Arlington off Strotz Road.

Paddle Route. From Arlington (Haller) Park (RM 17.8), the Stilly flows slowly over a sandy bottom, past sand and gravel bars and a few riffles, the banks lined with stately cottonwoods. Expect rocks and logs in the water, which is clear most of the year, and a few tight chutes at low water, a few sweepers at high water. Soon the left bank is encased in waste concrete dumped on the riverside. The noise of machinery and barnyard smells invade the river from adjacent gravel pits and dairies; beaver sign attests to the presence of the nocturnal rodents, and birds are abundant, including robins, black-headed grosbeaks, killdeer, mallards, spotted sandpipers, house finches, and Steller's jays. Bald eagles may still have a nest near the river.

The Stillaguamish is a broad, slow river lined with grasses. In addition to the cottonwoods, paddlers will find maples, Douglas-fir, western red cedar, and hemlock. At RM 12 (just above the double I-5 bridge) Bed Rock Rapid offers a minor challenge. Be ready for occasional logjams that create tight corners. But the biggest challenge is just 0.25 mile below I-5: a low diversion dam that may best be portaged or lined. At certain water levels it creates what could be a dangerous hydraulic keeper (reversal current) across the face of the dam. It can be scouted from Gulhagen Road off Pioneer Highway.

The river begins to swing broadly through its floodplain under bridges (railroad and

Opposite: Small sloughs off the lower Stillaguamish are worth exploring.

highway), past a trailer park with a gravel beach (river right) opposite a steep bluff (river left). The river margin is vegetated with willow, alder, and cottonwood that provide habitat for deer and numerous birds, including the varied thrush and king-fisher. The lower 3 miles, under tidal influence, offer marine species. At low tide, mudflats dominate both banks. The take-out is on river right at RM 1.8.

10 North Fork Stillaguamish River

Location: West of Darrington to Arlington
Distance: 18 miles
Paddle time: 4 to 5 hours
Season: Year-round except flood stage; may be too low August through September
Rating: Class 2
Hazards: Sweepers, logjams, Class 2 rapids
Shuttle: 6.4 miles; pavement
Flow information: USGS website
River gauge: 12167000 near Arlington
Historic flows: Average 1893 cfs; maximum 44,000; minimum 117
Maps: USGS Arlington, Oso; Bicycling in Snohomish County map, from Ride Store in Lynnwood
Information: REI/Outdoor Recreation Information Center; Snohomish County Tourism Bureau; Washington Department of Fish and Wildlife website for Wildlife Areas and Access Points

The North Fork of the Stillaguamish is a lovely stream that flows westward from a few miles west of the North Cascades timber town of Darrington to Arlington through a bucolic valley of old farms and small homesteads. It offers grand views of the North Cascades peaks and, in the winter, a bit of eagle watching. Its rural valley fosters varied wildlife and makes the short paved shuttle route ideal for bicycling. The climate is mild enough for the river to be runnable any time there is enough water. There can be too much water, however, for the river floods with heavy winter rains and spring snowmelt. Few boaters want to be on it at flood stage. Floods often rearrange the river's form and furniture and may create logjams.

Access. To reach the take-out just north of downtown Arlington, take Exit 208 from I-5 and head east on Pioneer Highway (SR 530). Turn left onto SR 9 and head north; turn right off SR9 and turn left onto Burke Avenue, then drive to N West park at the end of Avenue. This access is on the left (south) bank of the Stilly, east of SR 9 immediately below the confluence of the two forks that create the main river.

To reach the put-in, drive east on SR 530 for about 15 miles from Arlington, through Cicero and Oso, and turn left (north) onto Whitman Road (251st Avenue NE) near Halterman. Cross the abandoned railroad right-of-way that's proposed to become a trail. The access, which lies between the railroad bed and the river, is maintained and used regularly by the Evergreen Fly Fishing Club and is scheduled to become a unit of the Snohomish County Parks system. The put-in is on river left beneath the bridge.

An alternate North Fork put-in is the Washington Fish and Wildlife Department access off Monty Road at Cicero (near the SR 530 bridge, 8.7 miles east of Arlington). Although SR 530 follows the river and crosses it twice, there are few access points.

Paddle Route. The North Fork is rocky in its first few hundred yards, with a riffle or two before it reaches a dogleg to the left at the most severe rapid on this segment. It runs to the edge of the Mt. Baker–Snoqualmie National Forest, which borders the river for the next mile; then it swings south under the railroad and highway bridges to flow past Wheeler Mountain on the south side of the floodplain.

A number of vacation homes lie along the southbound stretch of the North Fork, which soon bends west in a broad, sweeping curve to the right, leaving a wide gravel bar on the right where steelhead fishermen gather to try their luck. Take care in boating past anglers. Courteous boaters avoid interfering with the activities of other river users.

The paddling gets progressively easier downstream, and the views upstream progressively improve. Whitehorse Mountain can be seen from a number of stretches below Oso, which can be recognized by the bridge that crosses the river just south of town (no access here) and by the entry of Deer Creek, which flows into the North Fork on the right southwest of Oso.

Barnyard smells mingle with the odor of fresh-cut cedar from the small mill

A winter paddler heads down the North Fork Stillaguamish; Whitehorse Mountain in background. (Steve Reutebuch photo)

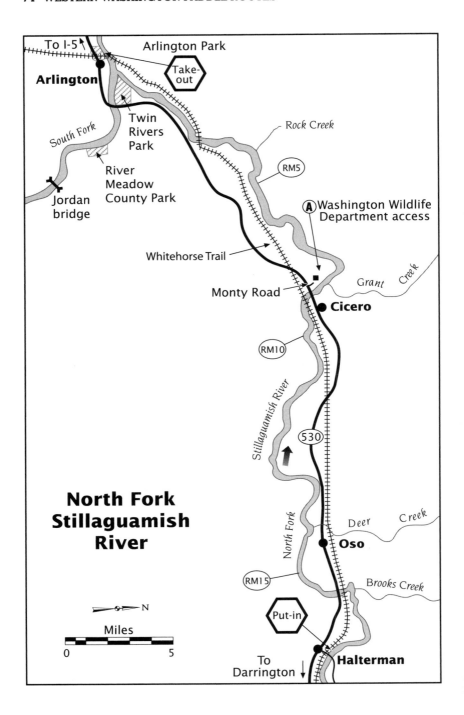

near Oso. In the summer you can smell the raspberries in adjacent fields. Spotted sandpipers, kingfishers, great blue herons, robins, and yellow warblers add color and variety to the trip, and old barns offer picturesque views.

Vacation homes and year-round residences line the riverbank, as do private picnic areas and trailers. Riverside vegetation includes blackberries, red osier dogwood, tall grasses, and the usual deciduous trees: tall cottonwoods, alders, and maples. The sound of farm machinery and logging trucks intrudes into the river corridor at times, but generally this is a quiet segment with distant views of North Cascades peaks and forested hillsides, marred here and there by inevitable clearcuts—this is logging country.

Access at Monty Road is steep, either a rough haul over riprap boulders or a long carry through blackberry bushes. This site could be a major access point, but at this writing it remains undeveloped. The eddy under the bridge offers quiet water for a take-out, and there is a small parking area (better used for loading boats than for parking) between the highway and the railroad.

The Monty Road access may be used for launching a run to Arlington, where the two main forks of the Stillaguamish converge just a few dozen feet above the Arlington (Haller) Park access. This stretch of river goes through a short, pleasant canyon and adds 9.5 miles to the trip. It can be run as an entirely separate trip.

11 South Fork Stillaguamish River

Location: Granite Falls area to Arlington
Distance: 11 miles
Paddle time: 4 hours
Season: Year-round, especially early spring through summer
Rating: Class 2
Hazards: Sweepers, logjams, rapids
Shuttle: 8.3 miles, mostly pavement
Flow information: USGS Washington website
River gauge: 12161000 near Granite Falls
Historic flows: Average not available; maximum 21.17 feet; minimum 2.99 feet
Maps: USGS Granite Falls, Lake Stevens, Arlington; Bicycling in Snohomish County map from Ride Store in Lynnwood
Information: Snohomish County Tourism Bureau; Verlot Public Service Center; Washington Department of Fish and Wildlife website for Wildlife Areas and Access Points

The South Fork of the Stillaguamish is another popular steelhead stream flowing through a rural area. Its background bluffs give it the appearance of an Ozark

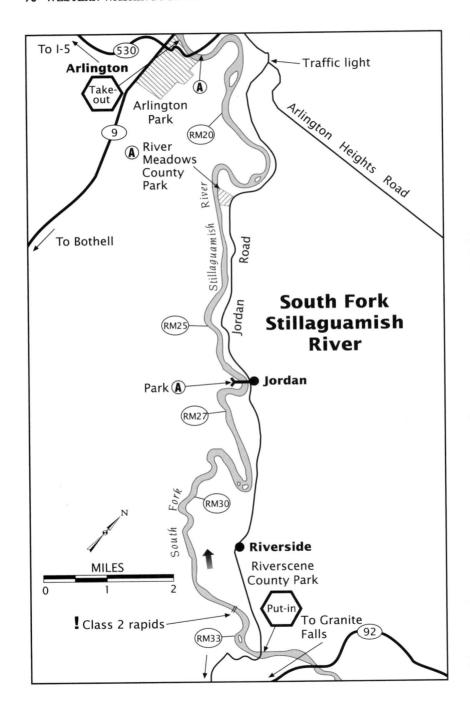

river, but its vegetation is strictly Pacific Northwestern. Most of the action on this broad but lively river comes within the first few miles of this segment. Alternating pools and riffles, the river is rocky. It's a good poling river, challenging enough in its moderate rapids to provide practice in basic canoeing techniques. This segment is a favorite trip for the area canoe club.

Access. Four access points on the South Fork from Granite Falls to Arlington offer opportunities for running several different segments: (1) beneath the bridge across the South Fork north of Granite Falls at Riverscene County Park; (2) beneath the suspension footbridge at Jordan, 7 river miles downstream from Riverscene County Park; (3) at River Meadows County Park, another 4 river miles downstream; and (4) at Arlington (Haller) Park, immediately below the confluence of the two forks of the Stilly.

To reach the take-out just north of downtown Arlington, take Exit 208 from I-5 and head east on Pioneer Highway (SR 530). Turn left onto SR 9, then right onto Burke Avenue, then turn left and drive to the park at the end of N West Avenue. This access is on the left bank of the Stilly, east of SR 9 immediately below the confluence of the two forks that create the main river. Another river access is on the left bank along the Dike Road west of Arlington off Strotz Road.

To reach River Meadows County Park, go back to SR 530 and continue east through Arlington as though heading to Darrington. Turn right onto Arlington Heights Road at the red light about a mile beyond the bridge across the South Fork. In another mile, turn right again, onto Jordan Road, and follow it southeast toward Jordan. In about 3 miles turn right into River Meadows County Park, and drive down the hill to the parking area, which is within an easy carry of the riverbank.

To reach the upper launch site for this segment, drive back to Jordan Road (also known as the Granite Falls–Arlington Road), turn right, and drive the 8.3 miles to Riverscene County Park at the bridge across the South Fork just north of Granite Falls. The put-in is to the left of the road, river right, the upstream side of the bridge at Bergen Road (192nd Drive NE). To go more directly to the launch site, take SR 92 off SR 9 north of Lake Stevens and travel northeast toward Granite Falls. Just before reaching the city streets, turn left onto Jordan Road (Granite Falls–Arlington Road), which jogs around a bit but heads generally north to cross the South Fork. Immediately past the bridge, turn right into Riverscene County Park, which lies at Bergen Road.

On the drive from River Meadows County Park to the Granite Falls launch site, you will pass through Jordan, a tiny community with a small parking area (six cars at most) on the south side of the road. Access to the river involves crossing a suspension footbridge to a small park with a broad beach on river left beneath the bridge. It makes a strenuous carry, but it is possible to launch or take out here, dividing this run into a 7- and a 4-mile run, above and below this point.

Paddle Route. From the launch site beneath the bridge, the river is clear, rocky, and rapid, ideal for poling: shallow with a gravel or rocky bottom. Lovely

Eroded bluffs along the South Fork of the Stillaguamish

deep green pools are followed by easy 3- to 4-foot drops, good Class 2 water. Fully half the action of this segment occurs in the first mile.

Below a third drop (rapid) at a couple of small islands on the second turn, the river mellows and the wildlife (mergansers, ravens, spotted sandpipers, and great blue herons) appears—or rather, you have time to notice it. Houses, a series of miniature waterfalls, and a ledge of fossil shells appear on the left bank. It is a pool-and-drop river with sandy beaches often opposite shallow cliffs.

The banks are lined with vine maple, western red cedar, Douglas-fir, hemlock, alder, and (in season) bright yellow monkey flowers. The bird life includes bald eagles, several species of swallows, and ducks. The suspension bridge at Jordan, throwing its shadow into the deep pools at the edge of the park beach, marks 7 miles from the launch.

Below Jordan the river gets slower, broader, shallower, and more agricultural in the final 4 miles of this segment, a trend that continues all the way to Arlington. Many paddlers take out at River Meadows County Park because it is convenient (though a long carry in late summer, when the gravel bar widens with low water) and because the river slows below the park. To Arlington from the park is another 4 miles, a good hour's hard paddling on slow water.

SOUTH PUGET SOUND

12 Snohomish River Sloughs

Location: Northeast of Everett
Distance: 3 to 23 miles
Paddle time: 3 miles per hour
Season: Year-round
Rating: Tidal flatwater
Hazards: Contrary tides, powerboats
Shuttle: None necessary
Flow information: USGS Washington website
River gauge: 211555000 near Snohomish
Historic flows: Average not available; maximum 35 feet; minimum N/A (tidal)
Maps: USGS Marysville, Everett, Snohomish; NOAA charts 18423, 18443, 18444; Bicycling in Snohomish County map, from Ride Store in Lynnwood
Information: AquaTrek; Everett Chamber of Commerce; Marysville Parks and Recreation Department

The Snohomish River Sloughs—Ebey, Steamboat, Union, and the mouth of the river itself—offer more than 40 miles of paddling, a network of waterways in which a paddler could get lost, paddling for days with the tide, moving with the ebb and flow. Industrial development dominates the shoreline, but the area also serves as wonderful waterfowl habitat. The women's Olympic crew team and other rowers have used the lower river and some of its sloughs for training. Fishermen, many of them in powerboats, make regular use of the sloughs, as do hunters in waterfowl season. A copy of the *Snohomish River Estuary Recreational Guide* from Snohomish County Parks & Recreation will greatly enhance the paddling experience.

Access. Langus Riverfront Park on the lower main stem of the river, about 3 miles upstream from its mouth in Everett Harbor, offers the best access, with a boat launch, restrooms, picnic area, and boathouse on the southwestern edge of Smith Island.

The public boating access at the waterfront park in Everett charges a fee for launching, and it involves paddling across the face of Everett Harbor to reach the mouth of the river or any of the sloughs. Other potential accesses are at Lowell Riverside Park, 7 miles from the mouth, 4 miles above Langus Park; and at Rotary Park a mile upstream from Lowell off Snohomish River Road, 8 miles from the mouth of the river. A waterfront park in Marysville offers seventy-two parking spots and access to Ebey Slough from a four-lane boat ramp with no launch fee.

To reach Langus Riverfront Park southbound on I-5, take Exit 198 (North Broadway in Marysville) onto SR 529 (Pacific Highway); exit onto Frontage Road

Crew teams often practice on the Snohomish out of Langus Riverside Park.

and follow the signs to the park. To reach the park northbound on I-5, take Exit 195 and turn left onto East Marine Drive to SR 529 heading north, then take the first exit after crossing the Snohomish River and follow the signs to the park.

The 10th Street waterfront park in Everett can be reached by taking I-5 Exit 195 heading north onto Grand Avenue, which becomes East Marine Drive under I-5 as it swings northwest to loop around the north end of the peninsula on which most of north Everett is built. It becomes West Marine Drive as it swings south and the cross-street numbers begin to climb. At 10th Street, turn right into the waterfront park and boat ramp, where the launch fee is about $7.

For the Lowell access, take I-5 south to Exit 192 (Broadway/Lowell Road) and head south; turn left on Lenora Street and head for the river on what becomes Lowell River Road. At the edge of Lowell there is a carry access at a small park on the left bank left of the road. A mile beyond Lowell is a public access with boat ramp at Rotary Park on the left. The launch fee is about $3.

To reach the Ebey Slough boat launch in Marysville, head north on I-5, cross the river and its sloughs, take Exit 199 right onto Cedar Street, then left onto 1st Street to the Waterfront Park at 1404 1st Street NE (no launch fee).

Paddle Route. From a launch at Langus Riverfront Park, paddlers may head downstream toward the Everett waterfront and paddle south to the Port of Everett or turn north to paddle the sloughs. Careful scrutiny of tide charts will make this an easier and more pleasant trip. It is possible to paddle up Steamboat Slough, the first major waterway north of the river mouth, or Ebey Slough, which flows into Possession Sound a mile north of the river mouth. Union Slough splits off Steamboat Slough about a mile from its mouth.

The waterfront represents industrial development, a port for large oceangoing vessels. To the north lie log storage areas, largely at the mouths of the sloughs. Despite the development, this is good wildlife habitat for shorebirds, waterfowl, and bald eagles. As you paddle up the sloughs, you get farther from industrial activities and background noise of I-5 traffic, which dominates the lower 2 or 3 miles.

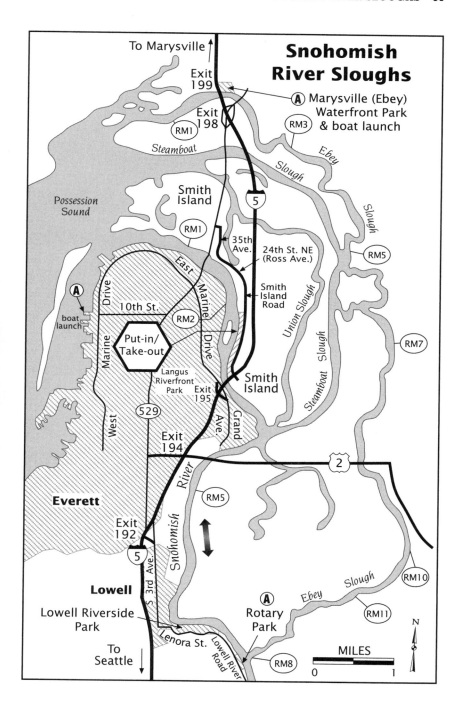

Snohomish River Sloughs

To Marysville↑

Exit 199

Ⓐ Marysville (Ebey) Waterfront Park & boat launch

Exit 198

RM1

RM3

Steamboat

Ebey

Slough

Slough

5

Smith Island

Possession Sound

RM1

RM5

35th Ave.

24th St. NE (Ross Ave.)

East Marine Drive

Smith Island Road

Ⓐ

boat launch

10th St.

RM2

Marine Drive

Union Slough

Grand Drive

Put-in/ Take-out

Steamboat Slough

RM7

Langus Riverfront Park

Exit 195

Smith Island

West Marine Drive

529

Exit 194

Grand Ave.

River

2

Snohomish River

RM5

Everett

Exit 192

RM10

5

Slough

Lowell

S. 3rd Ave.

Ebey

RM11

N

Lowell Riverside Park

Ⓐ

Rotary Park

To Seattle ↓

Lenora St.

Lowell River Road

RM8

MILES

0   1

Ebey Slough and Steamboat Slough entwine twice at RM 5.2 and RM 6.4 at high water levels (high tide). Union Slough and Steamboat Slough, having run 4.4 and 6.2 miles respectively, join at RM 4 on the lower Snohomish. Ebey Slough splits off the river at RM 8.1, flowing 12.4 miles to the Sound, the long way 'round.

Going upriver from the Smith Island launch at Langus Park, paddlers pass under the double span of I-5, skirt the industrial northeast edge of Everett, and meet the take-off point of the twin sloughs, Union and Steamboat, at RM 4. They skirt the ridge carrying I-5 and much of southeast Everett until they reach Lowell. Here the river turns abruptly away from the ridge and heads eastward, upstream.

For a longer run, it is possible to paddle downstream on the river from Cady Park in Snohomish (see Trip 13) to either of the take-outs suggested above. It is a 10-mile run and a 3-hour paddle from Cady Park to Langus Riverfront Park.

13 Snohomish River

Location: Sultan to Snohomish
Distance: 8 miles
Paddle time: 2 to 3 hours
Season: Year-round, especially summer
Rating: Tidal flatwater (up to Class 2)
Hazards: Logjams, sweepers, powerboats
Shuttle: 12 to 14 miles, pavement
Flow information: USGS Washington website
River gauge: 21150800 near Monroe
Historic flows: Average 9512 cfs; maximum 150,000; minimum 763
Maps: USGS Snohomish, Maltby, Everett; Bicycling in Snohomish County map, from Ride Store in Lynnwood
Information: Snohomish Chamber of Commerce; Snohomish County Tourism Bureau; Washington Department of Fish and Wildlife website for Wildlife Areas and Access Points

The Snohomish River begins where the Snoqualmie and the Skykomish join, roughly 20 miles from its mouth. More than half its length is under tidal influence, which reaches well above the town of Snohomish. This segment is mellow—a cool, clear green river with slow current and braided channel full of islands. Its backdrop changes by slow degrees from forested and mildly isolated, through agricultural, to developed. It offers good birding and easy paddling.

Access. Cady Park in Snohomish makes an excellent take-out for this segment. Two possible put-in points suggest themselves: (1) the Skykomish River Centennial Park public boat launch on the Skykomish immediately south of Monroe, 4 miles upstream from the confluence; and (2) the High Bridge public fishing access on the Snoqualmie, 2.8 miles upstream from the confluence.

To reach the take-out at Cady Park in Snohomish, take US 2 or SR 9 to Snohomish. From US 2, take the exit east of town, head west on 92nd Street SE (which becomes Second Street in Snohomish), turn left, and follow Maple Street to its end at Cady Park. From SR 9, take the exit west of town (Foster Slough/River Road), head east into town, take the fork to the right (First Street), turn right onto Maple Street, and follow it one block to its end at Cady Park.

For the access south of Monroe (see Trip 14), take US 2 east, turning right in Monroe at Lewis Street and heading south. Before reaching the bridge across the Skykomish immediately south of town, turn right onto a dirt road that constitutes a public boating access, a 14-mile shuttle. Ample parking exists on the east side of South Lewis Street near the bridge.

To reach the High Bridge access on the Snoqualmie, head south from Snohomish on SR 9, turning left at Rees Corner onto Broadway (called 99th Avenue SE and SR 96) to Cathcart, where 164th SE, coming in from the right, eventually becomes Elliott Road as you follow it east. It roughly parallels the river as you head upstream. About 3 miles after Elliott Road passes beneath the SR 522 overpass and 1.5 miles beyond taking a fork to the left, turn left onto High Bridge Road (also known as Tester Road). Just past the bridge, turn left into a public fishing access to launch. This shuttle is roughly 12 miles.

Paddle Route. The 4-mile run on the Skykomish from Monroe to the confluence can be tricky at low water, when the current flows strongly beneath sweepers. The Skykomish meanders from bank to bank, with large gravel bars forcing the current back and forth into bank vegetation. On one river trip, the author capsized his canoe beneath a sweeper near the left bank about 3 miles below Monroe on this stretch. The 2.8-mile lower stretch of the Snoqualmie is like a Southern swamp,

Canada geese rest on a Snohomish River gravel bar.

Snohomish River
(Sultan to Snohomish)

Skykomish River I
(Monroe to Confluence)

Skykomish River II
(Sultan to Monroe)

except for a riffle a few hundred yards above the confluence with the Skykomish; it is slow and sluggish (except at high water) and heavily forested. At the confluence, the two rivers meet, then flow around an island.

From the confluence of the Skykomish and the Snoqualmie, the Snohomish River passes under the long angular bridge of SR 522, then flows placidly past forested banks where tall cottonwoods line the river; Douglas-fir, hemlock, and western red cedar mark the ridges. Farmhouses and rural residences appear on the left bank. For 3 miles the river flows fairly straight, the channel braiding among islands; then it takes an abrupt turn to the right, the beginning of a huge S where the river widens and timber debris, anchored in a sandy bottom, provides benign obstacles to avoid. Shorts Road provides rough access along the final bend of the S between RM 16.3 and 16.5.

The river splits around islands, the water level determining how navigable a given channel may be. A private beach offers swimming and sunbathing opportunities at RM 15 as farmlands begin to dominate. Flocks of Canada geese and killdeer frequent the gravel bars; powerboats begin to appear. As paddlers near the town of Snohomish, they may notice the mouth of the Pilchuck River coming in on the right just after they pass beneath the first of two railroad bridges. The second railroad bridge announces the take-out less than a quarter mile downstream on the right bank at Cady Park.

14 Skykomish River I

Location: Monroe to confluence
Distance: 4 to 12 miles
Paddle time: 1 hour
Season: Year-round, especially summer
Rating: Class 2
Hazards: Logjams, sweepers
Shuttle: 4 miles, pavement
Flow information: USGS Washington website
River gauge: 21150800 near Monroe
Historic flows: Average 9512 cfs; maximum 150,000; minimum 763
Maps: USGS Monroe, Maltby; Bicycling in Snohomish County map, from Ride Store in Lynnwood
Information: Snohomish Chamber of Commerce; Snohomish County PUD; Snohomish County Tourism Bureau; Monroe Chamber of Commerce; Washington Department of Fish and Wildlife website for Wildlife Areas and Access Points

This short segment of the lower Skykomish is a delightful run and can easily be coupled with a run up the Snoqualmie to the High Bridge access (see Trip 13) or

Blacktail deer can be seen along many Western Washington rivers.

a run all the way to Snohomish (8 more miles). The area through which it flows is agricultural and full of wildlife. At high water it is a flush down a big river with few obstacles; at low water it requires more maneuvering because a few bends can carry most of the flow under some serious sweepers.

Access. Paddling or poling up the Snoqualmie to the High Bridge access offers a take-out option, but paddlers looking for a longer run might go all the way to Cady Park in Snohomish (Trip 13). The logical launch site is off South Lewis Street at the south edge of Monroe at Skykomish River Centennial Park.

To reach the launch, take US 2 into Monroe; turn right onto Lewis Street and drive south to the edge of town. Before reaching the bridge, turn right onto a dirt road, which offers access to the Skykomish River's right bank below the bridge. Parking is available on South Lewis Street.

Paddle Route. The Sky (short for Skykomish) is broad and deep here, and green most of the year. It soon shallows and, at low water levels, meanders from bank to bank between gravel bars. Farms line the banks, but agricultural activities do not intrude into the river corridor, and the area is full of wildlife: deer, beavers, raccoons, and numerous bird species, including ospreys and eagles.

At low water levels the river seems to disappear downriver; then the channel swings off to the left, where it hugs the bank after running over a shallow bar that pinches the current into a narrow chute. The current swings back to the right for a time, clear and green as it ripples over the shallows, then swings hard against the left bank under a sturdy sweeper that has upset a number of paddle craft over the years. Inexperienced paddlers may want to portage or line at certain water levels or take a different channel, even if the craft has to be walked through. Islands occur at higher water levels; in selecting routes, it is generally best to follow the stronger current, unless it leads into a logjam.

Within sight of the confluence there is a rocky promontory on the left bank that makes a nice lunch stop and a good diving platform to swim in the adjacent deep pool. Summer sunbathers and swingers of ropes from the SR 522 bridge can be observed at the beach on the right.

15 Skykomish River II

Location: Sultan to Monroe
Distance: 9 miles
Paddle time: 2 to 3 hours
Season: Year-round, especially summer
Rating: Class 1+/2–
Hazards: Sweepers, narrow chutes at low water levels
Shuttle: 9 miles, pavement
Flow information: USGS Washington website
River gauge: 12134500 near Gold Bar
Historic flows: Average 3948 cfs; maximum 102,000; minimum 298
Maps: USGS Sultan, Monroe; Bicycling in Snohomish County map, from Ride Store in Lynnwood
Information: Monroe Chamber of Commerce; Snohomish County PUD; Washington Department of Fish and Wildlife website for Wildlife Areas and Access Points

The Skykomish between Sultan and Monroe sweeps widely within its floodplain, meandering between huge gravel bars, the shoreline protected by giant cotton-woods. As it hugs the south side of its floodplain, it embraces steep hills that leave the river in shadow much of the year, a cold river where steelheaders gather to try their luck. The adjacent agricultural lands are hardly noticed from the river, so dense is the streamside vegetation in most of this stretch.

Access. To reach the take-out, drive east on US 2 into Monroe, and turn right (south) on Lewis Street to the bridge across the Skykomish at the south edge of town. Before reaching the bridge, turn right to a public fishing and boating access on the river's right bank. Parking is available nearby on the east side of South Lewis Street.

The launch site lies at the mouth of the Sultan River in Sultan. To reach it from the Monroe take-out, return to US 2, and head east to the west edge of Sultan. Before reaching the bridge across the Sultan River, turn left (north) into Sportsman Park. The launch site lies beneath the railroad bridge that parallels the highway bridge across the mouth of the Sultan River.

To reach the alternate access on the left bank 2 miles above Monroe, take Ben Howard Road, which parallels US 2 south of the river. To reach the east end of Ben Howard Road, take the bridge across the Sky in downtown Sultan. To reach the west end of Ben Howard Road, cross the bridge over the Sky south of Monroe and take the first left. The access is 2 miles from the SR 203 bridge, about 8 miles from the access in Sultan.

Paddle Route. From the launch site at the Sultan River mouth (RM 34.4), the Sky flows southwest in a huge open S to accept the offerings of Elwell Creek flowing in from the south (RM 31.7). The river is broad and swift, especially just before it reaches the south side of its floodplain against a steep hillside.

At the mouth of Elwell Creek the Sky angles west-by-northwest for 2 miles until it bumps into the ridge carrying US 2 between Monroe and Sultan. This wooded section screens the agricultural lands that flank the Sky through this segment. In summer, broad gravel bars offer ideal lunch stops; paddlers can pick sun or shade.

From its encounter with US 2, the Sky makes a beeline to the southwest. It runs headlong into that same steep hillside, which turns it west-by-northwest, bouncing it back and forth between its floodplain barriers. In less than a mile the fishermen's access on the left bank offers an out for the weary paddler.

An angler hauls his drift boat out of the Skykomish.

The Sky approaches US2 in another mile, then turns southwest for a 2-mile run past Monroe, where the take-out lies on the right (north) bank, just below the SR 203 bridge. Paddlers who have planned a longer run can continue to Snohomish (see Trips 13 and 14).

16 Skykomish River III

Location: Big Eddy to Sultan
Distance: 9 miles
Paddle time: 2 to 3 hours
Season: Year-round, especially summer
Rating: Class 2
Hazards: Logjams, sweepers, rapids, clay ledges
Shuttle: 8 miles, pavement
Flow information: USGS Washington website
River gauge: 12134500 near Gold Bar
Historic flows: Average 3948 cfs; maximum 102,000; minimum 298
Maps: USGS Sultan, Index
Information: Monroe Chamber of Commerce; Washington Department of Fish and Wildlife website for Wildlife Areas and Access Points

The Skykomish River from the Big Eddy below the Skykomish (US 2) bridge east of Gold Bar to Sportsman Park west of Sultan is a favorite segment for paddlers who like a little action. Most of it comes in the first half mile in a Class 2 rapid that can be seen from the launch site. There are a few other minor rapids and a series of waves, and one chute caused by blue-gray mud ledges halfway down the run. The adjacent highway and farmlands are unnoticeable, for the most part, and the wildlife is plentiful—a great picnic run with several massive gravel beaches at low water.

Access. To reach the take-out, drive east on US 2 to the west edge of Sultan. Turn left (north) into the park immediately before the bridge over the Sultan River adjacent to the Sultan Waste Water Treatment Plant.

To reach the put-in at Big Eddy, 8 miles to the east, drive back to US 2, turn left (east), and drive through Sultan, Startup, and Gold Bar. A mile beyond the east edge of Gold Bar, the highway crosses the Skykomish on a high bridge. Beyond the bridge, turn right down a bumpy dirt road to an access on the left (east) bank of the river above the railroad bridge. The put-in is just south of US 2 at the Big Eddy—a huge, deep green, mildly swirling pool. (The Big Eddy is visible from the US 2 bridge 2 miles east of downtown Gold Bar.)

Paddle Route. From the Big Eddy, a good place to practice paddling technique, the river dives under the Burlington Northern Railroad bridge and immediately

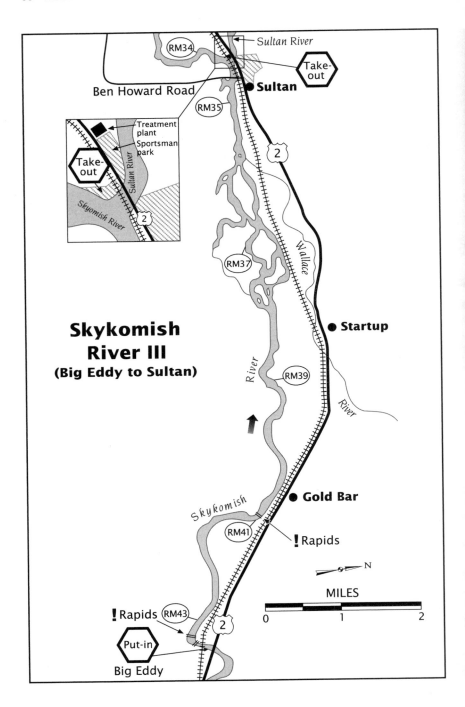

RM34

Sultan River

Take-out

Sultan

Ben Howard Road

RM35

Treatment plant

Sportsman park

Sultan River

Take-out

Skyomish River

2

2

Wallace

RM37

Skykomish River III
(Big Eddy to Sultan)

River

● **Startup**

RM39

River

● **Gold Bar**

Skykomish

RM41

! Rapids

N

MILES

0   1   2

! Rapids RM43

Put-in

2

Big Eddy

Big Eddy on the Skykomish near Gold Bar is a popular take-out for whitewater boaters and a put-in for a tamer stretch. (Brian Burns photo)

enters a Class 2 rapid. Below the rapid, the river doglegs to the right, moving quickly into a second, less-severe rapid. (One canoeist who failed to wear a PFD drowned in the first half mile of this river segment.)

The river broadens and shallows, becoming mellow for the next 3 or 4 miles, its banks lined with tall trees, its waters holding fish that entice anglers, kingfishers, great blue herons, mergansers, and ospreys. A blue-gray clay bank appears on the left, marking a peculiar geologic feature manifesting itself in a series of waves and strange currents that have flipped a few canoes. The hard clay bottom is near the surface at low water levels, but the water is difficult to read.

A few homes appear along the shore as the river splits around islands; paddlers generally take the right-hand channels. Either of the two big islands at RM 36 and RM 37 will serve as a lunch stop, but the second island is especially popular, summer or winter. It is a great place to skip rocks, and the big logjam offers some protection from any upstream winds. In the summer it makes a good swimming beach as well.

The Wallace River enters from the right just below the second big island as the river gathers itself together for the parade through town. Numerous houses line the right bank as the river approaches Sultan. After passing beneath the bridge across the Skykomish in Sultan—the one that leads to Ben Howard Road—there is only a quarter mile to make the take-out on the right, just below the mouth of the Sultan River, which makes a tricky landing at certain water levels.

17 Snoqualmie River I

Location: Tolt River mouth to confluence
Distance: 25 miles
Paddle time: 6 to 7 hours
Season: Year-round, especially autumn
Rating: Class 1
Hazards: Floods, sweepers, and logjams in the first half of the trip
Shuttle: 26 miles, pavement
Flow information: USGS Washington website
River gauge: 12149000 near Carnation
Historic flows: Average 3710 cfs; maximum 65,200; minimum 239
Maps: USGS Carnation, Monroe, Maltby; Snoqualmie Valley Map produced by Town Graphics
Information: Snoqualmie Valley Chamber of Commerce; Washington Department of Fish and Wildlife website for Wildlife Areas and Access Points

The bucolic nature of the lower Snoqualmie River characterizes this segment. Dairy farms line the river, adding to its nutrient base, especially during periodic winter flooding, and decorating the banks with farm litter and used equipment. Holstein cattle that graze its banks drink at the river, breaking down the banks and leaving their manure. Mountains, snow-clad in winter and spring, rise in the distance beyond forested hillsides periodically scarred with clear-cuts. This stretch of river is popular with anglers.

The final few miles of this trip flow through an isolated heavily forested area reminiscent of a Southern swamp. Ideal for summer and early fall paddling—rope swings hang from riverside trees, sandy beaches invite swimming and picnicking, blackberries ripen in August and September—this segment offers placid paddling through private lands with beautiful fall colors.

Access. Accesses can be reached from SR 203 between Fall City and Monroe. To reach the take-out, take High Bridge Road, a continuation of West Snoqualmie Valley Road NE, which roughly parallels the river on the west bank. Heading northwest, turn right onto Tester Road, which crosses the river on the High Bridge. It can also be reached from the east by turning south off the Old Snohomish Monroe Road southwest of Monroe.

To reach the Tolt River launch site, drive south on SR 203 to Carnation between Fall City and Monroe. Just south of Carnation, at the bridge across the Tolt River, turn west onto a dirt road immediately north of the bridge. This road leads to the mouth of the Tolt, where a rough access offers a launch on the right bank at Tolt Park.

For an alternate launch site at Taylors Landing, drive to Duvall in the lower Snoqualmie Valley: 8 miles south of Monroe, 14 miles northwest of Fall City on SR 203. Woodinville Duvall Road reaches Duvall from the west, crossing the Snoqualmie River as it enters town. Turn left onto SR 203, head north (toward Monroe), and drive 0.2 mile to the public fishing access left of the highway at Taylors Landing.

Paddle Route. From a launch at the mouth of the Tolt River, the Snoqualmie runs swift and deep past King County's John MacDonald Park, which includes a suspension footbridge across the river from which it is possible to watch salmon swimming upstream during their spawning runs. You can see them from your boat as well on this popular steelhead fishing run. After 2 relatively straight miles, the river makes a tight turn to the left and flows past Stillwater Wildlife Recreation Area on the right bank. Stillwater Park lies just below the wildlife area.

The flow slows, as the name "Stillwater" suggests, and meanders widely through

Anglers, some in chest-high waders, others in boats, fish the Snoqualmie River.

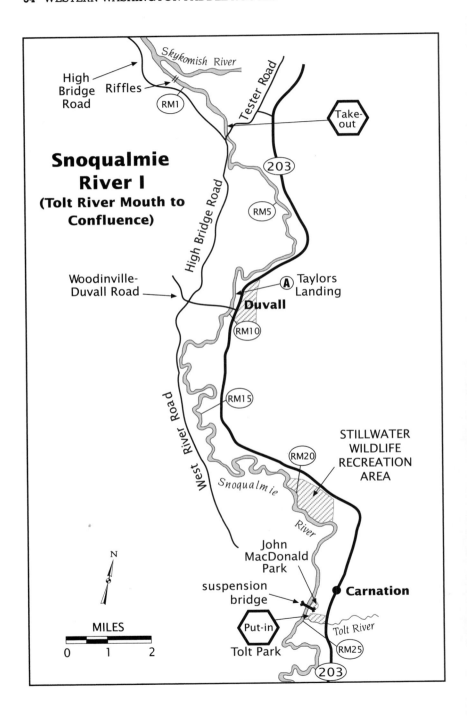

Snoqualmie River I
(Tolt River Mouth to Confluence)

its floodplain, creating numerous oxbows (abandoned meanders) that decorate the river valley, providing important wildlife habitat as well as hunting and fishing opportunities. As the river nears Duvall, it swings toward the east side of the valley and straightens for a mile or so past Duvall. Taylors Landing access lies at the north edge of Duvall.

From Duvall (RM 10) the river is deep, diked, and riprapped but placid and peaceful—an easy river to paddle, with little current, ideal for beginning paddlers. The river makes a straight run for a mile north, then doubles back upon itself in a tight S at RM 8.7. For the next few miles, it passes through pasturelands (adjacent to dairy farms) on the east side of the valley. At RM 6.2 the river crosses the King–Snohomish county line.

Nothing much changes on the river in Snohomish County except that it widens and begins a gradual snaking movement toward the west side of the valley. At RM 3.6 it takes a sharp turn to the north and picks up a little speed around a small island where the river narrows and shallows. In less than a mile (at RM 2.8) the river passes under High Bridge Road, the take-out.

Those who want a longer trip can continue down the Snoqualmie an additional 8 miles to its confluence with the Skykomish (see Trip 13). Below the High Bridge take-out the river enters its "Southern swamp" stage for the next mile before breaking out into a lively riffle a mile above the confluence.

18 Snoqualmie River II

Location: Fall City to Tolt River mouth
Distance: 11 miles
Paddle time: 4 hours
Season: Year-round, except at flood stage
Rating: Class 1
Hazards: Pilings, sweepers, logjams
Shuttle: 3 or 8 miles, pavement, some dirt
Flow information: USGS Washington website
River gauge: 12144500 near Snoqualmie
Historic flows: Average 2588 cfs; maximum 78,800; minimum 9.7
Maps: USGS Snoqualmie, Fall City, Carnation; Bicycling in Snohomish County map from Ride Store in Lynnwood; Snoqualmie Valley Map produced by Town Graphics
Information: Snoqualmie Valley Chamber of Commerce; Washington Department of Fish and Wildlife website for Wildlife Areas and Access Points

The Snoqualmie River between Fall City and Carnation, a bucolic stretch perfect for novice paddlers, may be bound by dikes much of the way, but the river is well

The Snoqualmie River sweeps quietly through its agricultural valley east of Seattle.

forested, offering views of its agricultural valley and distant peaks. It gives the beginning paddler few worries. There are occasional riffles, sweepers, and logjams; but the current is so slow, for the most part, that such obstacles serve as good training for more rambunctious river segments. An alternate take-out 3 miles into the trip allows a shorter run.

Access. To reach the take-out, drive to Carnation on SR 203 between Fall City and Monroe. Just south of Carnation, at the bridge across the Tolt River, turn west immediately north of the bridge onto a dirt road which leads to the mouth of the Tolt in King County's Tolt Park. Here a rough access offers a take-out on the right bank just below the Tolt mouth. A few dozen yards downstream lies an access on the right bank beneath the suspension footbridge across the Snoqualmie in King County's John MacDonald Park, but it requires a long carry. To reach this area, take the turnoff for the park between Carnation and the Tolt Bridge (north of the Tolt River).

To reach the suggested launch site, drive south on SR 203 to Fall City, crossing the bridge over the Snoqualmie into town. There are two alternatives: (1) turn right, park along the road within the next few dozen yards, and launch from the gravel bar beneath the bridge on river left; or (2) go straight toward Preston. Just after crossing the bridge over Raging River, turn left onto SE 44th Place, which leads to a boat ramp and a campground at the river's edge on the left bank. Either access is a good launch site.

The intermediate access, Richters Boat Landing, lies just off SR 203, 2.5 miles north of Fall City, at the northern terminus of Neal Road, which is blocked off immediately above the boat ramp; it can be reached only by turning into the north terminus of Neal Road from SR 203.

Paddle Route. From either Fall City launch site (RM 36.1 or 36.3), the river

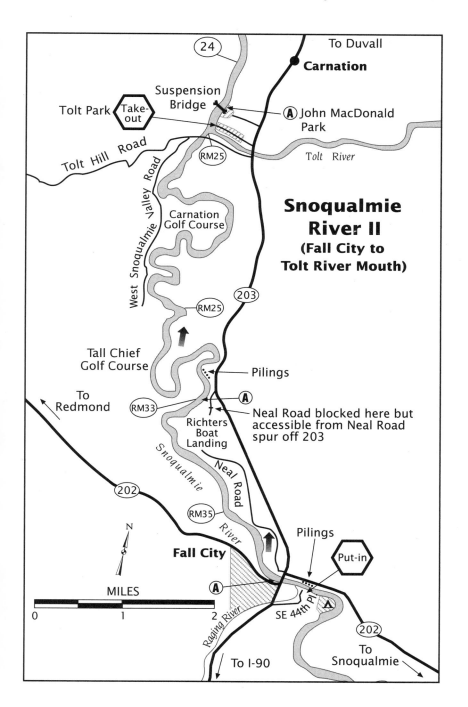

To Duvall

Carnation

24

Suspension
Bridge

Tolt Park
Take-
out

Ⓐ John MacDonald
Park

Tolt Hill Road

Tolt River

RM25

West Snoqualmie Valley Road

Carnation
Golf Course

Snoqualmie
River II
(Fall City to
Tolt River Mouth)

203

RM25

Tall Chief
Golf Course

Pilings

To
Redmond

RM33

Ⓐ

Neal Road blocked here but
accessible from Neal Road
spur off 203

Richters
Boat
Landing

Snoqualmie

Neal Road

202

RM35

River

Pilings

Put-in

N

Fall City

Ⓐ

SE 44th Pl

Ⓐ

202

MILES

0   1   2

Raging River

To
Snoqualmie

To I-90

flows northwest for a little over 2 miles between riprapped banks overgrown with blackberry bushes and lined with native vegetation. Adjacent farms go largely unnoticed. Some maneuvering is required at a few mild riffles and two stretches with old pilings in the river. At RM 33.7 the river turns abruptly to the right and in less than a mile passes the ramp at Richters Boat Landing. SR 203 comes close enough to be visible from the river twice in the next mile. Farms begin to encroach on the river corridor, and the banks in places are beaten down by cattle.

The river meanders widely for the next several miles, looping back and forth on the west side of the valley. It comes close to two golf courses some 5 miles apart. The river first aims at Tall Chief (RM 31), then runs north for a mile through farmlands. At RM 30 it begins a series of three east–west hairpin bends in the next 2 miles, all through pastures or croplands.

Through most of this segment the river is slow and deep, full of snags and tree trunks anchored in the sandy bottom. At RM 28 it begins a loop to the north, then abruptly south, and finally, northeast for 0.5 mile before it swings west again past Carnation Golf Course (river left). Once more it bends abruptly north adjacent to West Snoqualmie Valley Road, for the last mile to the Tolt Mouth take-out.

19 Snoqualmie River III

Location: Falls to Fall City
Distance: 4 miles
Paddle time: 1 to 2 hours
Season: Year-round
Rating: Class 2; Class 3 upstream
Hazards: Rapids, especially above Tokul mouth
Shuttle: 3 miles, pavement
Flow information: USGS Washington website
River gauge: 12144500 near Snoqualmie
Historic flows: Average 2588 cfs; maximum 78,800; minimum 9.7
Maps: USGS Snoqualmie, Fall City; Snoqualmie Valley Map produced by Town Graphics
Information: Snoqualmie Valley Chamber of Commerce; Washington Department of Fish and Wildlife website for Wildlife Areas and Access Points

The stretch of the Snoqualmie River between Snoqualmie Falls and Fall City is only about 4 river miles, but it offers good variety and is ideal for a bicycle shuttle. Many experienced paddlers go upstream from the boat launch to play in the Class 2 rapids above (within sight of the falls). Polers like to practice their skills in the rocky rapids of this upper section, but even novice paddlers can negotiate the river downstream, though at low water the rapids become rockier and tighter.

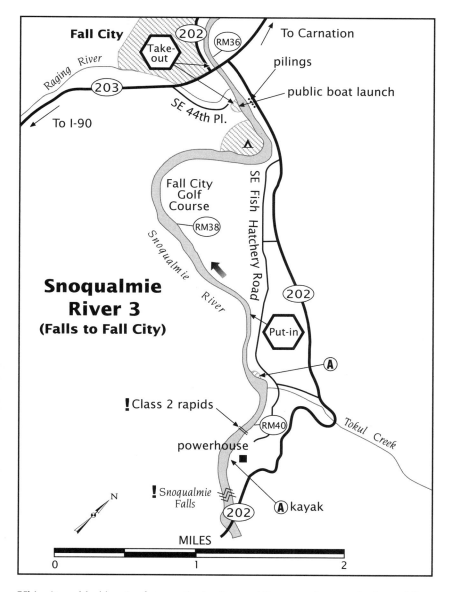

Fall City

202

RM36

To Carnation

Take-out

Raging River

pilings

203

public boat launch

SE 44th Pl.

To I-90

Fall City Golf Course

SE Fish Hatchery Road

RM38

Snoqualmie River

Snoqualmie River 3
(Falls to Fall City)

202

Put-in

Ⓐ

! Class 2 rapids

RM40

Tokul Creek

powerhouse

! Snoqualmie Falls

202

Ⓐ kayak

N

MILES

0   1   2

Ubiquitous blackberries festoon the banks providing succulent snacks for paddlers and birds; fishing is often good.

Access. Excellent access to this segment is available at two possible take-outs in Fall City and at the put-in on river right, a public fishing access just below the mouth of Tokul Creek along Fish Hatchery Road. Kayakers often drive to the power plant at the end of Fish Hatchery Road (Plums Landing), and launch from the trail immediately below the powerhouse to play in the rapids below the falls.

Drive to Fall City, taking SR 202. To reach the canoe/kayak take-out at Fall City Riverfront Park, turn west on SR 202 just south of the bridge; the take-out lies on river left, below the bridge.

To reach the boat ramp take-out 0.25 mile upstream, take SR 203 south from its junction with SR 202. After crossing the bridge over the Raging River, turn left immediately past the bridge onto SE 44th Place, which follows the Raging River downstream to its confluence with the Snoqualmie. The boat ramp lies on the dike left of the river a few dozen yards above the mouth of the Raging River.

The launch site lies a half-mile below Snoqualmie Falls. From Fall City, head north for a short distance, crossing the SR 202/203 bridge, then immediately turn right and follow SR 202 southeast toward Snoqualmie and North Bend. After a mile, turn right onto SE Fish Hatchery Road, which angles toward the river. Follow the road along the river to Plums Landing public boat launch to the right of the road, on the river's right bank.

To reach the kayak launch area, continue on the same road, cross Tokul Creek, and drive up the hill and around a couple of bends to the small parking area by a

A steelhead angler fishes the Snoqualmie downstream from Snoqualmie Falls.

gate (usually locked) at the powerhouse. Follow a trail to the river to the right of the fence around the power plant facility.

Paddle Route. This segment gets progressively tougher as paddlers head upstream from the boat ramp, progressively easier as they head downstream from the kayak launch at the powerhouse. Below the boat ramp the river has a couple of mild rapids and a few rocks to dodge at low water levels. The river broadens, deepens, and slows as it approaches Fall City.

Some riffles show in low water as the current swings from one side of the river to the other, but once the river flows into its big bend to the right, around Fall City Golf Course, it is lakelike: a long, narrow stretch of deep green water. The river turns abruptly to the left as it approaches SR 202 a mile east of Fall City; then it hugs that road for the rest of the way to Fall City. A few ancient pilings line the right bank. The left bank is busy with the campground, which covers the promontory around which the river makes its last bend to either of the two take-outs, both on the left—the boat ramp, just above the mouth of the Raging River, or 0.25 mile below at Fall City Riverfront Park.

20 Snoqualmie River IV

Location: Above the falls, North Bend to Snoqualmie
Distance: 4 miles
Paddle time: 1 to 2 hours
Season: Year-round
Rating: Class 2 first mile, Class 1 below
Hazards: Sweepers, logjams, rapids, major falls downstream
Shuttle: 4 miles, pavement
Flow information: USGS Washington website
River gauge: 12144500 near Snoqualmie
Historic flows: Average 2588 cfs; maximum 78,800; minimum 9.7
Maps: USGS North Bend, Snoqualmie, Bandera; Snoqualmie Valley Map produced by Town Graphics
Information: Snoqualmie Valley Chamber of Commerce; Washington Department of Fish and Wildlife website for Wildlife Areas and Access Points

This section of the Snoqualmie River is obvious from the road, but difficult to reach. Parking is limited at all of the precious few access points. A bicycle shuttle is ideal here. The river is a real gem, involving all three major forks of the Snoqualmie. It lies below Mount Si, which provides a spectacular background for the entire run. The river itself is delightful, with a few riffles, lots of deep pools, a largely natural shoreline, and numerous sand and gravel bars much used by anglers and picnickers. It is also a favorite for tubers and air-mattress floaters. This area is part of the Three Forks Natural Area of the Mountains to the Sound Greenway.

Access. To reach the take-out, drive southeast on SR 202 from Fall City toward Snoqualmie and North Bend. At the top of the falls at the northwest edge of Snoqualmie—just beyond Snoqualmie Falls Lodge and before crossing the Snoqualmie River—turn left onto Mill Pond Road. The take-out lies to the right (south) of the road, just beyond the bend of the river, at a small informal access point that requires roadside parking.

To reach the launch sites, drive east on Mill Pond Road to SE Reinig Road and continue east (upstream) alongside the river. SE 396th seems like the continuation of the main road, but SE Reinig Road turns right at the next intersection, at a bend of the river where a rough access on river right leads to a favorite summer play spot for swimmers and waders within sight of an old railroad bridge.

The main launch site offers access to the Middle Fork beneath the bridge on 428th Avenue SE, northeast of North Bend. To reach it, continue east on SE Reinig Road to a T intersection, turn right (south), go 0.6 mile to SE 92nd Road (a dead-end road) and turn left, then immediately right onto a rough dirt road to the Middle Fork. Parking is limited and vehicles cannot access the river directly, but a short carry offers launching possibilities beneath the bridge.

Paddle Route. At the Middle Fork launch site, the river is pleasant and picturesque: Mount Si looms over the paddler's shoulder, and downstream the river is wild in its scenic beauty but mild in its flow. At the first bend, however, the river turns a bit wild in its flow. After a little jog to the left, it makes a sharp swing to the right against a gigantic logjam that at high water could be a terror. At low flows it is merely a hazard to maneuver past, but there are numerous snags in the sometimes-swift water of this first mile.

Just below the logjam, the Middle Fork meets the North Fork head-on and the currents swirl together off a long sandy point bar. With a trail coming into this vicinity on the right, anglers and picnickers make use of the sandy bar on the right. The deep pools begin just below the confluence with plenty of debris in the river, but the current is so slow the logs and snags generally offer few major hazards; they're more likely just minor obstacles to maneuver around.

Pools and riffles alternate to the South Fork mouth on the left. The South Fork has occasionally been totally blocked by logjams. Winter floods tend to rearrange the river's furniture. SE Reinig Road runs along the right bank, offering steep access at a couple of points. A few rural homes line the bank as the river becomes one big, slow, deep channel.

As it turns left in a big bend beneath a railroad bridge, the river passes the swimming hole on the right at the junction of SE 396th and SE Reinig Road, a possible launch or take-out point. Soon the river swings back to the right beneath

Opposite: View of Mount Si from the Middle Fork of the Snoqualmie River

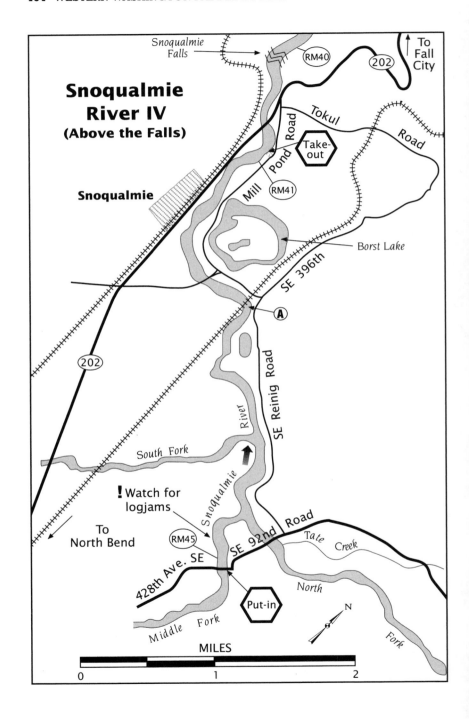

Snoqualmie River IV
(Above the Falls)

Snoqualmie Falls

RM40

To Fall City

202

Tokul Road

Pond Road

Take-out

RM41

Mill

Snoqualmie

Borst Lake

SE 396th

A

202

SE Reinig Road

River

South Fork

Snoqualmie

! Watch for logjams

To North Bend

RM45

SE 92nd Road

Tate Creek

428th Ave. SE

North

Put-in

Middle Fork

Fork

N

MILES

0   1   2

a railroad bridge. The edge of the town of Snoqualmie lines the left bank; a thin fringe of timber between the river and Mill Pond Road lines the right.

This slow, deep stretch continues around several bends, passing under another railroad bridge. Soon the protective railing along Mill Pond Road comes into view as paddlers see several planters pointing downstream anchored in the river bottom. When you see the planters and the guardrail, it is time to look for the take-out on the right immediately upstream from the railing.

21 Sammamish River

Location: Between Redmond and Kenmore
Distance: 2 to 13 miles
Paddle time: 4 to 5 hours
Season: Year-round
Rating: Class 1
Hazards: Trash and debris in the river
Shuttle: 12 miles, pavement
Flow information: None available
Maps: USGS Redmond, Kirkland, Bothell; NOAA chart 18447 (lower river)
Information: King County Parks and Recreation Division; Redmond Parks and Recreation Department; Washington Department of Fish and Wildlife website for Wildlife Areas and Access Points

The Sammamish River between Lake Sammamish and Lake Washington creates a passage for anadromous fish but no longer for boats. The Sammamish River Trail runs all the way from Marymoor County Park to Kenmore. The river flows slowly through an urban area that supports beavers, muskrats, and numerous species of birds, including many ducks and geese. It offers nearby access to fine restaurants, shopping areas, seven wineries and breweries as it passes through Redmond, Hollywood Corner, Woodinville, Bothell, and Kenmore.

Access. Abundant access to the Sammamish River suggests numerous short sections for brief after-work floats that are ideal for bicycle shuttles. The best launch site lies at Luke McRedmond Landing Park south of Redmond. Other accesses are at street ends in Redmond, at nearly every bridge crossing in the valley, at both sides of the river in Bothell, and at a public boat ramp in Kenmore. Additional access is available at several parks on Lake Washington.

For the last take-out before reaching Lake Washington, take NE Bothell Way (SR 522), which loops around the north end of Lake Washington. At 68th Avenue NE in Kenmore, turn south, cross the Sammamish River, and immediately turn right into a public fishing access on the left (south) bank of the river beneath the bridge (Kenmore County Park). There is substantial parking here, but the area is

Easy put-in for Sammamish paddlers

heavily used by powerboaters and is often crowded with vehicles and boat trailers. The nearest auxiliary parking is blocks away.

From the take-out in Kenmore, to reach the Bothell accesses, return to SR 522 and head east. As it enters Bothell, the road curves left (north). Just as it begins to curve back to the right (east) again), turn right onto Wilson Avenue into the park at Bothell Landing, an access on river right with parking and several nice shops and restaurants nearby. The other Bothell access is just across the river. Turn right off Main Street (a block north of NE Bothell Way and SR 522) onto 102nd Avenue, heading south over the Sammamish River. Take the first right after crossing the bridge, turning into a large parking area that offers access to the river's left bank—a good take-out or put-in point.

To reach the access points in the Sammamish Valley, retrace the route to SR 522, which soon becomes a freeway. Turn right toward Woodinville, take the Woodinville exit, and follow SR 202 south, first along the west side of the river, then along the east side after it crosses the river on NE 145th Street. Between Woodinville and Redmond it is possible to access the river at most of the crossings that intersect SR 202: 154th Place NE, NE 145th Street, NE 124th Street, or NE 116th Street (in Sammamish River County Park).

In Redmond you can access the river at several street ends and NE 85th Street abutting the Sammamish River Trail, but the best launch site is Luke McRedmond Landing Park off the south side of Redmond Way southwest of Redmond; it has a paved boat ramp, fifteen parking spots, and two handicapped parking spaces.

To reach the launch site, go east from I-405 on SR 520 (Exit 168B) and exit at West Lake Sammamish Parkway. Turn left onto the Parkway and go through the stoplight at NE Leary Way, staying left at the Y, to SR 901, West Lake Sammamish Parkway. Turn right at Redmond Way (SR 508) and right again onto 159th Place NE. Turn right immediately through a short section of parking lot and bear right into Luke McRedmond Park. (Most of the park lies south of Redmond Way.)

From I-405, go east on NE 85th Street (SR 908, Exit 18). After a few miles the road becomes Redmond Way. Turn right onto 159th Place NE, and immediately right into a short section of parking lot, and bear right into the park.

Paddle Route. A concrete weir built on the Sammamish River to raise the level of Lake Sammamish prevents paddlers from traveling by boat from Lake Sammamish to Lake Washington without a portage. The launch site on the east side of the river at Luke McRedmond Landing Park avoids the weir. The Sammamish River Trail parallels this segment all the way to Kenmore. Bear Creek enters from the right below the launch site as the river, flanked by condominiums, enters Redmond. It passes an office park and the Redmond City Hall. A number of good restaurants are within easy walking distance of the river.

Channelized for most of the stretch to Lake Washington, the Sammamish runs northward out of Redmond. Being cut into a uniform-sided trough does not severely detract from the river's aesthetic quality, its natural beauty, or its value as wildlife habitat: beavers and muskrats live in this stretch, ducks and geese nest here, along with red-winged blackbirds and marsh wrens. Look upstream for views of Mount Rainier. Swallows, spotted sandpipers, northern harriers, red-tailed hawks, kingfishers, killdeer, grebes, great blue and green herons frequent the area; cattails, feral iris, and wild sweet peas grow along the river; and blackberries ripen in season. Noisy electric pumps drain water from the river for nearby irrigation.

The water is slow, even sluggish, but there is usually a perceptible flow and a sense of the natural. The river passes open meadows, ball fields, turf farms, dairies, and scattered condos. It passes within a quarter mile of rural shopping centers as well as several wineries and breweries. Bikers, runners, anglers, hikers, skaters, hot air balloonists, and ultralight fliers, even dogsledders (with sleds on wheels) use the Sammamish River Trail and may be seen from the river.

As the river passes the Tolt Pipeline Trail, it swings northwest toward Woodinville, scrapes the edge of that growing community, and turns westward through a light industrial area. Even as it approaches the noisy overpasses that carry I-405 overhead, the river is flanked by small farms and residences. Soon it begins to

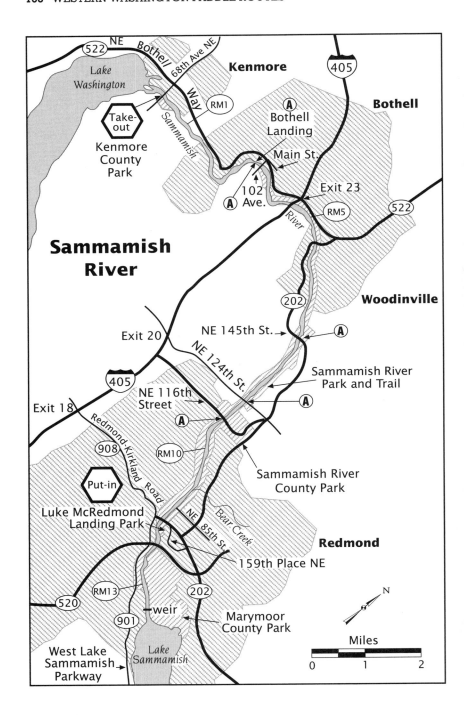

curve past suburban homes, golf courses, tree nurseries, and mobile home parks.

The river widens, making room for powerboats tied up at private docks. Canada geese mob the river in this area. Activity is steady along the trail that parallels the river. The closer the river gets to Bothell, the more the urban environment encroaches upon the natural. The take-out on the left bank in Bothell is a good place to stop after a 10-mile float. Bothell Landing on the right just beyond offers a pleasant park, more urban than bucolic.

The last 2.5 miles are largely urban-industrial; powerboats ply this stretch so continuously, especially on weekends and after-work hours, that it is less than pleasant for paddling. Still, it can be delightful in the early mornings and whenever you can have the river to yourself—antipodal paddling.

22 Issaquah Creek

Location: South end of Lake Sammamish, north of Issaquah
Distance: 1 to 2 miles
Paddle time: 1 to 2 hours
Season: Year-round
Rating: Class 1
Hazards: Debris from human activity, natural debris
Shuttle: None necessary
Flow information: USGS Washington website
River gauge: 12121600 near mouth
Historic flows: Average 130 cfs; maximum 3200; minimum 6.2
Maps: USGS Issaquah; East King County Map by Kroll Map Co. of Seattle
Information: Washington Department of Fish and Wildlife website for Wildlife Areas and Access Points

Issaquah Creek is a small, intimate stream. No shuttle is needed because it involves paddling up a creek from an access on the lake into which it flows, then returning. The creek offers a natural area in the midst of rapid urban development. It has a salmon run, muskrats, beavers, deer, coyotes, and abundant bird life, from bald eagles to marsh wrens, from green herons to nesting ducks. It is protected somewhat by Lake Sammamish State Park.

Access. The best access is from the boat launch at the southeast end of Lake Sammamish in Lake Sammamish State Park. From I-90 eastbound, turn off at Issaquah Exit 17 and take the East Lake Sammamish Parkway north about 3 miles to Lake Sammamish State Park boat launch area. Turn left into that facility and launch onto the southeastern lobe of Lake Sammamish. Paddle west to the mouth of Issaquah Creek.

Paddle Route. From the boat launch at Lake Sammamish State Park southwest to the low-lying delta of Issaquah Creek, paddlers may encounter a few power-boats, but paddling into the creek mouth and heading upstream leaves the noise, as well as the wind and most of the people, behind. A few trails in the vicinity may have hikers, but within a quarter mile (shortly after passing beneath the footbridge across the creek), they too should be left behind.

The channel may be blocked periodically by natural debris from recent storms, but boaters can generally work their way up the creek with either pole or paddle—though the pole may get snagged in overhead vegetation at times, for segments of the creek flow through a tunnel of trees and shrubs. Blackberry vines hang over the water but can be avoided. The berries can also be sought out for snacks in the late summer or early fall.

The creek winds through the trees and shrubs, gradually increasing in speed as it breaks into an opening here and there. At a sharp turn to the left, about half a mile from the mouth, a strong current flows around an island that may call for portaging or lining. However, especially with a pole, one can usually maneuver upstream. You may see anglers or a pair of lovers along the bank.

Steep cut banks a few feet high mark the creek's course through the meadows as it approaches SE 56th Street. In the summer these meadows are full of wild-flowers and goldfinches feeding on thistle seeds. In late spring, the creek harbors families of ducks, mostly mallards. Fall brings the salmon run, fun to watch as they work their way up to the hatchery in Issaquah. Paddlers can turn around at this

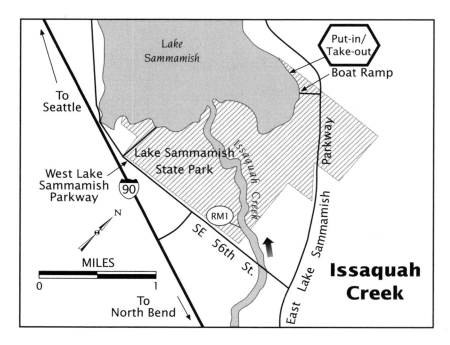

A wooden footbridge spans Issaquah Creek in Lake Sammamish State Park.

point and drift back down to the mouth, then paddle across the lake to the launch site, which is also the take-out.

23 Cedar River

Location: Maple Valley to Renton
Distance: 14 miles
Paddle time: 3 to 4 hours
Season: Year-round, especially summer
Rating: Class 2
Hazards: Logjams, sweepers, rapids, one headwall
Shuttle: 12 miles, pavement
Flow information: USGS Washington website
River gauge: 122119000 at Renton
Historic flows: Average 659 cfs; maximum 10,600; minimum 30
Maps: USGS Maple Valley, Renton; Cedar River Trail Park Map; East King County Map by Kroll Map Co. of Seattle
Information: Cedar River Trail Park; King County Parks and Recreation Division; King County Dept. of Natural Resources; Washington Department of Fish and Wildlife website for Wildlife Areas and Access Points

The Cedar River flows under the Renton Library and can be seen from the I-405 S-curves. A whitewater river in its youth, the Cedar in its final few miles offers an active paddling experience through a bucolic semirural area. The river is small and intimate, a rocky run with brushy bends, an occasional high bluff, lots of gravel bars, numerous bird species, and evidence of beavers and muskrats. Its run through downtown Renton is unique, with anadromous fish visible in the clear water, even beneath the library. The Cedar—along with the Missouri, the Yellowstone, and the Lower Snake—made American Rivers' list of the 10 Most Endangered Rivers in 1999 because of urban sprawl and water withdrawals. (American Rivers is North America's leading river conservation organization.) Nature also has a way of changing the river with occasional landslides and logjams.

Access. The last mile of the Cedar River before it flows into Lake Washington is flanked on the right by parklands with a convenient take-out at Riverview Park across the river from the Renton Airport. The launch site is a rough, often-rutted access at the edge of Maple Valley within sight of the SR 18 overpass.

To reach the take-out, find the Cedar River Trail and Park in Renton off North

The Cedar River flows under the Renton Library as it enters the city.

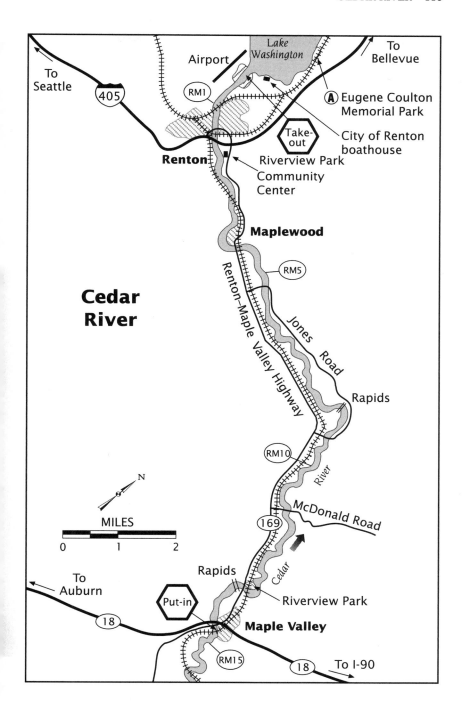

To Seattle

405

Airport

RM1

Lake Washington

To Bellevue

Ⓐ Eugene Coulton Memorial Park

City of Renton boathouse

Take-out

Renton

Riverview Park Community Center

Maplewood

RM5

Renton–Maple Valley Highway

Jones Road

Cedar River

Rapids

RM10

River

McDonald Road

169

N

MILES
0   1   2

To Auburn

Rapids

Put-in

Cedar

Riverview Park

Maple Valley

18

18

RM15

To I-90

6th Street from Logan Avenue North in the midst of the Boeing complex. NE Park Drive, which becomes Lake Washington Boulevard North, is a good way to get there from Exit 5 off I-405. A City of Renton boathouse (canoe and kayak sales and rental shop) is on the dock to the right at the mouth of the river.

Lake Washington Beach Park (Gene Coulton Memorial Park), which has abundant parking, is another potential take-out, but it involves paddling a mile across the lower end of Lake Washington, an interesting float through an industrial area.

To reach the launch site at Maple Valley, take the Enumclaw exit off I-405 to the Renton–Maple Valley Highway (SR 169). Heading east and south on this route, paddlers can scout much of the river, especially if they take the Jones Road cutoff that crosses the river, parallels it, and recrosses it well below Maple Valley. In Maple Valley, turn left off SR 169 just after crossing the river, then left again into an unpaved, unmarked riverside access between the highway and the railroad tracks. This is the launch site, unpretentious but adequate, 12 miles from the I-405 exit.

Paddle Route. From the launch site on river left (RM 14.7), the river is fast and rocky. It passes beneath SR 169 and SR 18 in quick succession, runs a fast mile through a brushy corridor, then passes under SR 169 again and the adjacent railroad bridge a mile northwest of Maple Valley (RM 13.5) to run east of the highway for several miles.

The river has a rural flavor. Wooded banks hide most but not all of the surrounding homes. Some short, simple rapids and the speed of the current keep paddlers busy as the river swings back and forth across its floodplain. At one moment it nudges the railroad embankment on the left; at the next it nibbles at the base of the bluff on the right; and at one point (near RM 12) it dives into the headwall on the right. Watch for logjams after high water.

The Cedar flows beneath a bridge (McDonald Road) at RM 11.1, parallels the railroad for a few hundred yards, swings back toward the bluff on the right, back again toward the railroad, and repeats this performance to slide beneath the Jones Road bridge at RM 9.3. Just below this point, the highway and the railroad turn due west, still paralleling one another quite closely; whenever you near the railroad tracks, the highway is adjacent.

Jones Road kisses the riverbank between RM 5 and 6. The river flows beneath the western Jones Road bridge at RM 5.3, then becomes more debris-ridden as the gradient mellows. A mile downstream the river curves left under both the railroad and the highway to make a big loop around Maplewood. It remains south of the highway for the rest of its course to Renton, but the railroad crosses to the south side of the river at RM 2.9.

The Cedar River mellows as it approaches Renton, getting slower, a little deeper, less rambunctious. Development intrudes here and there (a sand and gravel works on the left from which silty water trickles into the river, concrete or asphalt banks in places, buildings), but parklands also embrace much of the riverbank in the lower few miles. Once the river passes beneath the twin spans of I-405, the banks are concrete, the scene urban, including the river's passage beneath the library.

For the last 1.5 miles, expect to see people watching, waving, having their lunch along the river. Watch for fish in the river and gulls overhead, but don't be afraid to accept this as an urban world, not a bad place to stop for a drink or something to eat. Paddlers could even exit the river at one of the cross streets, but that might tie up traffic—better to go on the last mile to the suggested take-out.

24 Duwamish River/Waterway

Location: Fort Dent Park to Elliott Bay
Distance: 12 miles
Paddle time: 4 to 5 hours
Season: Year-round
Rating: Tidal flatwater (up to Class 2)
Hazards: Snags, tidal currents, powerboats, large ships, a tidal rapid (Class 2)
Shuttle: None necessary or 12 miles, pavement
Flow information: Tidal
Maps: USGS Seattle South, Des Moines; NOAA charts 18448, 18449, 18450; Port of Seattle map, On the Waterfront
Information: Port of Seattle Public Affairs

The Duwamish River and the "waterway" at its mouth provide a unique paddling experience, from fast-water chutes on the ebb tide to dodging oceangoing vessels around Harbor Island while admiring views of the Seattle skyline. The Green River becomes the Duwamish just below Fort Dent Park, where the historic Black River draining Lake Washington once joined. The Lower Duwamish is largely industrial, yet it harbors a great blue heron colony, and anglers still line the low-level Spokane Street Bridge to try for a variety of saltwater and freshwater fish.

Access. Numerous accesses exist for launching a small paddle craft onto the Duwamish River/Waterway, from the poor put-in at Fort Dent Park on the last mile of the Green before it becomes the Duwamish, to public access on Elliott Bay, below its highly developed saltwater mouth. All of the alternate accesses lie in the tidal reach of the waterway. They consist of several public accesses, most of them reached from either East or West Marginal Way.

(1) Jack Perry Memorial Viewpoint (Terminal 30 Access) is the lowest access on the river itself, at the lower end of the East Waterway where Alaskan Way South becomes East Marginal Way South, south of the Coast Guard Station (south of Massachusetts Street), where huge cranes rise into the sky to dominate the waterway. Driving south on East Marginal Way, turn right immediately south of the tank farm (fuel storage structures) at an area marked "Terminal 30, East Waterway, Interim

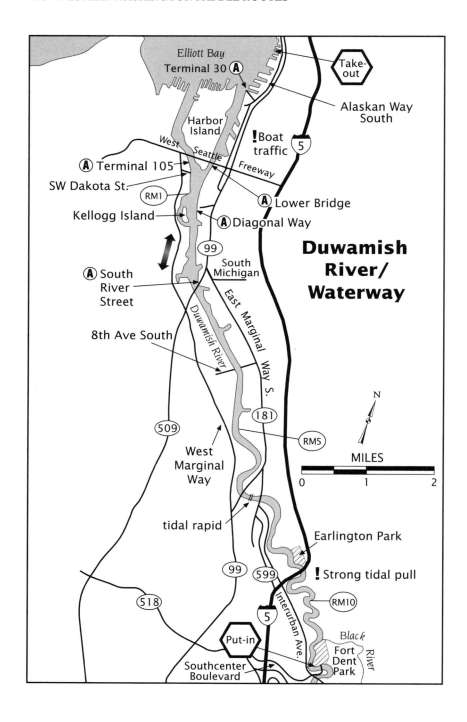

Elliott Bay
Terminal 30 Ⓐ

Take-out

Alaskan Way South

Harbor Island

! Boat traffic

5

West Seattle

Ⓐ Terminal 105

Freeway

SW Dakota St.

RM1

Ⓐ Lower Bridge

Kellogg Island

Ⓐ Diagonal Way

99

Duwamish River/ Waterway

South Michigan

Ⓐ South River Street

East Marginal Way S.

Duwamish River

8th Ave South

N

509

181

RM5

West Marginal Way

MILES

0   1   2

tidal rapid

Earlington Park

! Strong tidal pull

99 599

RM10

518

Interurban Ave.

5

Put-in

Black River

Fort Dent Park

Southcenter Boulevard

Public Access Site" to a Port of Seattle access with ample parking that marks the end of an 11-mile trip from Fort Dent Park.

(2) Lower Bridge site on the east shore of the East Waterway lies a few dozen yards below its split from the West Waterway, but it can be reached only from eastward traffic lanes on the lower bridge from West Seattle (beneath the new West Seattle Bridge). The access ramp is so close to the bridge you can't see it until you are there: immediately after the guardrail ends on the bridge over the East Waterway. There is room for only five or six vehicles to park at this take-out, the end of a 10-mile trip from Fort Dent Park, or the launch site for local exploring. (Transients have been known to live here.) An outgoing tide causes significant current through the bridge pilings. On high tides there is no clearance beneath the bridge.

(3) Diagonal Avenue South Public Shoreline Access (Diagonal Way site) is probably the best take-out or launch site on the lower waterway—plenty of parking, and the access is protected by a small indentation at the end of Diagonal Way. The turnoff to Diagonal Way is the second stoplight south of the viaduct carrying Old SR 99. It is located just opposite the lower (downstream) end of Kellogg Island.

(4) South River Street site, a boat ramp almost directly beneath the First Avenue South Viaduct, just south of the South Michigan Street ramp. Turn west onto South River Street, a very short street that bisects East Marginal Way a block south of South Michigan. The boat ramp is just east of the Viaduct over the Duwamish. This take-out terminates an 8-mile trip from Fort Dent Park.

(5) Terminal 105 Viewpoint lies on the west bank of the Duwamish just as the West Waterway splits around Harbor Island. Situated off West Marginal Way, it is a tiny park provided by the Port of Seattle. Just north of Southwest Dakota Street, this access is marked "Duwamish Public Access—Public Shore." A trip from Fort Dent Park ending here would be 10 miles long. (It is not intended as a boating access, but it can serve that purpose.) Parking is limited.

(6) Terminal 115 Viewpoint (follow signs from juncture of West Marginal Way, SW and SW Michigan to Second Avenue SW) involves a long carry.

(7), (8) River access is available at 8th Avenue South on both sides of the waterway from Marginal Way, East and West, respectively, in the neighborhood of South Park.

(9) The public access at Fort Dent Park (RM 11.7) is no more than a trail leading to a sandy beach (at low water levels) or an eddy (at high flows). To reach Fort Dent, get on southbound I-5 any of several different ways: West Seattle Freeway, Old SR 99, or East Marginal Way S. Travel toward Southcenter or the junction of I-5 with I-405. East Marginal Way S (also SR 181) may be the best bet because it puts you on Interurban Avenue, which crosses Southcenter Boulevard at the right place: at the left turn to Fort Dent Park. Heading south on I-5, take Interurban (Exit 156), follow it to the Southcenter Boulevard junction, and turn left. Crossing the lower Green River, enter Fort Dent Park and turn left at the south end of the parking area

The South River Street site is often used by Native American fishermen.

adjacent to an open field. The access is on the point of land at the south edge of the park, where the river loops back in a great horseshoe. Check it out on foot before you carry the craft and gear all over the park looking for the right place.

A dedicated boat-launching site (not a boat ramp) at Fort Dent Park would greatly enhance boating use of the lower Duwamish—a highly developed but nonetheless interesting stretch of river.

Paddle Route. From the launch site in Fort Dent Park, the river heads northwest, skirting the park and forming its western boundary. A fringe of trees on the left bank thinly veils development. Within a mile, a slough comes in from the right—all that remains of what was once the Black River, the historic outlet of Lake Washington. The confluence of the Green and the Black once created the Duwamish, named for the local Native American tribe of which Sealth (Seattle) was chief.

For the next 2 miles—to the I-5 crossing—the Duwamish meanders through Foster Golf Links, a lovely run and a good access site as well. Traffic noise whines down from the I-5 crossing. If the tide is going out, there is a strong pull by the river, gurgling past snags and industrial debris anchored in the muddy bottom. Earlington County Park embraces the right bank. There are bridges galore: 42nd Avenue South, East Marginal Way S (SR 181), Pacific Highway. Some of this stretch of river is lovely, almost isolated by the dikes raised to control its flooding. Beware of commercial traffic on the river. Groups of paddlers should stay together along one shore or the other.

From RM 5, the Duwamish is an industrial river but nonetheless interesting and paddle-worthy. Late in the afternoon and on weekends and holidays it can be a delightful place to explore, though powerboats often create an atmosphere less than desirable for paddle craft. At RM 0.8, the Duwamish splits around Harbor Island, creating a pair of busy waterways where paddling may not seem appropriate during the working day or at high tide, but where it can offer unique paddling opportunities.

25 Green River I

Location: Kent to Tukwila, lower reach
Distance: 6.5 miles
Paddle time: 2 hours
Season: Year-round
Rating: Class 1
Hazards: Woody debris anchored in the river for anadromous fish habitat
Shuttle: 8 miles, pavement
Flow information: USGS Washington website
River gauge: 12113350 at Tukwila
Historic flows: No average provided; maximum 22.63 feet; minimum 1 foot
Maps: USGS Renton, Des Moines
Information: Washington Department of Fish and Wildlife website for Wildlife Areas and Access Points

The lower Green River in this short stretch of placid but relatively fast water bound by dikes on both sides is worth considering, much of it flanked by parklands in west Kent and in Tukwila. It begins in a rural area marked by nurseries, berry fields, and old barns; traverses several miles of fertile farmland now devoted to housing developments; passes through Tukwila's industrial and commercial heart; then, after passing beneath I-405, ends at Fort Dent Park. It provides a link between the Green River in the Auburn–Kent area and the Duwamish River, allowing a continuous trip of more than 30 miles.

Access. Salmon enhancement projects and Native American fishing activities have discouraged development of additional river access for recreational boaters. Consequently, access is limited to the poor take-out at Fort Dent Park (RM 11.7) and a launch site in west Kent, just south of South 212th Street.

To reach the take-out, take the SR 181/Interurban Avenue exit from I-405 (Exit 1) a mile east of the I-5/I-405 interchange, and head north on Interurban Avenue. Turn right onto Southcenter Boulevard, which crosses the lower Green as it enters Fort Dent Park. Turn left at the first intersection in the park and stop as

The lower Green River flows through a protected parkway in Tukwila.

far south and as close to the open field on the southwest as possible. The take-out is at the bend of the river a hundred yards below the bridge and is reached by a long carry from the south parking area (see map for Trip 24).

To reach the launch sites, retrace the route to I-405, but do not get back on the freeway. Go straight ahead on SR 181 (Interurban Avenue, which becomes West Valley Highway) heading south. It touches bends of the river at three points and parallels it for several hundred yards. Parts of the paddle route can be scouted

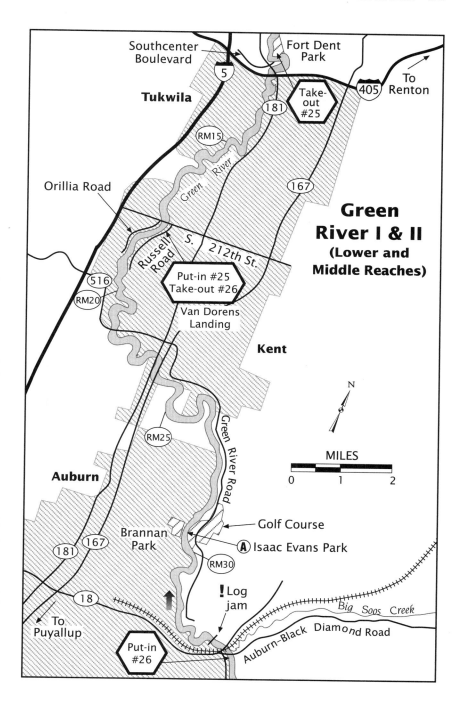

from the road. Turn right at South 212th Street in Kent, and follow it to the river. Launch on the east side of the river by turning left onto Russell Road just before reaching the river and follow it south to Van Dorens Landing, the best access on the river in this vicinity.

Paddle Route. The Green River is usually clear in the area of the launch site, swift and sandy-bottomed. Its grassy dike blocks out much of the surrounding development while domestic geese and wild birds make exploring this stretch worth the effort for bird-watchers. The river meanders in slow, easy curves, passing beneath bridges at South 212th Street and South 176th Street, where it begins a brief affair with West Valley Highway, which it hugs for half a mile.

Christensen Road embraces the left (west) bank. A greenbelt park and a bicentennial park help preserve the natural aspect of this stretch as it cuts through industrial backyards and commercial enterprises. After passing beneath the freeway, the lower Green leaves behind much of the developed world and takes on a more natural tone as it approaches Fort Dent Park. It makes a big horseshoe bend, flows beneath the bridge that leads into the park, and bends to the right. The take-out appears on the right, just around that final bend.

26 Green River II

Location: Auburn area to west Kent, middle reach
Distance: 16 miles
Paddle time: 4 to 5 hours
Season: Year-round
Rating: Upper mile, Class 2; remainder, Class 1
Hazards: Logjams, sweepers in upper mile
Shuttle: 15 miles, pavement
Flow information: USGS Washington website
River gauge: 12113000 near Auburn
Historic flows: Average 1316 cfs; maximum 28,100; minimum 81
Maps: USGS Des Moines, Renton, Auburn; Kent Parks and Recreation Department facilities map
Information: Kent Parks and Recreation Department; Washington Department of Fish and Wildlife website for Wildlife Areas and Access Points

The Green River from the mouth of Big Soos Creek 2 miles above Auburn through west Kent changes from a rural river, where steelheaders fish, to a suburban river that nibbles the edges of Auburn and Kent while following a natural course through agricultural lands and residential fringes. Much of the riverbank is riprap overgrown with blackberry bushes, grasses, and shrubs—ideal habitat for the many species of birds—a delightful stretch with poor access.

Note: Major logjams have blocked the river below the launch site in the past, but the river eventually works its way through and around them. Keep in mind that every high-water event may redecorate the riverscape. Always be on the look-out for sweepers, sleepers, and logjams on all Northwest rivers, especially after a flood. Check with local authorities and other paddlers.

Access. Only rough accesses lie between the suggested launch site at the mouth of Big Soos Creek 2 miles above Auburn and the take-out in west Kent. Adequate public access in or near Kent is badly needed to facilitate paddling this segment.

To reach the take-out in west Kent from I-405, take SR 181 Exit 1 and drive south on West Valley Road (SR 181). At South 212th Street, turn right (west). At the east end of the Green River bridge, turn left onto Russell Road east of the river to Van Dorens Landing.

To find the suggested launch site, go back to South 212th, turn right (east) back to SR 181, turn right and drive 2 miles south, then turn left (east) on the

Green River through Auburn

Kent–Des Moines Road (SR 516). Then turn right onto SR 167 heading south to Auburn. To reach the launch site, take SR 18 east out of Auburn, and turn right about 3 miles east of Auburn at the exit to the Auburn–Black Diamond Road. Just before that road crosses the Green River, turn right onto the road to Flaming Geyser State Park (SE Green Valley Road), then immediately turn left into a public fishing access adjacent to the bridge across from the mouth of Big Soos Creek. The launch site is on the left bank.

Green River Road on the east side of the river in Auburn offers several possible rough access points as it parallels the river downstream (north) toward Kent. Isaac Evans Park at the northeast edge of Auburn is one of these points.

Paddle Route. Directly across from the put-in, Big Soos Creek's confluence with the Green River is the most notable natural feature in an area dominated by man-made structures: the Green River (Auburn–Black Diamond Road) bridge, the Burlington Northern Railroad bridge, and the SR 18 bridge. The first mile of river seems like wilderness, with natural islands and forest debris (sunken logs, stumps, sweepers, and logjams). The river swings to the left around a bend usually full of downed trees. At times the river may be entirely blocked, but a portage around the obstacle is usually short and simple, especially at low water.

The river runs into the riprapped railroad embankment to the south as it gathers itself into one channel for an S turn at the eastern edge of Auburn. Soon houses begin to appear on the left bank, though the right bank remains forested. The diked banks are overgrown with blackberry bushes, grasses, and shrubs. Bird life abounds: great blue herons, spotted sandpipers, kingfishers galore, several species of swallows, many mallards and mergansers, frequently with young in late spring and early summer. During salmon migration season, you can see fish in the river.

The trip through east Auburn is delightful, as one of the nicer parts of town smiles on the river (rather than turning its back, as Kent seems to). The river flows beneath Porter Bridge (8th Street NE and SE 320th Street); loops past Isaac Evans Park on the right bank, Brannan Park on the left. Access to the river from either park is possible but involves a long carry. The Green then runs north past the Auburn Golf Course on the right.

Between Auburn and Kent the river is much used by tubers, rafters, and air-mattress floaters who gain access from Green River Road east of the river. The river is clear and shallow, with a few riffles and some deep pools—an ideal poling stream. The banks are natural enough to attract such bright-colored birds as orioles, goldfinches, and western tanagers.

In 2.5 hours from the suggested launch site, a paddler can reach Kent at the intersection of 78th Avenue S and South 259th Street. But there is no access, even though you can read the street signs from the river: a pity, for the paddler gets hungry and thirsty about this time, and South Kent stores suffer the loss of potential business. Tall grass and blackberry bushes dominate the landscape, and it is possible to discern a small dairy farm.

Below the SR 167 and SR 181 bridges, the Green is largely a big ditch—but it is a delightful ditch, its banks covered with eye-pleasing vegetation, its waters teeming with fish, wildlife, and birds. Domestic ducks and geese join their wilder cousins, while hikers, cyclists, and joggers join the parade along riverside trails. Van Dorens Landing is a few hundred yards downstream on the right bank at RM 18.2.

27 Green River III

Location: Rural reach east of Auburn
Distance: 7 miles
Paddle time: 2 hours
Season: Year-round
Rating: Class 1+/2–
Hazards: Logjams, sweepers
Shuttle: 8 miles, pavement
Flow information: USGS Washington website
River gauge: 12113000 near Auburn
Historic flows: Average 1316 cfs; maximum 28,100; minimum 81
Maps: USGS Auburn, Black Diamond
Information: Washington Department of Fish and Wildlife website for Wildlife Areas and Access Points

The Green River between Whitney Bridge (RM 40) and the mouth of Big Soos Creek (RM 33.6) flows through the bucolic Green Valley east of Auburn, an area similar to the Skykomish Valley between Sultan and Monroe. It meanders through croplands, orchards, and pastures between forested slopes. Local farmers sell produce along the Green Valley Road. Ancient evergreens stand as sentinels here and there, remnants of early days before the valley was logged.

Access. To reach the launch site at Whitney Bridge Park, take SR 18 east to Auburn–Black Diamond Road about 3 miles east of Auburn and turn right. Just before that road crosses the Green River, turn right onto SE Green Valley Road (signs suggest this is the way to Flaming Geyser State Park) and drive 8 miles, then turn right onto SE 219th Street. Within a hundred yards, turn right into the parking area at Whitney Bridge Park. The launch site, on river right, involves a short carry, but there is plenty of parking. A big barn across the river just upstream of the bridge marks the location.

On your drive to the launch site, you will pass the take-out: on the left immediately after turning onto SE Green Valley Road where Big Soos Creek flows into the Green River (see put-in for Trip 26).

Paddle Route. Downstream a half mile from the launch site, the river bends left, then runs straight between vegetated banks for another mile before it splits

Logjams such as this are not uncommon after floods on Green River's Middle Reach near Auburn.

around an island (RM 38) where fishing access extends for a half mile along the right bank. *(Note:* Logjams may be present after floods.)

Below the island the river bends right, straightens for another mile, then is augmented by creeks entering—first from the right, then from the left. There is walk-in access on both sides of the river at RM 36. The river courses through pastures of dairy cattle and horses, past neatly kept houses and vivid barns. Planted flowers grace many of the homes along the river. Local fruits and vegetables are available during summer.

The checkerboard lands of the Muckleshoot Indian Reservation lie above the river on the left. Most are above SR 164, which parallels the river for the final 3 miles of this stretch. Fishing and picnicking above and below Neeley Bridge often leave the banks littered, but the river flows clean and clear with strong current

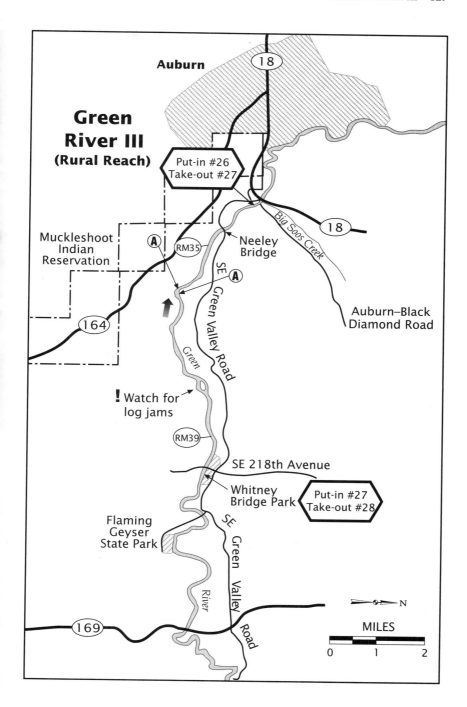

Green River III
(Rural Reach)

Auburn

18

Put-in #26
Take-out #27

Muckleshoot
Indian
Reservation

A RM35 Neeley
Bridge

Big Soos Creek

18

164

SE Green Valley Road

A

Auburn–Black
Diamond Road

Green

! Watch for
log jams

RM39

SE 218th Avenue

Whitney
Bridge Park

Put-in #27
Take-out #28

Flaming
Geyser
State Park

SE Green Valley Road

River

169

N

MILES

0   1   2

between forested banks, a pleasant float. The take-out has been badly littered in recent years by anglers, along with transients who often take up residence near the undeveloped boat ramp.

28 Green River IV (Yo-Yo Stretch)

Location: Flaming Geyser State Park to Whitney Bridge
Distance: 3 miles
Paddle time: Less than 1 hour
Season: Year-round
Rating: Class 2
Hazards: Rapids, logjams
Shuttle: Less than 2 miles, pavement
Flow information: USGS Washington website
River gauge: 12113000 near Auburn
Historic flows: Average 1316 cfs; maximum 28,100; minimum 81
Maps: USGS Black Diamond
Information: Flaming Geyser State Park; Washington Department of Fish and Wildlife website for Wildlife Areas and Access Points

A short and varied section of river, this segment, known locally as the Yo-Yo Stretch, is a favorite with paddlers who make the same run several times a day for practice. It is ideal for polers, who can work their way up from Whitney Bridge into the park and back down again in 2 hours for a good workout. It has small rapids, one short but serious Class 2 rapid, one interesting bedrock riffle, and a few deep pools with fine beaches and forested banks.

Access. Whitney Bridge offers good access, as do several places in Flaming Geyser State Park. Roadside accesses are also possible, and (with special permission) a few private put-ins—all within a short run.

To reach the take-out from SR 18 about 3 miles east of Auburn, turn right at the Auburn–Black Diamond Road exit. Just before that road crosses the Green River, turn right onto SE Green Valley Road, the route to Flaming Geyser State Park. Eight miles from the turnoff, turn right onto SE 219th Street. Within a hundred yards, turn right into the parking area at Whitney Bridge Park. Leave a shuttle vehicle here.

To reach the put-in, retrace the route to SE Green Valley Road and turn right, continuing toward Flaming Geyser State Park. The road crosses a bridge in less than a mile and enters the park. Follow the road to its end, park, and explore the area for river access. The river lies to the north; several points along a half-mile of riverfront offer hand-carry access.

Paddle Route. From any of the launch sites in Flaming Geyser State Park, the Green River is clear with just enough action to keep paddlers on their toes. In midsummer, it is crowded with tubers and sunbathers, kids floating on air mattresses, and riverside picnickers. Drifting through the park, boaters pass a few rock gardens and mild rapids, occasional beaver cuts, and (during the fishing season) frequent steelheaders—anglers after the prize game fish of the Northwest.

At the big bend of the river above Flaming Geyser Bridge, there is a pool so deep that even in the clear water you cannot see the bottom. A rope tied to an overhanging tree limb hints at summer play. A long rock garden (merely shallow water at high water flows) leads to the bridge. A gravel-and-sand bar is exposed at river left. It's a swimming beach in the summer, and a year-round take-out for those who want to float the stretch again.

Below the bridge, the river splits around a series of islands, the flow on either side runnable at any level above extremely low water. Be wary of current that wants to take a craft into sweepers along the shoreline. Around the bend is a small rapid, followed by a deeper section of river, then a bedrock area where the river shallows over sandstone and consolidated mud. It drops again into a deep

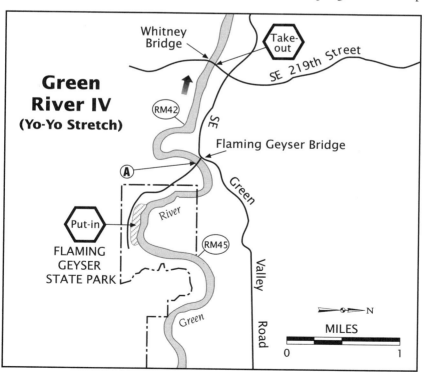

Horses cooling off in the Green River Yo-Yo Stretch

pool, then shallows out, deepens around a bend visible from the road, and gathers itself for an honest Class 2 rapid.

The head of the rapid can be seen but not scouted from the road. The river splits around a small island at high water levels and drops a few feet in 50 yards over a bouldery stretch of fast water. It can be lined on the right from a point that is ideal for scouting the river. Stop and scout it if you are uncomfortable with the rapid, but it is fairly straightforward, although tough to pole up. From the foot of the rapid to the take-out bridge, the river is broad and shallow, ideal for poling. The take-out is under the bridge, on river right within a 100-foot carry of the parking area.

The river from this access to the mouth of Big Soos Creek just east of Auburn is a 7-mile Class 2 run (see Trip 27) through a rural valley full of horse farms and pastureland, a delightful trip that will challenge beginning paddlers. The river is lined with huge trees and offers excellent habitat for birds and other wildlife as well as excellent fishing.

29 Nisqually River Delta/McAlister Creek

Location: Between Olympia and Tacoma
Distance: Up to 8 miles
Paddle time: 3 to 4 hours
Season: Year-round
Rating: Tidal flatwater (up to Class 2)
Hazards: Logjams, contrary tides, fog, storms
Shuttle: None necessary, up to 10 miles, pavement
Flow information: USGS Washington website
River gauge: 12089500 at McKenna
Historic flows: Average 1286 cfs; maximum 50,000; minimum 20
Maps: USGS Nisqually, Anderson Island; NOAA charts 18440, 18445, 18448
Information: AquaTrek; Nisqually National Wildlife Refuge; Nisqually Reach Nature Center; Washington Department of Fish and Wildlife website for Wildlife Areas and Access Points

The Nisqually Delta, one of the richest wildlife habitats in Puget Sound, is protected as the Nisqually National Wildlife Refuge. McAlister Creek and the Nisqually River, the two streams that create the delta, offer unique paddling experiences. More than 200 species of birds have been seen in the refuge, which also harbors numerous species of mammals, reptiles, amphibians, and fish, as well as such saltwater species as crabs, clams, and oysters—even seals. McAlister Creek, once known as Medicine Creek, was the site of early Native American treaties in western Washington.

Access. Luhr Beach on Puget Sound offers access to both McAlister Creek, which flows past it, and the mouth of the Nisqually itself, a mile or so across the tidal flats. Access to the lower Nisqually is available at RM 3.2 from public boat accesses just upstream from the twin I-5 bridges, off Old Pacific Highway/Pacific Avenue (formerly Old Nisqually Highway). Private access is available to McAlister Creek at Nisqually Plaza RV Park at the bottom of Nisqually Hill off I-5 (Exit 114); be prepared to pay a launch fee ($7 at publication).

To reach Luhr Beach access from I-5, take Exit 114 just west of the Nisqually River crossing. Turn right to follow Martin Way west toward Lacey, then turn right onto North Meridian Road and follow signs to the Luhr Beach public fishing access. Audubon's Nisqually Reach Nature Center is situated here.

For another route to Luhr Beach from I-5, take Exit 111 onto Marvin Road NE in Lacy, heading south to Martin Way East. Turn left and follow it to Meridian Road NE; turn left and follow signs to Luhr Beach.

To reach the access on the lower Nisqually at RM 3.2, take Exit 116 off I-5 and head southwest on Old Pacific Highway/Pacific Avenue toward Nisqually. A rough

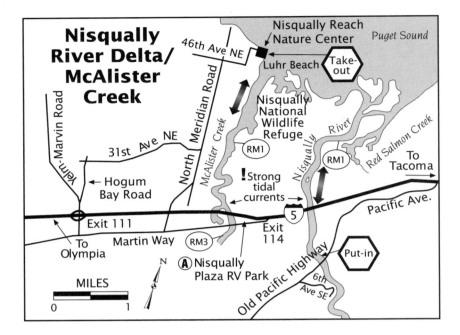

dirt (mud in wet weather) access, undeveloped and apparently unmaintained, lies to the right of the road 100 yards north of the bridge across the Nisqually.

To access McAlister Creek, take Exit 114 off I-5 and drive to the RV park behind the service station.

Paddle Route. From the launch site at the Old Pacific Highway bridge, the river is tidal and mellow with a few riffles at low tide. The houses disappear as a Native American fishing camp appears; the tribe for whom the river is named still fishes the streams in accordance with the Medicine Creek Treaty of 1854, signed on what is now McAlister Creek only a few miles away. The twin spans of the I-5 bridge loom ahead as the roar of freeway traffic intrudes into the river corridor—but not for long.

The river slows and takes on a mellow mood, creating a placid presence that one paddle partner suggested "could be in Guilford, Connecticut." Both banks are wooded. Soon the protection of the Nisqually National Wildlife Refuge makes its impact; the world grows still, natural, and wholesome, as the sound of freeway traffic subsides.

Depending on the tide level, the river may be tearing along to reach the Sound or backed up in a slow lake, but the setting is pleasant, calm, and quiet except for the sounds of nature or an occasional powerboat carrying Nisqually fishermen to set or check their nets. Look for gulls overhead, mallards and wood ducks in the eddies. Bird-watchers hike through the refuge on a trail along the left bank.

Blackberry bushes and beaver cuts mark the shoreline; Nisqually gill nets mark the river's surface.

As the craft reaches the open water of the Sound, a seal's head pops up. Duck blinds appear—yes, hunting is allowed on the refuge, but only during the open season, and gunners are required to use nontoxic shot. The dock at Luhr Beach is visible to the west. Shore birds, sea ducks, and geese frequent the area; bald eagles, great blue herons, and numerous gulls feed on the mudflats and in the nearby Sound.

You can reach the mouth of McAlister Creek by paddling a few hundred yards west; if the tide is right, paddling upstream is not difficult. The lower creek is broad, but a mile upstream it narrows and begins to meander, nuzzling the west bank where a steep, forested hillside turns it back to loop through the meadows to the east. The tide mark shows on the vegetation; salt burn kills leaves of vine maple, but the salt water doesn't seem to bother the sturdy trees that grow to the water's edge.

It is possible to paddle or pole up McAlister Creek to I-5, though the outgoing tide creates a fierce flow in the channelized creek where it has been narrowed and forced to loop around the bridge supports. Above the I-5 bridge you

Nisqually Delta National Wildlife Refuge

may find placid water (if you have studied the tide charts), but having left the refuge behind, you are in farmland. It may be time to head back downstream to the take-out at Luhr Beach.

OLYMPIC PENINSULA

30 Hoquiam River: East and West Forks

Location: North of Aberdeen and Hoquiam
Distance: East Fork 5 miles; West Fork 9 miles
Paddle time: East Fork 2 hours; West Fork 3 hours
Season: Year-round, but rainy in winter
Rating: Tidal flatwater
Hazards: Contrary tides, waterfront traffic at end
Shuttle: East Fork 7 miles; West Fork 9 miles, pavement
Flow information: Tidal
Maps: USGS Hoquiam, Humptulips; NOAA chart 18502
Information: Grays Harbor County Visitors Guide; Grays Harbor Chamber of Commerce; Washington Coast Chamber of Commerce; Washington Department of Fish and Wildlife website for Wildlife Areas and Access Points

The Hoquiam River proper, only 2.5 miles long, is totally urban; but above the point where its East and West Forks meet, it becomes almost rural. Both forks have lives and accesses of their own, as they loop widely back and forth in sinuous curves through marshy lands that protect the rivers from greater development. They offer peaceful paddling on tidal waters that are disturbed only by historic log storage and sport fishing.

Access. The take-out is on the Grays Harbor waterfront in southwestern Aberdeen. Developed boat launches exist on both major forks of the river and on the Little Hoquiam (see Trip 31), from US 101 on the West Fork and from East Hoquiam Road on the East Fork.

To reach the waterfront take-out in southwestern Aberdeen, from US 101 as it goes through Aberdeen turn south (left) onto 28th Street and head south past a log storage yard to the observatory and a pointer to the Port of Grays Harbor boat ramp. This boat ramp is only a few hundred yards east of the mouth of the Hoquiam River.

For access points on the West Fork, go back to US 101 (Lincoln Street) and follow it north out of Hoquiam toward two put-in points: (1) only 2.4 miles north of north Hoquiam, veer right onto a spur road (Fairfield Acres Access), then turn right again down a residential road and drive to its dead end, where a

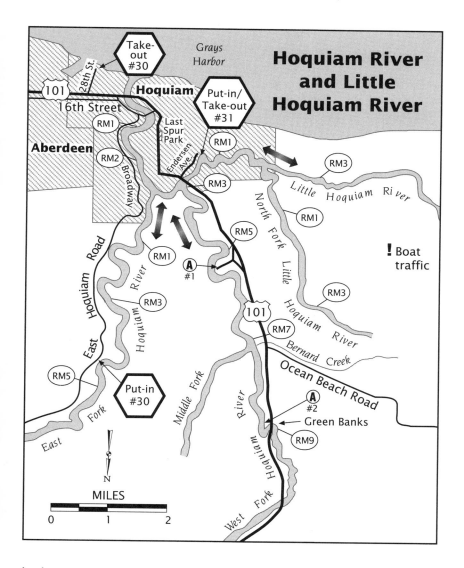

log boom serves as a public put-in at RM 5.3; (2) about 5 miles north off US 101, on the right (east) side of the highway, there is a facility known as Green Banks, dedicated in 1983 to public fishing access by ITT Rayonier, Trout Unlimited, and the Northwest Steelheaders Association.

For access on the East Fork, a boat ramp at RM 4.6 is 7 miles from the mouth of the Hoquiam. Go back to US 101 from the 28th Street take-out and follow it west to 16th Street (just before you reach the bridge over the Hoquiam). Turn right (the

Pilings on the Hoquiam River anchored rafts of old-growth timber cut decades ago.

sign says "Woodlawn") onto 16th Street, which soon becomes Broadway; follow it through Woodlawn, turning right onto East Hoquiam Road, which follows the river to a boat ramp (opposite 1702 East Hoquiam Road) 5 miles from US 101.

Paddle Route. Both forks of the Hoquiam offer interesting and contrasting paddling—both are tidal throughout these segments, and both can be paddled or poled upstream and down depending on tides.

East Fork. From the boat ramp, the East Fork is lined by mud banks at low tide. At high tide, it is lined by brushy shorelines with occasional stands of tall trees. Angler traffic attests to the aquatic life, as do kingfishers and great blue herons. There are a few homes along the bank, a number of pilings from earlier log storage areas, and more commercial development downstream as the river meanders through a marshy floodplain.

At RM 2.7, the river kisses the road and again at RM 1.5. At RM 0.5, commercial development begins in the form of forest-products and industrial facilities. The East Fork joins the West Fork at the north edge of Hoquiam, 2.5 miles from Grays Harbor. From RM 0.5 on the East Fork, you are still 3 miles from the waterfront take-out.

West Fork. The river plays hide-and-seek with US 101 from the put-in at RM 9 to RM 3, only 0.5 mile above the confluence of the East and West Forks at the north edge of Hoquiam. It is probably more heavily fished than the East Fork because of its proximity to the major highway and the developed fishing facilities. But for all of its access, it is still a relatively primitive paddle; few boats make use of it.

For its first 2 miles, the West Fork parallels the highway, passing between towering trees and along shrub-lined banks. Its Middle Fork joins it from the left just above RM 7, opposite the entrance of Bernard Creek from the right.

The river moves away from the highway below RM 7, swinging back to parallel the highway for nearly a mile (RM 6.5 to RM 5.7) before making a big loop on which access (1), the log boom, lies on the right bank at RM 5.3. It loops back near the highway at RM 4.8, then takes a long loop to the east side of its marshy floodplain before making one more move toward the highway to parallel it coming into town at RM 3. Here the Little Hoquiam joins it from the right.

Half a mile below its entry into Hoquiam, the West Fork is joined by the East Fork from the left. Totally tidal and surrounded by commercial and residential development for its last 2.5 miles, the Hoquiam flows into Grays Harbor at the west end of Rennie Island. To reach the take-out, paddle 0.5 mile up the Chehalis to the observatory on the Aberdeen waterfront.

31 Little Hoquiam River

Location: West of Hoquiam
Distance: 3 miles
Paddle time: 2 to 3 hours
Season: Year-round, but rainy in winter
Rating: Tidal flatwater
Hazards: Contrary tides, powerboats
Shuttle: None necessary
Flow information: Tidal
Maps: USGS Hoquiam; NOAA chart 18502
Information: Grays Harbor County Visitors Guide; Grays Harbor Chamber of Commerce; Washington Coast Chamber of Commerce; Washington Department of Fish and Wildlife website for Wildlife Areas and Access Points

Surrounding hills might be an eyesore of clear-cuts, but this small river's atmosphere suggests "wild" and its waters are full of life. Access lies at a small isolated park; its upstream reach offers among the most peaceful experiences paddlers could seek. Even though a new road and bridge have been built over its first fork, many nearby sounds are blocked by the ridge to the south. Even at tidal flux, it is so still and quiet that you can see insects alight on its surface and watch fish take them. Birds in flight can be identified by their reflection on the river's surface.

Access. Lundrens Landing, a small park in northwest Hoquiam, is the only access necessary because a craft can easily be paddled up and down this little stream.

To reach the access park, head north out of Hoquiam on US 101 (Lincoln Street), which turns left (west) near the north edge of town, then swings right at an angle to the northwest just before crossing the Little Hoquiam River. As the highway completes its swing to the northwest, turn left onto Queen Avenue, which becomes Endersen Avenue (a road at one end, an avenue at the other) at the first curve west of US 101. Follow it southwest to a bend in the Little Hoquiam River, where a small park and boat landing provides the put-in and take-out.

Reflecting on the Little Hoquiam River

Paddle Route. From the launch site, the river is often reflection-still except for occasional stirring by powerboats that use the boat ramp. Around the first bend upstream, the man-made world is left behind and paddlers enter a kinder, softer realm. Wonderful woodsy smells replace exhaust fumes, and bird songs nibble at the fading echoes of automobile and powerboat motors' roar. Hundreds of swallows fill the air at dusk or before a rain, and the only sounds are natural ones as the river weaves its way into the wilderness. Clear-cut scars dominate the landscape, but nature was here first and will endure. Even in the battle-scarred landscape, there are great blue herons, spotted sandpipers, kingfishers, green herons, gulls, nighthawks, and robins.

At dusk the river loops quietly into the darkening landscape. An insect hatch is happening: the surface of the river is alive with multi-strikes of tiny fish. Their feeding frenzy makes more noise than passing paddlers. A bridge looms ahead and the river splits beyond it. The right-hand fork is blocked by fallen trees in a few hundred yards. The main river meanders and curves for another mile. Then paddlers can head back down the quiet river toward the landing, moving with the tide, watching reflections in the water as nighthawks flit and dive and swoop, gathering insects. It's that kind of river.

32 Wishkah River

Location: Northeast of Aberdeen
Distance: 8 miles
Paddle time: 2 hours
Season: Year-round, but rainy in winter
Rating: Tidal flatwater
Hazards: Contrary tides, powerboats
Shuttle: 6.2 miles, pavement
Flow information: Tidal
Maps: USGS Aberdeen, Humptulips; NOAA chart 18502
Information: Grays Harbor County Visitors Guide; Grays Harbor Chamber of Commerce; Washington Coast Chamber of Commerce; Washington Department of Fish and Wildlife Web site for Wildlife Areas and Access Points

The Wishkah River flows into the Chehalis River in the latter's last mile at the point where the Chehalis gives up its ghost to Grays Harbor. One of several tidal rivers in the Grays Harbor area, the Wishkah offers exploratory paddle trips on different branches, providing unique insights into the area. The Wishkah, which circles through northeastern Aberdeen, flows out of the timbered forestlands from an area that includes two units of the Olympic Wildlife Area. It is a slow, narrow river, ideal for beginning paddlers.

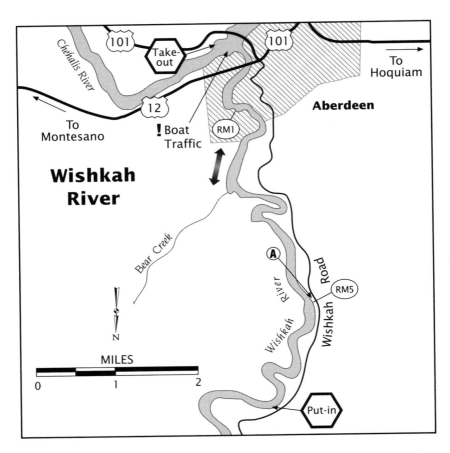

Access. To reach the take-out across the Chehalis River from the mouth of the Wishkah, follow US 101 south from H Street across the bridge over the Chehalis River. Highway signs point the way to Raymond and Westport. Turn left at the first stoplight with the main flow of traffic, then left again onto Boone Street just before you reach the South Aberdeen Fire Station on the left. (Since it may be difficult to make this turn in heavy traffic, it makes sense to go beyond the turnoff, double back wherever it is convenient and legal, and, as you head back toward Aberdeen, make the right turn onto Boone Street.) Boone Street leads to a public boat access on a short, rough, unmaintained street.

To reach the launch site several miles up Wishkah Road, recross the bridge over the Chehalis River and take US 101 (G Street) straight ahead to Market, turn right and follow it to B Street; turn left and follow it north. It forks right to become Wishkah Road, which closely parallels the river. Follow it out of town along the river to the boat ramp at RM 7.2 (5 miles from the left turn onto B Street).

Paddle Route. The Wishkah River is a small, intimate stream. It seems to have been diked at some time in the past, but whatever human control existed is so far removed in time that it appears natural enough; the banks are well vegetated and the bends seem appropriate to a natural river. It is largely rural with a few big trees along its banks and a house or two along the way. A slow-moving fishing boat may come putting along upstream, but there are few powerboats in so narrow a river.

The river swings left, then sharply right through marshy lands. It hugs the road between RM 5.4 and RM 5, and then swings away into the marsh—only to return for another kiss at RM 4.3. At RM 4 it begins a sharp S that ends as Bear Creek comes in from the left and the river approaches Aberdeen. The last 2 miles of this route flow through an urban area; the final 0.5 mile, through downtown. US 12 crosses the river a hundred yards from its mouth. The take-out involves paddling across the mouth of the Chehalis as it flows into Grays Harbor.

Log storage pilings on the lower Wishkah

33 Chehalis River I/Sloughs

Location: Montesano to Hoquiam-Aberdeen-Cosmopolis area
Distance: 13 miles to the observatory take-out at 28th Street
Paddle time: 3 to 4 hours
Season: Year-round, but best in summer
Rating: Tidal flatwater
Hazards: Contrary tides, big ships, powerboats
Shuttle: None necessary or 15 miles, pavement
Flow information: Tidal
Maps: USGS Aberdeen, Hoquiam, Montesano; NOAA chart 18502.
Information: Grays Harbor County Visitors Guide; Grays Harbor Chamber of Commerce; Washington Coast Chamber of Commerce; Washington Department of Fish and Wildlife website for Wildlife Areas and Access Points

The lower Chehalis and its associated sloughs combine a logging town and sea-port with amazingly pristine backwater paddling. The lower 3 miles of the river are almost totally urban, commercially developed, and export oriented, but above the 3-mile mark, six sloughs branch off into picturesque bayous reminiscent of Southern swamplands, except for the vegetation, which is strictly Northwestern. Three major tributaries covered by this book enter the Chehalis in this segment: the Hoquiam, the Wishkah, and the Wynoochee.

Access. Several boat launches provide abundant access to the lower Chehalis: one on the Aberdeen waterfront, another across the Chehalis from the mouth of the Wishkah, a third at RM 3, and a fourth a mile south of Montesano above the mouth of the Wynoochee. Paddle-craft access can also be negotiated from Morrison Waterfront Park at RM 1 below the mouth of Elliott Slough—the only one of seven sloughs that joins the river below RM 3.

To reach the westernmost access, follow US 101 (Sumner Street) west through Aberdeen. After entering Hoquiam, turn left (south) onto 28th Street to the Port of Grays Harbor boat ramp (gravel) by the observatory (hours: 7 AM to dusk).

Morrison Waterfront Park, another logical take-out for this trip, is located at what was the dock for the local fishing fleet until 1956. Traveling east on Wishkah Street (US 12), turn right onto Fleet Street just past the shopping mall at the east end of Aberdeen (just before US 12 starts to climb the hill east of town). This area offers access to the right bank of the Chehalis, less than a quarter mile above the mouth of the Wishkah.

To reach the boat ramp across from the mouth of the Wishkah, take US 101 south across the bridge over the Chehalis River (a sign says "to Westport and Raymond"). Turn left at the first stoplight (H Street; the main flow of traffic goes left at this light), then left again onto Boone Street as the road bends right just before you reach the South Aberdeen Fire Station. (This is an awkward turn in heavy traffic; it

The Chehalis River flows past Friends Landing near the mouth of the Wynoochee River.

may be best to go beyond it, turn around somewhere, and approach it from the other direction, as a right turn will be easier.) This is the old West Bridge approach with no sign or dock on a short moguly road, unmaintained and with little parking.

To reach the third access, in south Cosmopolis, return to US 101 and turn left past the South Aberdeen Fire Station, toward Raymond. Turn left at F Street and drive to the waterfront access provided by Weyerhaeuser.

To reach the boat ramp south of Montesano, the put-in, return to US 101. At this point there are two options:

(1) Turn left and continue toward Raymond, but in a few miles turn left on SR 107 toward Montesano on the South Bank Road. This location provides a look at Blue Slough and Preachers Slough, both south of the river. After SR 107 forks left and crosses the Chehalis River, 0.1 mile above the mouth of the Wynoochee River, turn right at a public fishing access sign into a parking area with a boat ramp. (2) From US 101, turn right and return to Aberdeen, turning right again in downtown Aberdeen onto US 12, heading east. At Montesano, turn right onto SR 107, drive a mile south of town (past a lumber mill), and turn left into the public fishing access (the launch site).

Paddle Route. The Chehalis is tidal throughout this segment: a big, deep river impacted by logging activities and heavily used by powerboats, many of which launch at the boat ramp south of Montesano at RM 13.3. Launching here, paddlers immediately pass beneath SR 107, then under the railroad bridge. The Wynoochee enters on the right, flushing the Chehalis with fresh mountain water.

The river flows southwest until it bumps into the railroad embankment (RM 11.6), then hugs that embankment for a mile before swinging slowly toward the north and encountering sloughs on the right: first Peels Slough at RM 9.5, then Higgins at RM 8.7. The river narrows, divides around an island (RM 8), and swings toward the south again.

At RM 6.8, Preachers Slough enters from the left, offering a side trip of more

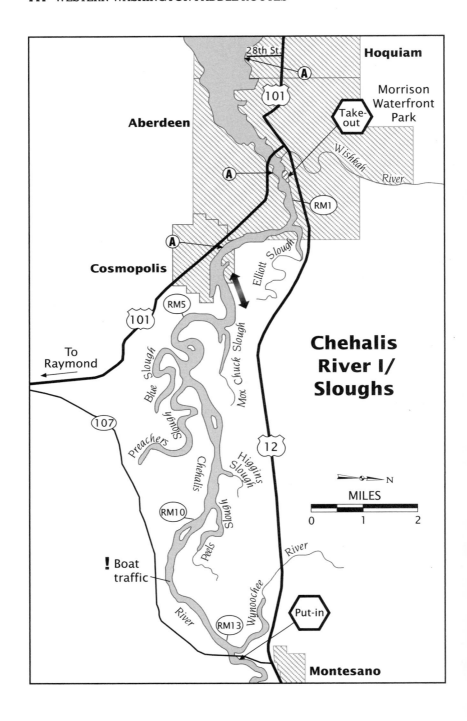

than 2 miles up the slough if the tide is high and there are no barriers. At RM 6.4, Blue Slough enters, also from the left (a side trip of nearly 3 miles up this one). Below Blue Slough, the river enters a tight S bend that takes it 1.5 miles to complete. Mox Chuck Slough enters from the right at RM 4.4, as the river bends left. The river straightens as it enters Cosmopolis (with the Weyerhaeuser mill visible on the left bank) and greets one more small slough on the left.

Slough exploring can take a lot of time. Just be aware that such side trips add to paddle time. Keep in mind too that tidal influence will alter tour time on the river; it is slow going against an incoming tide, but fair time can be made paddling upstream with the incoming tide.

From RM 3 the river is flanked on the left by the backyards of Cosmopolis, on the right by log export activities and facilities. The river here heads north and then makes a sharp left turn as Elliott Slough enters on the right at RM 1.3. Elliott Slough is largely a log-storage facility, and the Chehalis River from this point is totally engulfed by Aberdeen. In another mile the river loses itself in Grays Harbor.

34 Chehalis River II

Location: Porter to Montesano
Distance: 20 miles
Paddle time: 5 to 6 hours
Season: Year-round
Rating: Class 1+/2−
Hazards: Sweepers, logjams, high water
Shuttle: 18 miles, pavement
Flow information: USGS Washington website
River gauge: 12035002 near Satsop
Historic flows: Average 6425 cfs; maximum 53,500 (gauge not in service during record 1996–97 floods); minimum -819
Maps: USGS Montesano, Malone
Information: Grays Harbor County Visitors Guide; Grays Harbor Chamber of Commerce; Washington Coast Chamber of Commerce; Washington Department of Fish and Wildlife website for Wildlife Areas and Access Points

This long, looping stretch of the Chehalis offers excellent paddling on a clear-water river with numerous gravel bars for fishing, picnicking, or camping. For the most part it flows through private property, so be sure to camp below mean high water level or obtain permission from the local landowner. An easy river flowing through a broad valley, this lower segment provides good fishing as well as occasional views of distant mountains and nearer clear-cut forested hillsides. Several of its tributaries can also be canoed.

Access. To reach the take-out from US 12 at Montesano, take SR 107 south toward Raymond. Less than a mile south of Montesano, after passing a lumber mill on the left, turn left to a public fishing access on the right bank of the Chehalis, 0.25 mile above the mouth of the Wynoochee River.

To reach the put-in, return to US 12 and head east toward Elma, then southeast toward Porter. Turn right (south) at the northwest edge of Porter, toward Rony and South Bank Road, crossing the railroad tracks and the Chehalis River. As the bridge grade descends, turn left into a public fishing access area. The boat ramp is on the southwest bank of the river beneath the bridge at RM 33.2. *(Note: This also is the take-out for Trip 35.)*

To reach an additional access at the mouth of the Satsop, take US 12 to the Satsop exit (north to Satsop, south to the access) and turn off onto Keys Road. Access lies less than 2 miles from US 12 at RM 20.5.

Paddle Route. In this lower stretch, the Chehalis River is slow and lazy—sometimes influenced by tide—with a few easy drops. From the launch site on the left bank, the river runs northwest, gradually leaving the highway and flowing through farmlands. A short distance below RM 32 it starts a big S curve to approach the left edge of its floodplain. It curves less sharply in another big S bend as Eaton Creek enters on the left (RM 28.6) and Mox–Chehalis Creek enters on the right (RM 27.8).

The river straightens, paralleled by South Bank Road and the railroad. Delezene Creek enters from the left (RM 26.8). At RM 26—just after a powerline crossing—a third big S bend begins just south of Elma. Although the river is crossed by a bridge carrying the South Elma–Workman Road at RM 23.8, there is no access.

The river flows west as it passes beneath this bridge, curving in gradual bends for the next 3 miles. Workman Creek enters from the left, Fuller Creek

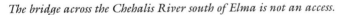

The bridge across the Chehalis River south of Elma is not an access.

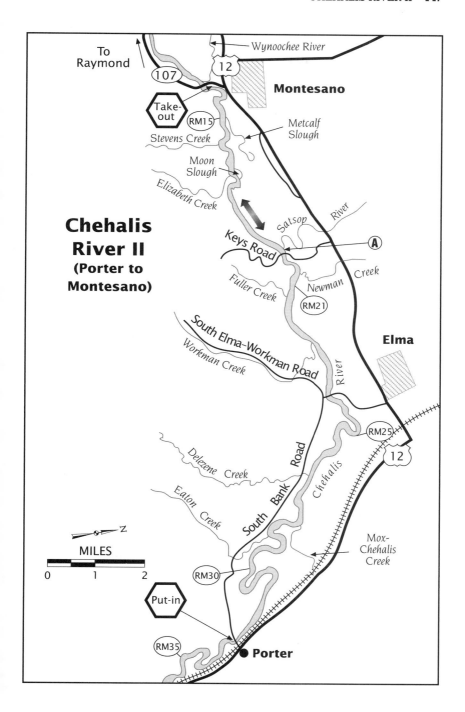

To Raymond

Wynoochee River

107   12

Montesano

Take-out   RM15

Metcalf Slough

Stevens Creek

Moon Slough

Elizabeth Creek

Chehalis River II
(Porter to Montesano)

Keys Road

Satsop River

A

Fuller Creek

Newman Creek

RM21

South Elma–Workman Road

Workman Creek

Elma

River

RM25

12

Delezene Creek

South Bank Road

Chehalis

N

MILES

0   1   2

Eaton Creek

Mox-Chehalis Creek

RM30

Put-in

RM35

● Porter

from the left at an island, and Newman Creek from the right. Just after the river flows beneath the bridge carrying Keys Road across the Chehalis, the Satsop River comes in from the right. The access here is between the Satsop mouth and the bridge.

As tributaries have added volume to the river, it has become bigger and broader. From the mouth of the Satsop, the Chehalis again flows along the south edge of the valley, paralleling the railroad for more than 2 miles before making a sharp right turn into a broad area, from which Moon Slough loops around an island in the vicinity of RM 17.

Elizabeth Creek enters from the left, opposite the island. Stevens Creek enters from the left on a sharp bend at RM 15.8, where the river touches the railroad embankment. After another mile of relatively straight river, Metcalf Slough enters from the right (RM 14.7). This area is tidal, and at extremely high tides the impact can be felt. One more big, sweeping bend, and the river parallels SR 107 south of Montesano, makes a final sharp right, and flows beneath a bridge. Take out at the boat ramp on the right beneath the bridge.

35 Chehalis River III/Lower Black River

Location: Oakville to Porter
Distance: 9 miles from put-in at Elma–Gate Road; from lower Black River, 18 miles
Paddle time: 3 hours; from lower Black River, 6 hours
Season: Year-round, but best spring through fall
Rating: Class 1+
Hazards: Sweepers, logjams
Shuttle: 8 miles, pavement
Flow information: USGS Washington website
River gauge: 12031000 at Porter
Historic flows: Average 4043 cfs; maximum 80,700; minimum 164
Maps: USGS Malone
Information: Grays Harbor County Visitors Guide; Grays Harbor Chamber of Commerce; Washington Coast Chamber of Commerce; Washington Department of Fish and Wildlife website for Wildlife Areas and Access Points

The Oakville-to-Porter run is a pleasant paddle on a moderate-sized Chehalis River as it flows through a broad, undeveloped agricultural valley. The banks are well vegetated with shrubs, grasses, second-growth timber, and nontimber species. The lower Black River is shallow and narrow, with a gravel bottom and abundant aquatic vegetation; its lower 2 miles revert to Southern swamp—slow with heavily wooded

The boat ramp near Oakville is a logical take-out or launch for trips on the middle Chehalis.

banks. The Chehalis between the mouth of the Black River and the Oakville access flows through farmlands, with fields often nudging the river itself. It has plenty of gravel bars and a lot of timber trash as well.

Access. All three accesses are easy to find; two are just off US 12, and one is only a mile by paved road from this main highway. To reach the take-out for this segment (the launch site for Trip 34), turn west from US 12 just northwest of Porter, cross the river, and turn left into a public fishing access parking area.

There are two ways to reach the put-in, roughly a mile northwest of Oakville:

(1) Northwest of Oakville (near Oakville High School) turn north onto Elma–Gate Road between the railroad and the river. The put-in is an undeveloped public fishing access on a slough that communicates with the Chehalis (at low water it may be blocked by a beaver dam). The access is left of the road north of Oakville

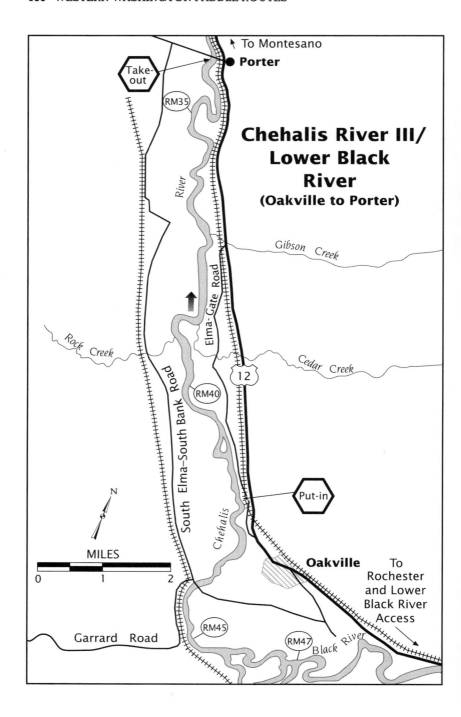

To Montesano

Porter

Take-out

RM35

Chehalis River III/ Lower Black River
(Oakville to Porter)

Gibson Creek

River

Elma-Gate Road

Rock Creek

Cedar Creek

12

RM40

South Elma–South Bank Road

Put-in

Chehalis

N

MILES

0 1 2

Oakville

To Rochester and Lower Black River Access

Garrard Road

RM45

RM47

Black River

on river right. (2) Heading southeast from Porter to Oakville on US 12, just after crossing Gibson Creek turn right 3 miles southeast of Porter onto Elma–Gate Road. This will save a couple of miles and provide an opportunity to see the river, which it parallels for about a mile.

To reach the lower Black River access off US 12, for a 9-miles-longer stretch of the Chehalis and lower Black, drive through Oakville, heading east toward Rochester; about 2 miles east of Oakville, immediately after crossing the Black River, turn right into a small parking area by a boat ramp on the left bank of the river (the take-out for Trip 36).

Paddle Route. At the launch on the lower Black River, masses of aquatic vegetation almost obstruct a paddle route down its narrow course through this section. Some routefinding may be necessary at the low water levels of late summer. The river flows past farmhouses and barns, past pastures and clearings. After a couple of miles of extreme meandering over a shallow gravel bottom (ideal for poling) with occasional riffles, the river slows to sluggish, winding between steep, thickly wooded banks.

From the mouth of the Black at RM 47, the Chehalis flows through a broad, intensively farmed valley where some fields extend to the river's edge. It meanders widely, involving a slough-like backwater on the right 0.25 mile below the confluence, and another on the left 1.5 miles below the confluence. At RM 45 the river reaches the left (southwest) side of its floodplain to parallel the railroad and Garrard Road for a mile, then flows beneath the bridge (RM 44) that carries South Elma–South Bank Road into Oakville.

From the bridge, the river curves northeast briefly through a heavily wooded area on the outskirts of Oakville. At RM 42.2, the undeveloped access (which may be difficult to see from the river unless it's been scouted carefully beforehand) lies on the right bank of a slough, which may be a beaver pond at low water levels.

For the next mile, the river mostly hugs the northeastern side of its floodplain, then makes a sharp turn back toward South Bank Road. It then swings slowly southwest, then loops back to the middle of the valley to flow northwest for several miles through alternating open areas and forested stretches, with pastureland and farms on either side.

Rock Creek enters from the left at RM 39.2, just as the river bends east. Cedar Creek enters from the right at RM 38.7, and Gibson Creek enters from the right at RM 37.2. The broad valley is full of isolated oxbow lakes and gravel deposits left by an earlier river. At RM 36 the river returns to the northeastern side of its floodplain briefly, paralleling the Burlington Northern Railroad tracks for a quarter mile, then begins a major double loop just south of Porter, to again nudge the railroad at RM 34. It loops left around Porter. The take-out lies on the left bank (across the river from Porter), upstream from the bridge.

36 Black River

Location: Littlerock area to US 12, near Rochester
Distance: 12 miles
Paddle time: 5 to 6 hours
Season: Year-round
Rating: Class 1
Hazards: Vegetation masses, fallen trees, sweepers
Shuttle: 10 miles, pavement
Flow information: None available
Maps: USGS Rochester, Oakville, Rochester; Capitol Forest Multiple Use Area Map by Washington Department of Natural Resources
Information: Washington Department of Fish and Wildlife website for Wildlife Areas and Access Points; Washington Department of Natural Resources, Forks Office

The Black River southwest of Olympia, a unique Southern river placed in the Pacific Northwest, is a placid fairyland stream full of beautiful butterflies and bird life during summer, fantastic colors in autumn, and wildflowers in spring and summer. Even in winter this black-water river suggests *The Hobbit* or *Willow* in its scenic beauty. Curling around the southeastern base of the Black Hills below Capitol Forest, it has excellent access, yet remains one of the most remote rivers in the state. Even in this 12-mile segment it offers great variety.

Access. Public access can be found on Littlerock Road south of Littlerock, at the oxbow bend of the river off Moon Road west of Rochester, and on US 12 between Rochester and Oakville. The routes are ideal for bicycle shuttles. Another access is on the Chehalis River 1.5 miles northwest of Oakville, about 5 miles below the mouth of the Black River for anyone who wants to make a longer run.

To reach the take-out on US 12 about 3 miles east of Oakville and 4 miles west of Rochester, take I-5 Exit 88 south of Olympia and head west on US 12. The boat ramp is on the left (south) side of the highway on the river's left bank (RM 4.2) at the bridge across the Black River.

To reach the subtle boat ramp off Moon Road (another possible take-out), return to US 12 and head east 2 miles to Moon Road, which Ts in from the left. Turn left onto Moon Road, then right in 0.25 mile onto School Land Road and head east toward Rochester for 0.25 mile. The access is to the left of the road on the left bank of the river at RM 8.7; a 7-mile trip results from a take-out here. From upstream on the river, this access is so well hidden it pays to leave a marker on the bank.

To reach the put-in south of Littlerock, continue east on School Land Road

Opposite: Black River near launch at Littlerock Road

into Rochester, turn left onto the Rochester–Littlerock Road, and head north for about 5 miles. The put-in for this trip is at a public fishing access left (west) of the highway, about 2 miles south of Littlerock, at RM 16.2.

(To reach the alternate take-out on the Chehalis River northwest of Oakville, return to US 12 and head west. Just west of Oakville, turn left onto Elma–Gate Road, which follows the river more closely than does US 12; within a mile there is an access point left of the road on the right bank of the river. A trip to this point adds 9 miles; see map for Trip 35.)

Paddle Route. Protected by marshes and pasturelands, both public and private, the Black River barely flows for the first 5 miles of this 12-mile segment. It is a long, deep lake fringed by water lilies, often overhung by streamside vegetation. Carved by the massive glacial melt in the Cascades at the end of the last ice age, the Black River takes its name from its dark water (stained with the tannin of its decaying vegetation) and from its source in the Black Hills.

From south of Littlerock, the first 3 miles hug the east side of the valley, never more than 0.5 mile from the highway and the adjacent railroad, which are hidden by dense vegetation that screens all but the sound of an occasional logging truck. At RM 13 there is a private boat ramp on the left bank without an access road; crayfish sun themselves on the corrugated concrete.

From this point the river swings gradually toward the west side of the valley. Mima Creek enters from the right at RM 12.3, 0.5 mile before the river nudges the Burlington Northern Railroad (RM 11.8) near the Black River Wildlife Area. From here it heads southwest for 1.5 miles, past isolated homes and tall conifers.

The river skirts a couple of farms near the northwest edge of Rochester and changes character completely at RM 10: It begins to loop in sharp, sudden curves, its bottom shallows into a series of dips, and the current picks up. The bottom is covered with thick mats of aquatic vegetation; in some places the clumps actually interfere with navigation, forming obstacles that nearly block the river.

Passing beneath a spur railroad bridge at RM 9.3, the river goes into its oxbow between RM 9 and RM 8. The access at RM 8.7 is so subtle that paddlers may miss it unless looking carefully; if you plan to take out here, you may want to leave a marker on the bank to make sure you'll recognize the spot when you reach it. The river is less than a dozen yards wide here. At RM 7 it passes beneath Moon Road between US 12 and Gate, which lies only a few hundred yards from the river.

The river continues its looping course, hemmed in by dense vegetation. Its bottom is shallow, full of aquatic growth in places but scoured clear in others. The current increases from time to time (thus the scouring effect). Rafts of water crowfoot, forget-me-nots, and wild mint grow in the water during the summer. Ancient pilings and logs host lush gardens of grasses, wildflowers, and shrubs.

When the Black River (US 12) bridge comes into view, it is time to take out unless paddlers plan to continue downstream another 4 river miles to the Chehalis (the lower Black embraces the Chehalis Indian Reservation, and paddlers

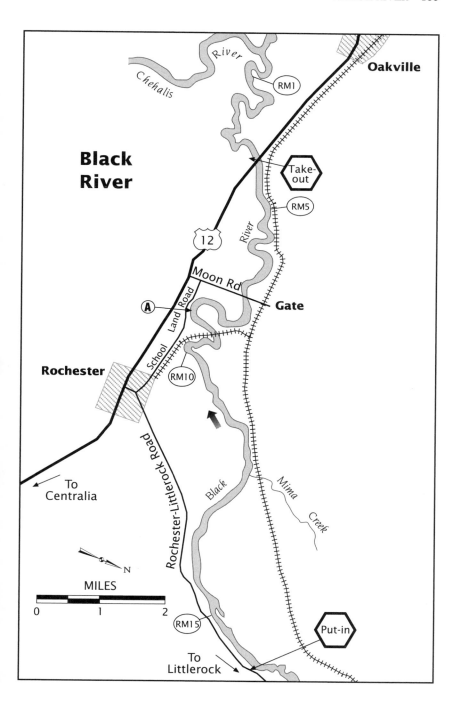

Black River

may encounter fish nets), and 5 more miles on the Chehalis River to the access northwest of Oakville. This is farming country, with some fields extending to the water's edge. There are small drops and deep pools, a few trashy corners with sweepers and snags, but lots of gravel bars.

37 Wynoochee River

Location: Lower main stem near Montesano
Distance: 6 to 16 miles
Paddle time: 4 to 5 hours
Season: Year-round
Rating: Class 2
Hazards: Timber trash, sweepers, diversion structure
Shuttle: Up to 15 miles, pavement
Flow information: USGS Washington website
River gauge: 12036000 at Aberdeen
Historic flows: Average 833 cfs; maximum 23,600; minimum 57
Maps: USGS Montesano, Wynoochee Valley
Information: Grays Harbor County Visitors Guide; Grays Harbor Chamber of Commerce; Washington Coast Chamber of Commerce; Washington Department of Fish and Wildlife website for Wildlife Areas and Access Points

The Wynoochee River flows south out of Olympic National Park, but a major dam that makes this river runnable throughout the year (though it may get a bit lean in late summer and early fall) creates a barrier between the pristine and the merely scenic. Several segments of the upper river are run by kayakers, and canoeists run a 19-mile segment above this 16-mile stretch, which is broken by an ancient diversion structure near RM 8. This segment flows through a broad farming valley to the Chehalis just south of Montesano. It is a pool-and-riffle river with plenty of gravel bars and fine views of low, timbered hills.

Access. The best take-outs are at public fishing areas south of Montesano on the Chehalis River: one, 0.25 mile above the mouth of the Wynoochee; the other, at Friends Landing 0.25 mile below it. Four accesses lie along the Wynoochee Valley Road north of Montesano: one about 4 miles northwest of town at the mouth of Black Creek (RM 5.5); another at the Cutover Bridge (RM 13.7); the third and fourth at the Old White Bridge site (RM 16).

To reach the take-out on the Chehalis River a mile south of Montesano, take US 12 to Montesano and turn south onto SR 107 toward Raymond. Less than a mile south, just past a lumber mill, turn left to a public fishing access on the right (north) bank, 0.25 above the mouth of the Wynoochee.

To reach the take-out at Friends Landing 0.25 mile below the Wynoochee

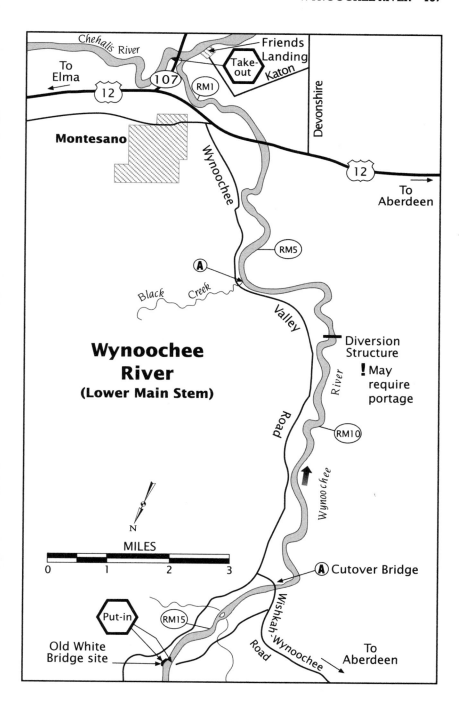

mouth, take Devonshire Road south off US 12, turn left onto Katon, and follow signs to the riverside park along the Chehalis.

To reach the first of four accesses via Wynoochee Valley Road, return to Montesano, head west on US 12 to Wynoochee Valley Road (it leads toward Wynoochee Dam), and turn right, following it northwest 4 miles to the Black Creek boat ramp left of the road on river left. A float from here to the take-out is less than 6 miles. To locate the Cutover Bridge access site (a shortcut to the Wishkah River), continue north on the Wynoochee Valley Road for 6.2 miles, then turn left on Wishkah–Wynoochee Road to an access on the left bank (east side) at RM 13.7.

The river is accessible from either side of the river at RM 15.7. To reach the right bank (west side) of the river, go west on Wishkah–Wynoochee Road, cross

The Wynoochee's pristine character is seen from a roadside viewpoint at river mile 11.3.

the river on the Cutover Bridge, and turn right almost immediately, then follow the road 2 miles to the west side of the Old White Bridge site at the end of the road. To reach the left bank (east side of the river), return to Wynoochee Valley Road, turn left, and drive 2.5 miles to a public fishing access sign. Turn left again, following the road to the riverbank. These two upper accesses are directly across the river from each other.

Paddle Route. From the Old White Bridge site, the river flows relatively straight for nearly 3 miles, its banks overgrown with grasses, native shrubs, wildflowers, and ubiquitous blackberry. An island lies at RM 14.8, with two small creeks entering the river from opposite sides. The river flows beneath the Cutover Bridge at RM 13.6, bends sharply left at RM 13.2, and begins a series of slow meanders that continue for the next 6 miles. A diversion structure at RM 8.1 may have to be portaged.

Several times the river kisses Wynoochee Valley Road from RM 12 south to RM 2.6, where US 12 crosses the Wynoochee. Throughout this segment the river flows past farmlands; an occasional barn or farmhouse is visible from the river, but the agricultural scene rarely intrudes. Wildlife occurs along the river (birds, raccoons, deer), and anglers often ply their sport during their seasons.

Despite the obvious urban scene at Montesano and traffic on US 12, which the Wynoochee parallels for a mile, the river remains relatively wild all the way to its meeting with the Chehalis south of Montesano.

38 Satsop River: Lower Main Stem, East and West Forks

Location: Between Aberdeen and Olympia, north of US 12
Distance: East Fork 10 miles; West Fork 11 miles; main Satsop 4 miles
Paddle time: 3 to 4 hours each
Season: Year-round, except late summer or early fall
Rating: Class 2–
Hazards: Timber debris, sweepers, pilings in fast water
Shuttle: East Fork 11 miles, West Fork 12 miles; pavement
Flow information: USGS Washington website
River gauge: 12035002 near Satsop
Historic flows: Average 6425 cfs; maximum 53,500; minimum 147
Maps: USGS Elma, Wynoochee
Information: Grays Harbor County Visitors Guide; Grays Harbor Chamber of Commerce; Washington Coast Chamber of Commerce; Washington Department of Fish and Wildlife website for Wildlife Areas and Access Points

The lower Satsop and its lower East and West Forks form a network of small, intimate clear-water streams that flow out of the southern Olympics through rain-forest

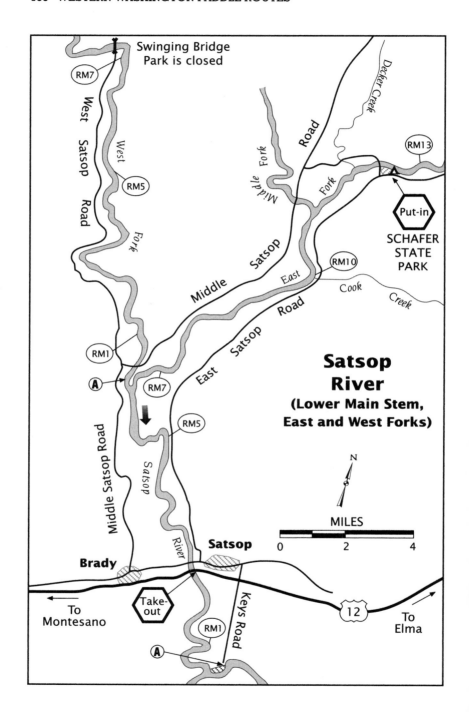

vegetation. The area is largely cut over, but second-growth areas still offer high-quality habitat for wildlife and paddlers. The pool-and-drop character of the river offers challenges to the paddler, and the scenery provides an exciting and varied backdrop.

Access. Both of the uppermost accesses (one on each fork) lie in parks. The one on the West Fork offers a steep but manageable launch, but Swinging Bridge Park has been closed for several years. It is included here in the hope it will someday be reopened; it was one of Weyerhaeuser's most popular parks and the only launch site on the West Fork. The one on the East Fork lies in Schafer State Park. The alternate access near the juncture of the two forks is rough but adequate.

The two suggested take-outs, both on paved roads and both featuring boat ramps, provide excellent access to the lower main stem. One lies off US 12 near the town of Satsop; the other on the Chehalis at the Satsop mouth.

(1) To reach the main take-out boat ramp on the Satsop main stem, travel east on US 12 between Montesano and Elma near Satsop. The boat ramp, on river left below the US 12 bridge, is accessible only from the eastbound lane, but there are several traffic crossovers. A trip down the main stem river from the forks is only a 4-mile run. An alternate take-out lies on the Chehalis River, less than 0.25 mile above the mouth of the Satsop. Take Keys Road south off US 12, just east of the bridge, and follow it 1.3 miles to a public fishing access. (2) The steep, unmaintained boat ramp take-out on the lower West Fork lies within sight of the confluence and can readily be used as a take-out for runs on either fork (if you can find access to the West Fork) or as a launch site for the short run on the main river. To reach this handy access, head east from the boat ramp on US 12 to the next exit (Satsop), and turn left (north) toward Satsop. Turn left again into that small town and head west to Brady, even smaller. In Brady, turn right onto Middle Satsop Road and drive about 3.5 miles to the boat ramp (a public fishing access right of the road, on the right bank of the West Fork).

To reach the East Fork put-in, turn right from the forks access and head north on Middle Satsop Road. At the road fork 0.25 mile north of the forks access, stay right and follow the signs 4.7 miles to Schafer State Park. It is possible to launch from the park with a short carry to the river. (The park also can be reached by taking the East Satsop Road north from the Satsop–Brady Road just west of Satsop, east of the bridge across the Satsop.)

Paddle Route. The East Fork in popular Schafer State Park is lean on water in late summer, but most of the year it is readily runnable by canoe or kayak. It will be challenging at times because of the tight corners, timber debris, low water, and sweepers, but it offers an insight into an isolated, intimate rain-forest river.

Almost immediately paddlers will float beneath the bridge that brought them to the park. As the river bends out of sight of the bridge, a tiny creek enters on the right, followed by Decker Creek also on the right (RM 12). The river corridor is lined with tall trees; though roads parallel the river on opposite sides, they rarely intrude upon the river itself.

Children like to wade at the Schafer State Park launch site on the East Fork of the Satsop River.

Below Decker Creek the river makes a jog to the right, then a quick jog to the left over a rocky bed, to meet the Middle Fork, which enters from the right at RM 11. A long, gradual curve to the left and the mouth of Cook Creek appears on the left at RM 10. At this point East Satsop Road is near enough to touch as the river curves back to the right for a straight mile. A trio of small creeks enters from the right between RM 9.2 and 8.2, as the river meanders through its floodplain for the final 2 miles to a confluence with the West Fork at RM 6.4.

Downstream from the forks, the river slows, meanders more widely, creating a few islands as it flows through farmlands. At RM 3 it straightens for a run through old bridge pilings just above the Satsop-Brady Bridge, then a railroad bridge and the double span of the Satsop River (US 12) bridge. The take-out is on the left bank immediately below the highway bridge on the Chehalis. Or, continue on to the alternate take-out at the mouth of the Chehalis.

The West Fork launch site at RM 7.2 (should it ever reopen) is marked by a footbridge across the river, the namesake of Swinging Bridge Park. Immediately there is a sharp turn to the right, and the park is lost from sight in a narrow gorge overhung with huge rain-forest trees. The road is near the river for the next 5 miles but so far above it that it never intrudes.

Three small streams enter from the left in the next 3 miles. The gorge and forest end, and meadows appear. Deer may be seen, as well as raccoons and muskrats—even foxes—and numerous bird species, especially in late spring and early summer.

At RM 3.7 the river makes a sharp bend to the right, then at RM 3 an even sharper bend back to the left.

The final 3 miles of the West Fork meander through meadowlands, as the river takes on a pool-and-drop character. It flows beneath Middle Satsop Road, which leads to Schafer Park, and enters a small gorge in its last half mile to join the East Fork in a huge deep pool.

39 West Fork Humptulips River

Location: North of Hoquiam/Aberdeen
Distance: 6.5 miles
Paddle time: 1 to 2 hours
Season: Year-round, but best at high water, November to May
Rating: Class 2–
Hazards: Logjams, sweepers
Shuttle: 4.5 miles, pavement, some dirt
Flow information: USGS Washington website
River gauge: 12039005 below US 101
Historic flows: Average 1338 cfs; maximum 33,000; minimum 82
Maps: USGS Quinault Lake; Olympic National Forest and Park Map
Information: Olympic National Forest; Washington Department of Fish and Wildlife website for Wildlife Areas and Access Points; Washington Department of Natural Resources, Forks Office

A rain-forest river rising along the southern boundary of Olympic National Park, the Humptulips River is charming for its name as well as its lush vegetation and pristine character—even in an area where the forests have been butchered for decades. This short, serpentine segment of the West Fork flows past steep bluffs of conglomerate and sandstone, alternating between pools and shallows with occasional modest drops. There are logjams and sweepers, sometimes a tree across the river, but such obstacles can be portaged. The meaning of Humptulips has been disputed: It means either "cold area" or "tough to pole."

Access. To reach the take-out, turn off US 101 onto Donkey Creek Road (FR 22) about 3.5 miles north of where 101 crosses the Humptulips River near the village of Humptulips. Drive 4.9 miles to a bridge across the West Fork of the Humptulips; just beyond the bridge, turn left onto a dirt road that gives access to the river. A mountain bike is ideal for the short shuttle.

To reach the launch site, return to Donkey Creek Road, turn left, and drive 2.9 miles to Fish Trap Road (FR 7940) which branches off to the left (west). Turn onto Fish Trap Road and drive for about 2 miles, then turn sharply right, following this rough logging road along the river for about a quarter mile. After crossing

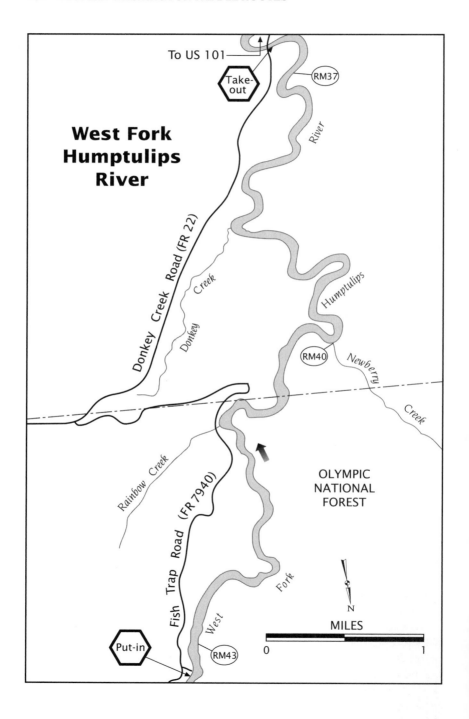

To US 101

Take-out

RM37

**West Fork
Humptulips
River**

River

Donkey Creek Road (FR 22)

Creek

Donkey

Humptulips

RM40

Newberry

Creek

Rainbow Creek

Fish Trap Road (FR 7940)

OLYMPIC
NATIONAL
FOREST

N

Fork

West

Put-in

RM43

MILES

0   1

a bridge over Rainbow Creek, a small tributary with a tiny waterfall on the right, follow this road, staying left at the fork, to a river access, to launch on the left bank of the river (RM 43.2).

Paddle Route. The West Fork of the Humptulips flows south from the launch site (RM 43.2) over a shallow, gravelly bottom, through lush rain-forest vegetation (big-leaf maples festooned with ferns overhanging the river, hemlocks, and western red cedar). It pools occasionally, swinging back and forth between gravel bars and dropping over minor rapids. After a few hundred yards it bends right, then sharply left to snake southward for a mile to the mouth of Rainbow Creek entering from the left (RM 41.2). Fish Trap Road crosses Rainbow Creek by a bridge visible from the river, which turns abruptly right, then right again in two sharp bends to form three sides of a square box between dense streamside vegetation.

The river then loops north for a final bend through Olympic National Forest and flows southwest. The hidden bluffs begin to emerge to form vertical riverbanks of

Paddling the Humptulips past a conglomerate cliff

conglomerate. Tiny falls and dripping springs water the ferns and flowers that grow on the bluffs, a spectacular sight. Newberry Creek enters from the right (RM 40). The river loops its way south, then east in two big horseshoe bends, as it approaches Donkey Creek Road.

Donkey Creek enters from the left (RM 38.4), and the river bends southward again. At RM 38 it nudges the road (unnoticeable because it is well above the river and screened by vegetation) before swinging back to the west for 0.25 mile to the mouth of a tiny tributary creek (RM 37.7). Then the river swings south again for its last meandering mile to the take-out. The bluffs have been left behind, and on the flats the river swings between gravel bars and overhung banks, where a tree occasionally falls to block the entire river or create a sweeper. The take-out lies at a wide gravel beach on the left bank as the river swings east to flow beneath the Donkey Creek Road bridge (RM 36.7).

From this point it is possible to continue downstream all the way to Grays Harbor. Many of the river access points in the next several miles (not shown on map) have been closed by local landowners to protest a county ban on gravel mining intended to protect water quality and enhance the river's ability to propagate anadromous fish. A good public access is less than a mile downstream from 101 at Hanson Road (marked "Public Fishing Access") that turns west about a mile south of the Humptulips Store.

40 Queets River

Location: Queets Campground to Hartzell Creek, southwestern Olympic National Park
Distance: 12 miles
Paddle time: 3 to 4 hours
Season: Year-round, but best at high water, November to May
Rating: Class 2+/3–
Hazards: Class 2+ rapids, sweepers, logjams
Shuttle: 12 miles, gravel
Flow information: USGS Washington website
River gauge: 12040500 near Clearwater
Historic flows: Average 4353 cfs; maximum 133,000; minimum 281
Maps: USGS Salmon River; Olympic National Forest and Park Map
Information: Forks Chamber of Commerce; Olympic National Park; Washington Department of Fish and Wildlife website for Wildlife Areas and Access Points

A big, fast, cold river, the Queets flows out of the Olympic Mountains through coastal rain forest. Frequent winter floods rearrange the logjams and create new

Poling Sams Rapid on the Queets River

ones. Serious Class 2 rapids challenge paddlers, but it is the best wildlife river in the Northwest with elk, deer, otters, beavers, minks, coyotes, ospreys, and eagles as well as an occasional bear. Its meandering floodplain offers spectacular views of Olympic peaks, its ultimate source. The river is milky with rock flour from headwater glaciers.

Access. All of the launch sites and take-out points for this trip are reached from the Queets River Road in Olympic National Park, which leaves US 101 in the northern part of the Quinault Indian Reservation. (The shuttles are ideal for a mountain bike.) Turn north off US 101 onto Queets River Road about 7 miles east of the bridge across the Queets River, near its mouth (17 miles west of Quinault Lake). Follow Queets River Road north, then east. The take-out at Hartzell Creek (RM 11) is only 2 miles from US 101.

To reach any of the alternate accesses or the suggested put-in, continue east on the gravel road toward Queets Campground at the end of the road. At the

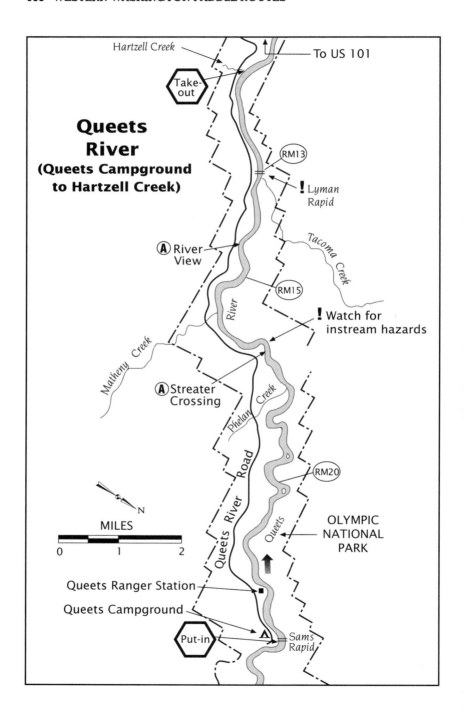

Hartzell Creek

To US 101

Take-out

Queets River
(Queets Campground to Hartzell Creek)

RM13

! *Lyman Rapid*

Ⓐ River View

Tacoma Creek

RM15

! Watch for instream hazards

River

Matheny Creek

Ⓐ Streater Crossing

Phelan Creek

Queets River Road

RM20

N

MILES

0   1   2

OLYMPIC NATIONAL PARK

Queets

Queets Ranger Station

Queets Campground

Put-in

Δ

Sams Rapid

campground, scout out a launch in, above, or below Sams Rapid (RM 23.2), which lies on the bend of the river that flows around the campground. Alternate access points are at Streater Crossing (RM 17.1), about halfway between Sams Rapid and the suggested take-out, and at River View (RM 14.4), about 3 miles southwest of Streater Crossing (4 miles northeast of Hartzell Creek).

Paddle Route. From Sams Rapid—a long, curving rock garden on the bend of the river at the campground put-in—the Queets flows southwest through a broad valley. Ancient trees that have survived the clear-cutting so devastating in this area appear along the bank: gigantic old Sitka spruces, huge cottonwoods, big-leaf maples covered with mosses, and massive Douglas-firs.

The river meanders through braided channels from one side of its floodplain to the other: first hugging the north side (RM 22.3), then bending south past the Queets Ranger Station to approach the south side (RM 21.3), then heading west for a mile, splitting around small, low islands throughout these first few miles. Beware of logjams and sweepers, large rocks, and confluence currents.

The Queets flows around a sizable island above RM 20. Either side is normally passable, but paddlers must judge the flow for themselves in low water because annual winter floods rearrange the bars, islands, and logjams, determining where the current goes. At the end of some horseshoe turns, the river again hugs the ridge on the right (north) at RM 18.

The straight stretch from RM 18 to RM 17 flows southwest through excellent elk habitat. A favorite spot for elk is the meadowland near the mouth of Phelan Creek, which enters the Queets from the left (south) at RM 17.8. Streater Crossing (RM 17.1) on the left (south) bank is a logical halfway point roughly 2 hours (6 river miles) from Sams Rapid. To find this spot from the river, scout it out from the access road on the drive up and establish a marker that will identify it from the river.

Below Streater Crossing, the river makes an abrupt left turn, with a nasty little rock and, at this writing, a sweeper on the far left. At low water, the hazard may be difficult to avoid, but it can be lined on the right. Several small rock gardens interrupt the flow of the Queets in this vicinity; they require some skill in maneuvering to negotiate successfully. The road roughly parallels the river from RM 16.8 to the take-out; but it is rarely visible, never obtrusive. Mount Olympus is visible to the east from several points along this stretch of river.

Matheny Creek flows into the Queets from the left (RM 15.8) just before the river enters a shallow S bend that ends at River View, a possible access (RM 14.4) on the left bank. The river corridor is well vegetated throughout this stretch, though massive clear-cuts can be seen on the surrounding hillsides outside the gerrymandered national park boundaries. Tacoma Creek enters from the right (RM 13.1), and the road (always on the left bank) parallels the river closely for the final 2 miles.

The toughest rapid on this stretch of river, Lyman Rapid, is immediately below Tacoma Creek's mouth. (Rocks that created the rapid were no doubt deposited at the tributary's mouth during high water.) There is a ledge system of bedrock on the left from which to scout the lower part of this long rapid. Below the rapid the river continues in a southwestern direction, with a steep bank on the left and open meadows on the right where you may see elk. A small rapid (more of a rock garden) leads to a deep pool at a slight right bend of the river just above the take-out. From the left bank, Mount Olympus is visible on clear days.

41 Clearwater River

Location: Southwest of Olympic National Park
Distance: 11.5 miles
Paddle time: 3 to 4 hours
Season: Year-round, but best at high water, November to May
Rating: Class 2–
Hazards: Sweepers, logjams, moderate rapids
Shuttle: 8 miles, pavement
Flow information: USGS Washington website
River gauge: None on Clearwater; refer to 12040500 downstream on the Queets
Historic flows: Average 4353 cfs; maximum 133,000; minimum 281
Maps: USGS Destruction Island; Olympic National Forest and Park Map
Information: Forks Chamber of Commerce; Olympic National Forest; Olympic National Park; Washington Department of Fish and Wildlife website for Wildlife Areas and Access Points

True to its name, and despite massive clear-cut logging in the drainage, the Clearwater is as healthy a stream as paddlers can canoe in western Washington. It abounds in aquatic invertebrates that provide good fish food. It is an intimate river: small and winding in its upper reaches, broader but nonetheless charming in its lower miles. Although logging operations scar the surrounding hills, little evidence of timber cutting exists on the river itself. Its shoreline vegetation is dense and natural—excellent habitat for certain wildlife species.

Access. Access to the Clearwater is by way of Clearwater Road, a paved second-grade highway (narrow, with plenty of sharp turns). To reach the Clearwater, turn north off US 101 about 2.5 miles west of Queets Road onto Clearwater Road, which is about 4.5 miles east of the US 101 bridge over the Queets and 19.5 miles northwest of Quinault Lake. In about 2 miles Clearwater Road crosses the Queets River near the Clearwater mouth. In less than a mile beyond the bridge (just after a Department of Natural Resources logging road enters from the right), turn left into the take-out at the DNR Clearwater Picnic Bar on the left bank of the river, 0.8 mile from its mouth.

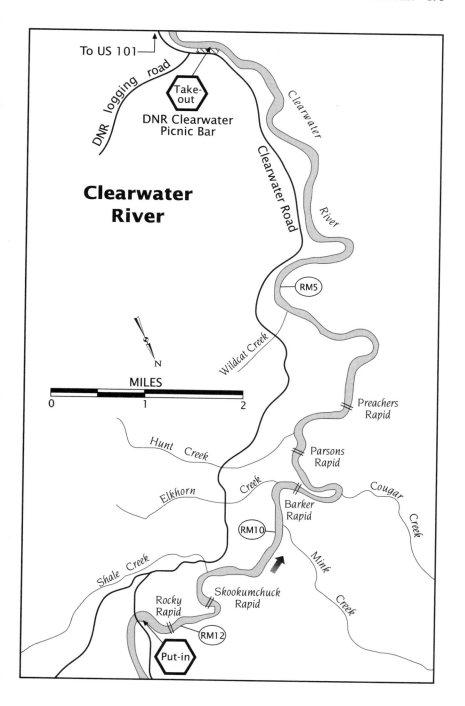

To US 101

DNR logging road

Take-out

DNR Clearwater
Picnic Bar

Clearwater

**Clearwater
River**

Clearwater Road

Clearwater

River

RM5

N

MILES

0   1   2

Wildcat Creek

Preachers
Rapid

Hunt   Creek

Parsons
Rapid

Elkhorn   Creek

Cougar

Barker
Rapid

Creek

RM10

Shale Creek

Mink

Skookumchuck
Rapid

Creek

Rocky
Rapid

RM12

Put-in

To reach the put-in, return to Clearwater Road and turn left (north), following it 8 miles to where it crosses the Clearwater River on a high bridge (stay left at all branch roads). The put-in beneath the bridge is a steep, rough carry down the north side of the road, west of the river.

Paddle Route. At low water levels, the first 100 yards of this run may require paddlers to lie flat in the bottom of the canoe to avoid overhanging trees. No doubt at higher water levels there is more current in midriver, away from the sweepers. In short, the first few hundred yards suggest the intimate character of this clear-water river: lots of shallows, riffles, sweepers, and minor logjams that can be gingerly negotiated.

At the put-in bridge (RM 12.3), a deep pool serves as a reflection pond for everything in sight. But the huge pool narrows and shallows to barely negotiable chutes and to riffles so shallow paddlers may have to walk their craft through in late summer. The river flows west after it breaks out of its initial bend at Rocky Rapid (so named on the USGS maps, but not all that severe). Then it makes a short, sharp horseshoe. Skookumchuck Rapid lies at the apex of the horseshoe, but it's generally no big deal; it flows into a sweeping curve that ends flowing westward again as Shale Creek enters from the left (RM 11). This area is engulfed in dense rain-forest vegetation.

Mink Creek enters from the right (RM 10) on a mile-long, straight stretch flowing southwest. Wide gravel bars force the current into the trees in some places. Barker Rapid lies halfway between Elkhorn Creek (river left), and Cougar Creek (right). The Clearwater bends northwest, then southeast in a sharp horseshoe, with

A logjam near the launch for the Clearwater River

Cougar Creek entering at the apex of the bend (RM 8.8), which opens toward the south for half a mile. Parsons Rapid, another insignificant riffle, shows up on the map at RM 8.

Then the river makes a quick right and left in rapid succession, as Hunt Creek enters from the left (RM 7.8) to mark a westward run for half a mile, then swings south to Preachers Rapid at RM 7.1. Below Preachers Rapid, the last named rapid on the river, the river flows southeast for nearly a mile after it breaks out of the bend (RM 6 to RM 5.2) and heads for the access road.

Wildcat Creek enters from the left (RM 5.3) before the river bends sharply south. The river continues southwest, hugging the left side of its floodplain, with the road just above. Another horseshoe bend to the west and back subtracts a mile as the river reaches for its confluence with the Queets and once more edges the road (RM 3.7). The river widens in its final 3 miles, flowing through a broad valley where a few farms suggest civilization but logging is still king.

Informal, private, and pirate (not officially designated) campsites appear along the last 2 or 3 miles of the Clearwater. A broad gravel bar on the left, opposite a low cut bank on the right, marks the take-out at the DNR picnic area, used all summer for family camping.

42 Hoh River

Location: Minnies Bar to Dickson Ranch
Distance: 20 miles
Paddle time: 4 to 5 hours
Season: Year-round, but best at high water, November to May
Rating: Class 2
Hazards: Logjams, sweepers, fast, cold water
Shuttle: 4.5 miles, pavement and gravel
Flow information: USGS Washington website
River gauge: 12041200 at US 101
Historic flows: Average 2538 cfs; maximum 62,100; minimum 249
Maps: USGS Forks, Destruction Island; Olympic National Forest and Park map
Information: Forks Chamber of Commerce; Olympic National Park; Rainforest Paddlers, Inc.; Washington Department of Fish and Wildlife website for Wildlife Areas and Access Points

The Hoh is the famous rain-forest river that serves as the centerpiece of the developed portion of Olympic National Park. The segment described here is downstream from the park. A big, cold, fast river even in its lower portions, the Hoh offers excellent fishing and challenging boating, though this segment has no real rapids.

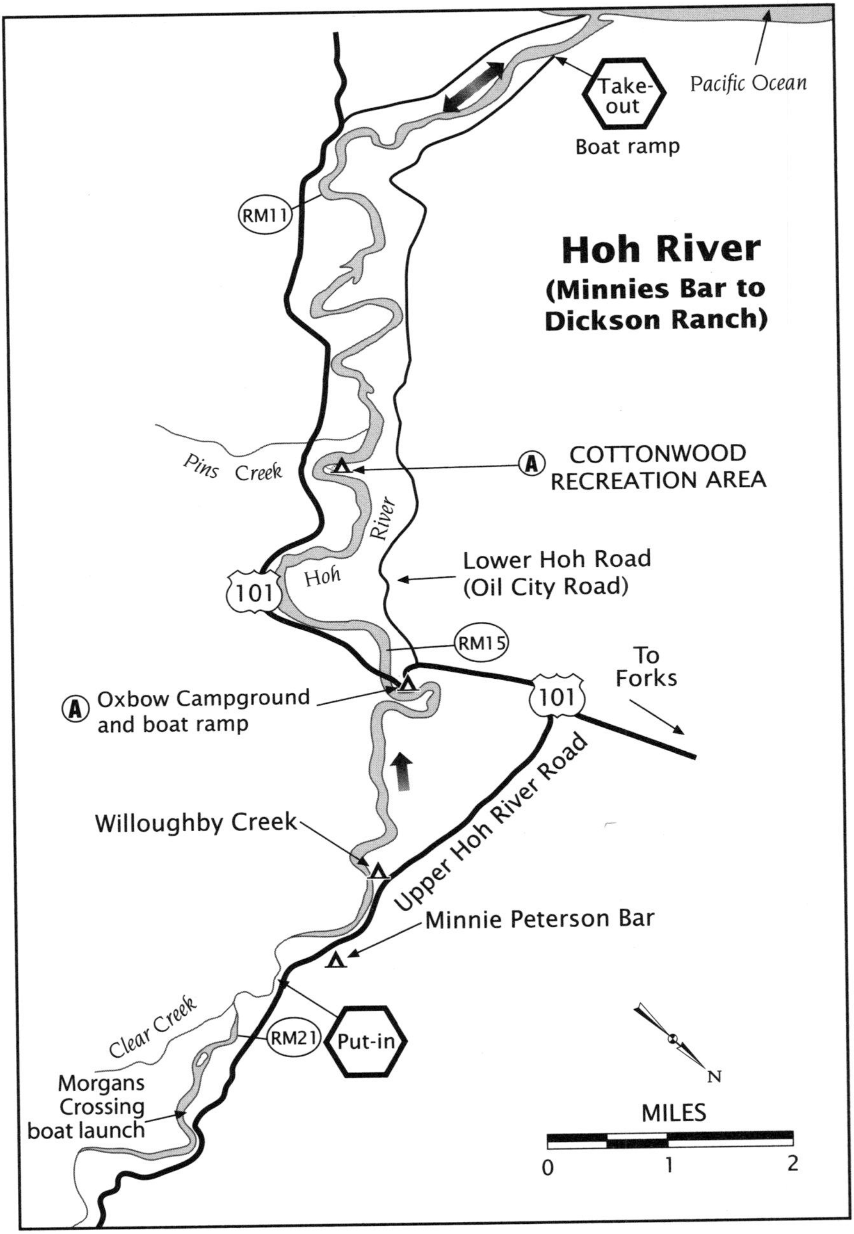

Take-out

Boat ramp

Pacific Ocean

RM11

Hoh River
(Minnies Bar to Dickson Ranch)

Pins Creek

Ⓐ COTTONWOOD
RECREATION AREA

Hoh River

101

Hoh

Lower Hoh Road
(Oil City Road)

RM15

To Forks

101

Ⓐ Oxbow Campground
and boat ramp

Upper Hoh River Road

Willoughby Creek

Minnie Peterson Bar

Clear Creek

RM21 Put-in

Morgans
Crossing
boat launch

N

MILES

0   1   2

The lower portion flows between parallel roads (US 101 on the south and the Lower Hoh Road to Oil City on the north), but roads rarely intrude on the river. It meanders and braids through a mile-wide floodplain to offer picturesque vistas and interesting wildlife habitat. While the Hoh floods every winter, it meanders enough to clear itself of most serious logjams, but they remain a serious possibility.

Access. Access is from Minnies Bar, a gravel bar just below the park boundary (RM 21.6); two Department of Natural Resources (DNR) facilities; and a private boat ramp near the river's mouth (RM 1.3). A DNR boat ramp just off US 101 near its Hoh River crossing at RM 15.5 is busy as a take-out for fishermen and a launch site for paddlers running the lower stretch. A campground off the Lower Hoh Road offers access near RM 11. The Hoh can be run nearly all the way to its mouth, an all-day float.

To reach the take-out for the fast-water upper section, about 15 miles south of Forks, turn off US 101 onto Oil City Road (Lower Hoh Road), which roughly parallels the river on its north side. Drive southwest about 2.5 miles and turn left toward DNR's Cottonwood Recreation Area, a primitive camping area that can serve as a boat launch. The shuttle is so short that a mountain bike makes an ideal shuttle vehicle.

The lowest take-out, a boat ramp just above Kathy Dickson's ranch, enables boaters to run the lower stretch of the Hoh. To reach it, just keep heading southwest on Oil City Road until you see the Dickson home; the take-out lies left of the road on the river's right bank. Ms. Dickson has not charged a fee, but she appreciates a small donation and a carry-out-your-own-trash policy.

To reach the Minnie Peterson launch site, take Oil City Road back to US 101 and turn left, then right on the Upper Hoh River Road toward the Hoh Rain Forest in Olympic National Park. River access is on the right side of the road from a huge gravel bar on river right. A boat ramp of sorts provides vehicle access to the bar.

Paddle Route. From the launch site (RM 21.3), paddlers will enjoy the river's power and push, but the speed of the current means they will have less time to react to problems, most of which occur at high-water levels in the winter or early spring. It is difficult to describe the route because it changes so much from season to season. As water level drops, the Hoh finds its route, braiding among gravel bars and islands, many of them burdened with logs and woody debris. The 7-mile run to US 101, the latter half away from the road, may test the paddler's routefinding and river-reading ability, but serious obstacles are usually an exception to the rule.

The Hoh is deep, swift, and cold at the DNR boat ramp near US 101, a busy place for a paddle craft, but within a quarter mile the river takes the craft beyond the bend, beneath the bridge, and west for a mile. RVs may be camped on the left bank as the river bends south. Paddlers may want to stop at RM 14 and visit the largest known spruce tree, the Helen Clapp Spruce. It stands (without its top) less than a quarter mile from the river. The spruce was once 248 feet high, but lost its

Inflatable kayaks easily negotiate riffles, rapids, and logjams on the Hoh.

top in a storm; it is 17 feet 9 inches in diameter and was once calculated to contain 50,500 board feet of lumber.

As the river continues its course south, it flows over a riffle (mild rapid) just as it touches the roadbed of US 101 (RM 13.6). Below the riffle it begins a westward curve, flows around an island (RM 13.4), passes a favorite fishing hole known as Allens Bar (RM 13), and swings north. The river braids and meanders through massive gravel bars, swinging back and forth between the bounds of its floodplain. At RM 12 (where it reaches the northern edge of the floodplain in one of its curves) lies a DNR fishing access with limited parking, accessible from the Oil City Road. The river swings in a big bend around a promontory gravel bank that serves as Cottonwood Campground (DNR) at RM 10.7, a possible take-out.

In the 9 miles downstream from Cottonwood to the lower take-out, paddlers will see the river broaden, split around islands, and continue its meandering, braided course to tidewater, then fluctuate with the tide in its lower few miles. Its lower reach splits around a few sizable islands, forms a few sloughs at high tide, and offers an interesting paddle that few people experience.

43 Quillayute River/Lower Dickey River

Location: West of Forks
Distance: 6 miles
Paddle time: 1 to 2 hours each
Season: Year-round, but best at high water, November to May
Rating: Tidal flatwater
Hazards: Sweepers, logjams, contrary tides
Shuttle: 4 miles, pavement
Flow information: None available (tidal)
Maps: USGS La Push, Quillayute Prairie; Olympic National Forest and Park map
Information: Forks Chamber of Commerce; La Push Marina (Quillayute Reservation); Olympic National Park; Washington Department of Fish and Wildlife website for Wildlife Areas and Access Points

The Quillayute is one of the shortest rivers in Washington. Formed at the confluence of the Bogachiel and Soleduck Rivers, it flows less than 6 miles westward to the Pacific. The Quillayute is totally tidal—as is the section of its tributary, the Dickey River, covered here. True rain-forest rivers, they both provide delightful paddling through corridors of gigantic trees covered with mosses and ferns. There are logjams, to be sure, and sweepers, but the flow is so mild in these relatively flat-terrain rivers that they present no real problem unless the whole river is blocked (as has been the case on the lower Dickey) or the tides cause strong currents.

Access. Both the put-in and the take-out for the Quillayute are from boat ramps directly accessible from La Push/Mora–Ocean Beach Road (SR 110), northwest of Forks, off US 101. The upper Dickey is accessible from Mina Smith Road, but such access may be meaningless if the frequent logjams exist on the lower Dickey. The best access to the Dickey, which involves traveling upstream (not a problem due to its tidal character), is from the boat ramp on the lower Dickey a mile west of the entrance station in this portion of Olympic National Park. With tribal permission, the Quillayute boat ramp on the left bank near the river's mouth at La Push may be used as a take-out.

To reach the Quillayute take-out and the put-in for an upstream exploration of the Dickey, drive west from the La Push turnoff from US 101 about a mile northwest of Forks on SR 110. Follow this road all the way into Olympic National Park, about 14 miles from US 101. Heading west, note Leyendecker County Park as the road forks. The boat ramp at the park will serve as a launch site for the trip down the Quillayute, which begins here at the confluence of the Soleduck (right) and the Bogachiel (left) rivers. (This is also the take-out for Trip 44.)

A mile west of the park entrance station, turn left to a boat ramp on the left bank of the lower 0.1 mile of the Dickey. This boat ramp will serve as a take-out for a 4-mile trip down the Quillayute from its point of origin or a put-in for a paddle (or pole) up the Dickey River or down the Quillayute to La Push.

To reach the launch site at Leyendecker County Park, simply retrace the route 4 miles to the boat ramp between the rocky Soleduck and the Bogachiel. A National Park Service campground (Mora Campground) lies near the Quillayute–Dickey confluence.

Paddle Route. The Bogachiel drops over a ledge into one of the deepest pools on a Northwest river; this is where the Quillayute is born. From the confluence of the Soleduck and the Bogachiel (RM 5.7), the Quillayute narrows briefly as it flows out of this deep pool. The road to its mouth crosses the Soleduck on the right as the Quillayute makes a long, straight, slow run toward the Pacific between borders of tall trees. The river meanders and braids among massive gravel bars left along the river by winter floods.

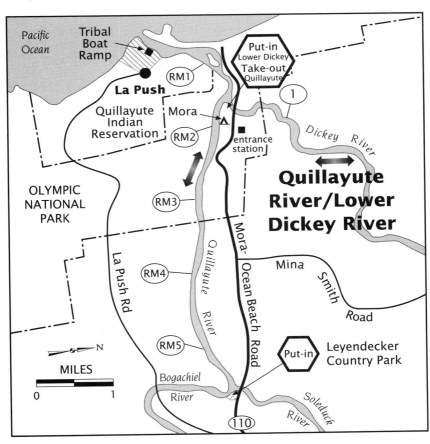

Timber litters the beach near the mouth of the Quillayute River at La Push, a possible take-out.

As the river heads west below RM 3.3, it enters Olympic National Park and flows slightly north of west for nearly 2 miles. It makes its final left turn to the ocean just below the mouth of the Dickey, which enters from the right (RM 1.6). The take-out lies on the lower Dickey, only 0.1 mile from the Dickey's entry into the Quillayute. Simply paddle or pole upstream on the Dickey; the boat ramp is on the right (river left on the Dickey). With tribal permission, you can run all the way to the Quillayute boat ramp at the river's mouth.

The Dickey is a smaller, more intimate river. Its navigability varies from season to season as logjams come and go with local flooding. Paddling or poling up the Dickey from the Quillayute offers a special experience as the river meanders through lush rain-forest vegetation.

44 Bogachiel River

Location: Bogachiel State Park to confluence
Distance: 7 to 15 miles
Paddle time: 4 to 5 hours
Season: Year-round, but best at higher water, November to May
Rating: Class 2–
Hazards: Logjams, sweepers, modest rapids
Shuttle: 14 miles
Flow information: USGS website
River gauge: None, but some info can be gleaned from 12043000 on the Calawah River, a Bogachiel tributary
Maps: USGS La Push, Forks; Olympic National Forest and Park Map
Information: Forks Chamber of Commerce; Olympic National Forest; Washington Department of Fish and Wildlife website for Wildlife Areas and Access Points

The Bogachiel River ("muddy waters") is a frequently flooding river of the Olympic Peninsula known to have washed out US 101 on its way to its confluence with the Soleduck River. It is a prime steelhead stream and receives much fishing pressure. Most of its course flows through private timberlands, but there are a few public access points. Much of it is forested, though there is also agricultural land along the way, largely unobtrusive. Its waters clear whenever the rains stop long enough to let the river drop its suspended load of rock debris, sand, and silt.

Access. Access to the put-in is provided at Bogachiel State Park on US 101, a few miles south of Forks, and at Smith Road across the river from the park. Campsites are available at the state park. Access to either of two suggested take-out points is from La Push (Mora–Ocean Beach) Road, which turns off US 101 a mile northwest of Forks.

The ultimate take-out for this segment of the Bogachiel is its end, its confluence with the Soleduck to create the Quillayute (Trip 43). To reach this point, drive northwest from Forks on US 101 and turn left (west) onto La Push/Mora Road (SR 110); it will become the Mora–Ocean Beach Road as you stay right at the Y. Drive to Leyendecker County Park (only 0.3 mile from the Y on the left side of the road). The boat ramp is between the Bogachiel, which flows from the left, and the Soleduck, which flows from the right.

An alternate access, a possible put-in for a shorter run downstream or a take-out for a shorter run from the state park, lies off La Push (Mora) Road about 3.4 miles east of Leyendecker County Park. Return to Mora Road and turn right (east); it joins La Push Road at the Y. Continue another 3 miles eastward and turn right onto Wilson Road to a public fishing access about 0.4 mile south.

To reach the launch site at Bogachiel State Park, return to La Push/Mora Road, and turn right (east); turn right when you reach US 101. Go through Forks, and continue south to the state park on the right about 7 miles after returning to US 101. Turn into the state park and seek an appropriate launch site, choosing from several riverside campsites available. Another launch site lies across the Bogachiel from the park: cross the river on the Russell H. Barker Memorial Bridge on US 101 and turn right onto Smith Road, then right again into a large gravel parking area that provides a carry to the river beneath the bridge.

Paddle Route. From either launch area (RM 15.6), the Bogachiel flows west for half a mile, turns gradually south, then abruptly northwest (RM 14.7) through Department of Natural Resources (DNR) lands. Then it heads northward in a series of loops, one of which kisses US 101 (RM 12.8). The river is clear most of the year and flanked by gravel bars backed by tall trees. The banks are wooded.

Grader Creek enters from the right (RM 10.4) shortly after the river turns west and leaves US 101 for the last time. Mill Creek enters from the right (RM 9.7) as the river continues to flow slightly north of west. At RM 8.7 a state steelhead rearing pond is just off the river on the right bank, accessible from Bogachiel Way southwest of Forks (no river access here). In another few hundred yards (RM 8.4) the Calawah River joins the Bogachiel from the right.

Moving southwest now, the river turns gradually south (RM 8). Weeden

Boat ramp at river mile 5.5 on the Bogachiel River

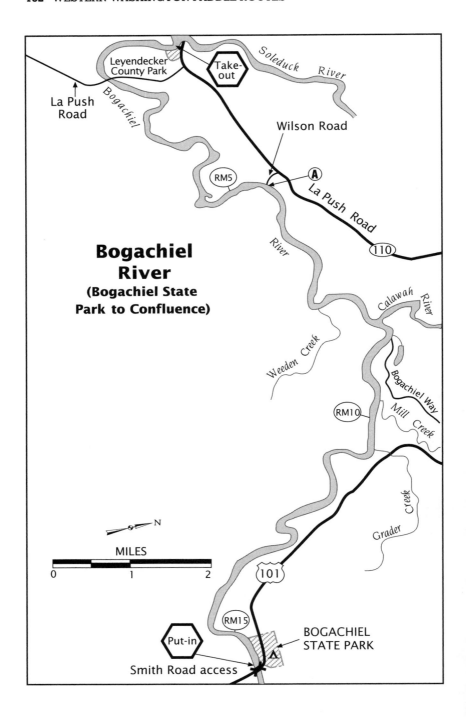

Leyendecker County Park

Take-out

Soleduck River

La Push Road

Bogachiel

Wilson Road

RM5

A

La Push Road

110

Bogachiel River
(Bogachiel State Park to Confluence)

River

Calawah River

Weeden Creek

Bogachiel Way

Mill Creek

RM10

Grader Creek

N

MILES

0   1   2

101

RM15

Put-in

BOGACHIEL STATE PARK

Smith Road access

Creek enters from the left, and the river makes an abrupt bend to the northwest, then back to the southwest. The alternate access appears as a boat ramp on the right. Below this intermediate access point, the river continues to bend back and forth, making a southward swing for a mile, then turning abruptly west at a big pool (RM 4.6) on the bend. A slough comes in from the right just beyond the bend (RM 4.4). In half a mile the river heads north again, then begins a broad double U as it continues its meandering course to its confluence with the Soleduck.

45 Strait of Juan de Fuca

Location: North Shore, Neah Bay to Port Townsend
Distance: Variable
Paddle time: Discretionary
Season: Year-round, except during threat of storm
Rating: Tidal flatwater and open ocean
Hazards: Storms on saltwater, tidal rips, logjams in rivers
Shuttle: None needed; point to point varies with destination
Maps: USGS Port Townsend North, Gardiner, Sequim, Dungeness, Morse Creek, Port Angeles, Angeles Point, Joyce, Disque, Twin Rivers, Pysht, West of Pysht, Slip Point, Clallam, Sekiu, Neah Bay, Cape Flattery; NOAA charts 18471, 18465, 18460, 18464, 18468, 18484, 18485; Olympic National Forest and Park map
Information: Dungeness Kayaking; Dungeness National Wildlife Refuge; North Olympic Peninsula Visitors Center in Port Angeles; Port Angeles Boat Haven Marina; Port Angeles Chamber of Commerce; Port Townsend Chamber of Commerce; PT Outdoors; Sequim Bay State Park; Sequim-Dungeness Valley Chamber of Commerce; Sound Bikes & Kayaks; Washington Department of Parks and Recreation Boating Information; Washington State Travel Information; Washington Department of Fish and Wildlife website for Wildlife Areas and Access Points

The North Shore of the Olympic Peninsula has become a mecca for sea kayakers. When the wind is still, the fog has lifted, and the sun is out, paddling the protected waters along the Strait of Juan de Fuca can be exhilarating. Canoe and kayak shops and liveries have sprung up in Port Townsend, Sequim, Port Angeles, and other towns along the North Shore to serve a growing cadre of paddlers. More than a dozen boat ramps and accesses lie along the shoreline. Paddlers may observe sea mammals and birds, explore tide pools and the mouths of rivers flowing into the Straits; they can beachcomb, picnic, and camp.

   Access. Access to most of the boat ramps along the eastern aspect of the North Shore can be reached from US 101, the main highway that loops around the

Olympic Peninsula. It leads to Sequim and Port Angeles; it also offers access to Port Townsend by way of SR 20. Road signs and local maps provide waterfront access information. Access to Port Townsend Bay and Admiralty Inlet can be found near the Port Townsend–San Juan Ferry dock at the eastern tip of Port Townsend. There is a boat ramp off Water Street between Port Hadlock and Irondale that provides access to Skunk Island and Oak Bay, but tidal currents in Portage Canal can be severe.

Gardiner, a Port of Port Townsend facility east of Sequim, offers access to Sequim Bay, as does Marlyn Nelson Park near Port Williams northeast of Sequim. The most popular launch site for paddling the protected waters of Dungeness Bay is at Cline Spit near the base of the spit, accessible from Sequim–Dungeness Road north out of Sequim. Ediz Hook protects Port Angeles Harbor, which you can access at the city park and pier.

West of Port Angeles, a number of launch sites can be reached from SR 112, which provides access to the western North Shore all the way to Neah Bay. This highway leaves US 101 near the Elwah River, which once pumped so much water into the Strait of Juan de Fuca that its protected eddy provided fresh water well out into the salt water. Access to Freshwater Bay lies at Salt Creek Recreation Area from Freshwater Bay Road off SR 112.

Farther west, a boat ramp at the mouth of the Pysht River accesses the Strait. Four public boat ramps lie on Clallam Bay, including one at Sekiu. Two more are at the mouths of Snow Creek and Sail River, and two on Neah Bay. They all make it possible to explore the mouths of north-flowing rivers. The Sail River boat ramp and both of the Neah Bay boat ramps lie on the Makah Indian Reservation.

This trip overview is shorter on details than any of the other trip summaries because it takes in a number of possible trips. Paddlers should check with sources listed above under Information.

Paddle Route. From Neah Bay to Port Townsend, paddlers can explore the shoreline of the Strait of Juan de Fuca and various river mouths along the North Shore. Some intrepid sea kayakers even cross the Strait to Vancouver Island or paddle into the San Juan Islands. The more protected waters along the coast are especially popular: Port Townsend Bay, Discovery Bay, Sequim Bay, Dungeness Bay, Port Angeles Harbor, Freshwater Bay, Crescent Bay, and Neah Bay. The whole North Shore is home to bald eagles; various sea mammals from seals and sea lions to dolphins and whales may be spotted from time to time.

River mouths may occasionally be blocked by logging debris and sandbars, especially after winter storms, but most of the rivers can be accessed from salt water at high tide. Washington Department of Fish and Wildlife officials often clear river mouths of silt, sand, and woody debris to allow salmon to migrate up the North Shore rivers. Most of them produce coho, chinook, and chum salmon.

The mouth of the Elwah is worth a visit for its eagle population. Once the dams are gone, the Elwah may return to its historic role as the producer of great

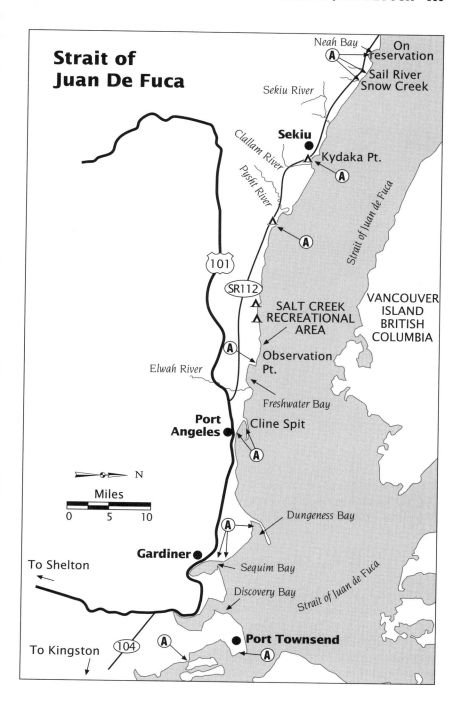

Strait of Juan De Fuca

Neah Bay

On reservation

Sail River
Snow Creek

Sekiu River

Clallam River

Sekiu

Kydaka Pt.

Pysht River

Strait of Juan de Fuca

101

SR112

SALT CREEK
RECREATIONAL
AREA

VANCOUVER
ISLAND
BRITISH
COLUMBIA

Observation
Pt.

Elwah River

Freshwater Bay

Port
Angeles

Cline Spit

N

Miles

0   5   10

Dungeness Bay

Gardiner

Sequim Bay

To Shelton

Discovery Bay

Strait of Juan de Fuca

To Kingston

104

Port Townsend

Paddling from the Elwha River mouth into the Strait of Juan de Fuca
(Patrick Maxwell photo)

fish, especially King Salmon. The lower 10 miles of the Pysht River are fairly flat with a gravel bottom ideal for poling; its pools and riffles provide fine salmon habitat, producing runs that paddlers can enjoy watching during migration.

The Clallam River, flowing north from the Olympic foothills, has a low gradient. Its tidal reaches can be paddled if the major sandbar at its mouth is open (if it isn't, you can easily portage over the bar). The Sekiu River northwest of Clallam Bay flows easterly into the Strait out of the northwest aspect of the Olympic Peninsula. Its low gradient pool-and-riffle lower reaches offer excellent poling possibilities.

The Hoko River northwest of Sekiu involves a convoluted lower reach, which includes a major oxbow loop that invites exploration.

The mouths of all these rivers and a number of other rivers and small streams can be explored from various launch sites along the North Shore. It is vital to study tide charts, listen to weather reports, and keep a sharp eye on weather patterns if you plan to paddle the waters along the Strait of Juan de Fuca.

SOUTHWEST WASHINGTON

46 Willapa River and Sloughs

Location: Near Raymond
Distance: 10 miles plus sloughs
Paddle time: 3 to 4 hours
Season: Year-round
Rating: Tidal flatwater
Hazards: Contrary tides, powerboats
Shuttle: 10 miles, pavement
Flow information: USGS Washington website
River gauge: 12013500 near Willapa
Historic flows: Average 636 cfs; maximum 12,800; minimum 14
Maps: USGS Raymond, South Bend; NOAA chart 18405; Willapa Bay
Water Trail Map of Access Points
Information: Port of Willapa; Washington Department of Fish and Wildlife
website for Wildlife Areas and Access Points; Washington Water
Trails Association

The lower Willapa River and its convoluting sloughs offer an interesting look at a small West Coast timber and fishing town as well as an opportunity to paddle some quiet rural waters and explore a protected saltwater bay. Fishing is good in the Willapa at certain seasons, and the boating is dependable year-round because of the tidal influence on this entire segment. Oyster fishing still thrives in the bay, but timber is king in Raymond, a town bisected by the river.

Access. Excellent take-out access exists off US 101 northwest of South Bend, about 2 miles from the river's mouth as it flows into Willapa Bay. An excellent put-in access lies at the mouth of Wilson Creek (RM 12), a 10-mile shuttle for a 10-mile run; ideal for a bicycle shuttle.

To reach the take-out, drive west on US 101 out of Raymond and through South Bend. At the northwest edge of South Bend, to the right of the highway, lies a small turnout with a boat ramp on the left bank of the lower Willapa River as it broadens to become Willapa Bay.

To reach the put-in, return to Raymond on US 101 and cross the bridge over the Willapa River. Almost immediately beyond the bridge, turn right onto Willapa–Monohan Landing Road and follow it about 4 miles to the public fishing access to the right of the road at the mouth of Wilson Creek. A boat ramp with ample parking is on the river's right bank.

Paddle Route. The Willapa River is placid at the launch site, unless the wind is up. The river, tidal all the way, hugs the road for the first 0.5 mile, past tall,

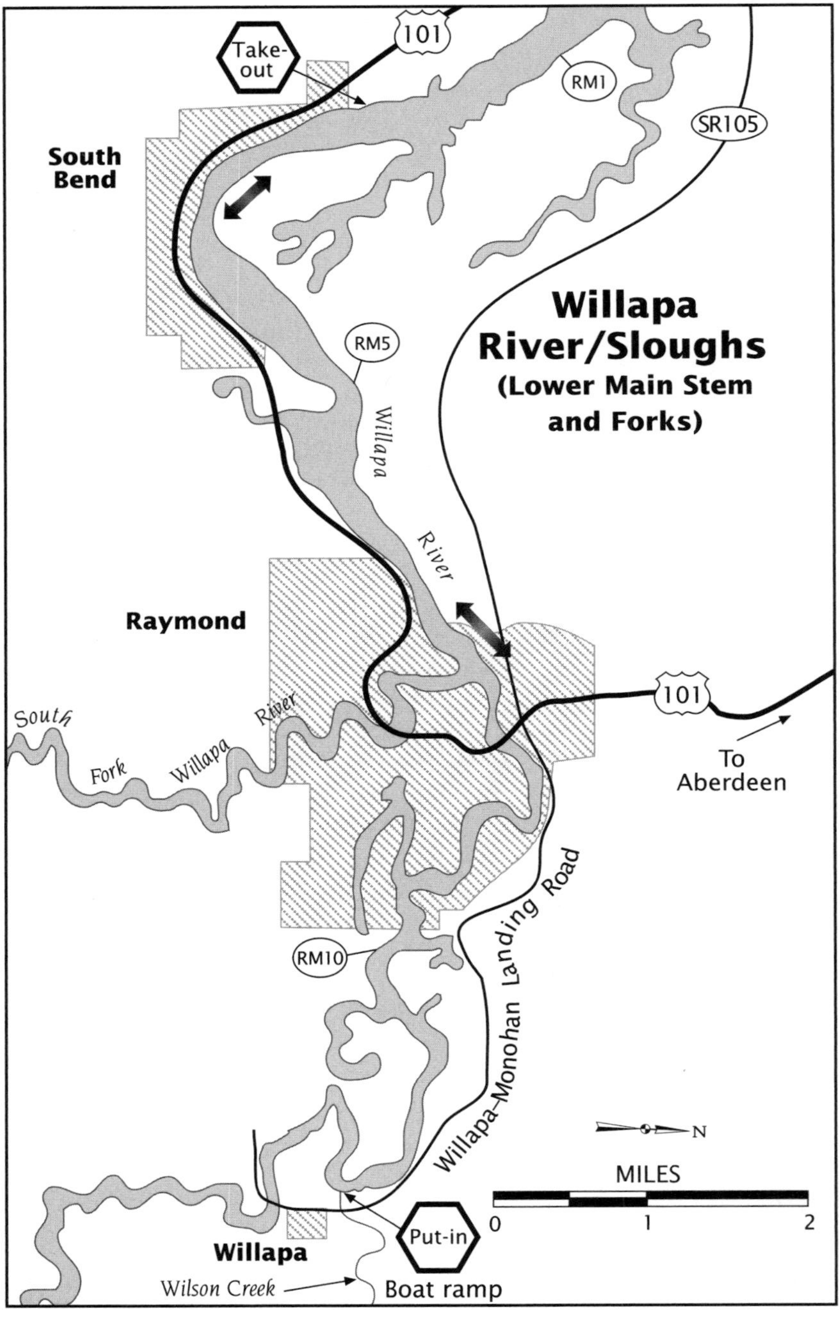

101

Take-out

RM1

SR105

South Bend

RM5

Willapa River/Sloughs
(Lower Main Stem and Forks)

Willapa River

Raymond

River

101

South Fork Willapa River

To Aberdeen

RM10

Willapa–Monahan Landing Road

N

MILES

0   1   2

Willapa

Put-in

Wilson Creek   Boat ramp

scattered conifers and ancient pilings. It bends left to flow west and run straight for about a mile through low-lying marshlands, then bends left again to head southwest. At RM 10.4 a major slough branches off to the left (south) to double back to a point very near a loop of the river a mile below the launch site.

The river broadens and becomes almost sluggish unless the tide is flowing out. Two other minor sloughs branch off to the right in this vicinity, and another branches off to the left just as the river reaches the east edge of Raymond, a town dominated by the timber industry.

From here for the next 3 miles the river loops through town, bordered by timber-related activities including a massive Weyerhaeuser sawmill. The small homes of a typical company town dot the slopes beyond the timber-processing facilities and huge piles of sawdust awaiting export. Sizable ships enter the harbor to carry away what used to be a waste product but is now a valuable resource.

The South Fork of the Willapa meets the main stem near the west edge of town and can be explored as a side trip. From the junction of the two forks, the river flows southwest, broad and busy with boating traffic (commercial fishermen, oyster gatherers, timber-related vessels). It's an interesting experience to dodge power craft in a paddle-powered boat. Most of the powerboat pilots are courteous drivers.

Another small slough heads south as the river narrows at RM 5, and South Bend begins on the left bank. The Willapa swings past South Bend in a broad U

The Willapa River can be a reflection pool at Wilson Creek launch site.

as a slough that branches off to the right at RM 2 sends its tentacles almost to the base of the open end of the U. The boat ramp that serves as take-out is hard to miss; it lies at the western edge of South Bend.

47 Palix River/North River/Smith Creek

Location: East side of Willapa Bay
Distance: 2 to 7 miles
Paddle time: Depends on tides and choice
Season: Year-round
Rating: Tidal flatwater
Hazards: Contrary tides, logjams, storms
Shuttle: None needed
Flow information: Tidal
Maps: USGS Western Quad, Bay Center, South Bend, Aberdeen SE, Nemah, North Nemah; NOAA chart 18405
Information: Bay Center Marina; Port of Willapa; Washington Department of Fish and Wildlife website for Wildlife Areas and Access Points

The Palix River, the North River, and the North's tributary, Smith Creek, flow into the northern and eastern aspects of Willapa Bay, all of them tidal and accessible from near their mouths. Their bottoms are silt and sand with some gravel, ideal for poling, but since they are largely protected from wind, they can usually be paddled as safely as any tidal stream on the coast. They offer access into a roadless forested landscape, much of it cut over in recent history. Despite siltation and logging debris, all of them produce salmon: coho, chinook, and chum. The lower reaches of these rivers offer ideal habitat for numerous species of birds as well as many small fur-bearing animals such as weasels, mink, and raccoon. Exploring this trio of tidal rivers offers boating fun, self-education, unique challenges, and productive fishing.

Smith Creek, the North River, and the Palix River all have protected wildlife areas.

Access. Access is easy from paved highways and boat ramps, one near the mouth of Smith Creek just off SR 105 west of Raymond for Smith Creek and nearby North River; the other off US 101 southwest of Raymond for the Palix.

To reach the Smith Creek access, drive west out of Raymond on SR 105, which leaves US 101 north of the Willapa River bridge at the north edge of Raymond. Just after crossing the mouth of Smith Creek, turn right into a large parking area; the boat ramp is on the southwest corner of the parking area.

To reach the Palix River boat ramp, take SR 101 southwest out of Raymond driving through South Bend along the shore of Willapa Bay. After rounding Range Point and passing Stony Point, cross the bridge over the Palix River. The boat ramp is on the left.

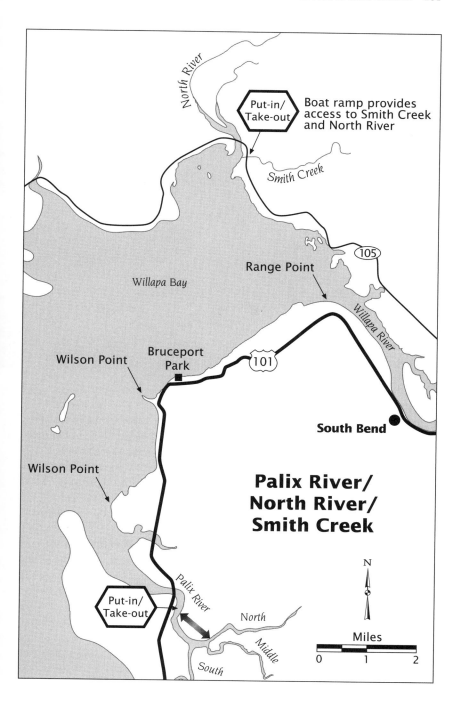

North River

Put-in/
Take-out

Boat ramp provides
access to Smith Creek
and North River

Smith Creek

105

Range Point

Willapa Bay

Willapa River

Wilson Point

Bruceport
Park

101

South Bend

Wilson Point

**Palix River/
North River/
Smith Creek**

N

Put-in/
Take-out

Palix River

North

Middle

South

Miles

0   1   2

Smith Creek in the Johns River Wildlife Area

Paddle Route. Smith Creek flows into the North River 0.3 mile from the North River mouth. Tidal influence on Smith Creek reaches inland a little more than a mile, but campers have been known to paddle or pole upstream for 4 or 5 miles if no logjams bar the way. It has become popular with weekend canoe campers. Roadless for its lower 7.7 miles, it has a sandy bottom with a little gravel, good for poling. Smith Creek's headwaters, which are crossed by US 101 about 11.7 miles from its mouth, have been logged extensively; logging and logging road construction have caused siltation, but it still produces salmon.

At the limit of tidal influence lies a large island; flows around the island vary with the latest high-water activity: just read the water and run. Above the island the creek narrows and meanders, making a broad S turn between RM 0.8 and 1.3 and again at RM 2. It bends sharply back upon itself about 3.4 miles above the island. Bear Creek, with several miles of significant chinook spawning water, enters at RM 3.8. How far you can travel upstream depends upon logjams, tide, and your own stamina and technique.

The North River has been run all the way from the US 101 crossing between Aberdeen and Raymond, but it is prone to logjams. It's preferable to run it upriver from its confluence with Smith Creek, accessible from the Smith Creek boat ramp less than 0.1 mile from the North River. The SR 105 bridge over the North River at RM 0.5 seems to block entrance to the river above the bridge, but paddlers can easily work their way through the booms and bridge pilings.

Above the bridge on the river's right bank (on your left as you go upstream) lies a commercial fishing resort. The river's lower 3 miles make a huge C curve open to the east. Above RM 3.2 it runs straight northeast for nearly a mile, then bends sharply right and left in less than a quarter mile. At RM 4.3 it straightens for a 2-mile run north to the mouth of Hatchery Creek (RM 6). An S-turn between RM 6 and 7 takes you to the first cascades and the first logging road. This may be as far as most paddlers wish to go.

The Palix River, only 1.5 miles long in its tidal basin, offers 10 miles of paddling or poling pleasure, an opportunity to explore several tidal reaches from an easy access. The Palix consists of three forks that split off within its first 2 miles. All of them are tidal: the South Fork joins the North Fork at RM 1.5; the Middle Fork joins the North Fork at RM 1.7. Paddlers in sea kayaks or canoes, or polers in open canoes and johnboats, can access any of the forks from the boat ramp in less than an hour. This is flat terrain. Boaters can explore roughly 5 miles of the North Fork, 4 miles of the South Fork, and 1.5 miles of the Middle Fork, all of it well protected from storms and ocean waves.

48 Grays River/Seal Slough

Location: North of Columbia River
Distance: Grays River up to 10 miles; Seal Slough 2 miles; Deep River 7 miles
Paddle time: 3 mph at slack tide
Season: Year-round, but best in rainy season, September through May
Rating: Tidal flatwater (up to Class 2)
Hazards: Contrary tides, wind on the bay
Shuttle: None necessary, or 3 to 10 miles, mostly pavement, some gravel
Flow information: Tidal
Maps: USGS Grays River; NOAA charts 18521, 18523
Information: Wahkiakum County Visitor Information; Washington Department of Fish and Wildlife website for Wildlife Areas and Access Points

Grays River is a small tributary of the Columbia River named for Captain Robert Gray, who discovered the Columbia (the river was named for his ship, the *Columbia Rediviva*). Seal Slough is a tributary of Grays River that enters it about 2 miles from its mouth. Nearby Deep River feeds into Grays Bay about 2 miles west of the mouth of Grays River. All these segments are tidal. Washington's only extant

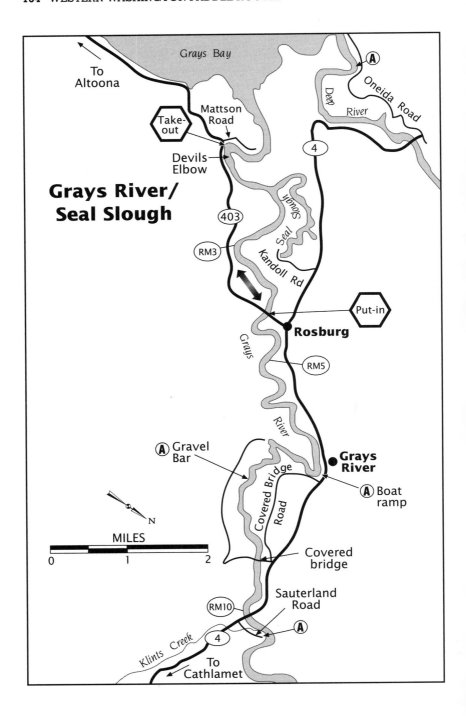

Grays Bay

To Altoona

Ⓐ

Deep River

Oneida Road

Mattson Road

Take-out

Devils Elbow

Grays River/ Seal Slough

4

Seal Slough

403

RM3

Kandoll Rd

Put-in

Rosburg

Grays

RM5

Grays River

Ⓐ Gravel Bar

Covered Bridge Road

River

Grays River

Ⓐ Boat ramp

Covered bridge

N

MILES
0   1   2

RM10

Sauterland Road

Klints Creek

4

Ⓐ

To Cathlamet

covered bridge lies on Grays River at RM 9.6, a mile above the upper extent of tidal influence. While this region is extremely rainy, it offers excellent birding and unique paddling opportunities through a historical landscape. Lewis and Clark camped briefly on the west shore of Grays Bay the fall of 1805.

Access. Public access is available at a boat ramp just south of the Rosburg Store, near the Rosburg Community Hall, and at a boat ramp in the village of Grays River. There are informal launch sites at a private campground less than a mile from the mouth of the Deep River; at a private boat dock at Devils Elbow, the last bend of Grays River before it enters the bay; and at a gravel bar at RM 8 near the confluence of the East and West Forks of Grays River north of SR 4.

The best launch site may also be the best take-out if the tides are played right: the boat ramp 0.3 mile south of Rosburg at RM 4.2. To reach it, turn south off SR 4 at the Rosburg Store (between Naselle and Cathlamet) onto Altoona Road (the sign says "Dead End—7 miles") and drive a short distance. Turn right onto a parallel road west of the highway heading west just as the highway rises to cross Grays River on an elevated bridge. The unmarked road leads to the Rosburg Community Hall. The boat ramp is a few dozen yards southwest of the building.

To paddle downstream to the Bay and perhaps explore Seal Slough on the way, paddlers may want to leave a shuttle vehicle (a bicycle is ideal) at Devils Elbow (RM 1), about 3 miles by road from the launch site. To reach it, return to Altoona Road (SR 403) and turn right; cross the bridge and head south for less than 3 miles to Mattson Road and turn right. Park alongside the road, preferably on the left-hand (southwest) side. It is best to ask permission to use the private dock to the right of the road for launching or taking out.

To reach two other accesses, return to SR 4 and turn right, heading northeast. Take Covered Bridge Road south (right) off SR 4 at the village of Grays River and launch at the boat ramp at a sharp bend of the river off Covered Bridge Road. The gravel-bar access at RM 8 (upstream of the covered bridge) can be reached by crossing the bridge and following Covered Bridge Road to a point about 2 miles above the bridge. A rough road offers access to a big gravel bar left of the road, on the left bank of the river.

For a longer run of Grays River above tidewater, launch at the rough access near the confluence of the river's main forks. Return to SR 4 and head east toward Cathlamet. Two miles from Grays River village, the highway crosses Grays River. Turn left onto Sauterland Road; follow it to where it peters out at a school bus turnaround; then follow the track to the riverbank (RM 10.6). A standard vehicle will make it in most road conditions.

To reach the launch site on the Deep River, return to SR 4 and head west. Just after crossing the Deep River, turn left onto Oneida Road. There is rough access from the road 4.7 miles from the highway and a commercial campground access 5.2 miles from the highway. (The paving ends 3.7 miles from SR 4.)

Paddle Route. From the boat ramp near the Rosburg Community Hall, paddlers can head upstream toward the covered bridge (if the tide is coming in) or downstream on the outgoing tide. Either route offers a unique experience. Both the upper Grays River and the stream below the covered bridge are Class 2.

Heading upstream between blackberry-festooned banks, paddlers weave northeast through agricultural lands about 3 miles to the village of Grays River. A boat ramp is located here at a tiny park at the south edge of town on Covered Bridge Road.

From the village the river swings abruptly south and then east through pasturelands, to flow beneath the covered bridge (RM 9.6). Going upstream beyond this point is likely to be difficult for two reasons: (1) the tidal influence subsides 1 mile below the bridge; and (2) in summer the water usually becomes shallow.

Heading downstream, paddlers encounter blackberry banks and thick bank vegetation of red osier dogwood and viburnum as the river loops widely through dairy farms and pasturelands, bordered by dark, brooding Sitka spruce trees that in places overhang the shore. It turns left to flow south for a mile, then swings right to flow westward, past occasional rural homes and backyard logging operations where second- and third-growth forests survive and wildflowers (lotus, jewelweed, tall orchids) abound in summer.

Just below RM 2, Seal Slough enters from the right and can be followed all the way to the old Finnish Church just off SR 4, a full 2 miles north by water. Taking a right turn at the fork 1.3 miles upstream, the paddler can go almost another mile up the branch of the slough that leads to Kandoll Road a few hundred yards west of Rosburg.

The lower 2 miles of Grays River are totally tidal, lined with tall trees and houses, boat docks, and moored boats. If the tide is right, boaters can paddle

A covered bridge over the Grays River about 10 miles from Grays Bay and the Columbia River

down to the bay, explore its northern reaches, even enter Deep River 2 miles to the west. If a shuttle vehicle has been left at the lower end of the Deep River, paddlers can take out there along a stretch of river lined by small houses, fishing shacks, and moored boats.

To run the upper stretch of Grays River, launch at the forks access (RM 10.6) off Sauterland Road. From here the river is small, winding, and shallow in summer, with splits around brushy gravel islands and tight corners, a moderate Class 2 river unless it is flooding, which it may be much of the year, given the heavy rains of the area. The river flows south as it begins a sharp S curve which ends beneath the SR 4 bridge over Grays River. Then it moderates as it enters agricultural lands, still lined by trees and shrubbery as it meanders through the valley to flow beneath the covered bridge.

49 Cowlitz River

Location: Salmon Hatchery to I-5
Distance: 8 to 22 miles
Paddle time: 4 to 5 hours
Season: Year-round
Rating: Class 1+/2–
Hazards: Minor rapids, sweepers, logjams
Shuttle: 8 miles, pavement
Flow information: USGS Washington website; Tacoma Public Utilities
River gauge: 14238000 at Mayfield Dam, 14243000 at Castle Rock
Historic flows: Average 6214/6757 cfs; maximum 68,400/139,000; minimum 451/998
Maps: USGS Castle Rock, Toutle, Onalaska; Lewis County map
Information: Lewis County Tourism in Chehalis; Department of Fish and Wildlife website for Wildlife Areas and Access Points; Washington Department of Natural Resources Castle Rock office

The Cowlitz is one of the premier steelhead fishing rivers of the Northwest, but it also yields salmon and trout. It is more of a mountain stream—a big one to be sure, but a mountain stream nonetheless—east of I-5 in the vicinity of Toledo. This stretch, which has shorter alternatives, is the most scenic and pristine of the Cowlitz. It offers views of Mount Rainier and Mount St. Helens as well as excellent fishing, good birding, and boating on a big open river that moves with good speed. It is rural but with little evidence of the adjacent farms, except for an access in a cow pasture.

One boater has called it "the best river this side of the mountains for new boaters," a personal opinion, but it suggests the quality of experience available on the upper Cowlitz. It may be challenging to some paddlers, but downstream it gets progressively tamer. Expect to see wildlife, such as bald eagles and ospreys, deer and beavers. The river is broad, tree-lined, and rural, almost wild in nature. Its forested banks give it a more pristine appearance than its surroundings suggest. This is a good run for sea kayaks.

Access. The Cowlitz lies a few miles south of US 12, but the launch site is reached from Spencer Road, which parallels the river on the north side. Spencer Road also provides access to public fishing areas at Massey Bar and the state trout hatchery. The shuttle drive offers views of both Mount St. Helens and Mount Rainier.

Although the take-out is almost immediately beneath the Cowlitz River bridges on I-5, it is complicated to reach. Take Exit 60 off I-5 onto Toledo-Vader Road and head east toward Toledo. After 2 miles, turn right at Jackson Highway in Toledo; follow it through town, crossing the Cowlitz and turning right onto South Jackson Highway, 0.3 mile from the bridge. Follow this highway southwest to Mandy Road; turn right onto Mandy, then left onto River Road. Continue under the I-5 bridges to the public fishing access just west of the freeway. The access also can be reached from Exit 57, about 3 miles south of Exit 60.

To reach Spencer Road en route to the launch sites, take Exit 60 off I-5 and head east to Toledo, turning left as Toledo-Vadar Road Ts onto the main north–south street in Toledo, which becomes the Winlock-Toledo Road. In less than a mile (just past Toledo High School), veer right at the Y toward Lewis and Clark State Park, and head northeast on North Jackson Highway. At 1.3 miles from the Y, turn right at the Cowlitz Mission Historic Site; after 0.3 mile, turn left onto Spencer Road and head east toward the launch site at Cowlitz Salmon Hatchery.

Paddlers will pass two other river accesses along the way: Massey Bar and the Cowlitz Trout Hatchery. To reach the launch site, continue to follow Spencer Road. After about 11 miles, there is a stop sign at Fuller Road. Go straight ahead 0.2 mile to a yield sign, which offers a free right turn; stay right (essentially straight ahead) into the Cowlitz Salmon Hatchery, and follow the road to the public fishing access several hundred yards below the barrier dam below Mayfield Dam. The launch site is on the right bank of the river. Many people camp here.

To reach the Cowlitz Trout Hatchery access, return to Spencer Road and turn left at the sign to Cowlitz Trout Hatchery. Follow the road to the public fishing access (a double boat ramp 0.7 mile from the turnoff). It is roughly 5 miles between the salmon hatchery and the trout hatchery, about the same between the trout hatchery and the turn-off for the Massey Bar access.

To reach the Massey Bar access, return to Spencer Road and head west. Turn left onto Buckley Road, which leads to what looks like a dead end. Veer right onto a gravel road, which winds down a hill into a cow pasture. On an open flat by the river, the launch site is on the right bank of the river. It's a boat ramp heavily used by steelhead fishermen for drift boats or dories.

Paddle Route. This 22-mile reach of the Cowlitz can easily be run in a day. The author has poled it from the salmon hatchery to the I-5 take-out in 4 hours

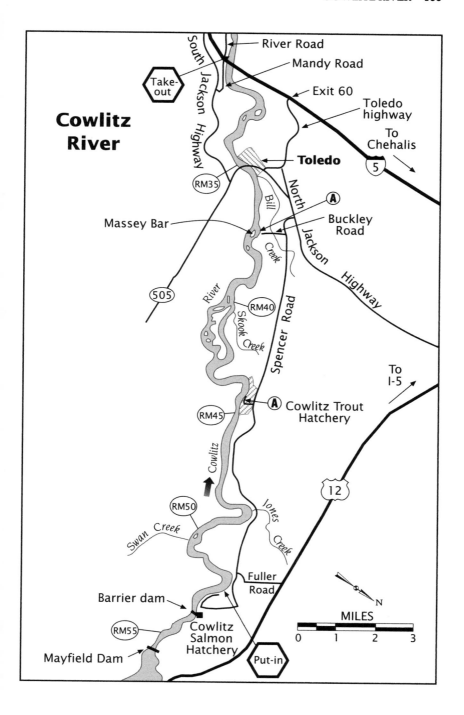

Cowlitz River

Take-out

River Road

Mandy Road

Exit 60

Toledo highway

To Chehalis

South Jackson Highway

RM35

Toledo

Bill

North Jackson Highway

Ⓐ

Massey Bar

Buckley Road

Creek

505

River

RM40

Skook Creek

Spencer Road

To I-5

RM45

Ⓐ Cowlitz Trout Hatchery

Cowlitz

12

RM50

Jones Creek

Swan Creek

Fuller Road

Barrier dam

RM55

Cowlitz Salmon Hatchery

Mayfield Dam

Put-in

MILES

0   1   2   3

N

Solo canoeing the Cowlitz River

and 15 minutes of river time in midsummer when the river was relatively low.

Immediately below the salmon hatchery boat ramp, the river bends sharply to the left. Within a quarter mile, paddlers are out of sight of civilization, heading south along a pristine corridor between tall trees where eagles and ospreys fish along with kingfishers and great blue herons. The river is shallow except at flood stage and amazingly intimate for so large a river.

The river bends sharply to the right 1.5 miles below the launch site, as two small streams enter from the left and an island appears in midriver. Either side of the island should be negotiable; in low water the flow will be obvious. From this bend, the river flows northwest for another 1.5 miles between tall cottonwoods and conifers with an understory of alders and native shrubs.

The river bends sharply once more to the left near Spencer Road. A small creek enters from the right, creating a serious rapid, a modest Class 2. (It can be scouted from the road while you are driving to the launch site.) The river flows south briefly, then bends back to the west at a steep bluff on the left bank.

Once the river takes its westward course, it flows relatively straight for 3 miles, the last 0.5 mile along the Cowlitz Trout Hatchery grounds. The access is at the lower (downstream) end of the hatchery property, 8 river miles from the start of this segment.

From the double boat ramp at this public fishing access, the river is broad and shallow, its banks well forested. The river bends to the left (there is private access on the left bank, just below the bend). Ospreys, eagles, kingfishers, and great blue herons fish the clear waters in this vicinity.

As the river bends to the right again, it becomes braided, but the main channel generally is obvious. Pasturelands lie on the left, a slight bluff on the right. Many islands provide lunch stops and excellent birding in summer. Skook Creek enters on the right a mile before the river gathers itself together—still broad, clear, and fast. It makes one more swing to the north against the bluffs before it reaches the Massey Bar boat ramp on the right bank of a shallow bend to the south.

From the access at Massey Bar, the river is broad and fast, clear and shallow, its banks riprapped with basalt blocks. In low water, a riffle shows just below the put-in. The river flows through open country with a fringe of vegetation along the banks, swinging gradually to the left to pass Toledo (on the right bank in about 3 miles). Bill Creek enters from the right just before Toledo. The river passes beneath the Toledo-Vader Road bridge and swings right—still broad and shallow for the most part, though a few deep stretches alternate with riffles. Walking access used by fishermen in steelhead season lies along the inside (right bank) curve at the bend below town. The river gradually deepens, flows around an island or two, and swings left at a point where the river is less than a mile from I-5 and the sound of highway traffic may intrude.

The river parallels I-5 about a mile from the freeway as it flows south, then curves right to flow westward in a long, straight stretch for more than a mile. The take-out is on the left bank 100 yards below the double span of the I-5 bridges. A few good river access points lie along River Road, which is the extension southwest of the road along the Cowlitz.

50 Lower Kalama River

Location: Ending at Columbia River
Distance: 8 to 10 miles
Paddle time: 2 to 3 hours
Season: Year-round; may be too low in late summer, too high in winter flood stage
Rating: Class 2–
Hazards: Sweepers, logjams, modest rapids
Shuttle: 6.4 miles, mostly pavement
Flow information: None available
Maps: USGS Kalama; NOAA chart 18524
Information: Cowlitz County Tourism in Kelso; Department of Fish and Wildlife website for Wildlife Areas and Access Points; Washington Department of Natural Resources Castle Rock office

One of the best steelhead tributaries of the Columbia, the Kalama has some fine whitewater stretches above this segment. At the lower reaches, this clear, swift stream provides a few challenging miles of modest rapids before it breaks out of its confining canyon a few miles from the Columbia into which it flows. The paddler is suddenly thrust into a modern world of freeways, a decommissioned nuclear power plant, and grain elevators feeding ships carrying food for a hungry world. Despite logging trucks on adjacent roads, as well as rural homes and vacation cabins along its shoreline, the Kalama is a pleasant run less than an hour from Portland.

Access. One take-out on the lower 0.5 mile of the river and another on the right bank of the Columbia River a few dozen yards downstream from the Kalama

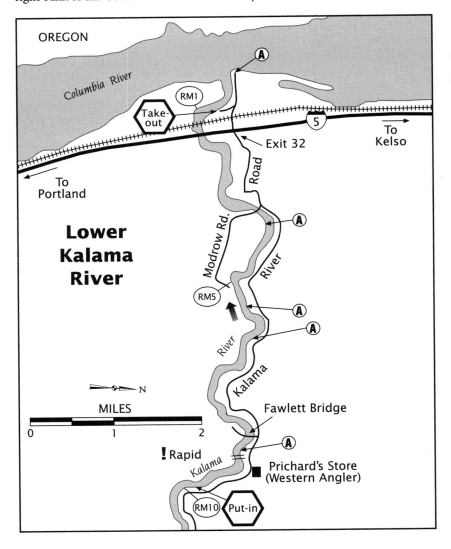

mouth offer convenient access at the end of this trip. Since Kalama River Road hugs the river for much of this segment, there are a number of possible launch sites from the roadside.

The take-out for this segment can be reached from I-5 by taking Exit 32 (Kalama River Road) 2 miles north of Kalama. It is also 7 miles from the SR 4 Exit 39 south of Kelso. Head west over the railroad tracks to a public fishing access left of the road, on the last bend of the river.

To reach the access on the Columbia River itself, follow the county road past the public fishing access to where the road officially ends. Then turn left, following signs that lead to a sportsman's club; but instead of turning left into the sportsman's club, go straight to the Columbia River beach on the right bank, a few dozen yards below the mouth of the Kalama.

To get to the launch areas, return to the county road that crosses over the railroad tracks and I-5 to become Kalama River Road, and follow it upstream (east). There are several roadside accesses, but the farthest upstream that is still Class 2 water is opposite a red barn on the left, 6 miles from the I-5 exit. The rough launch site is on the right (south) of the road, on the right bank of the river.

Other possible launch sites include the one at Prichard's Store (Western Angler), 0.6 mile downstream from the red barn put-in (RM 8.6); public fishing access areas at RM 6 and RM 5.4; and on the left bank just above the Modrow Road bridge (RM 3.5). Modrow Road crosses the Kalama River at this point as it heads south, then east to access the residents living south of the river.

Paddle Route. At the red barn put-in there is only roadside parking, and no boat ramp (just a rough carry to the right riverbank). The river gets busy quickly. An island forces a choice of routes; right is usually better. A big rock in midriver offers another challenge, then Prichard's Store (known as Western Angler) appears on the right bank across the road.

Below Prichard's Store is a solid Class 2 rapid that can be cheated, but its tail waves offer some nice standing waves. Kingfishers and ouzels make their presence known. Beaver cuts line the bank, and peeled sticks cover the sandy bottom in the eddies. Fern-festooned cliffs steer the river through a forested gorge, and a kinky cable crosses the river not far above Fawlett Bridge, where a Class 2 swing rapid lies on a sharp left-hand bend.

This rapid can be tricky. The current flows strongly along the left bank, which is essentially a cliff, and the right side of the river is a rock garden. Strong eddies mark the confluence of counter currents, but experienced paddlers should have few problems here. (If this rapid, which can be scouted from the road, seems too challenging, launch just downstream at the public fishing access a mile below.)

A waterfall on the left adds to the scenery, as does the presence of birds (Steller's jays, chickadees, more kingfishers). The river widens to shallow riffles. A series of waterfalls appears on the left and houses on the right, along with some domestic mallards. The public fishing access, well used by steelhead anglers, lies on the right;

Even the Kalama, a Columbia tributary, is influenced by tides.

a large rock is in midriver. The right channel is normally the way to go.

Licorice fern grows here in the shade of Douglas-fir, western red cedar, hemlock, grand fir, maple, and alder. Old houses appear on the left bank, and the river glides past a fish hatchery near a problem rapid. A gravel bar on the right pinches the river into a narrow, turbulent channel on the left. Watch for logjams and sweepers. Another access lies at a riffle on a big bend where cabins appear on the left, and there is a pipeline on the right at a green bridge with a logjam.

The green gas pipeline and a gauging station mark the entry into civilization. Soon Modrow Bridge comes into view with the fishing access on the left bank under the bridge. The river is out of the canyon now, and it widens and slows. Oak trees and planted orchards appear. Red osier dogwood lines the banks, and tall cottonwoods replace the conifers of the canyon.

There are a few sweepers, but the current is now so slow that they seem not to matter. The Trojan Nuclear Power Plant (see photo) has been removed from the land opposite the mouth of the river, and gulls join ravens and robins along the shoreline. Livestock appears, and the sound of the freeway intrudes even as more beaver cuttings suggest wilder times and places. The final mile is almost sluggish; on windy days paddlers will probably want to take out at the public fishing access 0.5 mile above the mouth rather than fight the wind and experience the waves on the Columbia.

northern cascades

51 Ross Lake

Location: From Colonial Creek Campground in North Cascades National Park
Distance: Up to 50 miles round-trip
Paddle time: 3 to 7 days
Season: July to October
Rating: Flatwater
Hazards: Extreme winds and cold water
Shuttle: None
Lake level information: Current lake levels available through Seattle City Light recording; North Cascades National Park website
Lake levels: Normal full pool, 1605 feet
Maps: USGS Hozomeen Mountain, Pumpkin Mountain, Ross Dam; any good map of Ross Lake National Recreation Area
Information: Ross Lake National Recreation Area Wilderness Information Center in Marblemount; Ross Lake Resort

Ross Lake *can* be reached by gravel road through British Columbia. But paddlers should be thankful it's a long and inconvenient trip for the masses from Seattle. Otherwise, this North Cascades gem would surely be overrun. As it is, the powerboats that ply the lake are mostly modest fishing craft (jet skis have been prohibited since 2000—a decision that should earn some park overseer a prize). That leaves the 24-mile-long lake and its views of granite peaks mostly to canoeists and kayakers—including Boy Scouts for whom an up-and-back trip on Ross Lake is a popular way to earn a 50-miler merit badge.

Although it looks natural in its setting of fir, hemlock, and cedar, Ross Lake is one of three back-to-back reservoirs on the upper Skagit River. Together, Ross, Diablo, and Gorge dams provide a quarter of the electricity used by Seattle. Ross Dam was completed in the late 1950s, about a decade before Congress created the 505,000-acre North Cascades National Park complex that includes Ross Lake National Recreation Area. Seattle City Light draws down the lake as much as 140 feet in winter, leaving an ugly ring. The lake is usually at full pool from July through early October. Managed primarily as wilderness, the park complex contains nearly half the glaciers found in the lower forty-eight states. That ice gives Ross Lake its deep blue color and keeps its water at about 50 degrees in summer. Diablo Lake, where this trip begins, rarely climbs out of the 40s. Bring a swimsuit—just don't expect to use it much.

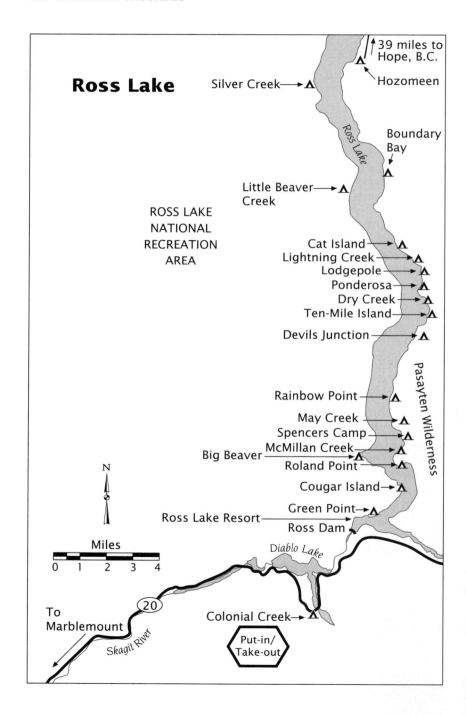

Access. Before beginning their trip, visitors must reserve specific campsites from the National Park Service. Free permits are available no more than 24 hours before the start of a trip at the Wilderness Information Center in Marblemount. Paddlers may not get their first choices for campsites. But with nearly fifty campsites in the nineteen boat-in campgrounds, obtaining a permit has not so far been a problem.

The southern end of Ross Lake can be seen from an overlook on the North Cascades Highway (SR 20). But it can't be reached from there by car, so paddlers begin and end their trip at the Colonial Creek Campground on Diablo Lake, located along the highway 10 miles east of Newhalem. It's a 5-mile paddle up Diablo Lake, through a spectacular chasm where the Skagit River once flowed freely, to the base of Ross Dam. A gravel road of 1.7 miles winds around the dam, climbing 600 feet from Diablo Lake to Ross Lake. Most visitors don't make the portage by foot; rather, they pay Ross Lake Resort $25 (per boat) for a shuttle on a flatbed truck. It can be arranged on the spot by picking up the telephone at the base of the dam. The 1950s-era resort is the only development on Ross Lake. Comprised of a cluster of fourteen floating cabins near the dam, it's a great place to spend the first or last night of the trip.

Paddle Route. A trip on Ross Lake should include time for hiking. Trails lead—always up—through primeval forests to waterfalls, alpine lakes, and vantage points. The lake holds native rainbow trout but is not particularly productive for fishermen. Bait fishing is prohibited, and single, barbless hooks are required. The lower mile of most tributary streams are closed to fishing, and some are closed

Ross Lake can capture a paddler's attention for days, with secluded campsites and even boat-up accommodations at Ross Lake Resort.

entirely. Paddlers stand the best chance of avoiding the lake's famously strong winds by traveling early or late in the day. Still, it's wise to include an extra day in the itinerary, since strong winds can force paddlers from the water. Rangers are generally understanding of those who get off schedule due to the weather.

Generally, the island camps and those on points of land offer slight relief from the mosquitoes that can torment campers at more sheltered spots, such as Big Beaver. Campers should closely follow park guidelines designed to prevent drawing black bears, deer, and other wildlife into camp. The North Cascades National Park complex is one of the few places in Washington where an extremely lucky visitor might spot a grizzly, wolf, lynx, or wolverine. Confirmed sightings are rare.

52 Similkameen River

Location: Palmer Lake to Shankers Bend
Distance: 13 miles
Paddle time: 5 hours
Season: Generally April
Rating: Class 1; Class 2 lower 5 miles
Hazards: Rapids on final 5 miles
Shuttle: 13.5 miles, pavement
Flow information: USGS Washington website
River gauge: 12442500 near Nighthawk
Historic flows: Average 1649 cfs; maximum 45,800; minimum 65
Maps: USGS Palmer, Oroville; Okanogan National Forest map
Information: Washington Department of Fish and Wildlife in Ephrata

Few places accessible by road are as remote as the Similkameen River in north central Washington. The arid valley once attracted miners. Now, only a few ranchers and orchardists survive, with visitors coming to fish the lakes in spring or hunt mule deer in fall. The river itself is largely overlooked, since fishing is poor and access tough.

The Similkameen originates near British Columbia's Manning Park. After being joined by the Pasayten River, which flows from Washington's Pasayten Wilderness, the Similkameen runs 126 miles to the confluence with the Okanogan River. Provincial Highway 3 was built along the river for virtually its entire course in Canada. The relatively short stretch of river in Washington is roughly paralleled by a smaller road.

This trip takes paddlers from Palmer Lake, down its sluggish outlet creek, and into a river that starts out broad and smooth but gains speed and excitement. The final 5 miles are accented with Class 1–2 rapids. For best paddling, look for flows of about 2000 cubic feet per second.

Access. The most obvious place to end the trip is Enloe Dam, about 3.5 miles

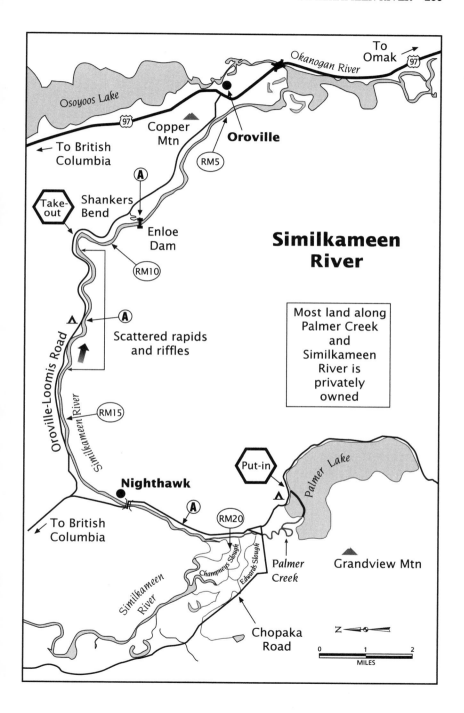

Similkameen River in Northcentral Washington

west of Oroville on Oroville–Loomis Road. An unmarked dirt road that leads to the dam is suitable only for sturdy vehicles with high clearance. The rough, narrow access road drops about 300 feet in a mile.

The trip described here ends 1.5 miles upstream from the dam at Shankers Bend, where Oroville–Loomis Road comes close to the river. Parking for several cars is available in a dirt turnout on the opposite side of the road from the river (look for the graffiti-covered section of a concrete irrigation canal). A rough trail leads about 100 feet to the water.

To reach the put-in, continue west on Oroville–Loomis Road for 12 miles to a small Department of Natural Resources (DNR) campground at the north end of Palmer Lake.

Two alternative accesses include a difficult-to-spot Washington Department of Fish and Wildlife fishing access 1.5 miles upstream from the community of Nighthawk and an informal campsite 4.5 miles downstream from Nighthawk.

Paddle Route. From the DNR's Palmer Lake campground, it's a short paddle to Palmer Creek. Watch for loons on this lovely lake and mountain goats on Grandview Mountain over the western shore. The creek itself meanders 3 miles through a flat, broad cow pasture, where farmers long ago placed car bodies along the banks to prevent erosion. The creek serves as an outlet stream for most of the year, but reverses itself in spring, as the Similkameen rises. At those times, Palmer Lake has two inlet creeks and no outlet. As the lake rises, it overflows onto the pasture at its north end. The lake holds smallmouth bass.

From its confluence with Palmer Creek, the Similkameen runs sluggish for about 5 miles before growing steeper, swifter, and narrower. Rock gardens are common. Canoes will scrape bottom when the flow is much less than 2000 cfs. Paddlers can avoid most of the rapids by taking out at the informal campsite about 6.5 miles downstream from the confluence of the creek and river. The site also can be used as a put-in for a quick trip through the roughest water.

Shankers Bend, where the trip ends, is the start of the 70-acre pool created by Enloe Dam. More than 100 feet tall, the dam generated a small amount of power for about fifty years before being abandoned by the Okanogan County Public Utility District in 1959. Environmental groups concerned with the return of salmon runs have suggested dismantling the dam, which has no fish ladder. The PUD wants it relicensed. The deep gorge below the dam has Class 3 rapids.

53 Methow River

Location: Winthrop to Twisp
Distance: 10 miles
Paddle time: 2 to 4 hours
Season: Virtually year-round
Rating: Class 1+
Hazards: Diversion dam across river; strainers
Shuttle: 8 miles, pavement
Flow information: USGS Washington website
River gauge: 12448500 at Winthrop
Historic flows: Average 1072 cfs; maximum 24,400; minimum 134
Maps: USGS Winthrop, Blue Buck Mountain, Twisp East; Okanogan National Forest map
Information: Okanogan–Wenatchee National Forest Visitor Center in Winthrop

In 89 miles from its sources in the North Cascades, the Methow River offers something for every paddling skill level on its way to the confluence with the Columbia River near Pateros (see Whitewater Trip 10). Commercial rafting companies and skilled whitewater paddlers flock to the Class 3 and Class 4 water in the Black Canyon below Carlton. More casual paddlers tend to look farther upstream, where pristine waters originating in the Pasayten and Chelan–Sawtooth Wilderness Areas don't rumble quite so violently.

The Methow (pronounced MET-how) upstream from Winthrop weaves through

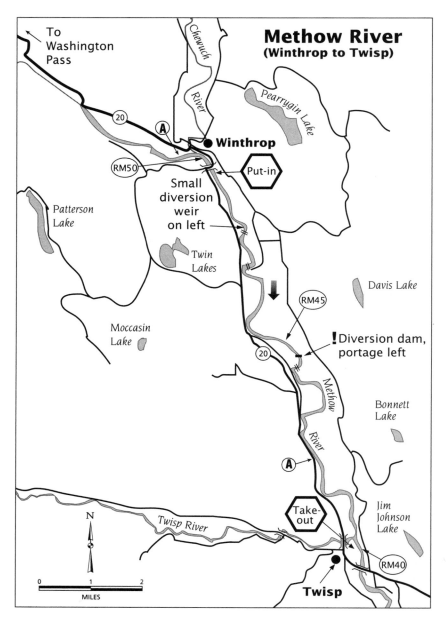

a scenic valley, past small ranches and tall cottonwoods. The only drawbacks for paddlers are the high odds of encountering logjams, which are especially dangerous in high flows.

This trip winds through the gentle portion of valley downstream from Winthrop. The shores are lined with ponderosa pines and cottonwoods towering above willows, serviceberry, and bitterbrush. Strainers are always a possibility, but the likelihood of logjams is much lower than in the stretch upstream from Winthrop.

The Methow from Winthrop to Twisp has two rapids ranging to nearly Class 2, depending on flow. Bald eagles, ducks, and deer are regularly seen along the river in winter and spring. Anglers can catch rainbow and cutthroat trout. Steelhead and chinook salmon run upriver in fall.

Access. Two good put-ins are available in Winthrop. One is at the Red Barn Community Park just across the SR 20 bridge on the upstream side of town. If flows are low, the better put-in is at the gauging station near the SR 20 bridge on the downstream end of town. The parking area is on the downstream side of the bridge, river left.

To reach the take-out, drive south from Winthrop on SR 20 about 8 miles to Twisp. Just south of the bridge over the Twisp River, turn east between the pizza place and the Chevron service station (the unmarked street is called Twisp Avenue), and drive to the second stop sign. Turn left into Twisp Community Park. Scout the best spot for a take-out.

Paddle Route. The Methow River can be floated most of the year, but low water can assure bottom-bouncing in the upper stretches in August and September and portions of winter when flows dip below 300 cubic feet per second. Occasional surges in February can make great winter floating. Runoff generally

Methow River near Winthrop in February

peaks between mid-May and early June, with flows around 6300 to 10,000 cfs. Paddling is not advised during peak flow levels. At any flow level, even the easier stretches of river demand that paddlers have skills to handle a few sharp turns and eddylines.

Development of scattered private homes along the river accelerated in the 1990s. Unfortunately, there is little public land above the high-water mark.

A diversion dam spans the river 5 miles downstream from Winthrop. To paddlers, the dam shows up in the distance as a perfectly straight line of water from bank to bank with concrete fixtures on each side. Portage river left. With careful scouting at some flow levels, canoeists can paddle over the diversion dam slightly left of center, but they must negotiate dangerous rocks and standing waves just below the dam. In low flows, paddlers can step out of their boats on river right and line down over the wooden diversion.

The river continues in placid stretches interrupted by riffles and the occasional sharp turn to keep paddlers on their toes.

The Methow Valley has several campgrounds managed by the Okanogan National Forest as well as at Pearrygin Lake State Park. Late-summer visitors can reap the harvest of fruit orchards from roadside stands that line the lower stretches of the river.

Another good paddle trip, with water ranging to Class 2, runs 12.5 miles from Twisp downstream to the fishing access off SR 20 in Carlton. This stretch has no diversion dam to negotiate, but some stretches can be challenging, depending on the flow. USGS maps needed for that section are Twisp East and Methow. For a more difficult route downstream from Carlton, see Whitewater Trip 10.

54 White River

Location: Sears Creek to Lake Wenatchee
Distance: 7 to 8 miles
Paddle time: 2 to 4 hours
Season: Generally April through October
Rating: Flatwater
Hazards: Deadheads, strainers, or logjams; weir near mouth of river; wind on Lake Wenatchee
Shuttle: 4 to 14 miles, pavement
Flow information: None available
Maps: USGS Lake Wenatchee; plus Wenatchee National Forest map
Information: Wenatchee National Forest, Lake Wenatchee Ranger Station

The White River ends on a quiet note at Lake Wenatchee, understating its wild run and lofty beginnings from one of Washington's most impressive volcanic

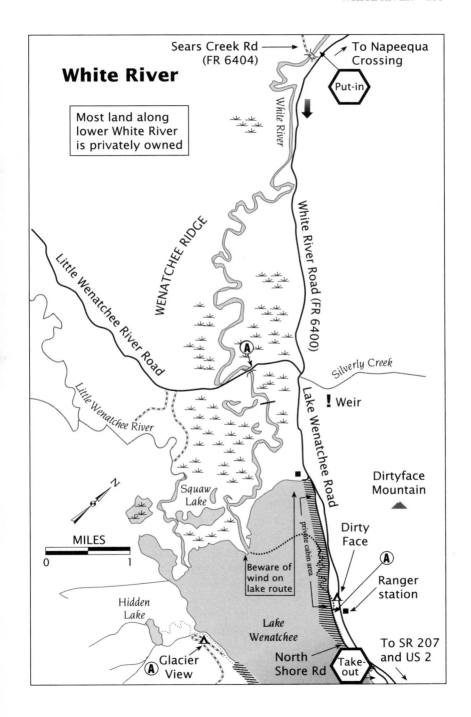

White River

Most land along lower White River is privately owned

Sears Creek Rd (FR 6404)

To Napeequa Crossing

Put-in

White River

WENATCHEE RIDGE

Little Wenatchee River Road

White River Road (FR 6400)

Little Wenatchee River

A

Silverly Creek

! Weir

Lake Wenatchee Road

N

MILES

0   1

Squaw Lake

private cabin area

Dirtyface Mountain

Dirty Face

A

Ranger station

Beware of wind on lake route

Hidden Lake

Lake Wenatchee

A Glacier View

North Shore Rd

Take-out

To SR 207 and US 2

Snow and cedars on White River in April

peaks. The river is named for the pulverized rock from the White River Glacier on the south flank of 10,541-foot Glacier Peak. This "glacial flour" colors the water during summer, but the stream clears when winter weather chills the glacial drip and the river is fed mostly by groundwater and snowmelt.

The upper reaches of the river are wild, as the stream plunges about 3000 feet in elevation in 15 miles through the Glacier Peak Wilderness. But soon after it tumbles over White River Falls, the river mellows to the temperament of a spring creek. Cedars loom over the water for a while before giving way to cottonwoods.

The stretch from Sears Creek to Lake Wenatchee can be enjoyed as early as paddlers can slide a boat down the snowbanks to the water. The season lasts as late in the fall as the ice and snow allow. The area offers plenty of hiking, plus sailboarding and other recreation at Lake Wenatchee. The last week of September or first week of October is prime time to see the brilliant fall color display on this stretch of the White River.

Access. From US 2 about 16 miles northwest of Leavenworth, turn north (near milepost 85) onto SR 207 toward Lake Wenatchee State Park. Cross the Wenatchee River, then bear left at a fork, where SR 207 ends and becomes Lake Wenatchee Road. To reach the best take-out option, bear left onto North Shore Drive toward the YMCA camp. Go about a mile on North Shore Drive to where the shoulder widens and a short walk through the woods leads to a beach popular with windsurfers. You've gone past this access if you start driving by a bunch of lakefront homes.

Another take-out option is farther west on Lake Wenatchee Road in front of the Lake Wenatchee ranger station, which is about 9 miles from US 2. There's a track leading down from the station to the lake.

To reach the put-in, continue northwest on Lake Wenatchee Road for 0.5 mile. Turn right at a fork onto White River Road (FR 6400). (The left fork becomes Little Wenatchee River Road.) Drive 2.5 miles on White River Road to the put-in at the bridge for Sears Creek Road (FR 6404).

Paddle Route. Although the surrounding area is managed by the Wenatchee National Forest, most land along this float is privately owned. In summer and fall, sandbars provide room for shore breaks. The work of beavers is obvious along the river, and the banks are tree-lined and steep in many areas. Blowdown trees are common. These "strainers" can be dangerous. Always be on the watch for logjams around bends. The river generally flows slowly enough so that if necessary, boaters can ferry to shore and portage with little difficulty.

A weir on the river causes a riffle during high flows. During low flows, floaters may have to line boats over the minor structure.

The biggest challenge can be the wind that crops up regularly on Lake Wenatchee. A contingency plan if you encounter a big wind is to pull out at the Little Wenatchee River Road bridge. The flow is gentle enough here to paddle downstream to the mouth and back upstream if necessary.

Other potential take-out points include the Forest Service's Glacier View Campground (14-mile road shuttle from put-in) just south of the White River mouth, and Lake Wenatchee State Park, a 5-mile open-water paddle down to the east end of the lake.

The area has several camping options, including an excellent campground with showers at Lake Wenatchee State Park.

The White River attracts a run of sockeye salmon in August and September, plus some chinook salmon and steelhead. It also holds rainbows and cutthroats and the increasingly rare bull trout.

For a side trip, consider driving to White River Falls campground, about 10 miles upstream from the Forest Service ranger station. An unofficial trail leads down to an overlook of the falls, which block passage for fish as well as paddlers. Other access to the falls is via the trailhead north of the campground at the end of White River Road. Hike south on Panther Creek Trail 1522.

55 Wenatchee River

Location: Cashmere to Wenatchee
Distance: 10 miles
Paddle time: 3 hours
Season: Generally March through July
Rating: Class 1; avoidable Class 2+
Hazards: Bridge abutments, changing river channels, rapids; wind at confluence with Columbia
Shuttle: 9 miles, pavement
Flow information: Chelan County Public Utility District
River gauge: 12462500 at Monitor
Historic flows: Average 3205 cfs; maximum 45,900; minimum 208
Maps: USGS Cashmere, Monitor, Wenatchee; Wenatchee National Forest map
Information: Wenatchee Valley Chamber of Commerce

No one should be surprised that the Wenatchee River is perhaps the most popular floating stream in Washington. The 54-mile river is like a paddler's Wal-Mart, offering most everything one could want with cheap convenience. Various stretches range from flatwater to violent whitewater. Tributaries such as the Chiwawa spice up the action for experts. A four-lane highway parallels the lower Wenatchee, making shuttles a whiz. Backpacking destinations in the alpine areas above the river are so popular, the Wenatchee National Forest's Leavenworth ranger station conducts lottery drawings for trail permits. The area is studded with national forest and state park campgrounds.

That's just a sampling of the attractions. Flowing down into the rain shadow on the east side of the North Cascades, the Wenatchee is a destination for hordes of paddlers and rafters escaping the dreary weather in western Washington. Conversely, locals flock to the river to seek relief from the sunny weather that has made the Wenatchee area a hotbed for the orchard industry.

Numerous commercial rafting companies as well as kayakers prefer the Class 3–4 whitewater stretch from Leavenworth to Cashmere. (For a stretch of somewhat tamer rapids along that area of the river, see Whitewater Trip 9.) Just upstream from Leavenworth, the river constricts into Tumwater Canyon, a violent bouldered channel that rates Class 5 or worse.

Canoeists can find more Class 2 paddling from the source of the river at Lake Wenatchee downstream to Plain. This stretch is accessible by paved road, but has a more forested and remote nature than the lower river. More Class 2 can be found from Plain downstream to Tumwater Campground, the last possible takeout before entering the dangerous water of Tumwater Canyon.

The trip described here, from Cashmere to Wenatchee, generally rates as easy during moderate flows. Some sections of waves and rapids provide challenges for those who want them, but less experienced paddlers can avoid difficulty in most conditions, with the exception of peak spring flows that normally occur sometime in May.

Access. The put-in is west of Wenatchee. From US 2/97 at Cashmere (milepost 112), exit south at the stoplight onto Cottage Avenue. Cross the bridge over the Wenatchee River. Turn right onto Maple Street (at Village Inn Motel). Continue straight to the put-in at Riverside City Park. (For an alternate put-in that is best in low flows, enter Cashmere on Cottage Avenue, cross the bridge over the river, and immediately turn left onto Riverfront Drive. Go 0.2 mile to an undeveloped put-in across from a power substation.)

To reach the take-out, drive east on four-lane US 2/97, following the exit signs to Wenatchee. SR 285 bends south and becomes Wenatchee Avenue at the north end of town. Turn east (toward the Columbia River) at the stoplight onto Hawley Street, which bends right and becomes Miller Street. Turn right (south) on Walla

April on the Wenatchee River

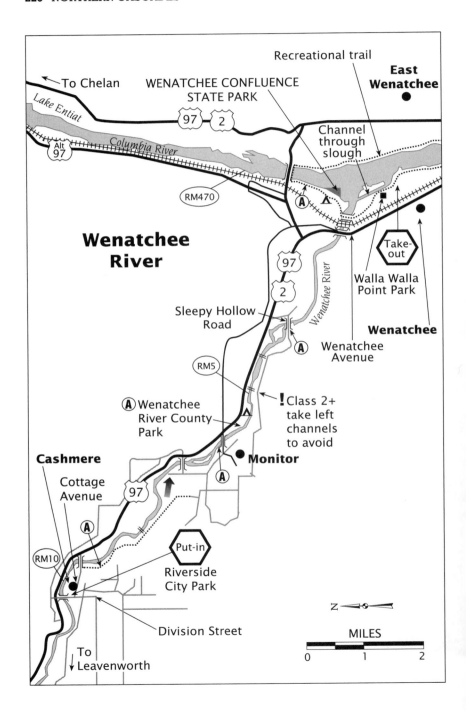

Walla Street toward Eagle Hardware. Then turn left (east) into Walla Walla Point Park (open 6:00 AM to midnight; no camping allowed). Take the left fork on the park access road and leave a vehicle in a parking slot near the restrooms. The take-out is by the footbridge over the inlet to the cove.

Other access points in this stretch include:

(1) Fishing access on the upstream, river-right side of the bridge at Monitor. From US 2/97, turn south on lower Sunnyslope Road (between mileposts 117 and 118), then right on Sleepy Hollow Road to the access at the bridge. (2) Wenatchee River County Park, near Monitor, off US 2/97 at milepost 115. (3) Boat launch at the end of Orondo Street in Wenatchee. (4) Wenatchee Confluence State Park boat launch, just north of Wenatchee River mouth.

Paddle Route. Floods, such as the 40,000 cubic-feet-per-second event in 1995, can make big changes in the lower Wenatchee River by creating new channels. Keep this in mind as you read this description, and as you paddle the river from year to year.

Ideal flows for paddling range from 1500 to 6000 cfs. Lower flows expose too many rocks. Flows higher than about 8000 cfs create swift currents with water flooding into the shoreline brush, erasing eddies and posing bigger consequences for little mistakes. Getting off the river could be difficult if you dump in high flows.

Several islands force paddlers to make route choices. One channel generally is better than another, but this can change from year to year. Paddlers must make the call on a given day. Virtually all sharp river bends—especially those against riprapped banks—have larger waves that can be run for fun or avoided by keeping tight to the inside shore.

The second of seven bridges you'll pass under on this trip is at Monitor. Just downstream from Monitor is a good pit stop at Wenatchee River County Park on river left.

Pay particular attention to Class 2+ rapids in the right channel of the island just downstream from the county park. (The rapids can be scouted before launching from Sleepy Hollow Road on the south side of the river.) To avoid the rapids, take the left or center channel at the island. The left channel has a sharp turn and a possibility of strainers. The center channel is likely to be the clearest option.

Just before the confluence with the Columbia, look for a channel into the trees on river right after passing under a series of three bridges. The channel offers a wind-sheltered route through a slough toward the take-out. The area is a refuge for wildlife, particularly birds, waterfowl, and muskrats. At the end of the slough, paddle out through an opening into the Columbia. The big river is a reservoir here, backed up behind Rock Island Dam. Turn right and go a short way before paddling under the footbridge to the take-out cove at Walla Walla Point Park.

Anglers should check state regulations for special seasons on hatchery-raised salmon and steelhead.

inland northwest
paddle routes

56 Lake Lenore

Location: South of Coulee City
Distance: Up to 9 miles round-trip
Paddle time: 2 to 5 hours
Season: Generally March through November
Shuttle: None
Rating: Flatwater
Hazards: Wind
Shuttle: None necessary
Maps: USGS Banks Lake, Moses Lake; Grant County map
Information: Washington Department of Fish and Wildlife in Ephrata

Here's a place to catch a whopper cutthroat trout while paddling the path of great Ice Age floods that carved Grand Coulee roughly 15,000 years ago.

Lake Lenore is 4 miles long, bordered on the east by SR 17 and on the west by cliffs that drop precipitously more than 1200 feet from the coulee rim. The weather tends to be warmer here than at the eastern and western edges of Washington, making this a particularly pleasant destination in fall and early spring. Anglers will be pleased to know that these choice periods also coincide with the best fishing for the large Lahontan cutthroat trout, which can weigh up to 6 pounds. Summer can be hot here, making early morning and late evening the best times for paddling or fishing.

The lake is popular with anglers, but remains quiet since laws prohibit boats with gas motors. The Washington Department of Fish and Wildlife also enforces catch limits and gear requirements that are much more restrictive than in the state's general fishing waters. Check the fishing regulations pamphlet for details. The Lahontan cutthroat trout is an import from Nevada. The high alkalinity of Lenore left the lake fishless until biologists learned that the Lahontans were specially adapted to these waters.

Access. Lake Lenore is easy to reach on SR 17 heading north from Moses Lake, Washington, or heading south from the junction with US 2 west of Coulee City.

From this junction, drive south on SR 17 about 16 miles (to milepost 80.2) and turn west on an unmarked dirt track that winds down to a put-in or take-out point at the south end of Lake Lenore. The access at the north end is at milepost 84.8.

When driving south on SR 17 from Coulee City, be sure to take note of several other attractions. The Dry Falls overlook is 2 miles south of the US 2 junction. The entrance to fine camping at Sun Lakes State Park can be found 3.7 miles south of the junction. The access road to the archeological sites at Lenore Caves is

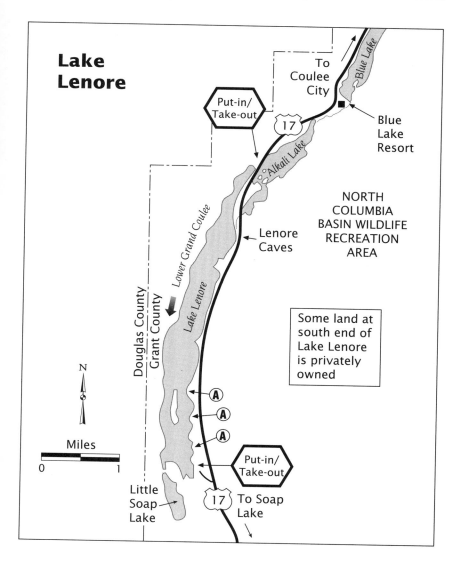

Fishing for Lahontan cutthroat trout on Lake Lenore

near the north end of Lake Lenore on the opposite (east) side of SR 17. A rocky trail leads past shallow depressions where nomadic cave dwellers sought shelter thousands of years ago.

Additional access is available at four points on the lake's east shore, including three access points along a 1-mile stretch north of the southern put-in. A state Fish and Wildlife vehicle access permit is required.

Paddle Route. Launch at either end of the lake, depending on the wind, and hug the west shore, where there are no roads, trails, or development along the cliffs. The lake generally is ice-capped from December through February. Spawning cutthroat trout become visible along the shoreline in March and April, particularly at the north end of the lake.

Most of the land around the lake is public, managed by the state or the U.S. Bureau of Reclamation. However, some private land development has occurred, notably at the south end of the lake. Anglers congregate at the north and south ends, leaving the scenic middle of the lake mostly deserted. Listen for chukar partridges clucking in the cliffs above.

At several points, paddlers can pull boats out onto the rocks and scramble up scree slopes to plateaus midway up the cliffs for good views. Watch for rattlesnakes.

Other than a few outhouses, no services are found on Lenore. Camping resorts are found at several nearby lakes.

57 Yakima River Canyon

Location: Ringer to Roza Dam
Distance: 9 to 19 miles
Paddle time: 6 hours
Season: Virtually year-round
Rating: Class 1+
Hazards: Heavy wind, strainers, scattered rapids
Shuttle: 20 miles, pavement
Flow information: USGS Washington website
River gauge: 12484500 at Umtanum
Historic flows: Average 2416 cfs; maximum 41,000; minimum 138
Maps: USGS Ellensburg South, Kittitas, Wymer
Information: U.S. Bureau of Land Management in Spokane

Since 1990, catch-and-release regulations have transformed the Yakima River into one of the most productive trout streams in the Northwest. Born in the snowfields of the Cascades, the stream runs swift and cold. It is home to large caddis flies and stone flies that produce trout as strong as Ellensburg stallions. The Yakama Tribe and others have worked in recent years to restore salmon and steelhead to the river, as well.

The Yakima River originates east of Snoqualmie Pass at Keechelus Lake and flows 215 miles to the confluence with the Columbia River near Richland.

One need not be an angler to appreciate the river and the arid canyon that guides its route between the cities of Ellensburg and Yakima. Slowing after its fall from the mountains, the water runs gently at the base of steep, open slopes where bighorn sheep sometimes are seen, and chukar partridges can be heard laughing at weak-legged mortals. Those who come to the canyon in winter are likely to spot bald eagles. Spring visitors find desert wildflowers. Prickly pear cactus and rattlesnakes are other notable residents.

Canyon Road, as SR 821 is known, runs along the east side of the river, which is a mix of private and public land. No houses stand on the opposite shoreline, which includes the L. T. Murray Wildlife Recreation Area and is largely inaccessible by road.

Access. To reach the most popular put-in from I-90, take Exit 109 at Ellensburg, Washington, and drive south on Canyon Road. About 3.5 miles from I-90, turn right onto Ringer Loop Road, and drive another quarter mile to a Washington Department of Fish and Wildlife boat launch.

Three U.S. Bureau of Land Management river accesses and a private campground give paddlers an opportunity to customize a trip of anywhere from 9 to 18.5 miles. All accesses are along Canyon Road.

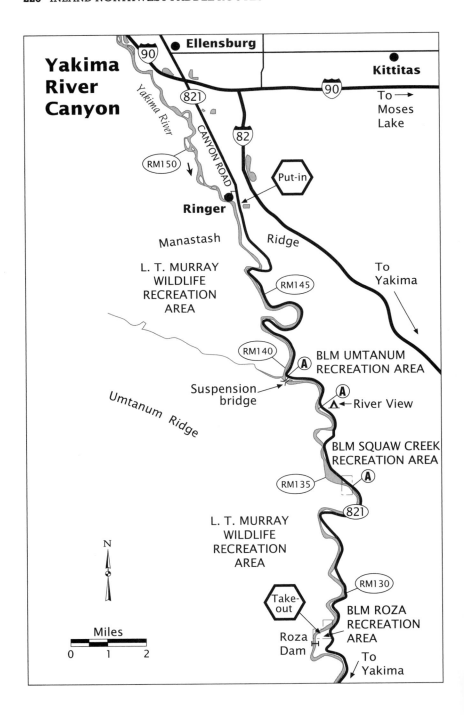

The first access is the BLM Umtanum Recreation Area, 9 miles downstream from Ringer. The take-out is on river left, just upstream from the suspension footbridge.

The private River View Campground is 10.5 miles downstream from Ringer. The owners charge fees for parking, launching, and camping.

The BLM Squaw Creek and Roza Recreation Areas are 13 and 18.5 miles downstream from Ringer. The Roza access, just upstream from Roza Dam, is the farthest upstream that powerboats are allowed on the Yakima.

Paddle Route. Upstream reservoirs keep the Yakima River high during summer, when farmers need water to grow apples, timothy hay, and other crops. Although there are no significant rapids, paddlers can count on a swift run with few eddies during the artificially high water. After running bank to bank from April to August, the river drops in fall and winter. These "off-seasons" also bring

Canoeing the Yakima River

relief from the powerful winds that plague the canyon in spring, and the heat and party-rafters that bear down on the river in summer. There is no off-season for the trains that rumble through the canyon to wake up campers.

Spring and summer flows at the Umtanum river gauge typically run more than 3000 cubic feet per second, dropping to an average of 2100 cfs in September and a little more than 1000 cfs in November.

58 Winchester Wasteway

Location: Dodson Road to Potholes Reservoir
Distance: 25 miles
Paddle time: 12 hours or overnight
Season: Generally March through mid-October
Rating: Flatwater
Hazards: Waterfall, thorn bushes; winds on Potholes Reservoir; hunting
Shuttle: 16 miles, pavement
Flow information: U.S. Bureau of Reclamation in Ephrata
River gauge: No number
Historic flows: Average 120 cfs; maximum 210; minimum 71
Maps: USGS Winchester SE, Corfu, Mae; Grant County map
Information: Mar Don Resort; Potholes State Park

Just decades ago, a river did not run through it. The topography was there, carved by post–ice age floods. But this stream within the Columbia Basin desert did not emerge in modern times until water was pumped from the Columbia River and spread onto croplands that had been mostly sage and cactus for thousands of years.

Irrigation runoff has been routed into a natural channel en route to Potholes Reservoir, forming one of the most wonderfully obscure paddling adventures in the lower forty-eight states. There's plenty of water for floating, but you'll want to bring drinking water from home.

Spring and early summer are magical times on the wasteway. Nesting waterfowl make a racket that goes on day and night: The symphony includes the trill of red-winged blackbirds, the clamor of Canada geese, the whine of coyotes, the ratcheting of sandhill cranes. It's worth making a primitive camp in the sand and sage and spending the night just to hear the serenade. Another option is to paddle down from the put-in and pole or paddle back out in the same day, passing the bulrushes and towering plumes of nonnative tall reed grass called phragmites. The flow in the section downstream from Dodson Road southwest of Moses Lake is easy to negotiate in either direction.

By late March, paddling conditions can be excellent, although campers can wake to a thick layer of frost on their tents. The leaves have not yet burst from

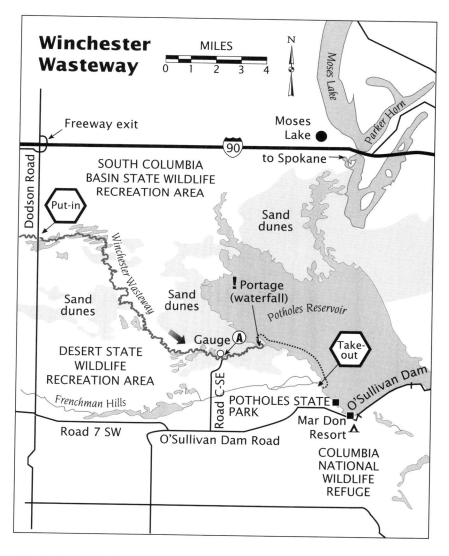

their buds to hide the thorns on the overhanging brush. By April, the vegetation is considerably greener and water is warm enough in the off-channel sloughs to produce good fishing for bass and perch. By June, the grasses begin to turn brown and small potholes dry up in the desert. But the wasteway keeps flowing, boosted by increased irrigation to Columbia Basin crops. Minimum flows ranging from 75 to 90 cfs generally run from December through mid-April. Runoff events, if any, typically occur from mid-January to mid-February. Maximum flows usually occur

Desert waterfall downstream from gauge on Winchester Wasteway

from mid-October through early November, ranging from 170 to 190 cfs.

Waterfowl hunters usually close the floating season on the wasteway, setting out decoys along the sloughs in hunts that begin in mid-October.

Access. To reach the put-in from I-90, take the Dodson Road exit about 10 miles west of Moses Lake, Washington, and head south 3.3 miles to the state-maintained parking site. Paddlers who want to do the through-trip to Potholes Reservoir can make the shuttle by continuing south on Dodson Road; then take the first paved left (east) onto Road 7 SW (Frenchman Hills Road), continuing east on O'Sullivan Dam Road to Potholes State Park. Novices—and paddlers who want to keep canoe bottoms pristine—can avoid the tougher section of the wasteway by taking out at the gauging station at roughly the midpoint of this trip. This take-out is accessible from Road C-SE off O'Sullivan Dam Road just west of Potholes State Park.

Paddle Route. A sense of humor is more useful than a map and compass for navigation in the wasteway. Paddlers may hit dead ends in the dunes and have to backtrack to find the channel. A few miles later, the channel is so narrow and fast you'll be draw-stroking frantically to pivot the canoe into a 90-degree turn. You might have to wade through cattails or duck under branches.

Summer weed growth can obscure the channel in some places. Stir mud with a paddle or watch for weeds bending downstream to track the channel current when the route opens into sloughs or dead-ends against sand dunes. The channel can be shallow in some spots, requiring paddlers to drag canoes briefly over sand.

The wasteway downstream from Dodson Road flows through state-managed land. Sand dunes provide numerous areas for primitive camping.

The lazy nature of the wasteway changes near the gauging station at the Road C-SE access. From here down, paddlers are likely to become acquainted with the thorns of Russian olive trees. The tripper in the bow can avoid them with prayer and a deft draw. The paddler in the stern might put more stock in armor. The channel gets fast and narrow, twisting and rocky in the last leg to Potholes Reservoir.

Downstream from the gauge, on a calm day, paddlers can hear the falls and have a leisurely 100 yards to get out on river right. On a windy day, first-timers might not detect the falls until they are within 25 or 30 yards. That's still plenty of time if you're not daydreaming.

The water gushes over concrete-like caliche cliffs in a three-stage fall that roars 25 feet down into a deep bowl. The portage around the falls offers its own adventure down a sand dune.

From the falls, a maze of sand dune islands must be negotiated out to Potholes Reservoir. Civilization appears in the form of fishing boats. Head northeast at first, then southeast into the reservoir, skirting the outside of the brushiest dunes toward the tall poplars of Potholes State Park. Only experienced paddlers should attempt this 3-mile open-water stretch in foul weather. The reservoir can be windy, but some protection can be found by snugging up to the lee along the west shore.

59 Hutchinson and Shiner Lakes

Location: Columbia National Wildlife Refuge
Distance: 3 miles round-trip
Paddle time: Variable
Season: March through September
Rating: Flatwater
Hazards: Wind
Shuttle: None
Maps: USGS O'Sullivan Dam; free Columbia National Wildlife Refuge map
Information: U.S. Fish and Wildlife Service, Columbia National Wildlife Refuge in Othello

The hundreds of lakes and ponds in the Columbia National Wildlife Refuge are an unexpected benefit of Columbia Basin agriculture. Most of the coulees and canyons were dry before irrigation came to the region. Now, the 23,100-acre refuge and surrounding state and private land support uncounted masses of migrating ducks, geese, sandhill cranes, and other birds.

Of all the drive-to waters in the refuge, paddlers find the most solitude on 50-acre Hutchinson Lake and 30-acre Shiner Lake, which are joined by a narrow channel. Special regulations discourage the crowds that mob other nearby lakes each spring and fall. The U.S. Fish and Wildlife Service does not allow hunting, camping, or swimming at Hutchinson and Shiner, which are closed for all uses from October until March. Gasoline-powered boats are prohibited.

The two lakes are not stocked with trout, the most popular gamefish in the region. Fishing can be good for bluegills and bass, and while nearby Potholes Reservoir draws fishermen from around the region, these two small lakes are growing in popularity with local anglers, many of whom fish from the bank.

Access. To reach Hutchinson Lake from Othello, Washington, drive north on Broadway Road, past the Nestle potato processing plant and Potholes East Canal. Broadway turns west and becomes McManamon Road at the canal. From there, it's about 7 miles to the well-marked gravel road that leads to Hutchinson Lake, which is a mile off the pavement.

Paddle Route. From the boat launch on Hutchinson Lake, most paddlers head east on the main lake, then through a narrow passage to Shiner. The channel often is too shallow and weed-choked for bigger boats, but canoes and kayaks normally have little trouble.

Stained basalt walls rise from the lake, broken in places where visitors can leave

Shiner Lake in the Columbia National Wildlife Refuge

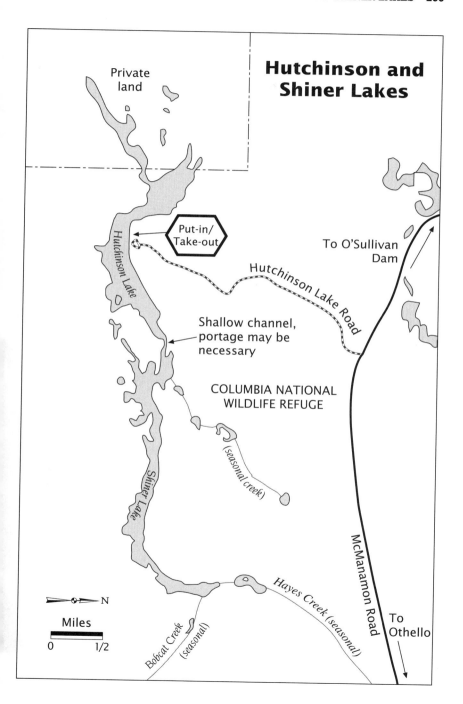

Private land

Hutchinson and Shiner Lakes

Put-in/Take-out

To O'Sullivan Dam

Hutchinson Lake

Hutchinson Lake Road

Shallow channel, portage may be necessary

COLUMBIA NATIONAL WILDLIFE REFUGE

(seasonal creek)

Shiner Lake

N

Miles

0   1/2

McManamon Road

Hayes Creek (seasonal)

Bobcat Creek (seasonal)

To Othello

their boats for a hike through the sage-covered scabland. Watch for cliff swallows that make their nests on the rocks, as well as great horned owls. Rattlesnakes are fairly common in summer.

It's little more than 1.5 miles from the Hutchinson Lake boat launch to the east end of Shiner. Paddlers can easily explore both lakes in the first or last hours of daylight, when wildlife viewing is best. That leaves plenty of time to catch a brace of hatchery trout at one of the more crowded lakes in the refuge, and set up camp where it is permitted.

60 Crab Creek

Location: Smyrna to Beverly
Distance: 7, 11, or 18 miles
Paddle time: 10 hours or overnight
Season: Virtually year-round
Rating: Class 1, with one avoidable Class 2 rapid
Hazards: Strong winds, fences, hunting
Shuttle: 17 miles, pavement and gravel
Flow information: USGS Washington website
River gauge: 12465000 near Irby
Historic flows: Average 63 cfs; maximum 8370; minimum 0
Maps: USGS Beverly and Beverly SE
Information: Washington Department of Fish and Wildlife in Ephrata

Starting as a trickle north of Reardan, Washington, the state's longest "creek" winds across three central Washington counties before dumping into the Columbia River. In many places, it feeds marshes that are oases for wildlife. To pre-irrigation farmers, the stream meant hope; they built their homes along its banks during rare wet years, assuming it would always provide enough water for their crops and families.

But for all its length—more than 175 miles—Crab Creek lacks staying power in this region where annual rainfall is measured in single digits. In places north of Moses Lake, the creek goes underground. The skeletons of farmhouses that were abandoned during drought years are scattered along the banks.

Make no mistake; this is harsh, if fascinating, country. Folks who normally spend their weekends prowling the Northwest's thick forests may feel exposed and vulnerable. When night falls, they'll be stunned by the wide-open view of the stars.

This trip covers Crab Creek's final 18 miles, mostly through land managed by the State Fish and Wildlife Department. It makes a wonderful overnighter for families, with the option of cutting the distance to 7 or 11 miles.

Depending on the season, paddlers will see red-winged and yellow-headed blackbirds, herons, cinnamon teal, and other waterfowl. Birds of prey are common and chukar partridges call from the Saddle Mountains, a stark Ice Age range that stands 1500 feet above the valley floor. Beavers gnaw on the rare trees and campers can count on a chorus of coyotes to sing them to sleep.

This trip serves as a reminder that no wild area can be assumed protected. As of 2007, as the state looked to build a new dam for water storage, lower Crab Creek was on the short list. The resulting reservoir would flood the creek and surrounding lands—as well as Nunnally Lake, a favorite of Washington fly-fishermen—so that the water could be released into the Columbia at times when irrigators elsewhere are taking too much. The plan makes perfect sense to those who see nothing but sagebrush and a muddy creek that's far too abused to support salmon and steelhead. Those who have paddled the creek know that it's rich in life that is too often on the losing end of human development.

At the base of the Saddle Mountains on Crab Creek

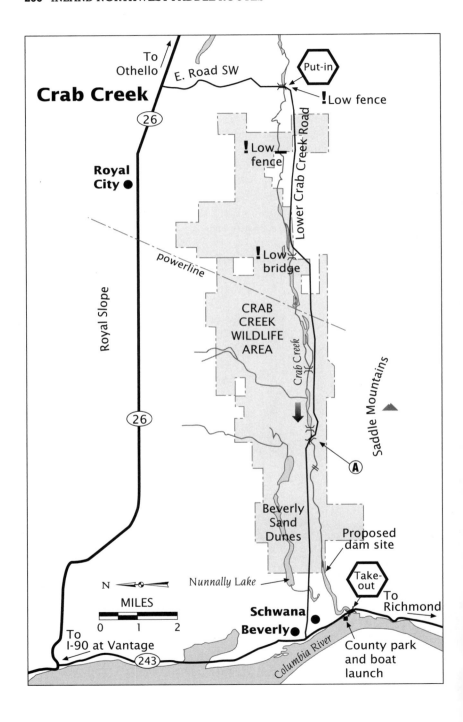

To Othello

E. Road SW

Put-in

Crab Creek

! Low fence

26

! Low fence

Lower Crab Creek Road

Royal City ●

! Low bridge

Royal Slope

powerline

CRAB CREEK WILDLIFE AREA

Crab Creek

Saddle Mountains

26

Ⓐ

Beverly Sand Dunes

Proposed dam site

Nunnally Lake

Take-out

To Richmond

N

MILES

0   1   2

Schwana Beverly ●

To I-90 at Vantage

243

Columbia River

County park and boat launch

Access. To reach the put-in from Royal City, Washington, drive 2 miles east on SR 26. Turn south on E. Road SW, and drive about 3 miles to Crab Creek. Park on the north bank, between the railroad tracks and the road, a few miles east of a spot on the map called Smyrna.

To reach the take-out from the put-in, continue south on E. Road SW, which turns west and becomes Lower Crab Creek Road immediately after crossing the creek. Drive west for 16 miles, to the town of Beverly, turn left on SR 243. Drive a mile to the mouth of Crab Creek, where there's a county park and boat launch on the Columbia River. Theft has been a problem at the park; leave nothing valuable in your car.

(For the most direct route to Beverly from I-90, take Exit 137 on the east side of the Vantage bridge. Drive south a mile on SR 26, then 7 more miles on SR 243.)

An alternative access is the bridge where Lower Crab Creek Road crosses the creek. It is 6 road miles east of Beverly.

Paddle Route. Paddlers come to their first, and most dangerous, hazard not more than 20 yards from the put-in, just as they emerge from under the E. Road SW bridge. A barbed-wire fence that spans the creek may offer too little clearance for canoes at high water. Check it out before beginning the trip.

Watch for a second fence with slightly more clearance about 2 river miles downstream from the put-in, and a footbridge with extremely low clearance about 5 river miles from the put-in. Other landmarks are an abandoned railroad bridge (roughly 8 river miles from the put-in) and a dilapidated wooden bridge that no longer reaches entirely across the creek (about 10 miles from the put-in). The second access is less than a mile downstream from that wooden bridge.

For the first 7 miles of this trip, Crab Creek flows slowly, meandering in some places, broadening into marshes in others. Downstream from the railroad bridge it builds speed and narrows.

Below the second access, the creek is swift and narrow, and hemmed between steep banks. It's about 1 mile from the second access to the only significant white-water, a short Class 2 rapid where the stream rounds a sharp corner and drops over a rock shelf. No obvious portage goes around the rapid, but a route can be picked along either bank. A large eddy is just downstream.

About a mile below the rapid, the creek widens and slows, passing the Beverly Sand Dunes, a popular playground for motorcyclists and other off-road enthusiasts. (The dunes can serve as an alternate take-out, but only for boaters with four-wheel-drive vehicles.)

The final mile of the stream fluctuates with the Columbia River, creating an ugly, inland tidal flat. Be careful if you step out of the canoe here; the mud is several feet deep in places.

Flows on Crab Creek vary with the weather and irrigation runoff. Since the gauging station is 100 miles upstream, its readings are a poor standard for this trip. Typically, however, spring offers the best combinations of good flows and friendly weather. Summer brings intense heat, along with mosquitoes and the occasional rattlesnake. Winter can leave a crust of ice along the shoreline. Duck hunters use streamside blinds in the fall, but this part of Crab Creek is too muddy for good fishing, so it is virtually unused the rest of the year.

Paddlers should be aware that westerly winds strong enough to push a boat upstream can hit during any season. They are most prevalent in the late afternoon and evening.

61 Columbia River I (Hanford Reach)

Location: Vernita to Ringold
Distance: 33 miles
Paddle time: 2 days
Season: Virtually year-round
Rating: Class 1 to 2
Hazards: Strong winds, powerful eddies, boils
Shuttle: 25.5 miles first day, 35 miles second day, pavement and gravel
Flow information: USGS Washington website
River gauge: 12472800 below Priest Rapids Dam
Historic flows: Average 118,000 cfs; maximum 693,000; minimum 4120
Maps: USGS Vernita, Coyote Rapids, Locke Island, Hanford, Savage Island; Benton, Grant, and Franklin County maps
Information: Hanford Reach National Monument; Washington Department of Fish and Wildlife in Ephrata

For all practical purposes, this is two trips, not one, on the last major free-flowing stretch of the Columbia. While the nuclear plants that line the western shoreline of Hanford Reach no longer operate, the Department of Energy keeps things under tight wraps. The public is allowed ashore only in the Wahluke Wildlife Area, a portion of the Hanford Reach National Monument. Camping or overnight parking is prohibited. A boat-in campsite at White Bluffs has been proposed.

The trip involves 18 miles of paddling the first day and 15 miles the second. While there are no rapids, paddlers should beware of strong eddies and crosscurrents. The size and remoteness of the river means capsizing could be fatal. Strong winds can develop suddenly, and summer brings intense heat. Paddlers should carry plenty of water.

Access. To reach the put-in from I-90, take Exit 137 on the east side of the Columbia near the bridge in Vantage, Washington. Drive south a mile on SR 26, then 28 miles on SR 243. The access, used mostly by anglers, is a rough track through the sagebrush to the river's edge, just upstream from the Vernita bridge on river left. Vehicles with low clearance might scrape rocks.

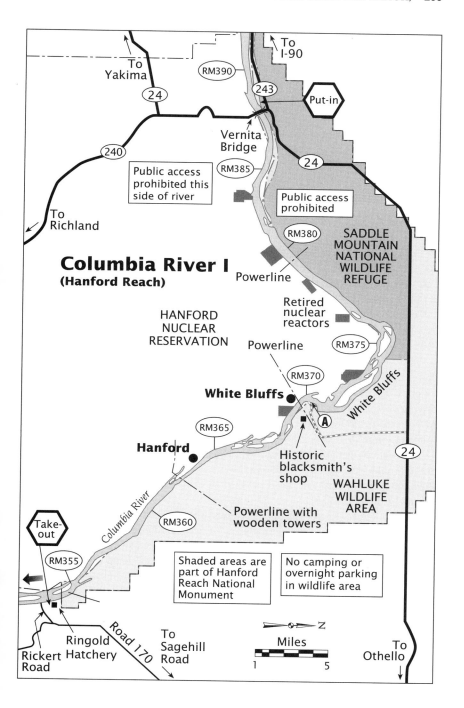

To I-90

RM390

To Yakima

24

243

Put-in

Vernita Bridge

240

RM385

Public access prohibited this side of river

24

Public access prohibited

To Richland

RM380

SADDLE MOUNTAIN NATIONAL WILDLIFE REFUGE

Columbia River I
(Hanford Reach)

Powerline

HANFORD NUCLEAR RESERVATION

Retired nuclear reactors

Powerline

RM375

RM370

White Bluffs

White Bluffs

RM365

Ⓐ

Hanford

Historic blacksmith's shop

24

WAHLUKE WILDLIFE AREA

Columbia River

RM360

Powerline with wooden towers

Take-out

RM355

Shaded areas are part of Hanford Reach National Monument

No camping or overnight parking in wildlife area

N

Road 170

To Sagehill Road

Miles

To Othello

Ringold Hatchery

Rickert Road

1   5

Columbia River Hanford Reach near White Bluffs (Julie Titone photo)

To reach the middle access, drive east from the Vernita Bridge 19 miles on SR 24. Just past milepost 63, turn right at the entrance to the Wahluke Wildlife Area. Follow the access road, which alternates between gravel and very rough pavement, about 4 miles to the only significant crossroads. Turn right and drive another 1.5 miles to the White Bluffs access. Overnight parking is not allowed. The State Fish and Wildlife Department sometimes closes this access in winter and spring to protect waterfowl. Check with the agency's Ephrata office.

The take-out is near the Ringold Fish Hatchery. From the middle access, continue east another 10 miles on SR 24, turning right on Sagehill Road, near milepost 74. At 11 miles, Sagehill comes to a T with Road 170. Turn right again, driving about 4 miles to a Y in the road. Stay left, on what is now Rickert Road. At 2 miles, turn right on the road to Ringold Fish Hatchery and in less than a mile follow a rough dirt road a few hundred feet to the river.

To reach the Ringold take-out from US 395 near Connell, drive west on SR 17 about 2 miles, through the town of Mesa. Turn left on Road 170 and drive 9 miles through Basin City to the junction with Sagehill Road. From that point, follow the above directions.

Paddle Route. Ignore the ominous nuclear reactors to the west (where cleanup will continue for decades and trespassing is a federal offense), and Hanford Reach looks little different than it did when European settlers first arrived. Few other trips in the Inland Northwest offer better wildlife viewing. Eagles and hawks ride the air currents created by 400-foot cliffs known as the White Bluffs. White pelicans drift over the river. The Reach's seventeen islands are predator-safe fawning grounds for mule deer in the spring and a sanctuary for 70,000 ducks and geese in late fall and early winter.

The Reach supports about 90 percent of the wild fall chinook salmon that still spawn in the Columbia. They draw scores of anglers in all manner of powerboats in autumn. Anglers also find healthy numbers of giant sturgeon, one of the oldest species on Earth. This is the last toehold for the Columbia River limpet and the Columbia pebblesnail. Biologists still are discovering new species of plants and insects on the land surrounding the Reach.

The White Bluffs are rich in fossils, including bones of extinct bison, horses, and mastodon. Remains of a blacksmith's shop still stand near the White Bluffs access, where the military camped during the Yakama Indian War (1855–1858). The access was a ferry crossing until the government ordered residents to move from the area so it could begin weapons production in secret. Farther downstream on the western shore, the Hanford school has stood empty since the 1940s.

Even in areas where public access is allowed, it is illegal to disturb fossils, artifacts, or the remains of buildings.

Discharges from Priest Rapids Dam can significantly alter flow in the Reach during a day.

62 Columbia River II (Lake Roosevelt)

Location: Hawk Creek to Keller Ferry
Distance: 20 miles
Paddle time: 2 to 3 days
Season: Year-round, best when near fullpool
Rating: Flatwater
Hazards: Strong winds
Shuttle: 38 miles, mostly pavement
Lake level information: Lake Roosevelt National Recreation Area
Lake levels: Normal full pool 1280 feet; normal high pool, 1290; normal low pool, 1208
Maps: USGS Olsen Canyon, Lincoln, Creston, Whitestone Rock, Keller Ferry, Keller; 1:100,000 scale Coulee Dam map; Lake Roosevelt National Recreation Area map
Information: Colville Confederated Tribes Parks and Recreation; Grand Coulee Dam Chamber of Commerce; Lake Roosevelt National Recreation Area

The Northwesterners who championed construction of Grand Coulee Dam had timing on their side. Americans were desperate for work and the president was looking for big projects to rally a nation demoralized by the Great Depression. The dam project did both, employing 8000 people, bringing irrigation to 500,000 acres of desert, and providing the electricity that would support Boeing and other economic mainstays—eventually helping to win World War II. No one—at least no one of influence—gave much consideration to the environmental and social costs of the project that was completed in 1942. Where once there was a rapids-studded river set deep in canyons, there now is a 130-mile-long lake named for the president who made it happen. In place of the salmon that had fed uncounted generations of people, there are pen-reared trout and Midwest imports such as walleye and small-mouth bass.

It's a changed and diminished place, but still a good place. Lake Roosevelt is a sunny paradise for boaters and sport fishermen, with twenty-two boat launches, twenty-nine campgrounds, and endless camping on isolated beaches. Basalt cliffs carved by Ice Age floods rise hundreds of feet over the lake and continue hundreds of feet below its surface.

The trip described here is a good introduction to the lower third of Lake Roosevelt National Recreation Area, where rainfall averages about 10 inches a year (half the average of more northern portions of the lake) and summer temperatures are typically in the 90s. Many other trips are possible, as well, linking boat launches, campgrounds, or undeveloped beach campsites along the 630 miles of Lake Roosevelt shoreline. Of particular interest to paddlers are the flooded lower reaches of the lake's primary tributaries, the Kettle, Colville, Spokane, and Sanpoil rivers. In fact, this trip could easily be extended 10 miles up the Sanpoil, to a tribal campground.

Want ideas for more options? Ask any Boy Scout; many seeking "50-miler" merit badges are among the lake's 1.5 million annual visitors.

Access. To reach the put-in, drive north from Davenport, Washington, on SR 25. At the Fort Spokane Store (22 miles north of Davenport), turn left onto Miles–Creston Road. It is 9 miles to the well-marked gravel road that leads to the Hawk Creek campground and boat launch.

To reach the take-out from Davenport, drive west for 30 miles on US 2, to Wilbur. Turn right (north) onto SR 174, then take another right after just 0.5 mile, onto SR 21. It's 14 miles through wheat fields and down a steep canyon to the boat launch at Keller Ferry.

The trip between the put-in and the take-out can be shortened by following the Miles–Creston Road from Hawk Creek to Creston where it meets US 2.

Paddle Route. Although the drawdown varies depending on snowpack and other factors, the water level in Lake Roosevelt fluctuates enough in a typical year to cover an eight-story building. Low water is typically around May, when water managers are making room for runoff from the mountains. Some years, the drop is significant enough to show the top of Kettle Falls, near the upper end of the reservoir.

The lake is normally at full pool by summer, leaving plenty of sand for camping. Daily fluctuations of up to a foot are still possible, so beach campers should pitch tents well back from the waterline.

The Hawk Creek boat launch (38 river miles above Grand Coulee Dam and some 635 miles upstream from the Pacific Ocean) is left dry whenever the reservoir drops below 1281 feet, so cannot be used to launch trailered boats much of the year. Even at full-pool in summer, it tends to get less use than other launches, particularly those with marinas, so is often a quiet place to start a trip. Be fore-warned, however, that low water exposes a field of mud though which paddlers must tote their gear before launching.

When water levels are near full-pool, paddlers should delay their trip long enough to visit the dramatic waterfall at the head of Hawk Creek canyon. It's reached by paddling a quarter mile upstream from the boat launch. In lower water, reach the falls by foot, via a short, obvious trail from the campground. Between the boat launch and the harbor, paddlers go through a short, narrow, and dramatic gorge where the creek flowed in pre-dam days. Eagles often are spotted here.

The shoreline of the main reservoir is a mix of long beaches, quiet coves, and cliffs that turn dramatic during the first or last light of the day. Dome-like Whitstone Rock (at RM 623, or 27 miles above the dam) towers 600 feet over the water, and drops another 300 feet beneath the surface. Elsewhere, the open country provides distant views of the forested Kettle River Range, often lit up dramatically in summer by lightning.

Paddling Lake Roosevelt near Keller

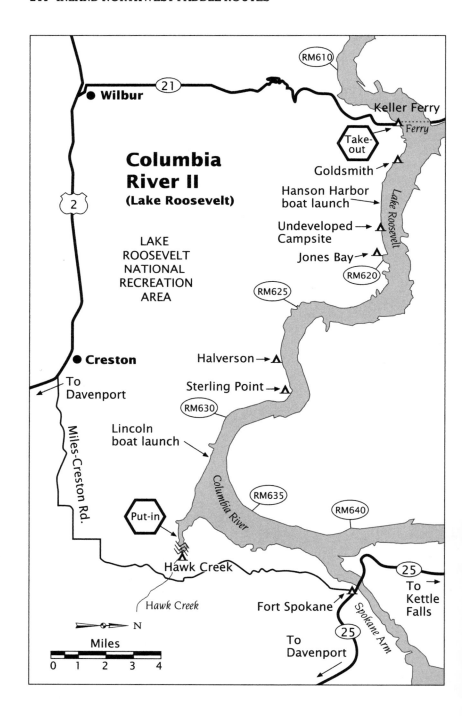

RM610

Wilbur 21 Keller Ferry

Ferry

Take-out

Goldsmith

Columbia River II
(Lake Roosevelt)

2

Hanson Harbor
boat launch

LAKE
ROOSEVELT
NATIONAL
RECREATION
AREA

Undeveloped
Campsite

Jones Bay

RM620

Lake Roosevelt

RM625

Creston

To
Davenport

Halverson

Sterling Point

RM630

Lincoln
boat launch

Miles-Creston Rd.

Columbia River

RM635

RM640

Put-in

Hawk Creek

Hawk Creek

Fort Spokane

25

To
Kettle
Falls

Spokane Arm

N

Miles

0 1 2 3 4

25

To
Davenport

Camping is plentiful, with the best boat-in sites for swimming and solitude at Sterling Point (RM 628) and Goldsmith (RM 617). There are outhouses at those and other developed campgrounds, and fire rings that can be used except during periods of drought. Beach campers, on the other hand, cannot have fires and must carry and use Coast Guard–approved Marine Sanitation Devices.

At this lower third of the lake, the southern shore is managed by the National Park Service as part of the Lake Roosevelt National Recreation Area. Boaters— even those traveling by canoe—pay $6 per car for a launching permit that's good for seven days. As of 2007, no fees were charged for beach camping or using boat-in campsites. The fee at drive-to campgrounds was $10.

The northern shore is managed by the Colville Confederated Tribes, which charge about $5 a night ($12 for three nights) for beach camping.

Campers should be alert for rattlesnakes on this portion of Lake Roosevelt. Black bears are more common to the north.

63 Columbia River III

Location: British Columbia to Northport
Distance: 10 to 20 miles
Paddle time: 3 hours
Season: Virtually year-round
Rating: Class 2
Hazards: Unpredictable currents, scattered whitewater, strong eddylines
Shuttle: 12 miles, mostly pavement
Flow information: USGS Washington website
River gauge: 12436500 at Grand Coulee Dam
Historic flows: Average 108,000 cfs; maximum 638,000; minimum 14,900
Maps: USGS Northport, Boundary; Lake Roosevelt National Recreation Area map
Information: Lake Roosevelt National Recreation Area in Kettle Falls

Tourists from every industrialized nation have visited Grand Coulee Dam, and growing crowds of boaters ply Lake Roosevelt, the reservoir behind the dam. But just upstream from the slack water is a short stretch of the Columbia River that often is overlooked, and still runs free. While there are no life-threatening rapids like those lost behind dams, this trip gives paddlers a sense for the power and majesty of the Columbia that challenged early explorers.

Boaters should be aware that while the Columbia looks tame from shore, it is possessed of unpredictable currents. The river is so broad that most of the rapids can be avoided with proper paddling skills. Still, there are powerful whirlpools, eddies, and crosscurrents that can jolt a canoe or toss water over the gunwales.

Capsizing can mean a long, exhausting swim in frigid water. More boaters die on the Columbia than on any other water in Washington, including Puget Sound. Beginning paddlers should not venture onto the river without several boats and experienced companions.

Access. Leave a shuttle vehicle at the boat launch in Northport, Washington, where the trip ends. The town is on the east side of the river on SR 25. To reach the boat launch heading north from town, veer right just before the highway crosses over the Columbia. Follow a well-marked road past a sawmill to the Northport City Park at the base of the bridge. Camping in vehicles is allowed at the park, but tents are not allowed.

To reach the put-in from Northport, drive north 11 miles on the Northport–Boundary Road (SR 251) to the tiny village of Boundary. Turn left on Waneta Road, which winds downhill about a mile to the Waneta border crossing. About 100 feet shy of the U.S. Border Patrol building, at the point where the guardrail ends, a dirt road leads about 100 yards to an old building site at the Great Northern Railroad tracks. Paddlers can park in the clearing, which is federal land, and carry their gear over the tracks and down an embankment to a prominent eddy where the trip begins. The route is easy to find despite the lack of a trail. Near the put-in is an informal campsite and fire ring.

Paddle Route. By the time it enters Washington, at the spot where this trip begins, the Columbia has already flowed more than 500 miles in Canada and still has 745 to go before reaching the Pacific Ocean at Astoria, Oregon. Downstream are seven massive dams, making this a rare unimpeded stretch of river. Not that it's entirely natural. At places here, the river is adorned with black-sand beaches that look inviting but should be avoided; that sand is actually metals-contaminated slag from the Tech-Cominco smelter 15 miles upstream in Trail, British Columbia. The company is also responsible for mercury contamination in the river, and is battling in court to avoid cleanup costs.

From the put-in, paddlers look out at an island that parts the river, creating some of the diciest whitewater of the trip. Unfortunately for thrill-seekers, it would take a tremendous effort to cross 100 yards of strong current to reach the froth. The hillside beyond the island, on the river's western shore, draws deer, bears, and other wildlife early and late in the day.

Farther downstream, the west bank is dotted with occasional houses and trailers, but the east bank remains relatively undeveloped. Paddlers are treated to views of lushly forested mountains and a riparian zone rich with deciduous trees and shrubs. The railroad tracks cross numerous ravines and gorges on picturesque wooden trestles. One such trestle is at RM 739, where Se River Creek tumbles down from Stone Mountain on river left. The highway shows itself only occasionally, and the sound of cars is drowned by the rush of the water.

There's a sprawling gravel bar on river right and Deadmans Eddy on river left at RM 738. Another mile downstream is a more significant landmark, the shallow mouth

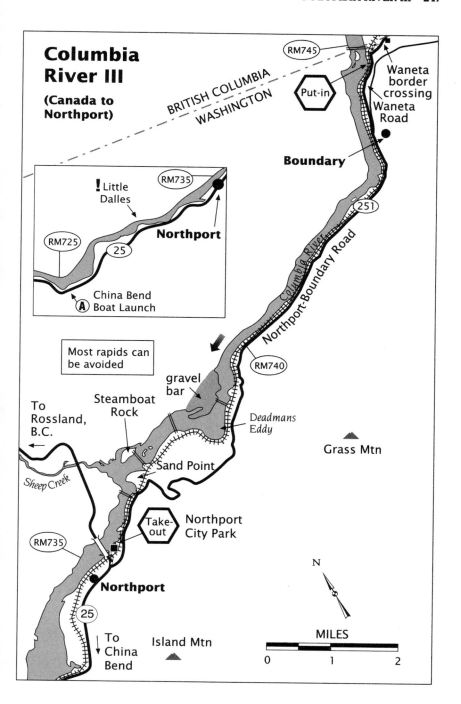

Columbia River III

(Canada to Northport)

RM745

Put-in

Waneta border crossing

Waneta Road

Boundary

251

BRITISH COLUMBIA
WASHINGTON

Columbia River

Northport-Boundary Road

RM740

gravel bar

Most rapids can be avoided

Steamboat Rock

Deadmans Eddy

Grass Mtn

To Rossland, B.C.

Sheep Creek

Sand Point

Take-out

Northport City Park

RM735

Northport

25

To China Bend

Island Mtn

! Little Dalles

RM735

Northport

RM725

25

China Bend
(A) Boat Launch

N

MILES

0   1   2

Columbia River near Northport, Washington

of Sheep Creek, which flows down from the Kettle River divide on river right. It's a good spot for wildlife-watching, with an abundance of shorebirds and waterfowl.

Fishing can be good at times for rainbow trout. This free-flowing stretch of river even holds a few native cutthroat trout, which, if caught, should be gently released.

Boaters who want a longer trip than the one described here may continue to the China Bend boat launch, 10 miles downstream from Northport. Some paddlers beach on the north shore and hike up to visit the remote China Bend winery. Beware of strong, unpredictable currents and sometimes dangerous whirlpools in the Little Dalles, where the river rushes through a narrow gorge. There is little opportunity for escape if a boat capsizes in this isolated stretch of river.

64 Walla Walla River

Location: Wallula Junction
Distance: 4 miles
Paddle time: 1 hour
Season: March through September
Rating: Flatwater
Hazards: Wind
Shuttle: 5 miles, pavement and gravel
Flow information: USGS Washington website
River gauge: 14018500 at Touchet
Historic flows: Average 559 cfs; maximum 20,300; minimum 0
Maps: USGS Wallula, Zangar Junction; U.S. Army Corps of Engineers Wallula Habitat Management Unit map
Information: McNary Dam in Umatilla, Oregon; U.S. Army Corps of Engineers in Walla Walla

The casual observer may miss the beauty in the final miles of the Walla Walla River. Its banks are steep and muddy, its backwaters shallow and uninviting. The

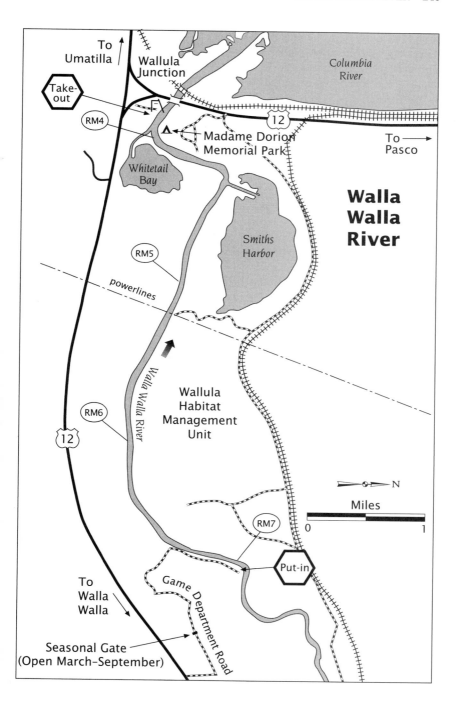

river is sluggish from the effects of McNary Dam on the Columbia River and stained brown from farm runoff. This stretch of the river does not support trout, although steelhead run upstream in winter. Transplanted channel catfish prowl the depths while big carp splash in the cattails. Even the put-in is difficult.

Yet there is beauty in the river bottom, which stands as a lush ribbon in an otherwise drab landscape. The U.S. Army Corps of Engineers plants wheat on either side of the river to attract wildlife. In spring and summer, paddlers may see flocks of nesting American avocets and migrating pelicans. In fall and winter, the valley is alive with ducks and geese, and is a popular spot for bird hunters. The Walla Walla begins in the Blue Mountains at the confluence of the North Fork and South Fork and runs 50 miles to the Columbia. Camping is available at Madame Dorion Memorial Park near the take-out.

Access. To reach the take-out, drive 17 miles south from Pasco, on US 12. Just south of the Walla Walla River, veer left at the Y known as Wallula Junction, then immediately take another left into a roadside picnic area. A rough dirt road leads from the picnic grounds to the river.

To reach the put-in, drive east on US 12 from Wallula Junction. Turn left on Game Department Road, about 3 miles from the junction. From October through February the road is gated and locked a half mile from the highway. Paddlers must portage their canoes another half mile to the river. If the gate is open, drive to the river, then turn right and drive another half mile upstream, launching at any of several openings anglers have cleared through the riverside brush. The bank is slick with mud, and stepping from the steep shoreline into a canoe can be tricky.

Paddle Route. Once on the water, there are few hazards to upset a canoe or kayak.

Walla Walla River in the Wallula Wildlife Habitat Unit

The Walla Walla is broad and deep, and the current is nearly imperceptible. Paddlers may wish to explore either of two ponds linked to the river by narrow sloughs.

65 Palouse Falls

Location: Lyons Ferry to Palouse Falls
Distance: 4 to 13 miles round trip
Paddle time: 5 to 8 hours
Season: Generally late February through May
Rating: Class 2, with upstream paddling
Hazards: Portaging or tracking canoes upstream through rapids over rocky, brushy shoreline; rattlesnakes, poison ivy; turbulence at base of falls
Shuttle: None
Flow information: USGS Washington website
River gauge: 13351000 at Hooper
Historic flows: Average 582 cfs; maximum 35,500; minimum 0
Maps: USGS Palouse Falls, Starbuck West
Information: Lyons Ferry Park near Starbuck

The lower Palouse River offers a mix of flatwater and running water leading into one of the region's most spectacular canoeable gorges. Basalt cliffs gradually close in as paddlers struggle upstream to the stunning amphitheater of Palouse Falls. Paddlers will have to use ropes to track their boats in several sections. Poison ivy lines the banks in places, and rattlesnakes are always a possibility. The reward is paddling into the pool and looking up 198 feet to where the huge column of water plunges off the rimrock.

Careful canoeists can frolic in the spray, but there is never enough room to paddle safely behind the falls. Indeed, in high spring flows, the falls create big waves, wind, and a vortex that wants to draw boats into the deathtrap. Enjoy this powerful sight from a safe distance.

On the return trip, expect three rapids ranging to Class 2.

Access. The trip begins and ends in Lyons Ferry Park at the confluence of the Palouse and Snake rivers. The park is between the small Washington towns of Washtucna and Starbuck on SR 261, with the park entrance at the north end of the highway bridge over the Snake River. Follow signs to the boat launch area. Also from near the park entrance, a gravel road leads a little farther north to a primitive launch for small boats near the old ferry exhibit. If the road is open, this launch saves boaters the effort of paddling around a large breakwater.

Paddle Route. The Snake River pool behind Lower Monumental Dam (some 20 miles downstream) floods the basin at the mouth of the Palouse, making it broad like a lake. The first 3 miles up the Palouse are slackwater suitable for novice paddlers and powerboats. Most paddlers with some experience can handle the current that gradually builds in a transition zone. The exact end of the slackwater depends on Palouse flows and the level of the Snake.

Shortly after the put-in, paddlers will come to the Marmes (pronounced MAR-mus) rock shelter, an archeological site discovered in 1962. In 1968, Washington State University scientists unearthed an ancient skeleton dating back 10,000 years—

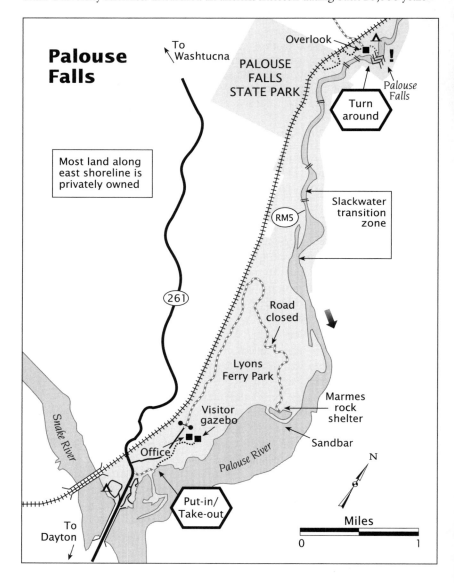

Palouse Falls

To Washtucna

Overlook

PALOUSE FALLS STATE PARK

Palouse Falls

Turn around

Most land along east shoreline is privately owned

RM5

Slackwater transition zone

261

Road closed

Lyons Ferry Park

Marmes rock shelter

Visitor gazebo

Office

Sandbar

Snake River

Palouse River

N

Put-in/Take-out

To Dayton

Miles

0   1

Ending a day on the lower Palouse near the confluence with the Snake River

the oldest human remains discovered at that time in the Western Hemisphere. Unfortunately, the find came one year before the site was to be flooded by Lower Monumental Dam. Progress was not about to be stopped, but the U.S. Army Corps of Engineers agreed to build a dike around the entrance to the cave—a last-ditch effort to preserve the dig site. The dike leaked. Water seeped in, and the cave is flooded by what is now called Marmes Pond. ("Marmes" is the name of the ranch family who once owned land at the shelter site.) A mudbar extends out from the dike. Powerboaters give it a wide berth as they head up the Palouse to fish for bass, crappies, and catfish.

The ideal flow for doing the entire trip is roughly 550 cubic feet per second measured upstream at Hooper. However, the upstream trip is still reasonable up to nearly 2000 cfs. Low flows make it virtually impossible to avoid rocks in rapids. High flows make upstream paddling more difficult and leave less room along the shore to track canoes around rapids. Some tracking is required regardless of flows. Bring long lines for both the bow and stern.

Once at the pool below the falls, canoeists can paddle into the pool and picnic in the basin. Just be careful.

In late April and early May, wildflowers such as arrowleaf balsamroot, lupine, and wild hyacinth bloom along the shore. This coincides with prime time for paddling— and the peak of the tick season. Park rules prohibit firearms, random camping, and campfires. A small campground is available at the Palouse Falls State Park overlook, which can't be easily reached from the river. There's a larger campground at Lyons

Ferry, which the State Parks Department turned over to private concessionaires during a budget crisis in 2002. Both parks feature short hiking trails.

66 Palouse River

Location: Palouse to Elberton
Distance: 8 to 16 miles
Paddle time: 5 hours
Season: Generally March and April
Rating: Class 1+
Hazards: Strainers, debris, sharp rocks
Shuttle: 6 miles, pavement and gravel
Flow information: USGS Washington website
River gauge: 13351000 at Hooper
Historic flows: Average 582 cfs; maximum 35,500; minimum 0
Maps: USGS Palouse, Elberton
Information: National Resources Conservation Service in Colfax

For most of the year from the US 195 bridge in Colfax, all you see is a skim of water beneath 20-foot concrete walls. The Palouse River doesn't look appealing to paddlers in a region with so many spectacular options. But the flood control channels are a clue that the Palouse isn't always a trickle. During the brief weeks of high water, knowledgeable paddlers head to the canyons up and downstream from Colfax, where the walls are basalt, rather than concrete, and the Palouse is still a river.

From its source in the Hoodoo Mountains of the St. Joe National Forest, the Palouse gathers from a tangle of small tributaries. When water conditions are right, the stream is floatable for about 120 miles from Laird Park Campground east of Harvard, Idaho, to the confluence with the Snake River. In that length, the river ranges to Class 4 in some stretches, with obvious portages around the flood control channels at Colfax and at the dangerous gorge upstream from Palouse Falls (see Trip 65).

This trip covers a manageable 16 miles. It starts in the small town of Palouse, and ends in Elberton, which is little more than a ghost town. There is one alternative access, at Eden Valley, to cut the trip in half. Most of the shoreline along this route is private land.

Access. To reach the Palouse put-in, follow SR 272 east from Colfax, Washington, for 17 miles. Turn right on Division Street and right again on Main Street, which leads in about a quarter of a mile to the city park. There is plenty of room for parking and launching boats at the park.

To reach the Eden Valley access (which can serve as take-out for the upper section or put-in for the lower stretch), turn north off SR 272 on Altergott Road. The gravel road is about 4 miles west of Palouse, and just west of milepost 8. Altergott crosses the river less than a mile from the highway.

The Elberton take-out is reached via Brown Road, which stems off SR 272 about 10 miles east of Colfax (7 miles west of Palouse). Drive north on this gravel road 3.5 miles to its intersection with Oral Smith Road, which immediately crosses the river.

Paddlers coming from the Spokane area can shave several miles off the trip to Elberton by turning east off US 195 at Dry Creek Road (the Garfield exit) just south of Steptoe. Drive 3 miles to Elberton Road, which is gravel, then another 3 miles over the Palouse River and through Elberton, to Oral Smith Road and the put-in.

Paddle Route. People accustomed to the Palouse region's signature rolling hills will be surprised at this river trip. Basalt walls rise 200 feet in places. Elsewhere, the river flows through open pine and fir forests.

Paddlers can see a variety of waterfowl and birds of prey. Broken shells provide evidence that freshwater mussels still survive in the muddy Palouse. River otters live here, too, perhaps drawn by the mussels. Sportsmen introduced Rio Grande turkeys to the region in the 1970s.

Timing is key. The most scenic portion of this trip—8 miles from Eden Valley to Elberton—is best experienced when water is flowing at roughly 800 to 1700 cubic feet per second. That window of opportunity typically comes during warm spells in March. At lower flows, paddlers must walk through long stretches, and canoes constantly scrape sharp rocks.

The upper 8 miles, from Palouse to Eden Valley, has a longer season and calmer water, but is cluttered with unsightly debris, including junk cars used to shore up denuded riverbanks. Some of the cars washed into the channel during the floods of 1996, giving paddlers the rare opportunity to perform eddy turns behind Fords and Buicks. Although less scenic than the

Palouse River near Elberton

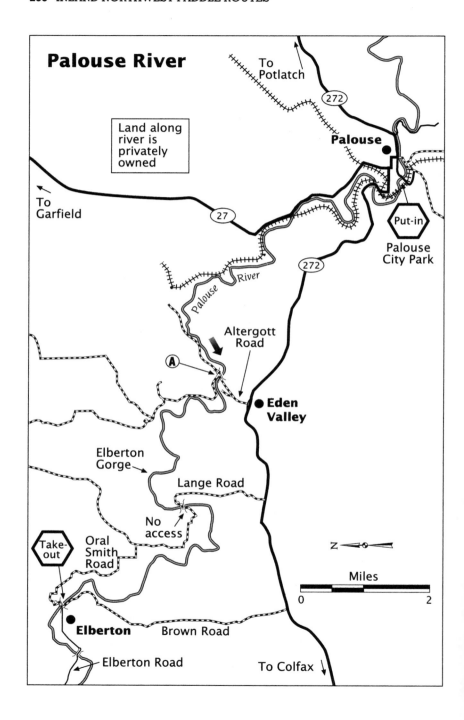

Palouse River

To Potlatch

272

Palouse

Land along river is privately owned

To Garfield

27

Put-in

Palouse City Park

272

Palouse River

Altergott Road

Ⓐ

● **Eden Valley**

Elberton Gorge

Lange Road

No access

Oral Smith Road

Take-out

Miles

0   2

● **Elberton**   Brown Road

Elberton Road

To Colfax

lower stretch, this is a good option for beginning paddlers, and can be run at flows as low as 400 cfs.

In 1995, the U.S. Geological Survey stopped recording river flows at Colfax, leaving paddlers to rely on the Hooper gauge, many miles downstream. Some guesswork is involved since readings at Hooper can be skewed by heavy flows on the South Fork of the Palouse. Generally, however, the flow at Elberton is half what it is at Hooper.

67 Bonnie Lake

Location: South of Cheney
Distance: 2 to 11 miles round trip
Paddle time: Half day or overnight
Season: March through October
Rating: Flatwater
Hazards: Wind
Shuttle: None
Maps: USGS Chapman Lake, Pine City; Spokane and Whitman County maps
Information: U.S. Bureau of Land Management in Spokane

Bonnie Lake isn't convenient. The 600-foot cliffs that surround it are known only to a few farmers, anglers, and canoeists. It can't be seen from any road, but is reached by paddling almost a mile up a sluggish creek that is nearly dry by August. Only canoes, rafts, and car-top boats with small motors can make the trip, so the lake is a fairly quiet getaway, an hour from Spokane.

Bonnie Lake is home to red-tailed hawks and turkey vultures in the summer, and bald eagles and a variety of waterfowl in the fall and spring. Raccoons feed on the lake's crayfish, as do bass, perch, and crappie. Keep your ears tuned for the cascading song of canyon wrens and the flurry of red-winged and yellow-headed blackbirds. This is rattlesnake country.

Be aware that strong winds are common in the afternoon. Few bays offer security in big blows, and vertical rock shorelines in some areas make beaching impossible. An easy 1- or 2-hour up-lake paddle could possibly turn into an epic on the return trip. Be patient.

Boaters must carry drinking water from home, since Bonnie Lake is a catch basin for runoff from surrounding farms and ranches.

Access. To reach the lake from the south end of Cheney, Washington, drive just over 17 miles south on Cheney–Plaza Road, the route to Turnbull National Wildlife Refuge. Past Turnbull, the road becomes Rock Lake Road. Turn left (east) on Belsby Road (formerly Miller Road). In 4 miles, this gravel road starts dropping into Hole-in-the-Ground, as the dramatic canyon between Bonnie and

South end of Bonnie Lake

Rock Lakes is known. At nearly 5 miles, the road crosses Rock Creek. The put-in is on the southwest side of the bridge, and the lake is out of sight to the northeast. Park as far off the road as possible so farmers can pass with combines and trailers. Don't block gates!

From the south, Bonnie Lake can be reached by taking Malden Road from Rosalia. A half-mile past Pine City, turn right onto Stephen Road. After a mile, take another right onto Hole-in-the-Ground Road, the second of twin dirt roads. It is 4 miles from this junction to the Rock Creek bridge.

Paddle Route. Paddlers heading up the narrow creek (the current is negligible) may wonder why they bother. Cattails, water lilies, and canary grass hem in the stagnant waterway, and the creek bottom is thick with mud. Cattle—and, sometimes, domestic bison—can startle boaters as they peer down from banks that rise 2 feet above the creek. Snakes, muskrats, and other creatures slip into the cattails as boaters pass. Watch for marsh wren nests hanging in the cattails. A half-mile upstream, visitors can see a rock arch high on the northwest cliff. Geologists believe the canyon, and the arch, were formed by floods at the end of the last ice age. This natural bridge apparently was hollowed out of a basalt wall by glacial flood eddies.

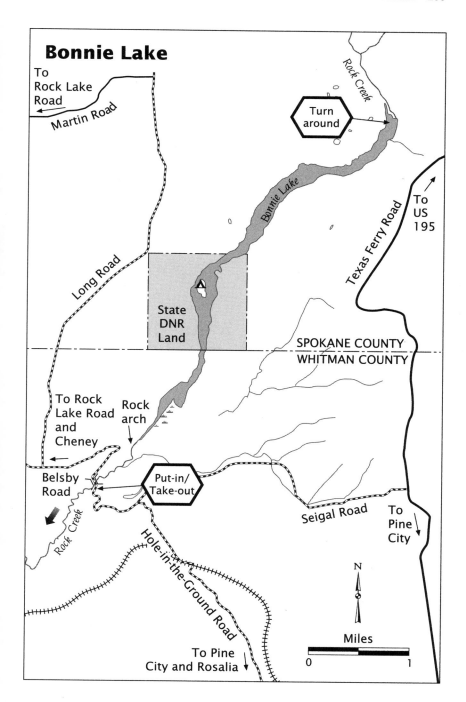

Bonnie Lake

To
Rock Lake
Road

Martin Road

Rock Creek

Turn
around

Bonnie Lake

To
US
195

Texas Ferry Road

Long Road

State
DNR
Land

SPOKANE COUNTY
WHITMAN COUNTY

To Rock
Lake Road
and
Cheney

Rock
arch

Put-in/
Take-out

Belsby
Road

Rock Creek

Seigal Road

To
Pine
City

Hole-in-the-Ground Road

To Pine
City and Rosalia

N

Miles

0   1

The cramped creek eventually opens into Bonnie Lake, which appears smaller than it is. Four miles long and a half mile wide, the lake fills the canyon, following the contours of cliffs. Only short stretches of the lake are visible at any time. Cliff swallows swarm at a canoeist's eye level, as they fly down from their nests in several basalt walls. Although the land surrounding the lake is privately owned, an island a third of the way up-lake is public land co-managed by the U.S. Bureau of Land Management and state Department of Natural Resources. It's a good place to camp, but this is no place for campfires. The evidence is in the charred ponderosa pines that stud the island. This area gets very dry beginning in late spring.

68 Fishtrap Lake

Location: East of Sprague
Distance: Up to 8 miles round trip
Paddle time: 3 hours
Season: Generally March through October
Rating: Flatwater
Hazards: Wind
Shuttle: None
Maps: USGS Fishtrap Lake; BLM Fishtrap-Miller Ranch map
Information: U.S. Bureau of Land Management in Spokane; Fishtrap Lake Resort

In less than an hour from the congestion of Spokane, a paddler can be plying the quiet waters of Fishtrap Lake. Blaring horns and cursing drivers are replaced by soaring raptors, songbirds, and waterfowl. Basalt cliffs take the place of office walls.

Just make sure it's not opening week of fishing season in late April, when congestion at the lake will be worse than it was downtown. Better to visit Fishtrap Lake in the quiet days before the opener, when the scattered aspens are just starting to wake to spring. Or wait until mid-May or later, when most anglers have given up the chase for hatchery-raised trout. Powerboats are common on the lake, but since water-skiing is prohibited, there is little reason for boaters to travel fast.

Access. To reach the lake, take Exit 254 from I-90 at Fishtrap (about 27 miles west of Spokane, Washington, and 10 miles east of Sprague), and drive south 2.5 miles on Sprague Highway Road. Turn left on Fishtrap Road, which leads to the Fishtrap Lake Resort on the north end of the lake. The seasonal resort offers campsites and boat launching for a fee. A Washington Fish and Wildlife Department vehicle access permit is required at the nearby public launch.

Paddle Route. The resort and a cluster of cabins and trailers that surrounds it are the only development on the lake. Yet the area has a colorful recreation history documented from 1900, when an area trapper established a rustic fishing resort with a few rowboats at the inlet, where Hog Canyon Creek flows into this basalt-rimmed lake.

In the early days, the resort workers would run a team of horses pulling a livery wagon up the road to the Northern Pacific railroad stop four days a week to shuttle campers who came from throughout the area to fish. The resort's stone house and hotel were built between 1910 and 1912. The large wooden dance hall that straddles the inlet was built just after World War I, becoming the gathering spot for lively Fourth of July celebrations. But the Depression took its toll, and the resort fell into disrepair. World War II hurt business further. The once-elegant hall in its scenic setting has been used as little more than a boathouse ever since.

As you paddle downlake from the resort or public launch, the land on the left (east side) is privately owned, with basalt cliffs and scree slopes sweeping up from the water to hide the vast sagebrush rangeland beyond. In spring and fall, turkey vultures seem to prefer the east shoreline snags for congregating and lounging.

The west side of the lake is mostly public land, thanks to Charles Miller, who sold his 8000-acre ranch to the U.S. Bureau of Land Management in 1992, preserving the shoreline from development. The land, with its 3500 acres of wetlands and hundreds of potholes, had been in Miller's family since 1871. It's now crisscrossed with public trails open to hiking, mountain biking, and horse riding.

Paddling Fishtrap Lake near Farmers Landing

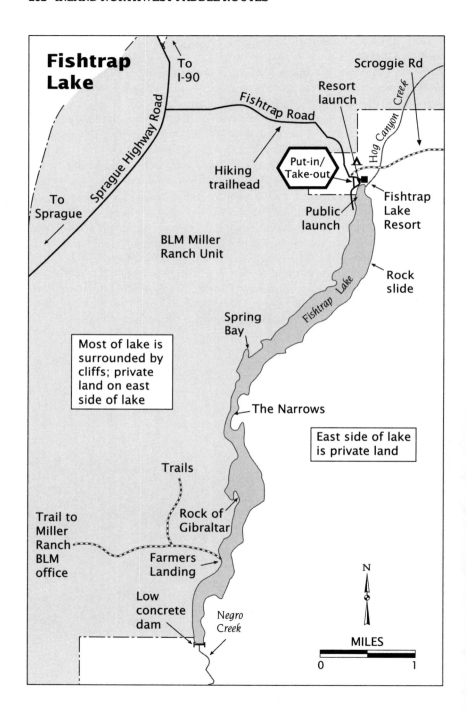

Fishtrap Lake

To I-90

Scroggie Rd

Resort launch

Fishtrap Road

Hog Canyon Creek

Sprague Highway Road

Hiking trailhead

Put-in/Take-out

To Sprague

Public launch

Fishtrap Lake Resort

BLM Miller Ranch Unit

Rock slide

Fishtrap Lake

Spring Bay

Most of lake is surrounded by cliffs; private land on east side of lake

The Narrows

East side of lake is private land

Trails

Rock of Gibraltar

Trail to Miller Ranch BLM office

Farmers Landing

Low concrete dam

Negro Creek

N

MILES

0   1

The west side in particular has cozy bays that attract ducks and turtles and smaller cliffs favored by cliff swallows. Paddle past Spring Bay before entering The Narrows. When the lake bulges to its widest point, a prominent point of rock, locally known as Gibraltar, warns that you've almost arrived at Farmers Landing, a good spot to pull out for people who would like to picnic or explore the public land by foot. An abandoned farm road leads through open pine forest to trails through the sagebrush-bunchgrass scablands above. Hikers might catch a glimpse of a variety of critters, including bluebirds, coyotes, wild turkeys, and mule deer. Check for ticks in spring. Camping is allowed only with a BLM permit that must be secured in advance from the Spokane office. Campers must pitch their tents at least a quarter mile from the lake. Campfires are prohibited.

Fishtrap Lake and the adjacent BLM land are popular with hunters from mid-October through December.

69 Hangman Creek (Latah Creek)

Location: Hangman Road to High Bridge Park
Distance: 5 to 11 miles
Paddle time: 3 to 4 hours
Season: Generally January through April
Rating: Class 1, some Class 2
Hazards: Blowdown trees; rocks in low water; two points of possible Class 2+ rapids
Shuttle: 8 miles, pavement
Flow information: USGS Washington website
River gauge: 1242400 at Spokane
Historic flows: Average 266 cfs; maximum 20,600; minimum 1
Maps: USGS Spokane SW; Spokane County map
Information: USGS Water Resources in Spokane

Hangman Creek is the delight of opportunists, the bane of procrastinators. Most of the year, especially in summer, the flows are too low for paddling. The exceptions are during midwinter thaws, late-winter runoff, and the occasional soaking rainstorm of summer and fall. Flows sufficient for paddling can develop in hours, and disappear nearly as fast. In these brief moments of opportunity, the creek is a standout paddle trip, complete with scenic rock and sand cliffs, wildlife, and playful rapids.

The official name for the creek is either Hangman or Latah, depending on which official source you cite. Hangman Creek became the common name after the military hanged several tribal leaders along the shores in 1858. Hangman Creek begins in the St. Joe National Forest and flows roughly 70 miles through farm valleys from southeast of Tensed, Idaho, through Tekoa, Washington, to the confluence with the Spokane River. From the forest, it flows in a fecund ribbon of rock and greenery through eastern Washington wheat country. Even where the creek wanders near the south edge of Spokane, it is an exceptional wildlife area. Paddlers will find sand beaches in lower flows. Wildlife includes beavers, muskrats, raccoons, great blue herons and other waterfowl, white-tailed deer, and hawks.

The upper sections of the river are rarely floatable. However, rafters and kayakers rush to run big flushes that create Class 3 and even Class 4 rapids in the canyon east of Spangle.

Access. From I-90 west of Spokane, Washington, drive 5 miles south on US 195. Turn left onto Hatch Road. Cross the bridge over Hangman Creek, continue a short way, and turn right on Hangman Valley Road. Drive 2.5 miles to a small turnout on the creek side of the road. (Remains of an old farm house may still be visible across the creek.) Do not block the private dirt road that leads closer to the water unless you have permission from the landowners. There is room enough for two cars to park by the road at this undeveloped put-in. Boats can be lowered directly off the road right-of-way to the water. Some boaters rate this a Class 2 paddle trip with a Class 3 put-in.

To reach the take-out, from the junction with Hatch Road, head north on US 195 for 4.3 miles and turn left (west) onto 16th Avenue (this is the last center turn lane before reaching I-90). The road bends north and becomes Lindeke. At the first stoplight, drive straight across Sunset Boulevard onto Government Way. Drive 1.3 miles and make a sharp right onto Riverside Avenue. Go a short way and cross the bridge over Hangman Creek. Parking is available upstream and downstream of the bridge. The take-out is on the downstream side of the bridge, river right.

Paddle Route. Gauging whether Hangman Creek is floatable can be tricky for the uninitiated. Half of the watershed is cropland. Gone are most of the forests, wetlands, and grass prairies that once filtered runoff, stored groundwater, and rationed flows into the creek through the year. Technically, flows above 1200 cubic feet per second are preferable to avoid banging on rocks in numerous riffles. Visually, if the creek is running fairly clear, it's too low to float.

For another rough gauge of whether this trip will leave the bottom of your boat unscathed, go to the Riverside Avenue bridge at the take-out. Look at the bridge abutment on river left. The river should be high enough to cover the concrete ledge at the base of the abutment.

The creek is susceptible to flooding that can alter the channel, form logjams, and drop trees into the water. The numerous riffles in this stretch are not a factor at adequate flows, but are definite boat denters in low flows.

The stretch from the put-in to Hatch Road includes only one significant rapid, which can rate up to Class 2 in high flows. The first major skill test comes downstream from Hatch after a placid pool leads to a sharp left turn upstream from Qualchan Golf Course and behind a subdivision. The short, rocky drop of Bridlewood Rapid can bounce boats in lower water. Large standing waves can swamp

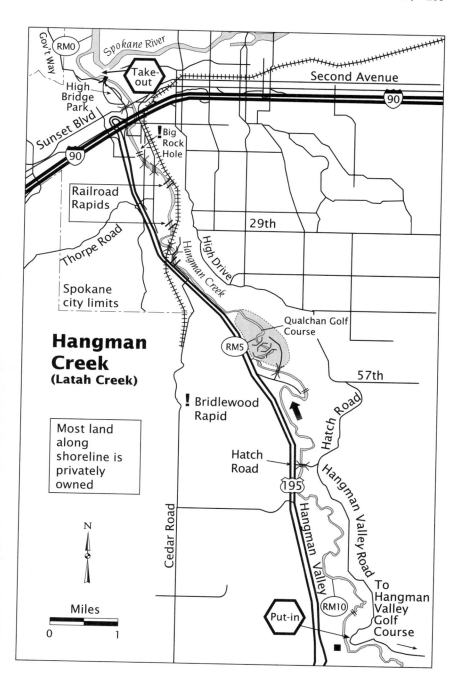

RM0

Gov't Way

Spokane River

Take-out

Second Avenue

90

High Bridge Park

Sunset Blvd

90

Big Rock Hole

Railroad Rapids

Thorpe Road

Hangman Creek

High Drive

29th

Spokane city limits

Hangman Creek
(Latah Creek)

Qualchan Golf Course

RM5

57th

Most land along shoreline is privately owned

! Bridlewood Rapid

Hatch Road

Hatch Road

195

N

Cedar Road

Hangman Valley

Hangman Valley Road

Miles

0   1

Put-in

RM10

To Hangman Valley Golf Course

boats in high or low water. Scout the rapid. Homeowners may be sitting on their decks to witness your mistakes.

Several bridges through Qualchan Golf Course pose little problem to alert paddlers, as long as logs or debris are not piled up and blocking the channel. Then the river braids into flats. Expect to bounce or step out of the canoe here in flows of less than 1200 cfs. Pass under steep, captivating sand cliffs with shallow caves carved by high water that scours out large chunks of rock.

After flowing along US 195, the creek makes a hard right turn at a railroad bridge (with a standing wave that can be avoided) followed by a hard left turn that can be tricky for some paddlers. From here, boaters will see the effect of man's hand in straightening Hangman Creek for flood control in the early 1930s. The channel becomes deeper, narrower, and boulder-strewn. The flows increase through a long stretch known as Railroad Rapids.

Perhaps the most notable obstacle is Big Rock Hole, a large midstream obstacle just past the Chestnut Street bridge. The big rock forms a challenging standing wave, and a hole at certain flows. Scouting is recommended.

The last stretch of the trip flows under the elegant arches of the old Sunset Highway bridge, past Spokane's rustic High Bridge Park to the take-out. If you were to proceed a short way beyond the take-out, you'd reach the Spokane River (see Trip 72). In summer, when Hangman Creek is too low to paddle, there is a large beach at the confluence. Beach patrons do not always wear swimsuits.

Bridlewood Rapids in high flows on Latah Creek

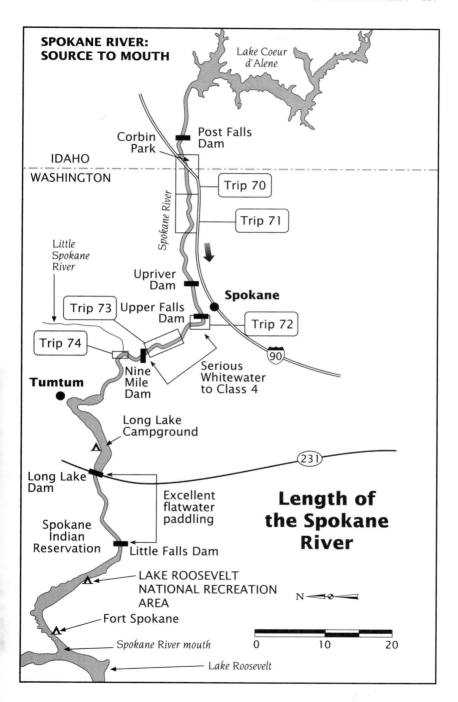

SPOKANE RIVER:
SOURCE TO MOUTH

Lake Coeur
d'Alene

Corbin
Park

Post Falls
Dam

IDAHO
WASHINGTON

Trip 70

Spokane River

Trip 71

Little
Spokane
River

Upriver
Dam

Spokane

Trip 73 Upper Falls
Dam

Trip 72

Trip 74

90

Nine
Mile
Dam

Serious
Whitewater
to Class 4

Tumtum

Long Lake
Campground

231

Long Lake
Dam

Excellent
flatwater
paddling

Length of
the Spokane
River

Spokane
Indian
Reservation

Little Falls Dam

LAKE ROOSEVELT
NATIONAL RECREATION
AREA

N

Fort Spokane

Spokane River mouth

0   10   20

Lake Roosevelt

SPOKANE RIVER: SOURCE TO MOUTH

Within minutes from downtown Spokane, paddlers can be launching boats to enjoy Spokane River stretches ranging from placid flatwater to Class 4 rapids. The ultimate Spokane River experience would be traveling the entire length, nearly 112 miles, including portages around seven dams and the thundering Spokane Falls in downtown. Sit-on-top touring kayaks are the perfect vessels for the trip, because they are maneuverable enough for most of the whitewater, seaworthy for the reservoirs behind the river's dams, and light enough to portage around several serious rapids. Wheels or shuttle vehicles would come in handy around the dams and other obstacles.

July and late September are good periods for optimum water flows throughout the river. Flows can be too high in spring. After dropping too low in August, the flows pick up again in fall.

Most paddlers, of course, will look for various river sections that fit their style and skills for day trips. The 16 miles downstream from Post Falls Dam is the longest free-flowing stretch. The river ranges from highly developed to surprisingly wild, from the buzz of I-90 to isolated wildlife sanctuaries. In and near Spokane, the shores contrast from river frontage lined with some of the region's most expensive homes to stretches settled by hobo camps.

SPOKANE RIVER SEGMENTS

Trips 70–73 take paddlers down portions of the Spokane River that are popular for good reason. But the river has much more to discover. For perspective, here is an overview of the river's entire 112 miles (mileages rounded):

Coeur d'Alene to Post Falls Dam (10 miles). From North Idaho College area, the original start of the Spokane River, the river is part of Lake Coeur d'Alene and has little current in water backed up behind Post Falls Dam. Homes, docks, powerboats, and jet skis are common. Put-in access near Cedars Restaurant; take-out at Post Falls City Park.

Post Falls Dam to Corbin Park (3 miles). A pretty stretch of river, but put-in access is difficult. The channels just downstream from Post Falls Dam are dangerous because of unpredictable surges from the dam.

Corbin Park to Harvard Road (7 miles). Splashy Class 1 rapids, strong eddies (see Trip 70).

Harvard Road to Plantes Ferry Park (8 miles). Rapids up to Class 2+ with play holes, the most popular stretch for canoeists and kayakers (see Trip 71).

Plantes Ferry Park to Upriver Dam (5 miles). Starts with riffles through boulders, then enters slack water behind Upriver Dam near Donkey Island. Flatwater continues past shoreline homes, under Argonne Road Bridge and Boulder Beach (good public access). Crew teams row here, but powerboats are common in the last 2 miles before the dam (no developed access).

Upriver Dam to Division Street (5 miles). From a boat launch below the dam, paddlers find interesting Class 1 paddling with huge willows and the Spokane Community College and Gonzaga University campuses adding a bucolic feel to an area that's largely industrial. The trip is possible with scouting, but no formal take-out is available.

Division Street to Maple Street (1.5 miles). Off-limits to boating. Section includes Riverfront Park, two hydropower dams, and Spokane Falls.

Maple Street to Meenach Bridge (4 miles). Class 1+ water with dangerous bridge abutments in faster water and rock gardens in low water. A whitewater park is proposed for this stretch (see Trip 72).

Meenach Bridge to Plese Flats (7 miles). Includes difficult rapids that range from Class 3 to Class 4 in some flow conditions. Recommended only for expert rafters and kayakers. Floaters pass a sewage treatment plant and a rifle club shooting range. Semideveloped access just downstream from Meenach Bridge, river right. Primitive access just downstream from treatment plant, river right. No take-out allowed at Riverside State Park Bowl and Pitcher Campground. Developed access at Plese Flats on river right downstream from Devils Toenail Rapid (upstream from Seven Mile Bridge).

Plese Flats to Nine Mile Dam (5 miles). Excellent flatwater paddling stretch on Nine Mile Reservoir with forested shoreline and basalt cliffs in Riverside State Park. Has current in high flows. The take-out is river left before dam (see Trip 73).

Nine Mile Dam to Nine Mile Resort (3 miles). Good access with little development in this stretch largely through Riverside State Park, but not necessarily a favorite of paddlers. From picnic site put-in on river right just downstream from Charles Road Bridge at Nine Mile Dam, it's a short float to the developed boat launch near mouth of Little Spokane River. From the launch, summer low water and weeds force paddlers into middle of river (Lake Spokane backed up behind Long Lake Dam) to contend with powerboat traffic. Nice facilities at resort, managed by Riverside State Park.

Nine Mile Resort to Long Lake Dam (22 miles). Dominated by powerboaters from late May into September, this flatwater stretch on Lake Spokane (a.k.a. Long Lake) isn't popular for paddling. One nifty spot worth exploring (late September is choice) is the granite coves along Riverside State Park's Fiske addition on the south shore. State-managed Long Lake Campground and boat launch, 5 miles upstream from Long Lake Dam, is closest access (paddle across the reservoir and a ways upstream). It's a longer paddle downstream from an undeveloped site, accessible year-round just west of Tumtum off SR 291. This route also requires paddling across the reservoir. Beware of wind.

Long Lake Dam to Little Falls Dam (4 miles). Perhaps the river's best flatwater section for getting away from it all. Wildlife-rich and virtually undeveloped (so far), with Spokane Indian Reservation on north shore and forest-ranch land on south shore. Rock cliffs and placid bays with lily pads and a few small, sandy beaches for swimming. A sweet full-moon paddle trip with no interference from lights. Put in at Avista picnic area on south shore between SR 231 (north of Reardan) and Long Lake Dam. Best to paddle downriver from here and back. Room for only one vehicle at rough take-out site near Little Falls Dam.

Granite coves in Lake Spokane at the Fiske addition to Riverside State Park are among the many features to discover in the length of the Spokane River.

Little Falls Dam to Columbia River (29 miles). No provisions were made to launch a kayak below Little Falls Dam. However, a rough carry down to water below the dam leads to several miles of nice paddling into the Spokane Arm of Lake Roosevelt with cozy beaches. The first good public access point is Porcupine Bay launch and campground, 18 miles downstream. By this point, the river is wide and often busy with boats coming from downstream sites in the Lake Roosevelt National Recreation Area. Paddlers could continue to Fort Spokane historic site, launch, and campground just before reaching the Columbia.

70 Spokane River I

Location: Corbin Park to Harvard Road
Distance: 7 miles
Paddle time: 2 hours
Season: Virtually year-round
Rating: Class 1+
Hazards: Bridge abutments; powerful eddies and turbulence in high water; boulders and strong eddylines in low water
Shuttle: 7.5 miles, pavement
Flow information: Avista Utilities for Post Falls Dam
Historic flows: Average 6139 cfs; maximum 49,800; minimum 67
Maps: USGS Post Falls, Liberty Lake
Information: Spokane County Sheriff marine deputies

Paddlers looking for a wilderness experience won't find it on the upper Spokane River. Scores of floaters on everything from inner tubes to driftboats dot the water on some days during summer. The Centennial Trail brings a parade of walkers, skaters, anglers, and bicyclists to the river's banks, and makes bicycle shuttles a pleasure. Yet there is a wildness about this stretch that serves as a natural attraction for Post Falls, Idaho, and the city of Spokane.

The 16 miles of river from below Post Falls Dam to the beginning of slackwater behind Upriver Dam flows through a setting of suburbs and industry. Yet most of the south riverbank within Washington is protected from development by the Centennial Trail corridor, which is managed by Riverside State Park and Spokane County. The shoreline above the high-water mark in Idaho is privately owned.

Serviceberry and mock orange bloom on the shores in spring, creating walls of white accented with the yellow of arrowleaf balsamroot. This wild habitat attracts quail, rabbits, and other creatures. Once or twice a year, someone reports seeing a cougar, bear, bobcat, or moose that has wandered down to the river, possibly from as far away as Mount Spokane. Ospreys are a common sight over the river, which provides rainbow and brown trout for both the birds and anglers.

The beauty of the Spokane River for Spokane–Coeur d'Alene area residents is that it can be sampled a section at a time, even on a whim after work. This section is choice for paddlers who want splashy riffles and possible play areas, but no unavoidable boat-swamping challenges.

Paddlers heading out to do this interstate trip should be prepared to comply with various rules. For example, Idaho's Kootenai County has required any small craft to carry a whistle or horn for emergency signaling. Idaho also requires all vessels to *carry* life vests for each person aboard. In Washington, however, Spokane County requires everyone floating the Spokane River to *wear* a personal flotation device.

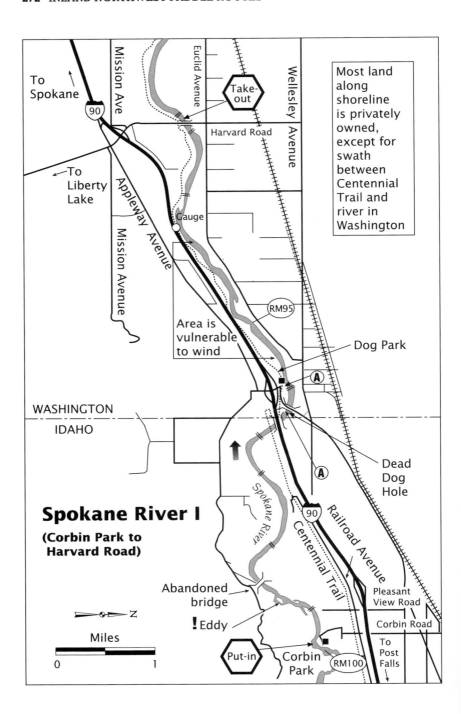

To Spokane

Mission Ave

Euclid Avenue

Take-out

Wellesley Avenue

Harvard Road

Most land along shoreline is privately owned, except for swath between Centennial Trail and river in Washington

To Liberty Lake

Appleway Avenue

Mission Avenue

Gauge

RM95

Area is vulnerable to wind

Dog Park

A

WASHINGTON

IDAHO

A

Dead Dog Hole

Spokane River I

(Corbin Park to Harvard Road)

Spokane River

Centennial Trail

Railroad Avenue

90

N

Abandoned bridge

Pleasant View Road

Corbin Road

! Eddy

Miles

0   1

Put-in

Corbin Park

RM100

To Post Falls

Access. To reach the put-in from I-90, take the Pleasant View Road Exit 2 at the west edge of Post Falls, Idaho. Go south to the stoplight and turn left (east) on Railroad Avenue. Go half a mile and turn right (south) onto Corbin Road, which winds down to the park along the shore of the river.

Travel to the take-out requires backtracking to I-90 and heading west toward Spokane, Washington. Take Liberty Lake Exit 296. At the intersection, turn north on Harvard Road. Cross the Spokane River bridge and immediately turn left into the access site.

Paddle Route. From the calm waters at Corbin Park, boaters soon get their first taste of splashy water. Rapids and eddylines for a mile below the put-in are as difficult as any found en route to Harvard Road. Use common sense in avoiding hazards posed by bridge abutments. Expect turbulence around big pilings at the I-90 bridge. Skilled kayakers like to play in Dead Dog Hole, created by a rock outcrop under the old state line highway bridge at river right just downstream from I-90.

Soon after passing under the I-90 bridge there is an optional take-out at the Centennial Trail access behind the

Paddling the upper Spokane River near Harvard Road

state line highway weigh station on river left. This is accessible from I-90's State-line Exit 299.

The river is tame from here to Harvard Road. However, boulders can be hard to avoid in low flows of late summer. Also, a headwind can slow your progress in more than a mile of straight stretches downstream from the state line. Be prepared for the eddy at the take-out just after passing under the Harvard bridge.

In spring flows of 19,000 cubic feet per second, paddlers can do this route in an hour. More typical summer flows under 3000 cfs combined with wind can triple the time and work. Late-summer flows under 1200 cfs require more skill to avoid rocks.

71 Spokane River II

Location: Harvard Road to Plantes Ferry Park
Distance: 8 miles
Paddle time: 2 to 3 hours
Season: Virtually year-round
Rating: Class 2
Hazards: Bridge abutments; powerful eddies and turbulence in high water; rapids
Shuttle: 9 miles, pavement
Flow information: Avista Utilities for Post Falls Dam
Historic flows: Average 6139 cfs; maximum 49,800; minimum 67
Maps: USGS Spokane NE, Liberty Lake; Spokane River Centennial Trail map
Information: Spokane County Sheriff marine deputies

This is the most popular and adventure-filled section of the upper Spokane River. Flora and Sullivan Rapids, both Class 2, are capable of swamping careless or unskilled paddlers. These waters are not as serious as the rapids in Riverside State Park downstream from Spokane, but floaters going from Harvard Road to Plantes Ferry Park can find a section to satisfy a wide variety of paddling skill levels. Kayakers and expert canoeists can be found almost any late spring or early summer evening playing in the waves and holes at Sullivan Rapids.

Access. To reach the put-in from I-90 east of Spokane, Washington, take Liberty Lake Exit 296. At the intersection, turn north onto Harvard Road. Cross the Spokane River bridge and immediately turn left into the access parking area.

To find the recommended take-out from I-90, take Sullivan Exit 291 and head north on Sullivan Road. After crossing over SR 290 (Trent Avenue), turn left (west) onto Wellesley Road. After driving 2 miles, you will see Plantes Ferry County Park begin where Wellesley bends left and becomes Upriver Drive. The take-out is just west of the main park entrance. To reach this take-out from farther west, take Exit 287 off I-90 and drive 2 miles north on Argonne Road. Turn east on Upriver Drive and go 2.2 miles to Plantes Ferry Park. Boats must be carried from the river up to the road.

You can vary this trip by taking advantage of access points at Barker and Sullivan Roads, both of which have well-marked exits off I-90 west of Liberty Lake.

Paddle Route. Spokane County law requires that life vests be worn by anyone floating the Spokane River, even inner tubers. Use common sense in steering clear of hazards posed by bridge abutments. Expect turbulence. Flow rates are very important for this section of river because of changes they make in rapids. Experience is the best teacher, but here are some general guidelines:

- Summer flows below roughly 6000 cubic feet per second create technical paddling through the rock garden at Flora Rapids. But skilled paddlers can

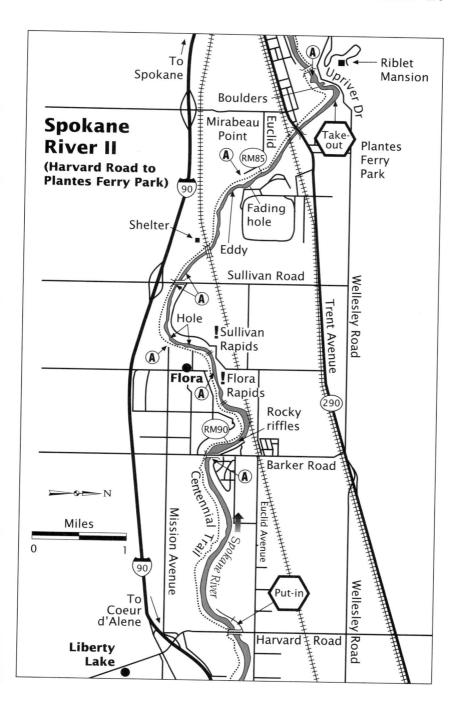

easily negotiate rocks around 2000 cfs, when the current is less pushy and more conducive to maneuvers.

- Rapids virtually wash out at flows above 15,000 cfs, but large standing waves will be waiting.
- Sullivan Rapids attracts kayaks and play boats in any flow below 20,000 cfs, but most play-boat paddlers simply come upstream from Sullivan Road in very low flows.
- Above roughly 22,000 cfs, water gets into brush along shore. Eddy-outs put paddlers in dangerous proximity of brush and trees. Hydraulics become powerful. Mistakes in strong current of this high, cold water can be disastrous.

Bridge abutments in the Spokane River at Sullivan Road

Once through Flora Rapids, watch for a big hole on river right at Sullivan Rapids. Tentative paddlers may want to take the fairly easy tongue leading through left-center of the rapids. Below Sullivan Rapids, keep to center to avoid a hole and rocks on river left.

Some riffles as well as strong eddies provide the only excitement downstream from Sullivan Road until paddlers reach Mirabeau Point. The area is characterized by fascinating rock formations sloping down to the bend on river left. Just beyond the large eddy at the bend, kayakers like to play in an unusual hole created only at flows above about 20,000 cfs. The hole grows to a crescendo for several seconds, then fades away, or "greens out," to nothing.

The take-out is at Plantes Ferry Park, where a nice eddy greets paddlers at a dirt launch. Paddlers can enjoy another riffle—turbulent in high flows—and a scenic boulder field below the Riblet Mansion by floating another half mile to a take-out at the Centennial Trail bridge. This is the last riffle before hitting slack water backed up behind Upriver Dam.

Some public land borders the river, most notably along the Centennial Trail on the south shore. Unless they know otherwise, boaters should assume other land above the high water mark is private.

Vandalism and break-ins can be a problem at Spokane River access sites. Leave valuables at home or put them in a waterproof bag and fasten them inside your boat.

72 Spokane River III

Location: Maple Street to Meenach Bridge
Distance: 4 miles
Paddle time: 1 hour or less
Season: Virtually year-round
Rating: Class 1+
Hazards: Bridge pilings, rocks
Shuttle: 4 miles, pavement
Flow information: USGS Washington website
River gauge: 12422500 in Spokane
Historic flows: Average 6689 cfs; maximum 49,000; minimum 49.7
Maps: USGS Spokane NW; Spokane County recreation map available from Northwest Map and Travel Book Center in Spokane
Information: Spokane County Sheriff marine deputies

A quick fix for that urge to play in a canoe starts on the Spokane River in downtown Spokane just downstream from magnificent Spokane Falls. The trip passes a proposed whitewater park and beach known for occasional nudity and runs through some decent opportunities to catch a brown or rainbow trout. If this sounds too

The Sandifur pedestrian bridge, built in 2004, uses some of the abandoned concrete railroad supports in the Spokane River near High Bridge Park. These in-stream obstacles pose a hazard to paddlers, especially in high flows. An optional put-in is available downstream from the bridge. A proposed whitewater park would further change the river features here.

good to be true, it probably is. The nude beach is along a rocky rapids. Boaters should pay attention to the river.

The trip can be paddled in as little as 30 minutes at flows over 6000 cfs. Houses are common along the river, but some stretches look surprisingly wild for a river in a city. Spokane County laws require paddlers to wear life vests while on the river.

Access. To reach the put-in from Monroe Street in downtown Spokane, Washington, drive to just south of the Monroe Street bridge over the Spokane River. Head west (downstream) on Main Street into Peaceful Valley. When you are almost at the bottom of the hill, bear right on a one-lane road toward Glover Field. Bear left on Water Street. The put-in is at the grassy park under the Maple Street bridge on the downstream side of the bridge pilings.

To reach the take-out, continue west on Water Street, past an old casket factory. Turn left at the end of the block onto Ash. Turn right onto Main. Turn left onto Elm. Then turn right onto Clarke.

This is a good point to scout a route through the footbridge pilings in the river. An optional put-in is just downstream from the bridge hazards. Also, this is the proposed site for a whitewater park and the trailhead for paths leading to the beach exposed at the mouth of Hangman Creek in low flows. Runners will recognize the following directions as part of the Bloomsday route that has attracted more than 60,000 runners for the annual fun run on the first Sunday in May.

Drive 0.8 mile and turn right onto Riverside Avenue. Cross Hangman Creek and bear right. At the stop sign, turn right onto Government Way. Drive nearly 1.5 miles to a stoplight and turn right onto Fort Wright Drive. Go 1.3 miles and bear right immediately after crossing the T. J. Meenach Bridge. (A sign says Riverside State Park.) At the stop sign turn right again, onto Pettit Drive. Head downstream along the Spokane River a quarter mile to a gated access on the river side of the road.

Paddle Route. Flow levels play a big role in the appeal of this float. The route is fairly easy in winter with flows around 6000 cubic feet per second. Spring flows

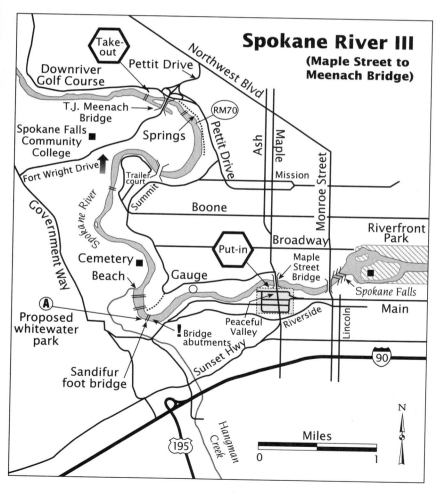

around 19,000 cfs wash out some rapids but create hard eddylines and serious hydraulics. The footbridge pilings upstream from the mouth of Hangman Creek are a concern at any level. Scout during the vehicle shuttle for proper alignment to avoid being swept into one of the in-stream pilings. The trickiest paddling could be in late summer when flows drop below 1200 cfs. The stretch going into the bridge pilings is rocky, as are the rapids that follow.

Downstream from the mouth of Hangman Creek, the paddling is fairly straightforward. Bigger waves can be skirted if desired. Some public land borders the river, but most of the shoreline is private.

This trip has two take-outs. Look for the first take-out shortly after passing under the Meenach Bridge near a street sewer outlet. Go another 100 yards for the next good take-out, which is somewhat camouflaged in willows. Scout it out during the car shuttle. Watch out for poison ivy.

Expect to see ducks, mergansers, blue herons, possibly even a bald eagle. The best trout fishing is just above and below the Maple Street bridge and below the three springs that pump cold water into the river just upstream from the Meenach Bridge on river right.

73 Spokane River IV (Nine Mile Reservoir)

Location: Plese Flats to Nine Mile Dam
Distance: 5 to 10 miles
Paddle time: 1 to 2 hours
Season: Year-round, best late spring through fall
Rating: Flatwater
Hazards: Wind, dam
Shuttle: 8 miles; none necessary after runoff
Flow information: USGS Washington website
River gauge: 12422500 in Spokane
Historic flows: Average 6689 cfs; maximum 49,000; minimum 49.7
Maps: USGS Airway Heights, Nine Mile Falls; Riverside State Park Spokane River Water Trail map
Information: Riverside State Park

This lazy stretch of the Spokane River, most of which is backed up behind Nine Mile Dam, appeals to leisure paddlers and power paddlers alike. Enjoy forested shorelines, basalt cliffs, and possibly a hike on trails up Deep Creek Canyon—all in Riverside State Park. After spring runoff subsides in June, there's virtually no flow, making out-and-back trips appealing from the nifty Plese Flats access. However, the paved Centennial Trail running along this stretch of river makes this trip especially appropriate for bicycle shuttles as long as bikes can be secured to avoid theft.

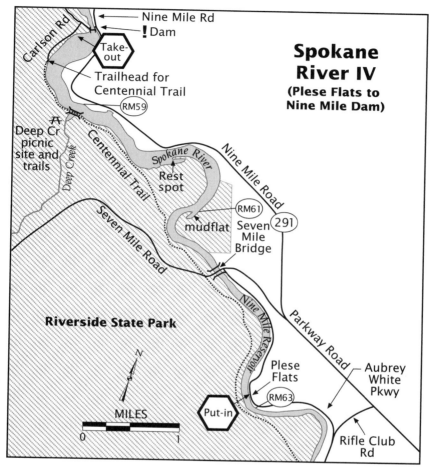

Access. To reach the Plese Flats put-in from the intersection of Assembly and Francis Avenue (SR 291) in north Spokane, Washington, turn west on Francis, which becomes Nine Mile Road. Drive 0.8 mile and turn left on Rifle Club Road. Drive 0.4 mile and turn right on Aubrey White Parkway. Continue downstream along the Spokane River 1.2 miles to Plese Flats river access.

To reach the Nine Mile Dam area take-out by vehicle, continue downstream on Aubrey White Parkway a short way and turn right on Parkway Road. Drive to Nine Mile Road (SR 291), turn left (northwest) and drive about 4 miles. Just after Nine Mile Dam, turn left and cross the river on Charles Road. Go a short way, turn left on Carlson Road, and look for an undeveloped parking spot near the water close to the dam-warning buoys on the left. The take-out is brushy and a bit of a haul.

To reach the take-out by bicycle from Plese Flats, pedal downstream on Aubrey White Parkway to Seven Mile Road. Turn left, cross the bridge over the river, and then turn right on the Centennial Trail. Ride to Carlson Road and turn right and down to the unimproved take-out area.

Paddle Route. The river still has current at Plese Flats (RM 63), but it dissipates quickly into the reservoir as June flows drop below 10,000 cfs. Summer paddlers have only the wind to gauge. Enjoy the paddling down past banks with huge willows. Look for teenage thrill-seekers jumping off Seven Mile Bridge. Frogs, turtles, and birds can be found in a shallow bay and mudflat around a right turn, river right, at RM 61. Another bay around a left turn, river left, at RM 60 offers a rest spot to pull out boats and picnic in a meadow or exercise legs on trails.

Paddle another half mile and note as you pass under the powerlines that the terrain is beginning to change, with the shoreline sand and gravel giving way to basalt rock and cliffs. Ponderosa pines are blending with hemlocks and an understory that indicates a cooler, wetter environment.

At RM 59, river left, paddle into the Deep Creek cove at the Centennial Trail bridge. Good hiking trails head up into the unusual geological formations in Deep Creek Canyon. Riverside State Park provides vault toilets near, but no other facilities along this route. There's a developed campground at the Bowl and Pitcher site upstream from the Plese Flats put-in.

Watch for game trails and beaver activity as you proceed downstream. As you

Kayakers heading under Seven Mile Bridge, Nine Mile Reservoir stretch of Riverside State Park

approach the take-out on river left before the warning buoys, note the silt flat that's been forming into an island since Nine Mile Dam was completed in 1908.

74 Little Spokane River

Location: Saint George's School to Spokane River
Distance: 3 to 6 miles
Paddle time: 3 hours
Season: Virtually year-round
Rating: Class 1
Hazards: Downed trees, deadheads
Shuttle: 7 miles, pavement
Flow information: USGS Washington website
River gauge: 12431000 near Dartford
Historic flows: Average 293 cfs; maximum 3170; minimum 62
Maps: USGS Nine Mile Falls, Dartford; Spokane County recreation map available from Northwest Map and Travel Book Center in Spokane
Information: Riverside State Park in Spokane

Floating the Little Spokane River, one can easily forget it's only a short way to the boundary of eastern Washington's largest city. The riverside habitat attracts a diversity of summering songbird species found in only a few places in the lower forty-eight states, according to Washington Department of Fish and Wildlife research. Mallards and widgeon sputter in back-eddies and marshes, while mergansers raft the main channel. Cedar waxwings flock to the river in early spring, painted turtles lounge on logs, beaver trails sneak into the grass, and white-tailed deer snort behind lush riparian plants. Wood ducks nest in boxes maintained by volunteers. Moose are frequently spotted.

Of all the wildlife, great blue herons are the most conspicuous, although large numbers of the birds no longer use a once-prolific rookery on the lower river. Herons are shy; it may be that an increased human presence led them to nest in cottonwoods elsewhere.

The feral yellow irises that line the stream bloom in late May and early June. In the 1920s their seeds spread by wind and current from the estates of wealthy landowners upstream. Though pretty, the irises have displaced native cattails in many places, contributing to the decline of some bird species.

A meandering 6 miles of the stream is open to floaters, from near Saint George's School to a developed take-out near the river's confluence with the Spokane River. The trip can be cut in half by launching or taking out at the Painted Rocks access. All three accesses are well marked. Both put-ins require a 100-yard portage to the water.

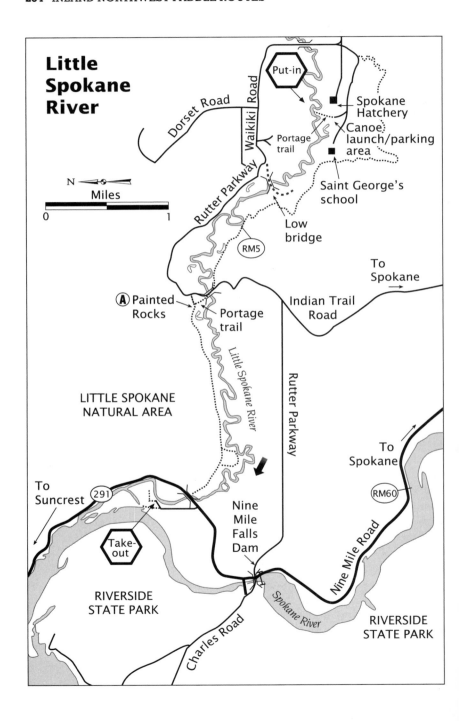

Little
Spokane
River

Dorset Road

Waikiki Road

Put-in

Spokane
Hatchery

Portage
trail

Canoe
launch/parking
area

Rutter Parkway

Saint George's
school

N

Miles

0   1

Low
bridge

RM5

To
Spokane

Ⓐ Painted
Rocks

Portage
trail

Indian Trail
Road

Little Spokane River

Rutter Parkway

LITTLE SPOKANE
NATURAL AREA

To
Spokane

RM60

To
Suncrest

291

Nine
Mile
Falls
Dam

Take-
out

Nine Mile Road

RIVERSIDE
STATE PARK

Charles Road

Spokane River

RIVERSIDE
STATE PARK

Little Spokane River in June

This stretch of the Little Spokane has no whitewater, and since it is fed in part by the Spokane aquifer, it is passable long after other rivers are too low to float. Possible downed trees, deadheads, two bridges, and several sharp turns present the only navigation challenges. Always check with state park officials during spring runoff, since passage under one residential bridge may be impossible and the gate to the upper put-in could be locked.

Access. To reach the upper put-in from Francis Avenue (SR 291) in north Spokane, Washington, drive north on Wall Street, veering left at 2 miles onto Waikiki Road. At 3 miles, the pavement ahead becomes Mill Road, and Waikiki turns sharply left. Follow Waikiki 1.3 miles to the turn-off for Saint George's School. The put-in is a well-marked parking lot a half mile down this paved road.

To reach the middle access at Painted Rocks, stay on Waikiki instead of turning toward the school. The road crosses the river, then bends sharply to the left, becoming Rutter Parkway. It is 3 miles from the Saint George's turnoff to the Painted Rocks (named for Indian paintings near the parking lot). A well-beaten path leads from the parking lot paralleling the road to the river put-in.

To reach the take-out from Painted Rocks, go south across the Little Spokane River and uphill to the junction with Indian Trail Road. Turn right, driving another 2 miles on Rutter Parkway. At the stop sign, turn right onto Nine Mile Road (SR 291). Go almost 1 mile and turn left (west) at milepost 10 onto the paved access road, which leads a quarter mile to the take-out site.

Paddle Route. Just downstream from the upper put-in, paddlers see the private campus of Saint George's School. Houses also are visible from the river. Most but not all of the shoreline has been purchased by Spokane County and the state of Washington. Rules forbid mucking about by foot along the river shores within the 1353-acre natural area. This is the only natural area in the State Parks system with special regulations prohibiting swimming, inner tubes, and air mattresses. State rules also prohibit bringing pets, alcoholic beverages, or firearms into the natural area. County rules require everyone on the river to wear life vests.

Paddlers leave the natural area as they pass under the SR 291 bridge. Swimming is permitted and pets are allowed along the river from here to the confluence with the Spokane River. The take-out is on river left a short way downstream from the bridge, just before a small set of rapids.

The Little Spokane originates near Newport, Washington. The river and its main fork run through Diamond, Sacheen, Eloika, and Horseshoe lakes (see Trip 75). This last segment is the only significant stretch the public can enjoy. In the 1960s, a foresighted group began lobbying to designate a section of the Little Spokane as a park. During the 1970s and 1980s, Spokane County and the State Parks department purchased more than 1000 acres along the lower river. Some landowners donated their shoreline property to the cause. This lower stretch was added to the state's scenic river system in 1991, giving it added protection.

Fishing is poor in much of the lower Little Spokane.

The river is popular, and the river ecosystem is showing signs of abuse: Not only are herons on the decline, delicate flowers have been trampled. Except in winter, it is a rare weekend when paddlers are alone on the river. To lessen the impact, members of the Little Spokane Scenic River Task Force suggest leaving the river to the birds and other wildlife during morning hours and in the early spring.

75 Horseshoe Lake

Location: Southern Pend Oreille County
Distance: 2 to 4 miles round trip
Paddle time: Variable
Season: Generally March through October
Rating: Flatwater
Hazards: None
Shuttle: None
Maps: USGS Fan Lake; Pend Oreille County map
Information: Washington Department of Fish and Wildlife in Spokane

Horseshoe Lake is one of several lakes and ponds strung like pearls along the Little Spokane River. Sacheen Lake suffers from too many houses, too many boats, and too many people. Weeds threaten to choke Eloika, which is the farthest downstream

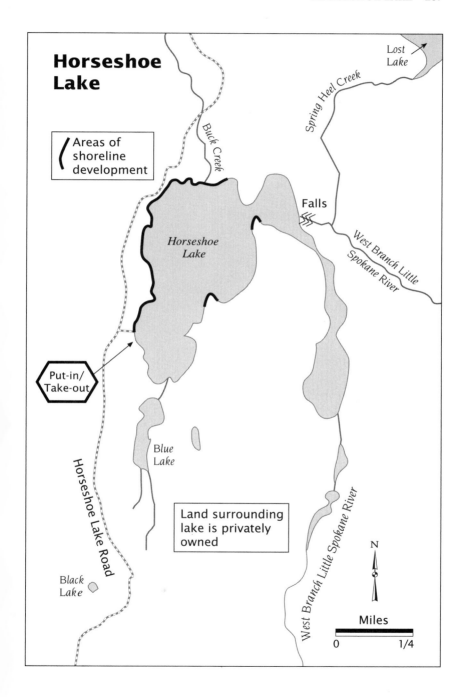

Horseshoe Lake

Areas of
shoreline
development

Buck Creek

Spring Heel Creek

Lost
Lake

Falls

Horseshoe
Lake

West Branch Little
Spokane River

Put-in/
Take-out

Blue
Lake

Land surrounding
lake is privately
owned

Horseshoe Lake Road

West Branch Little Spokane River

Black
Lake

N

Miles

0   1/4

Feeling the spray of the Horseshoe Lake falls at summer flows

and suffers the most from sewage, erosion, and the efforts of a farmer who long ago lowered the lake to gain cow pasture.

Steep banks and a lack of potable water have kept most development away from Horseshoe Lake. There are twenty or so houses on the main arm, but none on the eastern half of the horseshoe. At less than 200 acres, Horseshoe could easily be overrun with speedboats. Luckily for paddlers, the speed limit is 5 mph and fishing is notoriously poor.

Visitors are treated to a waterfall that tumbles some 50 feet. The falls, part of the West Branch of the Little Spokane River, is so strong in spring that it hides all boulders in its path. Most summers, it withers to a trickle.

The entire lake can be explored in an hour or two, with less than 4 miles of easy paddling, making this a great family outing.

Access. From US 2 about 20 miles north of Spokane, Washington, turn west onto Eloika Lake Road. Drive about 3 miles and turn north onto Division, a paved road that changes direction several times. Division becomes Horseshoe Lake Road (gravel) at 2.3 miles. It is another 5 miles to the lake and a state Fish and Wildlife Department boat launch, where the agency's vehicle parking permit is required.

Paddle Route. To reach the quiet side of the lake, paddle northeast from the launch and through a narrow gap between two points of land (a house sits on each). The waterfall is soon visible on the northern shore. From there, head southeast into the shallow eastern arm, where turtles are common.

With the exception of the launch, all land surrounding Horseshoe Lake is privately owned. So far, the owner has not prevented boaters from visiting the falls. Show your appreciation by picking up the trash left by others.

76 Little Pend Oreille Lakes Chain

Location: Starting from Lake Gillette
Distance: 1 to 5 miles round-trip
Paddle time: 2 hours
Season: April through October
Rating: Flatwater
Hazards: Ski boats
Shuttle: None
Maps: USGS Lake Gillette, Aladdin Mountain; Colville National Forest map
Information: Beaver Lodge Resort at Lake Gillette

One can only imagine paddling the Little Pend Oreille chain of lakes before roads pierced the Colville National Forest, bringing developers, vacationers, and powerboats to these small gems. Trappers surely found beavers in the four lakes that are linked by the slow-moving Little Pend Oreille River. They certainly found moose, bear, and other wildlife in the forests, meadows, and marshes that surround the lakes.

Today, houses and satellite dishes ring Lakes Sherry, Gillette, Thomas, and Heritage, which range from 26 to 163 acres. Motor size and speed are not restricted, so summer paddlers share the water with flotillas of anglers, water-skiers, and Jet Skis.

Still, the chain is well worth visiting, particularly in fall when most boaters leave and the hills turn amber with western larch. The channel between Lakes Thomas and Heritage is especially inviting, as it cuts through an

Paddling Lake Gillette on the Little Pend Oreille chain

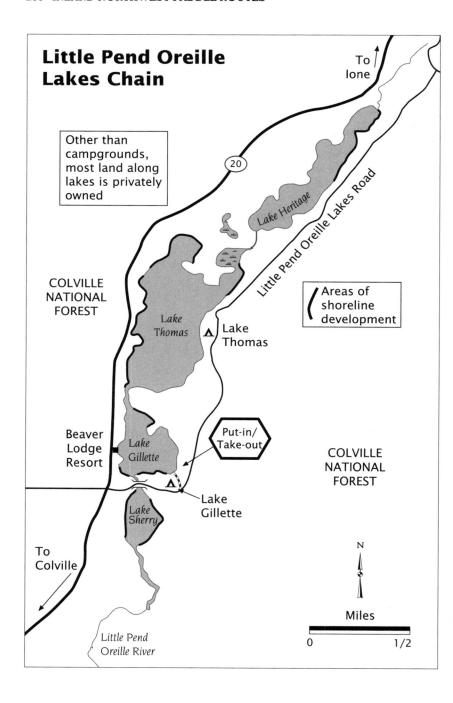

Little Pend Oreille Lakes Chain

To Ione

Other than campgrounds, most land along lakes is privately owned

20

Lake Heritage

Little Pend Oreille Lakes Road

COLVILLE
NATIONAL
FOREST

Lake Thomas

Lake Thomas

Areas of shoreline development

Beaver Lodge Resort

Lake Gillette

Put-in/ Take-out

COLVILLE
NATIONAL
FOREST

Lake Gillette

Lake Sherry

To Colville

N

Little Pend Oreille River

Miles

0   1/2

expanse of white-flowered lilies. The lakes are stocked with several species of trout. Crowds can be avoided during summer by paddling at first or last light, during moonlit nights, or on cool, cloudy days.

Access. To reach the lakes from Usk, Washington, drive north on SR 20. After about 32 miles, about 4 miles south of Ione, the road ahead becomes SR 31 and SR 20 turns to the west, toward Colville. Make the turn and drive 11 miles to Beaver Lodge Resort on Lake Gillette. The lakes also can be reached by following SR 20 east from Colville.

To reach the only public boat launch, drive 400 feet southwest from the resort to Little Pend Oreille Lakes Road. Turn left and drive a half mile to the Forest Service campground on Lake Gillette. (There is a second campground on Lake Thomas, less than a mile from the Gillette campground. It has no boat launch, but the portage from the road to a sandy beach is easy.)

Paddle Route. From Gillette, one can paddle south a short distance to Lake Sherry, or north to Lakes Thomas and Heritage. Round-trip from the campground to the far end of Lake Heritage is about 5 miles and can be paddled in a leisurely hour or two in calm weather.

77 Pend Oreille River (Z Canyon)

Location: Metaline to Boundary Dam
Distance: 12 miles
Paddle time: 5 hours or overnight
Season: Generally March through November
Rating: Flatwater, with turbulence at beginning
Hazards: Powerful eddies just downstream from SR 31 bridge; occasional powerboat congestion at Z Canyon
Shuttle: 11.5 miles, mostly pavement
Flow information: Boundary Dam powerhouse for pool levels
River gauge: 12395500 at Newport
Historic flows: Average 24,930 cfs; maximum 135,000; minimum 2420
Maps: USGS Metaline, Metaline Falls, Boundary Dam; Colville National Forest map
Information: U.S. Bureau of Land Management in Spokane

After negotiating a quarter mile of churning eddies and hydraulics on the Pend Oreille River near Metaline Falls, paddlers can relax. The flow eases into a scenic canyon spiked with several waterfalls, inlets, and shallow caves before backing up into flatwater behind Boundary Dam. (*Tip:* Start the trip before 9:00 AM. As the morning progresses, dam operations increase flows and cause more turbulence in the first section.)

At one stretch, the river constricts into Z Canyon, created by the channel's zig-zag through towering rock cliffs. The premier attraction comes near the end of the trip at the wet, windy base of 200-foot Pewee Falls. The falls don't have nearly the volume of Palouse Falls (see Trip 65), but they captivate boaters trip after trip.

The Pend Oreille River runs 114 miles from Idaho's Lake Pend Oreille through northeastern Washington and into Canada, where it flows into the Columbia River near Trail, British Columbia. The 12-mile stretch described here is by far the most scenic.

This route was rarely visited by paddling campers as late as the early 1990s. But the secret couldn't last, and several undeveloped campsites had been established by the late 1990s. Developed camping is available at the put-in and take-out. Anglers will find some fishing for trout, bass, and squawfish, although it's not as good as the bass angling upriver in the less scenic stretches near Ione.

Access. The trip starts down from RM 29 at Metaline, Washington, which is on SR 31 just a few miles upstream from the town of Metaline Falls. At the north end of Metaline, turn east onto Park Street, which winds down three blocks to the city park along the Pend Oreille River. Camping, water, restrooms, and a boat ramp are available. There's a less convenient put-in at RM 26.6 just north of Metaline Falls at Pend Oreille Village that avoids most of the early turbulence. A short portage is required from the old powerplant site to the river.

To reach the take-out, drive north from Metaline on SR 31 and turn west onto Boundary Road toward Crawford State Park. Drive 10 miles and bear right at the Y for the last mile down to Boundary Dam Campground and the boat launch. (*Note:* The left fork at the Y goes to Crawford State Park, a worthwhile side trip for guided summer tours into Gardner Cave.)

Paddle Route. When shuttling cars, consider a side trip to the northeast end of the SR 31 bridge near Metaline Falls for a bird's-eye view from RM 27 of the eddies just downstream. Carelessness near hard eddylines can topple canoes. The origin of the name Deadman Eddy, down from RM 26, isn't clear, but you don't want to find out the hard way.

As you head downstream, leave time to paddle into several inlets deep enough to hear tumbling waterfalls that are not apparent from the main river. Most of the falls are obvious, however. At RM 24.3, early in the trip, two cascades unofficially called Twin Falls pour into the Pend Oreille from opposite sides of the canyon.

Mining operations border the river near Metaline and Metaline Falls, but are high on a bench above and out of sight from the river. Some of the land passed early in the trip is privately owned. Lower in the canyon, the land is mostly managed by the U.S. Bureau of Land Management and the Colville National Forest.

A towering gray ridge of rock marks the entrance to Z Canyon at RM 22.5. A campsite is on river left just before the entrance. Listen for possible boat traffic before making the sharp right turn into the Z.

Cliffs near the Pend Oreille River's Z Canyon

Boundary Dam is regulated for power production by Seattle City Light. Full pool is 1990 feet above sea level. It is normal for the summer pool level to fluctuate 5 feet a day at the dam or up to one foot a day upstream at Metaline. In winter, fluctuations can be 15 feet a day. Expect fast flows and few places to pull off the river during spring runoff. An early-morning launch avoids some turbulence down from the launch.

Typically, the pool is at its highest level at 6:00 AM, and then gradually goes

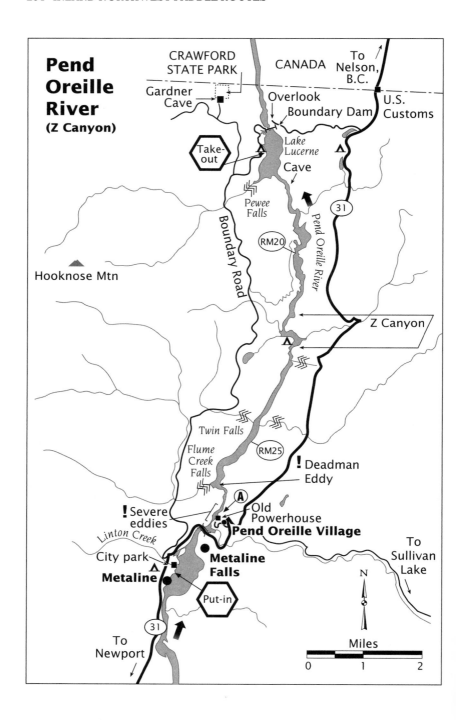

Pend Oreille River
(Z Canyon)

CRAWFORD STATE PARK

CANADA

To Nelson, B.C.

Gardner Cave

Overlook

Boundary Dam

U.S. Customs

Take-out

Lake Lucerne

Cave

Pewee Falls

Pend Oreille River

31

RM20

Boundary Road

Hooknose Mtn

Z Canyon

Twin Falls

RM25

Flume Creek Falls

! Deadman Eddy

A

! Severe eddies

Old Powerhouse

Pend Oreille Village

Linton Creek

City park

Metaline

Metaline Falls

To Sullivan Lake

N

Put-in

31

To Newport

Miles

0   1   2

down as it powers Seattle air conditioners. The lowest pool level of the day usually is around 10:00 PM. Levels above 1988 feet obscure entry to nifty shallow caves on river right (RM 18) before the bay to Pewee Falls. The 200-foot falls can be approached closely, but not too closely.

Stay river left when approaching the take-out at the campground. Do not go beyond the boat launch. Buoys mark the danger area near the gates of Boundary Dam (RM 17).

78 Kettle River I (Washington)

Location: Laurier to Orient
Distance: 12 miles
Paddle time: 3 hours
Season: Generally March through April, mid-June through early August
Rating: Class 1
Hazards: Possessive landowners
Shuttle: 9 miles, pavement and gravel
Flow information: USGS Washington website
River gauge: 12404500 at Laurier
Historic flows: Average 2878 cfs; maximum 35,000; minimum 70
Maps: USGS Laurier, Orient
Information: Lake Roosevelt National Recreation Area in Kettle Falls

Summer brings all manner of craft to the Kettle River in northeastern Washington. Inner tubes bob in the current along with rafts that serve as little more than floating platforms for parties. For canoeists, this trip is a fine alternative to staying home when most rivers are too low to paddle.

All is not well on the Kettle, however. Many landowners and local politicians insist the riverbed is private property. They say a visitor who steps out of his boat—even to wade in the river itself—must have permission to trespass. The issue became more divisive in summer 2003, when a handful of vocal landowners insisted the public does not even have the right to be on the water. Paddlers reported angry confrontations, prompting a courageous Ferry County prosecutor to issue a statement saying that private property ends at the high-water mark and public use of the river cannot be denied. That unpopular opinion is sure to be tested; the matter is far from settled.

This trip starts just shy of the Canada border (see Trip 79), near Laurier, and ends in the town of Orient. The river flows through open pastures and shaded forests. Visitors have a good chance of seeing white-tailed deer—in fact, deer are an after-dark hazard on area highways.

Access. From the town of Kettle Falls, Washington, follow US 395 west over the Columbia River, then drive north about 20 miles on US 395. At milepost 260, turn right into Orient and follow the town's main street about a half mile to a bridge over the Kettle River. The steep take-out—it may require two or more people to haul a canoe up the bank—is just upstream from the bridge, on the east side of the river.

To reach the put-in from Orient, continue north on US 395. Turn right onto Deep Creek Road, which is just past milepost 269 and less than a mile from Laurier and the Canada border. The gravel road twists downhill about a mile before coming to the bank of the Kettle. Follow it another mile to a bridge over the river at RM 32.

For years, river runners have used a rough path on the south side of the bridge to launch their inner tubes and boats. At times in recent years, someone has posted "No Trespassing" signs at the access, even though the public has a legal right to use public easements, such as at bridge crossings. With luck and perseverance, such intimidation tactics may fade away now that the Ferry County prosecutor has warned landowners that they cannot keep the public from the river. Just be aware that rules and attitudes can change here, for better or worse.

Between Orient and Laurier, about halfway between the two ends of Deep Creek Road (just past milepost 266), a highway turnout provides an alternate access for

Waiting for lower water on the Kettle River near Orient, Washington

those who would like to shorten the trip. Located at RM 26.5, it also is a safe spot for a shore break during the paddle. Road maps show the turnout as a rest area, but there are no restrooms or picnic tables, just a garbage barrel.

There is a bridge, but no public access, near RM 24, where Boulder Creek tumbles down from the west and Sand Creek enters from the east. Orient is at RM 19.5.

Paddle Route. For best boating, look for flows no greater than 4000 cfs. Traditionally, the best flows are in March, April, and July. Spring runoff usually chases sane boaters off the river during May and most of June, when flows sometimes top 20,000 cfs. (The average is 12,000 cfs in May and 9000 cfs in June.) Fall and winter can provide fine paddling, although the river often is low. The lowest water of the year normally comes in January, when the river's sources in Canada are frozen.

Camping is available at the National Park Service's Kettle River and Kamloops

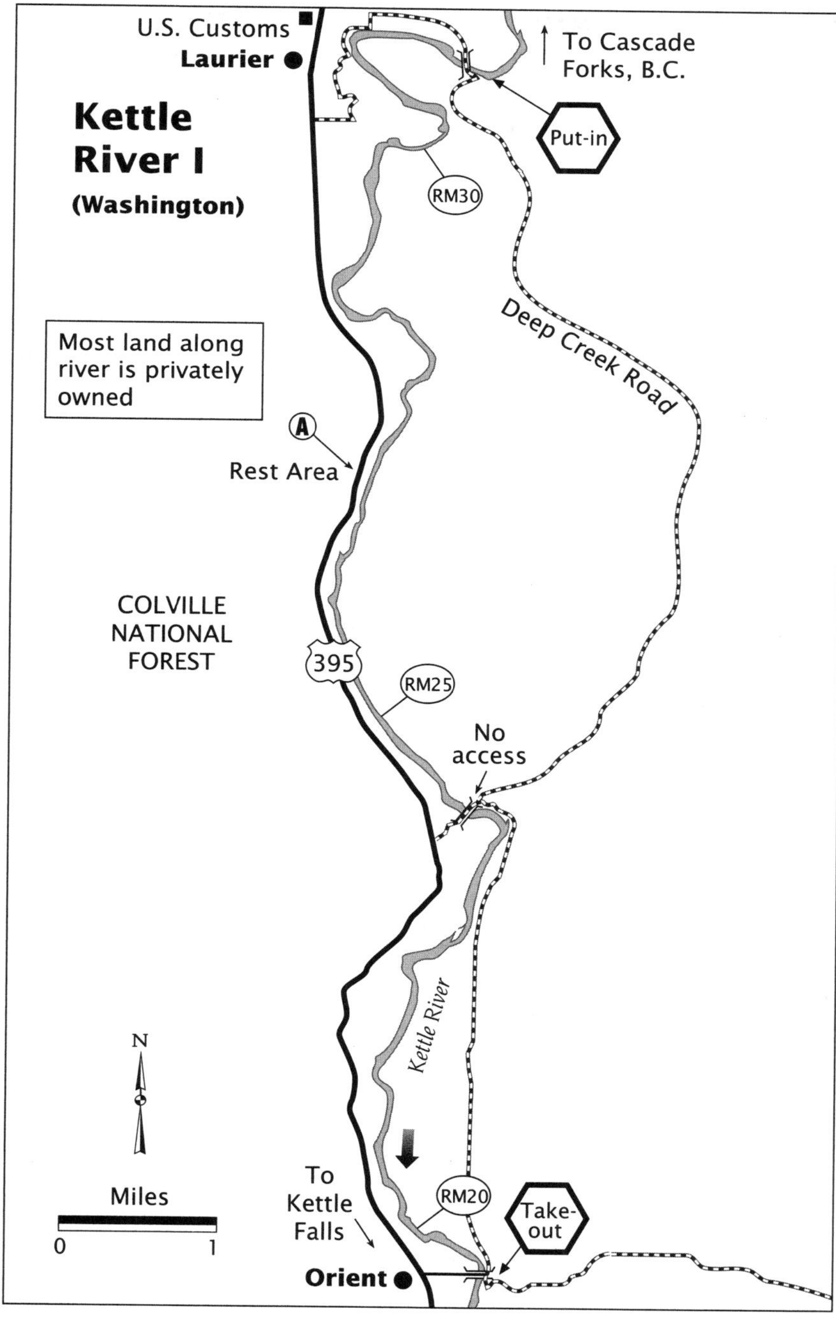

Kettle River I
(Washington)

U.S. Customs
Laurier ●

To Cascade
Forks, B.C.

Put-in

RM30

Deep Creek Road

Most land along
river is privately
owned

(A)
Rest Area

COLVILLE
NATIONAL
FOREST

395

RM25

No
access

N

Kettle River

Miles

0   1

To
Kettle
Falls

RM20

Take-
out

Orient ●

Islands campgrounds near the confluence of the Kettle and Columbia rivers. While staying in the campgrounds, set aside a couple extra hours to enjoy the 7 miles of sedate, family-friendly paddling on the lower river, from the community of Barstow (RM 11) to the Kettle River Campground (RM 8). Napoleon Bridge (RM 6) provides an alternative access. Side channels and wetlands are home to a host of waterfowl and other wildlife, including beavers, turkeys, deer, and bear.

Below Kettle River Campground, the river is influenced by the floodwaters of Grand Coulee Dam. Powerful rapids are exposed when the dam is drawn down, so scouting and common sense are required.

The Washington Department of Fish and Wildlife is trying to restore quality trout fishing to the Kettle River with special regulations. Check the current state fishing pamphlet.

BRITISH COLUMBIA

79 Kettle River II (British Columbia)

Location: Canyon Creek to Kettle River Provincial Park
Distance: Options providing trips ranging from 4 miles to 30 miles
Paddle time: 10 hours
Season: Generally mid-June and July
Rating: Class 1
Hazards: Strainers, debris
Shuttle: 24 miles, pavement and gravel
Flow information: Water Survey Canada in Penticton
River gauge: 08NN026 above Westbridge, 08NN003 on the West Fork
Historic flows: Average not available; maximum 15,925 cfs; minimum not available (35 on West Fork)
Maps: Canada EMR Almond Mountain 82 E/2, Greenwood 82 E/7
Information: Kettle River Provincial Park near Rock Creek (summer only); services contracted to Kaloya Contracting Ltd

An international stream, the 220-mile long Kettle River has its genesis in the West Kootenay region of British Columbia. It dips into Washington, turns north again into Canada, then makes one more border crossing for its final 33-mile run to the Columbia River near the town of Kettle Falls, Washington (see Trip 78). In the process, it offers many miles of paddling opportunities.

The trip described here starts in a forest of mixed conifers, then flows into a broad, lush valley of dairy farms, cattle ranches, and alfalfa fields. Deer are amazingly

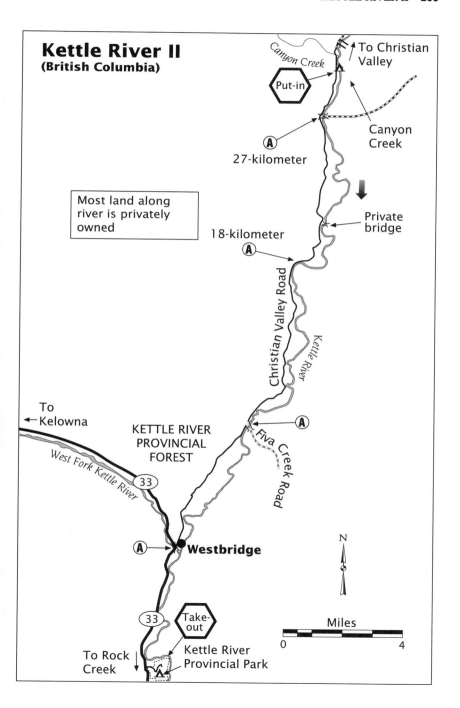

Kettle River II
(British Columbia)

abundant on the farms, and beavers are busy felling the cottonwoods that grow thick along the river. There are no notable rapids during normal river flows. The lower 4 miles are popular with locals on inner tubes.

Access. Kettle River Provincial Park makes a good base for a weekend of exploring, or a good take-out after a day of paddling. To reach the park from Curlew, Washington, drive northwest along the Kettle River for 16 miles on SR 501 (East Kettle River Road), to the Ferry/Midway border crossing (open 8:00 AM to 5:00 PM). One mile north of the international border, in the town of Midway, British Columbia, turn left on Provincial Highway 3. Twelve miles from Midway, turn right onto Route 33 in the town of Rock Creek, British Columbia. It is 4 miles from Rock Creek to the provincial park, which has ample camping and good river access through the picnic area.

Depending on the length of trip one desires, many options for launching are found upstream of the park.

To reach the closest put-in, drive 4 miles north from the park on Route 33 to Westbridge, British Columbia. Just before the highway crosses the West Fork of the Kettle River, turn left onto Westbridge Road (Route 33), which leads a few hundred feet to the river and the put-in at the base of the bridge. This launch is about a quarter mile upstream from the confluence of the West Fork and the main Kettle River.

Other access points are on the main Kettle, along Christian Valley Road, which starts in Westbridge and has kilometer markers showing the distance from that small village:

(1) The first Christian Valley access is just shy of the 8-km marker at Fiva Creek Road. Two or three cars can be parked on the east side of the river, where a steep trail leads to the water. (2) At 18 km, the road comes to the river's edge, providing decent access with parking for several cars on the road shoulder. (3) At 27 km, the road is again next to the river. A spur to the east immediately crosses the river and provides an obvious parking area and good place to launch. (4) Canyon Creek campground, at 32 km, is the final access on the gentle portion of the river. Upstream is a gorge with rapids too dicey for paddlers who lack whitewater skills and equipment. The campground is relatively undeveloped, with just two rough campsites and a pit toilet.

Paddle Route The route described here allows paddlers to customize their trips. Rough estimates of the river miles and required time between access points are:

- Canyon Creek to the 27 km access: 3 miles/1 hour
- 27 km access to 18 km: 8 miles/1.5 hours
- 18 km access to Fiva Creek Road: 8 miles/1.5 hours
- Fiva Creek to Westbridge: 7 miles/1.5 miles
- Westbridge to Kettle River Provincial Park: 4 miles/1 hour

One option for a quiet, 4-hour trip is the section from Canyon Creek to Fiva Creek, a total of 19 river miles. That trip offers a variety of scenery and excellent

Low water on East Fork Kettle River

wildlife viewing, with smaller crowds than those found farther downstream, near Westbridge and the provincial park. A group interested in a leisurely weekend could complete that trip one morning, then make a second trip from Fiva Creek to Kettle River Provincial Park the next. That itinerary would provide plenty of paddling and sightseeing for adults, plus ample shore time for younger members of the party. Consider bringing bikes to explore the Kettle Valley Railway, a rail-trail that crosses the park and through Westbridge en route to Penticton, British Columbia.

On summer weekends, the final 4 miles of the route (from Westbridge to the park) is best done early or late in the day to avoid the crowds that scare off all wildlife and sometimes give the river a parade-like atmosphere.

The provincial government maintains a river gauge on the main Kettle River above its confluence with the smaller West Fork. Another gauge is on the West Fork itself. Readings from the two gauges must be combined, and then converted to cubic feet per second, to accurately determine the flow below the confluence. The gauge on the main Kettle does not operate in winter.

In spring, the river is high and brown, reaching a peak of nearly 6000 cfs during a typical May. July flows average a tame 1500 cfs. By August, the river usually drops to about 400 cfs. Most winters reduce the flow to a trickle.

80 Granby River

Location: Ten-Mile Bridge to Grand Forks
Distance: 12 miles
Paddle time: 3 to 4 hours
Season: Generally March through July
Rating: Class 1 with avoidable Class 2
Hazards: Strainers, possible logjams; drop and turbulence near old dam site; rattlesnakes
Shuttle: 10 miles, pavement
Flow information: Water Survey Canada in Penticton
River gauge: 08NN002 at Grand Forks
Historic flows: Average 1071 cfs; maximum 13,475; minimum 8
Maps: Canada EMR Grand Forks 82 E/1
Information: Wildways Adventure Sports and Tours in Christina Lake

Only skeletons remain from the railroads, smelter, and dam that once rumbled, belched, and clogged the Granby River Valley near Grand Forks, British Columbia. May they rest in peace. At its source, the river remains undefiled. The Granby begins in a roadless wilderness of the southern Monashee Mountains and flows freely for 65 miles to its confluence with the Kettle River. The paddling options here attract a spectrum ranging from whitewater kayaking junkies to little kids in inflatable duckies.

The Granby's upper reaches have no road or trail access. The middle section is the realm of expert kayakers who can handle unpredictable waters such as the "Staircase" and "S-Curves," where serious drops are complicated by narrow rock gorges and logjams.

The lower Granby, however, is both easily accessible and accommodating to less experienced paddlers. But the floating season is short. Lingering winter weather can foil early-season excursions in this mountainous area. Peak runoff can raise the river to unsafe conditions sometime in late May or early June. By the end of July, the combination of low flows and irrigation pumps leaves the river too low for canoeing, although inflatables can continue to slide over the rocks.

Prime time is late June and the first few weeks of July, when the water warms; flows are just high enough for good paddling but low enough to expose the numerous sandy beaches.

Three bridges across the lower Granby are roughly at 10, 17, and 28 road miles upstream from Grand Forks, offering access points and options for paddling different stretches of Class 1 water. The scenery improves and the river becomes progressively more solitary as you head up the drainage. But the higher you go, the more susceptible the river is to logjams and strainers.

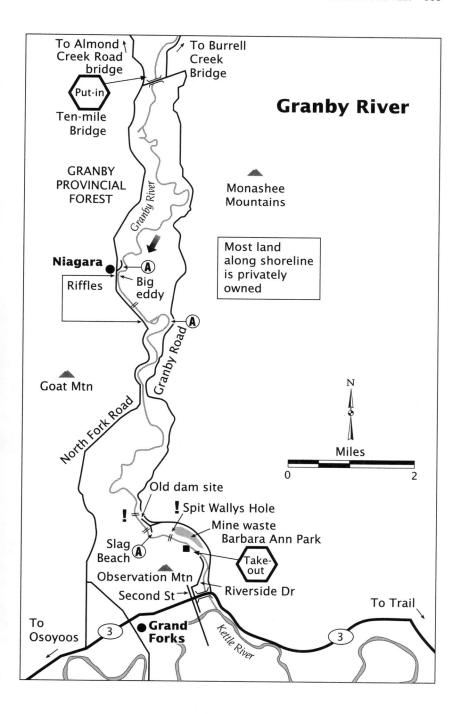

To Almond
Creek Road
bridge

To Burrell
Creek
Bridge

Put-in

Granby River

Ten-mile
Bridge

GRANBY
PROVINCIAL
FOREST

Granby River

Monashee
Mountains

Niagara

Riffles

(A)

Big
eddy

Most land
along shoreline
is privately
owned

(A)

Granby Road

Goat Mtn

North Fork Road

N

Miles

0   2

Old dam site

! Spit Wallys Hole

!

Mine waste
Barbara Ann Park

Slag
Beach

(A)

Take-
out

Observation Mtn

Riverside Dr

Second St →

To Trail

To
Osoyoos

3

●**Grand
Forks**

Kettle River

3

Access. This trip begins at Ten-Mile Bridge, also known locally as Humming-bird Bridge. The put-in is accessible by paved roads on both sides of the river.

For the east side, drive into Grand Forks, British Columbia, on Provincial Highway 3. At the east side of the bridge over the Granby River, turn north (upstream) onto Granby Road. Drive 1.4 miles and note a narrow, unmarked gravel road dropping down to the river just north of the black slag piles. This leads to the old dam site, an undeveloped picnic area, and a sometimes clothes-optional river access locally known as Slag Beach. Continuing north on Granby Road, pass another river access at 5.3 miles. At nearly 10 miles from Grand Forks, bear left at a Y to the bridge. The put-in is on the upstream side, river right.

Approaching from the west, from Highway 3 at the west edge of Grand Forks, turn north onto North Fork Road. Drive 7.5 miles and note the right turn onto Niagara Town Site Road, which leads down to a river access, where you can scout the small rapids in this stretch before continuing to the put-in. Continue another 2 miles up the North Fork Road to the bridge put-in, on the right.

Canoeists and kayakers enjoy surfing Spit Wallys Hole on the Granby River.

To reach the take-out, turn north off Highway 3 in Grand Forks and head north on Second Street (just west of the Granby River bridge). Turn right (east) at the stop, and then bend left (north) onto Riverside Drive. At 83rd Street, turn right and into Barbara Ann Park, where there is parking, lawn, and a sandy beach along the river.

Paddle Route. A 20-mile loop drive from Grand Forks to Ten-Mile Bridge via the North Fork and Granby Roads offers a neat way to get acquainted with this trip and scout the river. Bighorn sheep can sometimes be seen on the rocky slopes above. White-tailed deer are more common than people in the Granby Valley early on a summer morning or late in the evening as they feed in the vast bottomland meadows. The deer take refuge in the aspens, cottonwoods, and pines during midday, while playful otters are a possible sight anytime.

The river meanders through this broad section of the valley, sometimes braiding into channels. Small channels can be plugged with logjams, posing danger in high flows for paddlers who aren't paying attention downstream. In low flows, the smaller channels might simply run short of water.

The most challenging sections on this stretch include a big eddy followed by a stretch of riffles and rapids at Niagara (scout during shuttle drive). The last challenge begins at the old dam site. Look for an island of rock rubble and pilings in the middle of the river. The left channel has a serious drop. The right channel usually produces an easy tongue of flow leading down to a bend and several hundred yards of continuous riffles. At certain flow levels, it is possible to take on water near Slag Beach.

At the first sight of the big black slag piles, carefully scan the river-left half of the stream. Spit Wallys Hole doesn't look like much from upstream, but paddlers who aren't ready for serious surfing should give it a wide berth. At certain levels, this is a "keeper" hole that has been known to dump more than a few boaters and hold them in its frothy grasp. The hole is easily avoidable by staying river right.

The take-out is at the calm water and beach at Barbara Ann Park. A set of gauges at the upstream end of the park can be useful to boaters who regularly paddle the Granby, although they are difficult to read. The lower river paddles well at roughly 1 to 2.5 meters on these gauges, but these are not official measurements. Undeveloped campsites can be found along and near the Granby River, but the only official campgrounds are in the upper reaches, beyond the paved road above Burrell Creek. The first of several camping areas is nearly 30 miles upstream from Grand Forks. The rough road that goes upstream to Traverse Creek led to the only significant trail into the upper reaches of the Granby areas when it was protected as a 100,000-acre wilderness in 1995.

Rainbow trout inhabit the Granby, but large fish don't survive well in the lower stretches because of the skimpy flows that plague the river for much of the year. Upstream, where access is difficult, streamside habitat is healthy, and summer flows are cooler, the trout fishing can be superb for anglers with the mettle to get there.

81 Slocan River

Location: Perrys Bridge to Crescent Valley
Distance: 4 to 24 miles
Paddle time: 5 to 8 hours
Season: Generally April through mid-November
Rating: Class 1, with some Class 2
Hazards: Pilings from old logging operations scattered along river; logjams; afternoon wind
Shuttle: 20 miles, pavement
Flow information: Water Survey Canada website
River gauge: 08NJ013 near Crescent Valley
Historic flows: Average 3087 cfs; maximum 24,290; minimum 297
Maps: Canada EMR Passmore 82F/5; **Backroad Mapbook: Kootenays**
Information: Lemon Creek Lodge south of Slocan

The Slocan River flows out of Slocan Lake (see Trip 82) in the rugged Kootenay Range and runs 37 miles to its confluence with the Kootenay River upstream from Castlegar, British Columbia. The valley bustled during the gold mining boom in the 1890s. The modern attraction is the scenery and outdoor activities in clear waters that originate in Valhalla and Kokanee Glacier Provincial Parks.

The Slocan offers numerous options to accommodate long or short trips. The

Family paddling on the Slocan River

lower 3 miles downstream from Crescent Valley hold Class 3+ rapids that delight whitewater boaters. The upper river from Slocan Lake to Lemon Creek passes through a wildlife-rich slough, but tends to be plagued with logjams. The trip described below features the middle portion of the river, which offers the safest adventure for average paddlers.

Access. From Castlegar, British Columbia, drive north on Provincial Highway 3A toward Nelson 11.8 miles and turn west (left) onto Provincial Highway 6 toward Slocan. Take a vehicle odometer reading at this junction.

The take-out for this trip is 0.8 mile west on Highway 6 at the south edge of Crescent Valley. Parking is available on the river side of the highway. A steep trail leads down to a beach. Scout the take-out.

To reach the put-in, continue upstream on Highway 6. River access points along the way include (mileages are from the junction of Highways 6 and 3A): (1) the bridge just north of Crescent Valley off Pass Creek Road, 1.5 miles; (2) the Slocan Park bridge, 7.5 miles; (3) the Passmore bridge off Upper Passmore Road, 9.3 miles; (4) the Vallican bridge, 11 miles; (5) Winlaw Bridge off Winlaw Bridge Road, 16.5 miles.

The put-in for this trip is at Perrys Bridge, off Perrys Back Road, 21.2 miles north of the junction, or 2.5 miles south of Lemon Creek.

Paddle Route. The Slocan River is broad and gentle with splendid views upstream and down from the put-in to Winlaw Nature Park on river right. The park has a lawn, a covered pavilion, restrooms, and boardwalks. This is an excellent stop for a picnic and swim. Despite the glaciers in the mountains above, the Slocan is remarkably warm by early July. Winlaw Nature Park could be used as an access, but paddlers would have to portage 200 yards to the river. Whitewater stretches can be avoided by pulling out at Winlaw Bridge, just downstream from the park.

Just past Winlaw Bridge begins a long, fun stretch of rapids perhaps ranging up to Class 2 in very high or very low water conditions. Other than possible logjams, deadheads, and strainers, the floating is fairly routine from here to a nifty sand beach downstream from the confluence of Little Slocan River near Passmore. At a bend below the sand beach, large rocks create eddies and holes; good paddlers view the water here as a playground, but it could cause trouble for novice paddlers. Stay river right to avoid the obstacles.

The stretch from Passmore to the Slocan Park bridge has several rapids ranging between Class 1 and Class 2.

The only notable concern downstream from Slocan Park is a series of pilings that block the left channel at the last big bend before the take-out at Crescent Valley. Stay river right around the pilings. After rounding the bend and passing the last of the pilings, steer toward river left to prepare for the take-out. A series of rocks at the take-out could cause problems for novices in swifter early-summer flows. Scout this take-out during the vehicle shuttle.

The river is bordered mostly by private land with no legitimate camping

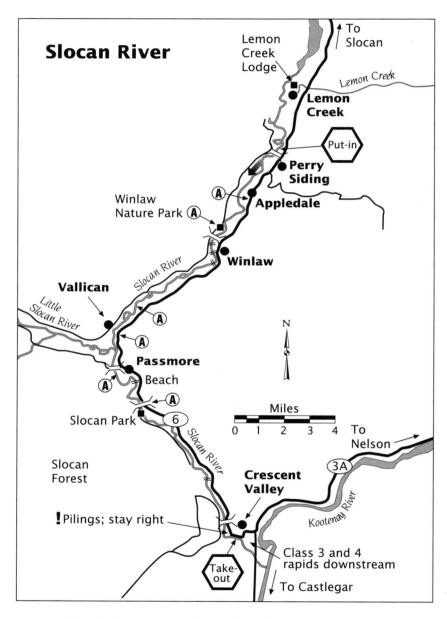

opportunities. Paddlers can find plenty of shoreline beaches during summer for stopping. The sand beach at the take-out is a popular local swimming hole.

Slocan River flows generally peak in June. The best paddling on this stretch is before or after peak runoff. The river can get quite low in late August. The easiest floating is at flows around 4500 cubic feet per second—enough to cover most rocks without creating severe hydraulics. Higher flows present more concern for possible logjams and strainers. Lower flows expose more rocks, requiring more maneuvering at a number of points.

The Slocan Valley has numerous attractions, including Nakusp Hot Springs Resort north of Slocan Lake, an abandoned 1890s gold mining town called Sandon, and a museum in New Denver for recalling the local World War II Japanese internment camp.

82 Slocan Lake

Location: Slocan to Wragge Beach
Distance: Up to 23 miles
Paddle time: 2 to 3 days
Season: Generally March through November
Rating: Flatwater
Hazards: Unpredictable winds; bears
Shuttle: 30 miles, pavement; optional 5 miles gravel
Maps: Canada EMR 82F/13, 82F/14 and 82K/3, plus Valhalla Provincial Park brochure
Information: Slocan Chamber of Commerce, Valhalla Provincial Park website

Sand beaches and isolated campsites dot the rugged, roadless, and mostly wilderness western shoreline of British Columbia's Slocan Lake. The water is clear enough to see paddle shadows 20 feet deep. Trails lead from the lake to waterfalls, alpine lakes, and spongy lichen-carpeted old-growth forests. A highway and three small towns are carved out along the east shore, but the lake is just big enough for paddlers to feel remarkably alone if they hug the western shoreline and the boundary of Valhalla Provincial Park.

The name Valhalla comes from the magnificent mythological hall for the bravest of slain Norse warriors. The views are inspiring from the lake. The best of the Valhalla, however, is waiting for those who hike the high-country trails to views of 9000-foot points such as Mount Dag and Gimli, Asgard, and Gladsheim peaks.

Access. From Castlegar, British Columbia, drive 12 miles north on Provincial Highway 3A. At the junction, turn onto Provincial Highway 6 toward Slocan and continue north about 28 miles. Turn left into Slocan. Go right at the first paved road, then left onto Fletcher Street, following signs to the village park and boat launch at the end of Main Street. The park's boat launch is the put-in for this trip.

To reach take-outs at the north end of the lake, continue north on Highway 6. Drive through New Denver, British Columbia, and go 10 miles. Turn left toward

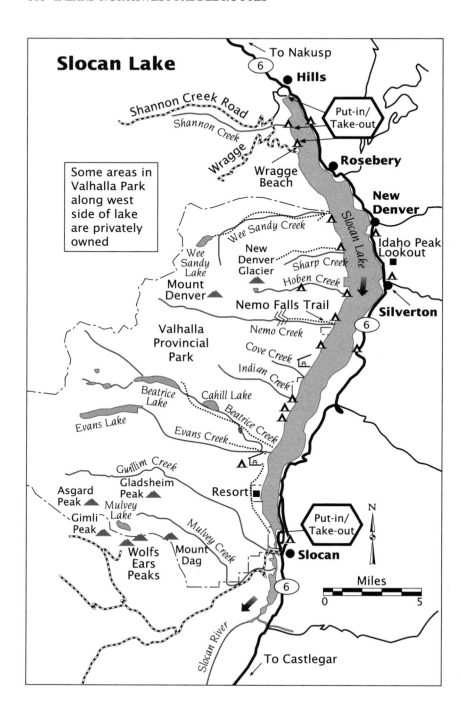

Slocan Lake

To Nakusp
6
Hills

Shannon Creek Road
Shannon Creek
Wragge

Put-in/
Take-out

Rosebery

Wragge
Beach

New
Denver

Some areas in
Valhalla Park
along west
side of lake
are privately
owned

Wee Sandy Creek

Slocan Lake

Idaho Peak
Lookout

Wee
Sandy
Lake

New
Denver
Glacier

Sharp Creek

Hoben Creek

Mount
Denver

Nemo Falls Trail

Silverton

Nemo Creek

6

Valhalla
Provincial
Park

Cove Creek

Indian Creek

Beatrice
Lake

Cahill Lake

Beatrice Creek

Evans Lake

Evans Creek

Guillim Creek

Asgard
Peak

Gladsheim
Peak

Mulvey
Lake

Resort

Put-in/
Take-out

N

Gimli
Peak

Mulvey Creek

Wolfs
Ears
Peaks

Mount
Dag

Slocan

6

Miles
0   5

Slocan River

To Castlegar

the bedroom community of Hills on Bonanza Road, which forks at a bridge across Shannon Creek. Choose from two options:

(1) Follow a paved road left a short distance to Alvorez Road, which leads to a day-use beach. Traditionally, overnight parking has been tolerated here but camping is not allowed. Asking permission is recommended. (2) Turn right at the fork, leaving the pavement, and head up Shannon Creek Road. Go left at another fork, following signs to Wragge Beach Forest Campground (5 miles from the Shannon Creek bridge).

Paddle Route. Where to start an end-to-end paddle tour on Slocan Lake is debatable. The prevailing wind reportedly comes from the north, but experienced paddlers say winds from the south are common. Early-morning starts are recommended to help avoid troublesome winds.

Boat launches and campgrounds are found at Slocan, Silverton, New Denver, and Rosebery. In addition to Wragge Beach, at least nine other

Peaceful morning on west shore of Slocan Lake

primitive campsites can be found along the northwest shore where there is no road access. Some have sand beaches, others are rocky. Nemo Creek Falls trailhead is popular with powerboaters, making the beach one of the busiest areas on the west shore. Evans Creek Camp, accessible by trail from Slocan, has a three-sided log shelter. Cove Creek Beach has a public cabin with room for up to six people.

Between campsites, the shoreline is rugged with granite outcroppings. Pictographs are found on rock walls on the west side of the lake in at least three places. The shoreline is lined with a mixed forest including cedar, hemlock, larch, grand fir, pine, lodgepole, spruce, yew, alder, birch, poplar, willow, and mountain ash. On the shore near Cove Creek, you can even find some ponderosa pines thriving at the northern extreme of the species' range.

The Valhallas are well-known grizzly country. Designated campsites have poles, usually near an outhouse, for hanging food. Watch for loons and ospreys. Anglers can catch rainbow trout, kokanee, and whitefish.

Although temperatures can be cold in winter, Slocan Lake rarely freezes, which made it a water highway for early-day mining and timber company barges. Rain is common every month of the year. Snow typically sticks to the shoreline in November and melts by April.

The spectacular collection of peaks and alpine lakes in the mountains ranging up from the lake were protected in the 122,500-acre Valhalla Provincial Park in 1983. At nearly 3 miles long, Evans Lake is huge by high-mountain-lake standards.

The park has not been as heavily used as Canada's more famous national parks to the north, primarily because the roads leading to the Slocan Valley are narrow and winding, and few access roads and trails have been developed in the park itself. Visitation, however, has been steadily growing. Backcountry camping fees are charged. Check the park website. Dogs are allowed in the park, but must be leashed. Fires are permitted only in designated campsites. Rangers recommend using only driftwood.

83 Elk River

Location: Hosmer to Morrissey bridge
Distance: 7 to 17 miles
Paddle time: 6 hours
Season: Generally July through October
Rating: Class 1+
Hazards: Possible logjams; high water during runoff
Shuttle: 15 miles, pavement
Flow information: Water Survey Canada website
River gauge: 08NK002 at Fernie
Historic flows: Average 1627 cfs; maximum 21,700; minimum 210
Maps: Canada EMR Fernie 82/G; Backroad Mapbook for Kootenays
Information: Fernie Chamber of Commerce

Most of the use on the Elk River is by rafts or drift boats oared by anglers keying in to the river's native bull trout and cutthroats. The fishing can be good in late summer and fall—so good that anglers don't invest the time a paddler might devote to appreciating the scenery. From the cottonwood-lined shores up to spectacular peaks, the Elk is an eyeful.

The river upstream from Hosmer, British Columbia, is smaller, with tighter turns and a steeper gradient. The large but graceful hoofed creatures for which the river is named make their home at the river's headwaters. The river below Morrissey, British Columbia, offers generally good floating, with some slack water to reach the alternative take-out at the bridge near the dam at Elko, British Columbia.

This trip features the most scenic portion of the 119-mile river, with stunning

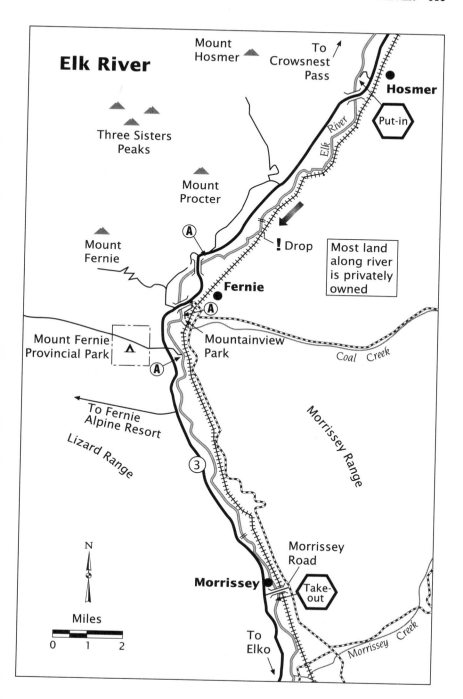

Elk River

Mount Hosmer

To Crowsnest Pass

Hosmer

Put-in

Elk River

Three Sisters Peaks

Mount Procter

(A)

! Drop

Most land along river is privately owned

Mount Fernie

Fernie

(A)

Mountainview Park

Coal Creek

Mount Fernie Provincial Park

(A)

To Fernie Alpine Resort

Lizard Range

Morrissey Range

3

N

Morrissey Road

Morrissey

Take-out

Miles

0   1   2

To Elko

Morrissey Creek

views of Mount Hosmer and other peaks. It flows through Fernie, British Columbia, a small ski-resort town where paddlers can easily eddy out for food or supplies. The river is especially scenic in late September and early October, when cottonwoods and aspens turn brilliant yellow. Since the river flows don't tend to settle down until the end of July, the fishing is best from August through mid-October.

Access. The put-in is in Hosmer. Check the odometer at the bridge over the Elk River at the north end of Fernie. Drive 6.4 miles north on Provincial Highway 3. Across from the Hosmer Hotel, turn left (west) into Hosmer on Main Street and then turn left on the main paved road. Go two blocks and turn left on Victoria Sreet. Drive to the put-in at the end of the road. Avoid blocking access to the boat access turnaround when you park.

To reach the best alternate take-out in Fernie, drive to the traffic light on the upstream side of the town's downstream bridge. Turn south (downstream) on 4th Street, then right (west) on 6th Avenue and continue along the river 0.4 mile to the Mountview access at the end of the road.

To reach the take-out, check the odometer at the Elk River bridge on the south (downstream) end of Fernie. Take Highway 3 south 8.5 miles and turn left (east) on Morrissey Road. (The turnoff is 9.5 miles north of Elko.) Just before the Morrissey bridge, bear right onto a dirt road to a rough boat launch and parking area.

Paddle Route. Massive 1995 floods rearranged the river channel shown on any previous map. The post-flood river wound up being straighter than it was before 1995. But because of the cottonwoods along this river and plenty of beaver

Mount Hosmer looms above an angler on Elk River near Fernie.

activity, there is always a chance for logjams that could create new bends and channels year by year.

This trip begins across the highway from the flank of Mount Hosmer, a mass of rock and snow that peeks in and out of view for the first half of the trip. One of the better views is looking upstream between the two bridges in Fernie, where one also looks up at stunning Three Sisters Peaks.

From Hosmer to Fernie, paddlers must negotiate a couple of snaky turns, plus one potentially upsetting drop as the stream approaches the railroad grade about two-thirds of the way to Fernie. The drop generally is not a factor in flows over 1000 cubic feet per second. But rocks can protrude almost unavoidably at flows less than 800 cfs. Look to slide by rocks at one side of the channel or the other. Generally, flows around 800 to 1000 cfs are ideal for paddling the entire trip. Higher flows can intensify Class 1+ spots between Fernie and Morrissey. Lower flows expose rocks in riffles.

The float from Hosmer to Fernie takes about 2.5 hours. It is possible to pull out at either bridge in Fernie. The northwest side of the upstream bridge is better suited to parking vehicles. A good access is just downstream of Fernie on river left in Mountview Park. This trip, however, continues through Fernie another 3 hours or more to the Morrissey bridge. This stretch has more riffles and tends to be closer to the highway as the river gradually flows into an area more heavily timbered with evergreens.

Land along the Elk River is a confusing mix of private and federal ownership. (Federal lands are called "crown lands" in Canada.) Maps accurately showing public land have not been readily available, thus camping along the river is not recommended. Developed camping is available at Mount Fernie Provincial Park, 1.2 miles southwest of Fernie off Highway 3.

84 Creston Valley Wildlife Area

Location: Nicks Island to Duck Lake
Distance: Up to 19 miles
Paddle time: 10 hours or overnight
Season: Generally April through October
Rating: Flatwater
Hazards: Powerboats on river; winds; hunting in fall
Shuttle: 19 miles, pavement
Maps: Canada EMR Creston 82/F2; Creston Valley Wildlife Area map
Information: Creston Valley Wildlife Interpretive Centre; Creston Chamber of Commerce

Like those in uncounted other river valleys, the vast wetlands of the Creston Valley were nearly lost to development and agriculture. A conservation project initiated by sportsmen made the difference, and led to creation of the 17,000-acre Creston Valley Wildlife Area in 1968.

Dikes hold back water that attracts ducks and geese. Biologists have counted more than 260 species of birds, with the greatest concentrations in spring and fall. It is British Columbia's most important inland stopover for migrating birds. Autumn visitors sometimes hear elk bugling from the tules, and see area creeks turned red with spawning kokanee salmon—which lend their name to the beer that is the pride of the nearby town of Creston.

The trip described here takes boaters from the meandering Kootenay River Channel—a quiet slough that was once the main riverbed—to the Kootenay itself. Many variations are possible. Although the river can be paddled year-round, other waters in the refuge freeze in winter, and Summit Creek can be too low for paddling even when there is ample water elsewhere.

Access. To reach the put-in from Creston, British Columbia, drive west about 5 miles on Highway 3, crossing the Kootenay River, Nicks Island, and the old river channel before turning left on West Creston Road. The road comes to the slough a little more than 4 miles from the highway, just upstream from the West Creston Highway bridge. There's room for only a couple of vehicles at the put-in, on the upstream side of river left.

To reach the take-out, drive north from Creston on Highway 3A, passing through the villages of Wynndel and Sirdar. Fifteen miles from Creston, at the north end of Duck Lake, the road starts downhill. Near the bottom of the hill, turn left onto the first gravel road, which is a public access to the wildlife area. The road is gated a short distance from the highway.

Paddle Route. Immediately after launching at the put-in and crossing under the West Creston Road bridge, paddlers must decide whether they will follow the old river channel or the river itself. The channel, which leads to the left, is by far the more interesting, providing the best views of wildlife and moderate shelter from the wind. But by late summer, it can be shallow and weed-choked. In that case, paddlers must bear right, crossing under another bridge and into the broad river, where boaters and skiers can be a nuisance on summer weekends and the wind can be ferocious.

From the put-in, the channel winds a lazy 6 miles to its confluence with Summit Creek at the north end of Nicks Island. Boaters can take a detour here, paddling upstream on Summit Creek about a mile to a sandbar where the water becomes shallow and the current is strong. From there, a rough road on the left leads to the abandoned Summit Creek Campground and its grove of 300-year-old cedars, which are worth exploring. The trees are hazardous during storms and officials faced the choice of cutting them down or closing the campground, leaving nowhere to camp in the wildlife area. Check at the Creston Valley Wildlife Interpretive Centre, which is open from late April through mid-October, for advice on camping outside the wildlife area.

After poking around the cedars, paddlers should head back down Summit Creek, to the old river channel and 2 miles beyond. They'll eventually come to the main stem of the Kootenay River, where the banks are too steep and brushy in most places to provide easy landing or views of the surrounding lowlands.

About 5 miles downstream from Summit Creek, the river splits, and boaters should turn right onto the East Branch of the Kootenay. In another 3 miles, it is possible to climb the dike on the right side of the river and look down into 3000-acre Duck Lake. The take-out, 6 miles after the river splits, is about 100 yards upstream from the Canadian Pacific Railroad bridge at the north end of Duck Lake. Boaters should watch carefully for the overflow pipe from Duck Lake on the right side of the river. A rough trail leads to the top of the dike, and it's a quarter-mile carry from the take-out to the parking area.

Flatwater in the Creston Valley Wildlife Area

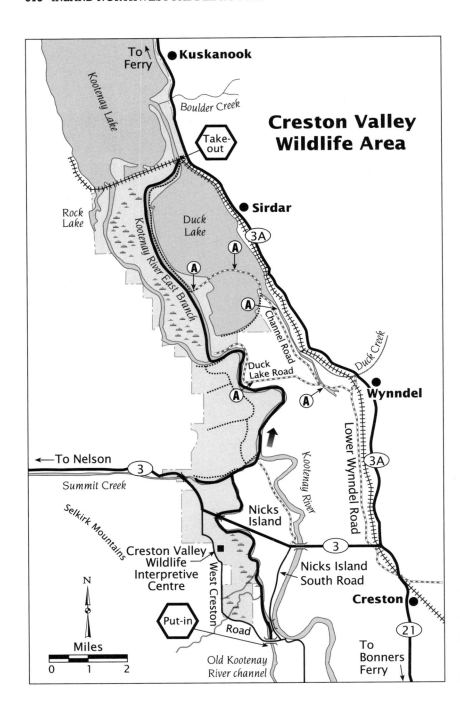

Families can enjoy peaceful paddling on Duck Lake, which sports good bass fishing and is off-limits to powerboats. The lake is a favorite nesting site for waterfowl, including five species of grebes, which perform elaborate spring courtship dances.

IDAHO

85 Moyie River

Location: Cooper Creek to Twin Bridges
Distance: 12 miles
Paddle time: 4 hours
Season: Generally June through early July
Rating: Class 1 to 2
Hazards: Scattered rapids; rock gardens at low flows
Shuttle: 10 miles, pavement and gravel
Flow information: USGS Idaho website
River gauge: 12306500 near Eastport
Historic flows: Average 688 cfs; maximum 8930; minimum 30
Maps: USGS Eastport, Meadow Creek; Kaniksu National Forest map
Information: Idaho Panhandle National Forests, Bonners Ferry Ranger Station

Born in the Purcell Mountains of British Columbia, the Moyie flows 58 miles in Canada and another 26 in Idaho before dumping into the larger Kootenai River about 10 miles east of Bonners Ferry, Idaho. Moyie Falls Dam holds back the river a few miles from the Kootenai. The spectacular gorge below the dam, which can be seen from US 2, is the view most people have of the river.

This trip starts a mile south of the Canada border and follows the river about 12 shady miles. The half-day trip is interspersed with rapids that can reach Class 2 at high water. Boaters will scrape and bounce through innumerable rock gardens when the flow is much less than 500 cubic feet per second. Camping is available at the put-in and 4 miles downstream from the take-out at the Meadow Creek Campground.

The Snyder Guard Station offers an ideal alternative to camping, for families or larger groups lucky enough to snag a reservation through the Bonners Ferry Ranger Station. Competition is fierce among those wanting to rent the 1908 ranger house, which was declared a historic landmark in 1982. The house and property are on river left, and make a fine, alternative take-out, 2 miles shy of Twin Bridges. Access is restricted to those with reservations, which come with the key to the gate that otherwise blocks entry from Meadow Creek Road.

Access. To reach the put-in from Bonners Ferry, Idaho, drive north about 30 miles on US 95. Turn right onto FR 2517, a gravel road that leads about a mile to Copper Creek Campground. A short carry leads to the river.

To reach the take-out from Copper Creek, drive 3 miles south on US 95 to Meadow Creek Road (FR 221). Follow Meadow Creek Road 6 miles to Twin Bridges, where the paved road becomes gravel. Look for a good take-out on the south side of the river, between the bridge for cars and its companion for trains.

Paddle Route. The Moyie is a classic mountain stream: cold, clear, shallow, and shaded with cedars and cottonwoods. Ospreys dive into its pools for cutthroat and hatchery-reared rainbow trout. Deer, elk, and other large mammals live along its banks.

Launching at the Cooper Creek campground, paddlers should be able to spot their first kingfisher before hitting the first set of mild rapids, about 1 river mile into the trip. There will be more, scattered throughout the 12 miles, their intensity varying along with the flow of the river. Three bridges (including one railroad bridge) are within 2 miles of each other, starting about 3 river miles into the trip. Once past that trio, there are no more bridges until the (aptly named) Twin Bridges take-out.

Summer low flows on the Moyie River

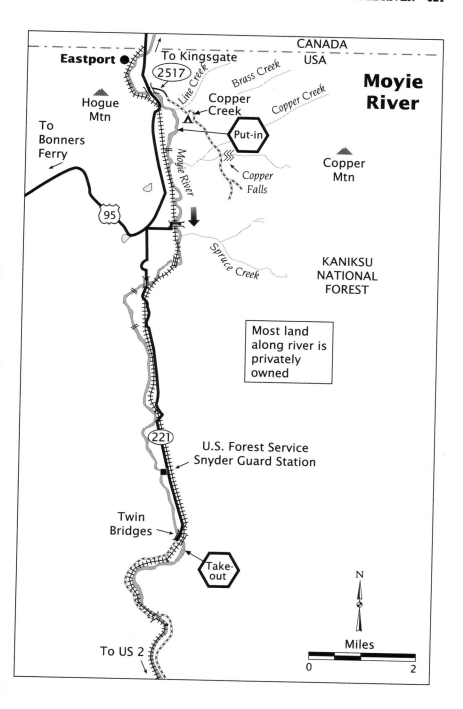

Moyie River

CANADA
USA

Eastport ●

To Kingsgate
2517

Line Creek

Brass Creek

Copper Creek

Copper Creek

Hogue Mtn

To Bonners Ferry

Moyie River

95

Copper Falls

Spruce Creek

Copper Mtn

KANIKSU NATIONAL FOREST

Most land along river is privately owned

221

U.S. Forest Service Snyder Guard Station

Twin Bridges

Take-out

To US 2

N

Miles

0   2

Below Twin Bridges the river gets progressively more technical, with Class 2+ whitewater in the 7 miles between the bridges and Meadow Creek Campground. Beginning and intermediate paddlers should end their trip at the bridges. By no means should they go beyond the campground, where the river becomes a playground for experienced whitewater paddlers.

The U.S. Forest Service held a series of meetings in 1975 to consider protecting the Moyie under the Wild and Scenic Rivers Act. Opposition from landowners was overwhelming, and the river remains unprotected. With the notable exception of the Snyder Guard Station, nearly all shoreline along this trip is private, and is dotted with cabins, houses, and "For Sale" signs. So far, the development does not detract from the journey.

86 Upper Priest Lake

Location: From Beaver Creek Campground
Distance: 6 to 12 miles round-trip
Paddle time: 4 hours or overnight
Season: Generally May through November
Rating: Flatwater
Hazards: Wind; occasional law-breaking powerboaters
Shuttle: None
Maps: USGS Priest Lake NE, Caribou Creek, Upper Priest Lake; Kaniksu National Forest map
Information: Idaho Panhandle National Forests, Priest Lake Ranger Station near Nordman; Idaho State Parks, Priest Lake State Park

Numerous options make this trip suitable for anyone from power paddlers to families heading for a day trip or campout at a North Idaho gem. By land, access to Upper Priest Lake is limited to muscle power. No roads lead to the 3.5-mile-long lake; no private development is allowed. This has left the lakeshore virtually pristine.

Unfortunately, the commotion of the larger Priest Lake creeps into Upper Priest because powerboats are allowed to motor up the 3-mile Thorofare separating the two lakes. Ironically, powerboaters flock to the upper lake on summer weekends to escape the madness on the big lake. Without restrictions on powerboats, the upper lake will ultimately be inundated with the noise, speed, and parties that plague other boating waters.

Meanwhile, Upper Priest Lake continues to be a premier paddling destination. Go in late spring and early fall for the best shot at solitude. During summer, the most pleasant paddling is on weekdays. But even on weekends, canoeists and kayakers can find themselves alone in paradise by paddling early in the morning and late in the day, when powerboat traffic is mostly gone.

Upper Priest Lake sand beach at Geisingers campsite

Heavy flow down The Thorofare from Upper Priest during runoff periods in April and May can make upstream paddling difficult. By late June, flows are barely perceptible.

Access. From Priest River, Idaho, drive 37 miles north on SR 57 to Nordman. Bear right onto paved FR 1339 toward Reeder Bay. Pass Reeder Bay Campground. From the Ledgewood picnic area, where the road number changes to 2512, continue north nearly 2 miles and turn into the Forest Service campground at Beaver Creek. Follow the signs to the lake access and put in on Priest Lake, or bear left and follow signs to the trailhead for Navigation Trail 291 and the 1000-foot portage trail to The Thorofare. Launching directly into The Thorofare is a good option (also shorter) should high winds develop and make the open water of Priest Lake dangerous to paddle.

This trip also can begin at Lions Head Campground, accessible from the east side of Priest Lake. From SR 57 at the south end of Priest Lake, turn east at Dickensheet Junction (see Trip 87). Go to Coolin, Idaho, and then drive about 24

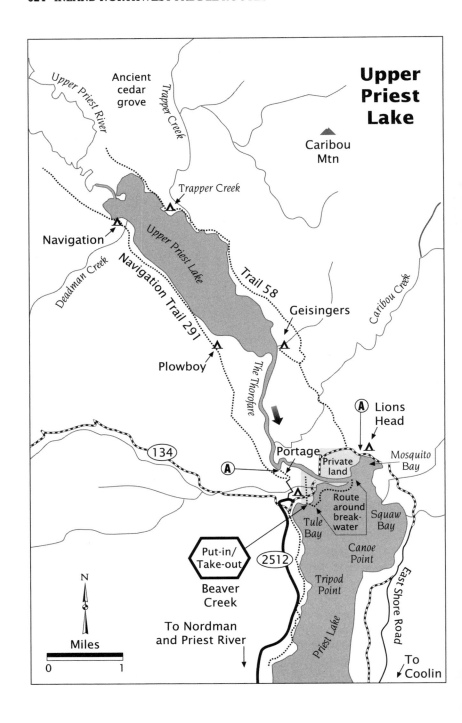

Upper Priest River

Ancient cedar grove

Trapper Creek

Upper Priest Lake

Caribou Mtn

Trapper Creek

Navigation

Upper Priest Lake

Trail 58

Deadman Creek

Navigation Trail 291

Caribou Creek

Geisingers

Plowboy

The Thorofare

Lions Head

Mosquito Bay

134

Portage

Private land

Route around break-water

Squaw Bay

Put-in/Take-out

Tule Bay

2512

Canoe Point

Beaver Creek

Tripod Point

Priest Lake

East Shore Road

To Nordman and Priest River

N

Miles

0   1

To Coolin

miles north on East Shore Road. The last few miles to the campground are gravel. The campground, managed by Priest Lake State Park, is less developed than others around the lake. RVs are discouraged by small sites and no power hookups.

Paddle Route. From the boat launch or from the sandy beach at Beaver Creek, paddle around the point toward the north end of Priest Lake. If the water is calm, set your sights on the right (east) end of the wooden breakwater fence in the distance. Turn left around the end of the breakwater pilings. The water is shallow with a sandy bottom here in Mosquito Bay. Paddle westward parallel to the fence. (*Note:* Should rough water arise unexpectedly, you can portage 100 feet over a sand spit at the west end of the wooden breakwater fence.) Continue west, paddling through a short gauntlet of private homes and into the entrance of The Thorofare. Here, thank God, development ends.

The Thorofare, generally protected by wind, adds a riverlike feeling to this flatwater trip. Powerboats are supposed to go up The Thorofare at no-wake speed. The narrow waterway is lined with brush and trees, offering only a few spots to comfortably pull onto shore. At summer levels, however, you can find numerous mud bars. The first place to get out and really stretch muscles is at the beach in front of Geisingers Campground at the outlet of Upper Priest Lake. Expect this popular campsite to be occupied.

The lake has three other pleasant semideveloped Forest Service campgrounds with outhouses. About ten undeveloped campsites have been hacked out along a shoreline that is generally too steep for camping. These sites, mostly on the east shore, range from solo-tent size to expansive enough for several tents. Sanitation can be a problem at these sites, since the steep terrain discourages some people from going as far from camp as they should for personal latrines. Upper Priest Lake is gin-clear, but bring your home-filled water containers, or be equipped with purification devices, as water from the lake or streams should always be treated before consumption.

The lake offers good options for hiking. Campgrounds at the west side of Upper Priest provide access to explore the shoreline on Navigation Trail 291. From Geisingers Campground, you can hook up with a trail that leads back to Lions Head Campground. The Trapper Creek Campground gives access to a trail that leads northwest along the lakeshore, past an old cabin site, and north to a forest of ancient cedars. If you prefer to do your exploring by boat, paddle to the northwest end of the lake and poke upstream as far as you can into the Upper Priest River.

Upper Priest Lake is in a Panhandle National Forests scenic area somewhat protected from chain saws. The Salmo–Priest Wilderness lies to the northwest. The watershed is home to a who's who of the region's endangered species, including mountain caribou, wolves, grizzly bears, and bull trout. Mycologists know the area for its abundance and variety of mushrooms: more than 1000 documented species.

87 Priest River

Location: Dickensheet to McAbee Falls
Distance: 25 miles (15 miles to Big Bend)
Paddle time: 12 hours or overnight (8 hours to Big Bend)
Season: Generally May through June; October
Rating: Class 1, with one Class 2 rapid
Hazards: Downed trees
Shuttle: 26 miles, pavement
Flow information: Avista Utilities or USGS Idaho website
River gauge: 12395000 near the town of Priest River
Historic flows: Average 1503 cfs; maximum 10,400; minimum 191
Maps: USGS Coolin, Outlet Bay, Prater Mountain; Kaniksu National Forest map
Information: Idaho Panhandle National Forests, Priest Lake Ranger Station near Nordman

Priest Lake is the jewel of North Idaho, set amid cedar and pine forests at the base of the craggy Selkirk crest. But while the lake is lined with cabins and resorts, and noisy with powerboats, the river that flows from the lake provides quiet paddling. Most land to the west of the Priest River is managed by the U.S. Forest Service; most on the east is the Priest Lake State Forest. Thus, development is limited to pockets of private land.

Autumn is prime time on the river. Each year, typically starting in mid-October, Avista Utilities company begins drawing down Priest Lake to make room for runoff that will refill the lake six months later. Water spills over Outlet Dam and into the river, creating ideal paddling just as fall colors peak. The mosquitoes are gone. Fall visitors may spot beavers that build dams on many of the creeks flowing into the river, or wood ducks that thrive on the ponds. The drawdown does not always occur like clockwork, and paddlers should contact Avista before committing to a trip.

The Priest River flows 44 miles from Priest Lake to its confluence with the Pend Oreille River. This trip is 25 miles long, with the option of shortening it by 10 miles.

Access. Those planning an overnight trip should leave a vehicle at the McAbee Falls take-out before driving to the put-in at Dickensheet Campground. To reach McAbee, drive north on SR 57 from the town of Priest River, Idaho. Turn right at 3.5 miles, and follow Peninsula Road about 5 miles to the river. Misnamed McAbee Falls is a Class 1+ rapid that starts under the bridge. The take-out is on the downstream side of the bridge, on river left.

To reach the put-in, drive north on SR 57 an additional 20 miles past Peninsula Road. Turn right at Dickensheet Junction, onto Coolin Road. In less than a mile,

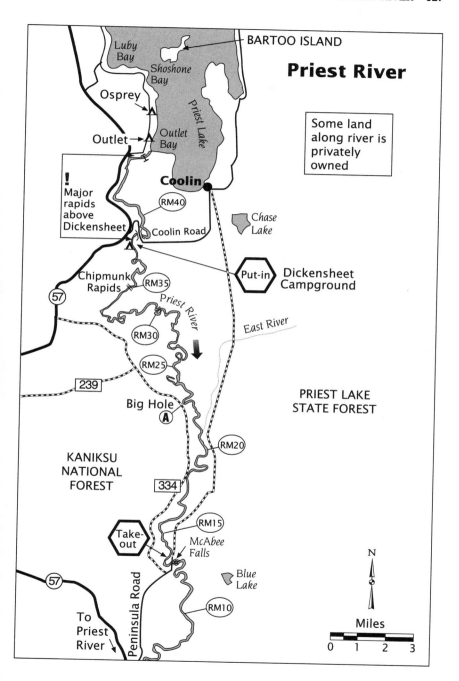

Luby Bay

Shoshone Bay

— BARTOO ISLAND

Priest River

Osprey

Priest Lake

Outlet Bay

Outlet

| Some land
along river is
privately
owned |

Coolin

RM40

Chase Lake

! Major rapids above Dickensheet

Coolin Road

Put-in Dickensheet Campground

Chipmunk Rapids

RM35

57

Priest River

RM30

East River

RM25

239

PRIEST LAKE STATE FOREST

Big Hole
Ⓐ

RM20

KANIKSU NATIONAL FOREST

334

Take-out

RM15

McAbee Falls

Blue Lake

57

RM10

N

Peninsula Road

To Priest River

Miles

0   1   2   3

Paddling after the first October snow on the Priest River

Coolin Road crosses the Priest River at state-owned Dickensheet Campground. Boaters can park in the campground close to the river.

For a single day on the river, paddlers should launch at Dickensheet Campground (RM 38.5) and take out at a spot called Big Hole, at RM 23.5.

To reach Big Hole from Priest River, follow Peninsula Road until just before McAbee Falls, then turn west onto FR 334. This dirt road, which is rough in places, weaves through the forest on the west side of the river, coming into sight of the water only occasionally. About 7 miles from Peninsula Road, a big bend in the river is visible from the road. There is room to park a car or two. A faint and steep trail leads about 100 yards to the river. (Drivers who miss this take-out will come to a cluster of houses in about a mile.) Two miles past Big Hole, Road 334 joins FR 239. SR 57 is another 5 miles beyond the junction, and from there it is 4.5 miles to Dickensheet Junction.

Hike to the river at Big Hole before starting a trip. Note a few landmarks at this take-out, which is as easy to miss from the water as it is from the road.

Paddle Route. Chipmunk Rapids (RM 35.5), about 3 miles downstream from Dickensheet, is the only significant whitewater of the trip. Little maneuvering is required, and the rapids should not pose a problem for intermediate paddlers. About 10 miles into the trip, the river begins a series of oxbows in a broad valley of private grazing land. Boaters will pass perhaps a dozen houses, cabins, and shacks before once again coming into public forest. Downstream from Big Hole, the river is mostly flat and meandering.

Several good campsites are downstream from Chipmunk Rapids, but campers must pay close attention to the Forest Service map to assure that they are on public, rather than private, land.

In the early twentieth century, the Priest River gained fame among anglers as the place to fill a creel with native cutthroat trout. Logging filled the stream with silt, and the decline was furthered by Outlet Dam, which causes the river to run low and warm in summer. Although the Priest still has the look of a prime trout stream, the fishing doesn't match the promise.

88 Pack River

Location: US 95 to Mouth
Distance: 4 to 23 miles
Paddle time: 8 to 12 hours
Season: Generally April through October
Rating: Class 1 and flatwater
Hazards: Tight turns; strainers, logjams; wind at Pack River Flats
Shuttle: 14 miles, pavement
Flow information: USGS stopped gauge readings near Colburn in 1992
Historic flows: Average not available; maximum 4330 cfs; minimum 36
Maps: USGS Colburn, Elmira, Oden Bay, Trout Peak; Kaniksu National Forest map
Information: Pack River General Store northeast of Sandpoint

The Pack River begins in northern Idaho's best alpine scenery along the crest of the Selkirk Mountains near Chimney Rock and Harrison Peak. It flows 45 miles before unloading into Lake Pend Oreille, one of Idaho's world-class freshwater destinations. Along the way, humans have left some disappointing clear-cuts and ill-advised roads. The small native cutthroat trout found high in the watershed do not do well lower in the drainage. But paddlers can find some wild moments.

The upper river, which starts in the Kaniksu National Forest, is narrow and swift. Skilled kayakers can find room to play in portions of the upper river when the flows are sufficient. Lower in the drainage, where the river becomes tame enough for average canoeists, most of the shoreline is privately owned. By putting

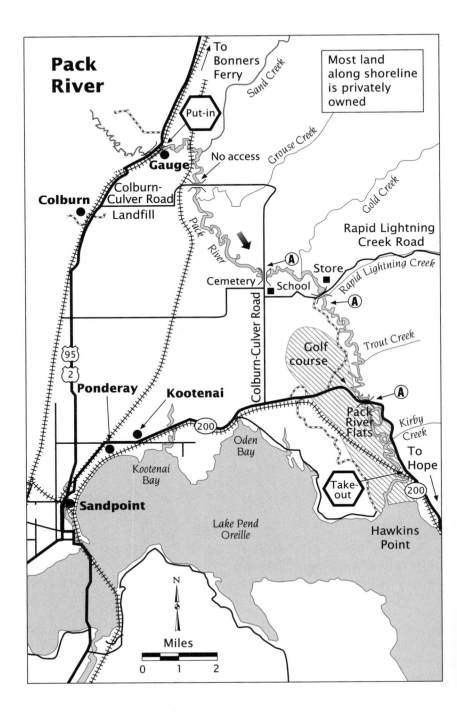

Pack River

Most land along shoreline is privately owned

in at bridges off Pack River Road, paddlers can find lively water roughly from Tavern Creek downstream to US 95. That section usually has enough water for paddling in June, but the flows can become too low in July. Be aware that the river upstream from US 95 has some tight turns that are prone to dangerous logjams.

The river from US 95 downstream to the mouth is the most accommodating to paddlers, offering several options for customizing the length of the trip. Paddle the entire 22.5 miles, or break it up into half-day segments.

Access. From the junction with SR 200 north of Sandpoint, drive north on US 2/95 nearly 10 miles to the put-in and unimproved parking area on the east side of the highway just north of the Pack River bridge (milepost 485.8).

To reach the take-out, backtrack south on US 2/95 about 2 miles. Turn east onto Colburn–Culver Road (milepost 483.7) and drive 6 miles (east then south) to a school. An optional take-out is at the bridge just before this school. To make this a 12.5-mile trip, go to the other optional take-out by turning left (east) at the school onto Rapid Lightning Creek Road. Drive 1.5 miles to a take-out on the east side of the Pack River bridge next to the fire station. Do not block the fire station driveway.

To reach the mouth of the Pack River, continue south from the school on Colburn–Culver Road for 2.8 miles to the junction with SR 200. (This junction is at milepost 36 for paddlers coming from Sandpoint on SR 200.) Head east on the highway and drive 4.8 miles, past a golf course and across the river, to a dirt road (milepost 40.8) that leads down from the highway to the shore at Pack River Flats near a railroad dike.

Other optional take-outs are at SR 200 on the east side of the Pack River bridge (milepost 38.8) and at several pullouts off SR 200 along Pack River Flats.

Paddle Route. This lazy, winding tour through forested meadows can be negotiated by paddlers with modest skills in a wide range of flow levels. The trip goes quickly with higher flows in May and June. Lower flows can make for a long day. Although surrounding land is mostly private, sand and gravel bars offer options for stopping, swimming, or picnicking below the high-water mark. The trip offers a good chance of seeing wildlife, including

Pack River at SR 200 bridge

beavers, bald eagles, ospreys, moose, deer, wood ducks, and spotted sandpipers bobbing their tails along shore.

Once under the railroad trestle from the put-in, paddlers enter what is, although short, the wildest stretch of this trip. In the first 2 miles, the river bends around a forested knob. Cedars lean over the water. The conifer forest gradually gives way to cottonwood bottoms under attack by beavers. Cabins and homes crop up increasingly along the river, but detract little from the experience.

Float 3.7 miles to the first Colburn–Culver Road bridge, where there is no easy or legal access. After a long, straight stretch downstream from the bridge, the river meanders become very tight. Paddle past one side of a house; ten minutes later, you paddle past the other side of the same house. Pass the optional access at the second Colburn–Culver Road bridge 9.8 miles from the start, near the school. The lazy nature of the stream can lull paddlers. Always watch ahead for obstructions.

From the Rapid Lightning Road bridge, another good access, paddlers drift into prime moose country and past several sloughs worth investigating for waterfowl, ospreys, and other creatures. Cattle also graze here. In midsummer, sandbars can be wide and grass tall along the banks. Hidden in the brush are the mouths of tributary streams, including Trout Creek.

A rough, rocky take-out is at the SR 200 bridge. But the nearly 4 miles of flatwater paddling through Pack River Flats is pleasant, with a good chance of seeing more birds and wildlife. Paddlers generally can follow the river channel, or blaze a trail over the flats, which are flooded when the level of Lake Pend Oreille is high. Scout the flats from the road when shuttling cars.

89 Clark Fork River Delta

Location: From Johnson Creek access
Distance: Up to 7 miles round-trip
Paddle time: 4 to 6 hours
Season: Virtually year-round
Rating: Flatwater with some upstream paddling
Hazards: Deadheads; paddling upstream against stiff current in high flows; wind off Lake Pend Oreille
Shuttle: None
Flow information: Cabinet Gorge Dam
Historic flows: Average 22,410 cfs; maximum 153,000; minimum 3000
Maps: USGS Clark Fork
Information: Sandpoint Chamber of Commerce

Sea kayakers and canoeists alike will enjoy this loop tour with its fascinating combination of flowing and still waters at the northeast end of Lake Pend Oreille.

Where the Clark Fork Delta meets Lake Pend Oreille

After surging out of Cabinet Gorge Dam, the river eventually braids into three branches called the North, Middle, and South forks. The route described here has several shorter options or variations through these forks in an area informally managed as the Pend Oreille State Wildlife Management Area.

Attractions include the numerous undeveloped islands, and coves and inlets left as havens for a wide range of wildlife—including deer, mink, ospreys, bald eagles, waterfowl, and numerous songbirds. Fall foliage is an attraction in itself.

Access. From Sandpoint, Idaho, drive 25 miles east on SR 200 to the town of Clark Fork (milepost 55). At the east end of Clark Fork, turn south on Stevens Road. Cross the railroad tracks and bear left on the paved road. Immediately after crossing a bridge over the main-stem river, turn right. Drive 2.5 miles on Johnson Creek Road. At the Y with FR 278, bear right to get to the put-in at Johnson Creek access.

Paddle Route. Be prepared for changing conditions. Water levels on this route are affected downlake by Albeni Falls Dam, which can cause Lake Pend Oreille to fluctuate up to 11 feet during the year. The Clark Fork River is controlled by several upstream dams, including Cabinet Gorge, built in 1952. In midsummer, the dam can shut down to minimum allowable flows of 3000 cubic feet per second—plenty low enough to make portions of this route shallow and rocky, especially near two bridges at the upstream entrance to the South Fork. The minimum flows typically occur at night, when there is less demand for power. Scout the river channel from the road on the way to the put-in.

Some paddlers will shrug off low water as a good excuse to climb out of the boat and use fishing rods, since the waters hold trout, bass, and squawfish.

Follow the recommended route clockwise, heading downstream from the put-in. A rock beach at the mouth of the South Fork is a good picnic spot or campsite. If big winds develop, simply turn tail back into the protected waters of the South Fork.

The rest of the route is fairly easy, depending on your paddling skills, wind conditions, and river flows. For instance, on a typical June day, the flow of the

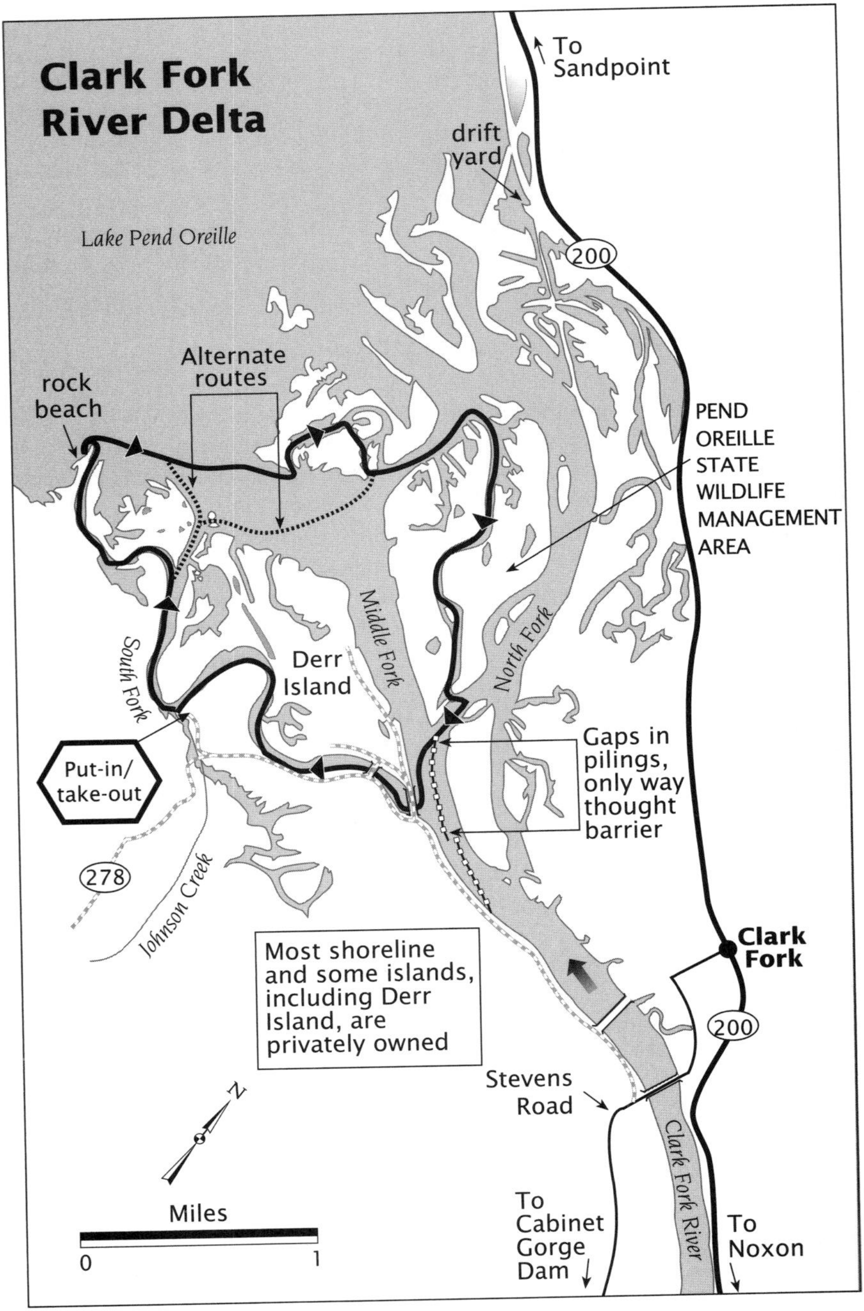

Clark Fork River Delta

To Sandpoint

drift yard

Lake Pend Oreille

200

Alternate routes

rock beach

PEND OREILLE STATE WILDLIFE MANAGEMENT AREA

South Fork

Middle Fork

North Fork

Derr Island

Put-in/ take-out

278

Johnson Creek

Gaps in pilings, only way thought barrier

Most shoreline and some islands, including Derr Island, are privately owned

Clark Fork

200

Stevens Road

Clark Fork River

N

Miles

0   1

To Cabinet Gorge Dam

To Noxon

Clark Fork River out of Cabinet Gorge Dam can be 33,000 cfs at noon, providing significant but not overwhelming current in the South Fork. By 5:00 PM, the river flow out of the dam may increase to 52,000 cfs, leaving the South Fork still reasonably easy to negotiate upstream. However, some paddlers might have difficulty navigating those flows against the stronger current in the upper Middle Fork.

The map shows two of several possible alternate routes to shorten the trip and avoid the Middle Fork.

When Albeni Falls Dam went online in 1955, much of the Clark Fork Delta area was purchased by the U.S. Army Corps of Engineers and turned over to the Idaho Fish and Game Department. However, portions of Derr Island and most of the islands west of the river mouth are private land. This route passes numerous hidden coves worth exploring, plus goose nesting platforms usually occupied in early May.

Pilings in the Middle Fork are designed to divert logs and other river debris to a drift yard at the end of the North Fork upstream from Hope. The drift yard is part of a project funded by Albeni Falls that collects about 10 acres of driftwood each year and prevents it from floating into Lake Pend Oreille.

Sightseers can follow the access road upstream to Cabinet Gorge Fish Hatchery. The hatchery normally is open to visitors during the day. The main attraction is in late fall, when returning kokanee are captured and stripped of eggs for propagation. Guided canoe and sea kayaking trips may be offered in this area.

90 Coeur d'Alene River I (Upper)

Location: Enaville to Old Mission State Park
Distance: 9 to 14 miles
Paddle time: 1.5 to 3 hours
Season: Virtually year-round
Rating: Class 1; some Class 2 possible
Hazards: Some sharp bends; strainers
Shuttle: 7 miles, pavement
Flow information: USGS Idaho website
River gauge: 12413500 at Cataldo
Historic flows: Average 2499 cfs; maximum 50,000; minimum 141
Maps: USGS Cataldo; Coeur d'Alene National Forest map
Information: Enaville Resort at Enaville; Idaho Panhandle National Forests, Coeur d'Alene River Ranger District, Fernan office; Idaho State Parks, Old Mission State Park

Drifting down the clear water, along the timbered shores of this stretch, a paddler might find it hard to imagine the dichotomies that history has brought together in the Coeur d'Alene River: native cutthroat trout against insensitive logging and mining; the long-gone Snakepit brothel at Enaville, Idaho, against the still-standing Jesuit Indian mission near Cataldo. Legacies good and bad live here. Be sure to visit Old Mission State Park, but don't swim or play in the dirt at the Mission Flats take-out. The area is contaminated with heavy metals from a century of Silver Valley mining.

Flows in this section of the Coeur d'Alene River typically are high enough for paddling most of the year. Exceptions to the rule include low flows during occasional weeks of extreme cold temperatures in winter and dry weather in late August or September. Also, the brief period of winter or spring flooding makes the river unsafe. Normally, however, the river gets a Class 1 rating, with no serious rapids.

The river from Enaville to Cataldo generally parallels roads, but swings away for stretches of solitude. The paved Trail of the Coeur d'Alenes also parallels this stretch, offering bike shuttle options. The river holds splashy riffles for play, plus a few tight turns to test paddling skills. The water is clear most

Coeur d'Alene River near Cataldo Mission

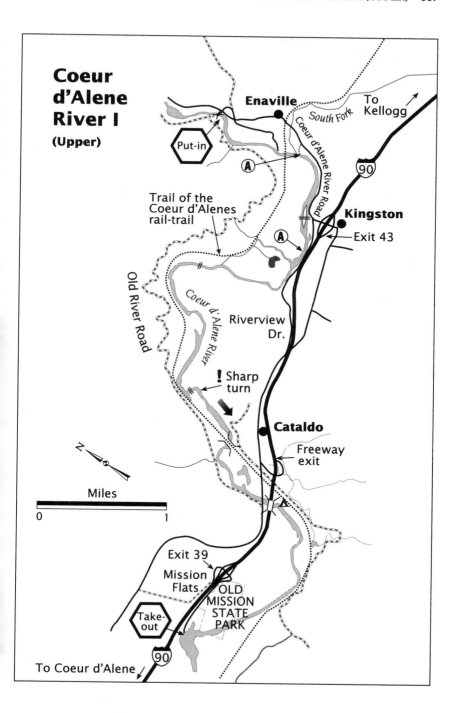

Coeur d'Alene River I
(Upper)

Enaville
South Fork
To Kellogg
Coeur d'Alene River Road
Put-in
Ⓐ
I-90
Trail of the Coeur d'Alenes rail-trail
Ⓐ
Kingston
Exit 43
Old River Road
Coeur d'Alene River
Riverview Dr.
❗ Sharp turn
Cataldo
Freeway exit
N
Miles
0   1
Exit 39
Mission Flats
OLD MISSION STATE PARK
Take-out
I-90
To Coeur d'Alene

of the year, with the bottom visible even in deeper holes. The area is prized for cutthroat trout.

The river begins near the divide that separates the drainage from Lake Pend Oreille. It flows 113 miles, collecting more water from the North Fork and South Fork before emptying into Lake Coeur d'Alene at Harrison, Idaho.

Access. To reach the take-out from I-90 between Coeur d'Alene and Kellogg, Idaho, take Exit 39, 1 mile west of Cataldo, toward Old Mission State Park. Go nearly a mile, following the frontage road paralleling I-90, past the historic Cataldo Mission, to the Mission Flats boat ramp.

To reach the put-in from the Old Mission Park exit, drive east on I-90 about 4 miles and turn off on Kingston Exit 43. Head north on Coeur d'Alene River Road, pass Enaville Resort, and be prepared to turn right on Old River Road at 2 miles from I-90. Bear left at the Y and cross the bridge over the Coeur d'Alene River. The put-in is near a tavern. Paddlers who leave vehicles on or near private property should always ask permission and get directions to preferred parking areas. A good alternate access is at the South Fork confluence.

Paddle Route. This stretch of the river is popular with swimmers and floating vessels of all types on hot summer weekends, but is virtually unused from fall through spring. Notable tricky spots include the standing waves and a sudden turn just after the river bends north away from Coeur d'Alene River Road. Also be on guard for the turbulence at a rock wall where the river turns 90 degrees to the right, shortly before flowing under I-90. This spot is easily avoided with a short portage if desired.

The last straight stretch to the Mission Flats take-out moves slowly, since it's on the verge of slack water backed up from Lake Coeur d'Alene.

The river's worst floods have been caused by rain-on-snow events during winter; for example, 79,000 cubic feet per second during the flood of 1974 and 40,000 cfs during floods in 1996 and 1997. However, high average runoff tends to be around 7000 cfs at Enaville for about two weeks between late April and early June. The lowest average flows tend to be around 145 cfs in August or September. Floating the river is a no-brainer at 2500 to 3500 cfs.

To extend this trip by about 5 miles, drive north on the Coeur d'Alene River Road to the turnoff to Bumblebee Campground. After crossing the bridge over the river, drive downstream, looking for undeveloped access points. The river offers good paddling farther upstream, almost to the confluence with Tepee Creek, when flows are adequate. The river is tighter and more technical in its upper stretches, as well as more susceptible to logjams. By sometime in July, the river gets too low for floating above Shoshone Creek.

This trip includes plenty of gravel beaches for stopping and picnicking. Although most surrounding land is managed by the Panhandle National Forest, much of the lower river area is privately owned. Several Forest Service campgrounds are along the river upstream from Prichard, which has limited services.

91 Coeur d'Alene River II (Lower)

Location: Killarney Lake to Harrison
Distance: 16 miles
Paddle time: 1 long day or overnight
Season: Generally March through December
Rating: Flatwater
Hazards: Powerboats; deadheads; wind; soil contamination from mine waste; hunting
Shuttle: 30 miles, pavement
Lake level information: Avista Utilities
Normal summer pool level: 2128 feet
Maps: USGS Lane, Medimont, Black Lake, Harrison; Coeur d'Alene National Forest map; Trail of the Coeur d'Alenes map
Information: Idaho Panhandle National Forests, Coeur d'Alene River Ranger District, Fernan office; Bureau of Land Management; Idaho Fish and Game (all in Coeur d'Alene); Friends of Coeur d'Alene Trails

Swarms of perch, crappie, and bass easily support predators that hunt this area from the air and underwater, as well as from boats. Ospreys, great blue herons, and waterfowl, including grebes and good numbers of wood ducks, are your constant companions on this grand sprawl of lakes and marshlands along the lower Coeur d'Alene River. Toothy northern pike lurk in the weedy shallows.

The Trail of the Coeur d'Alenes, a wonderful paved rail-trail, parallels this trip, providing options for enhancing the experience with bicycling.

The river channel is flanked by numerous wetlands and eight lakes that boaters can reach through narrow causeways. Slack water from Lake Coeur d'Alene virtually eliminates current in the lower river for much of the year. Paddlers willing to apply muscle power can customize numerous variations of this trip for a rewarding fishing or wildlife-viewing experience. The area bustles with wild creatures, including mink, muskrats, beaver, and shorebirds. Tundra swans migrate through in spring and fall, with the largest concentrations in March.

Be warned, however, that waste from the Wallace-Kellogg mining districts in the Silver Valley has been washing downstream for a century to coat the floodplain. Do not allow children to play in the benign-looking sand along the shores. Soils here are contaminated with heavy metals, including lead and zinc. After spring runoff, the metals seem to lock into the lake-bottom sediment, leaving the water safe for swimming. Boating in this area or even occasional forays onto the shores are not likely to harm people who exercise reasonable caution.

The wildlife reminds us that all is not well. Biologists have found the carcasses

Osprey with lunch on lower Coeur d'Alene River

of swans and other waterfowl dead from lead poisoning after consuming the roots of vegetation growing from the sediment.

Access. To reach the put-in from I-90 between Coeur d'Alene and Kellogg, Idaho, take Exit 34 toward Rose Lake. Go south on SR 3 about 5 miles and turn right onto Killarney Lake Road. Drive 3.5 miles to the Killarney Lake boat launch and campground, managed by the U.S. Bureau of Land Management.

To reach the take-out, go back to SR 3 and continue southwest about 17 miles to the junction with SR 97 (Harrison Road). Turn north and drive 7 miles to Harrison. The take-out is at the marina boat launch below the city park. Leave vehicles away from the resort area on a side street. Parking spaces are needed for the small town's businesses. It is only a short walk from the launch uphill to virtually anywhere in town.

Harrison is accessible from the south via Moscow and US 95. The take-out also can be reached from the north by turning off I-90 at Wolf Lodge Exit 22 and driving a tedious 28 miles south on curvy SR 97.

Use the Coeur d'Alene National Forest map for navigating to several other public access points along the lower Coeur d'Alene River, including: (1) Rainy Hill Campground and boat launch, managed by Panhandle National Forests at Medimont off SR 3. (2) Black Lake Resort boat launch off SR 3. (3) Thompson Lake boat launch, managed by the Idaho Fish and Game Department, on Thompson Lake Road northeast of Harrison.

Other river accesses can be found upstream from Killarney Lake at the town of Rose Lake and at Cataldo Mission. But the river from Killarney to Cataldo Mission is fairly featureless. Incidentally, the mission boat access area was the turn-around point for wooden ferries that once hauled timber up the river for the Silver Valley mines.

Paddle Route. The campground at 480-acre Killarney Lake is not inviting, as it shares tight quarters with the commotion of boat launching and parking. The first island north of the Killarney launch is largely private land, but farther north on the lake, Popcorn Island has a boat-in campsite with outhouses.

The first challenge for paddlers is finding the channel out of Killarney. The causeway is the largest of all the entries to the lakes along the river. But as you look southwest from the launch, the channel is hidden by a spit and expanses of tubular jointed vegetation standing tall like green stubble along the lakeshore. The dominant plant of the marshes is called equisetum, better known as horsetail. It has no food value for wildlife, but probably provides cover for waterfowl broods and warmwater fish. Look carefully across these marshes for the contrasting bright head of a great blue heron, the stealthy fish hunter of the waterways.

Idaho Fish and Game workers have planted wild rice, which flourishes in the marsh between Killarney and Hidden Lake. Waterfowl flock to the rice when the grain matures around the first of September.

Rather than using river miles, mileage for the tour described here begins at the Killarney launch and runs down the river. Paddlers can add miles and days to the trip, depending on how curious they are to explore the lateral lakes. After paddling from Killarney, turn west to head downstream on the Coeur d'Alene River. Points of interest include:

- **Rainy Hill** boat launch and RV campground, 4 miles on river left. Watch for the causeway that leads under a railroad trestle and concrete road bridge to Medicine Lake, 170 acres. Bear right and paddle under a larger bridge to reach Cave Lake and the scattering of buildings called Medimont. At 600 acres, Cave is the largest of the lakes along the lower river, but is shallow and loses much of its open water to weeds and marsh in summer. The lake has two resorts. (*Note:* Entry under the first road bridge to Medicine and Cave Lakes hinges on the pool elevation of Lake Coeur d'Alene. At spring levels above 2130 feet, clearance gets tight.)
- **Swan Lake**, 6.5 miles on river right. The entrance to this 370-acre lake appears out of nowhere on a broad treeless flat. The lake, with its rugged, roadless north shore, is one of the most isolated along the river, accessible only by boat. A rocky peninsula, which can become an island in high water, is state land with an undeveloped campsite.
- **Black Lake**, 8 miles on river left. Pass under a trestle, a favored swallow nest site, and up the causeway to the 350-acre lake, which has more homes than other lakes along the lower river. Water-skiing is popular. Public access is at a resort on the south shore, reached from Black Lake Road off SR 3.
- **Blue Lake**, 10.5 miles on river right. Surrounded by timbered private land, this 200-acre lake has remained undeveloped. But it's a target for water-skiers.
- **Thompson Lake**, 12.5 miles on river right. Pass a public boat launch as you head into this 400-acre lake, known for strict regulations to protect quality bass fishing. Some public land suitable for camping can be found on the lake's west arm, about half of which is marsh. Large floating islands can be found here, as well as stands of wild rice, which the Idaho Fish and

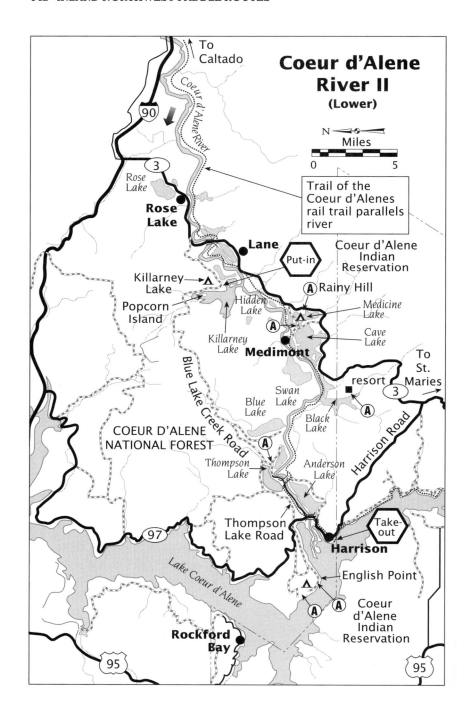

Coeur d'Alene River II (Lower)

Trail of the Coeur d'Alenes rail trail parallels river

Game Department leaves unharvested for the dining delight of waterfowl. From the boat access at the outlet, paddlers can walk through a cable gate to hike the dike road around Bare Marsh, a 200-acre wetland between Thompson and Blue Lakes.

- **Anderson Lake**, 15 miles on river left. The outlet to this 400-acre lake is just upstream from the SR 97 bridge over the Coeur d'Alene River. A road runs along the south shore.
- **Harrison**, 16 miles at river mouth. Buoys mark the river channel as it enters Lake Coeur d'Alene, but paddlers usually can take a shortcut through the shallow water, finding a direct route south to the marina at Harrison. Expect to see plenty of osprey activity here from spring through fall.

The best time to paddle along the lower Coeur d'Alene River during summer is early morning and late evening, when powerboat traffic is light and wildlife viewing is more pleasant. Prime time is before spring runoff in March and early April as well as September and early October, when few recreational boaters are on the water, and waterfowl migrations are in full swing. The stretch with the most remote feeling is between Swan and Blue Lakes.

The public boat ramps at Cataldo Mission, Killarney, Rainy Hill, and Thompson are popular staging areas for waterfowl hunters from mid-October into December.

Patches of public land, mostly on the north shore of the river, offer camping, picnicking, and hiking opportunities. Many boaters camp along the shores of the river, although some are tenting on private property. The Coeur d'Alene National Forest map is the best guide to the ample but scattered public land along the river.

Fishing in these lakes can be excellent for largemouth and smallmouth bass, perch, crappie, bullheads, and northern pike. Fishing regulations vary among the lakes.

92 St. Joe–Three Lakes

Location: Benewah Lake to Chatcolet
Distance: 5 to 10 miles
Paddle time: 2 hours
Season: Generally March through November
Rating: Flatwater
Hazards: Wind; powerboats; waterfowl hunting in October and November
Shuttle: 9 miles, pavement
Maps: USGS Benewah Lake, Black Lake, Chatcolet, Harrison; St. Joe National Forest map
Information: Idaho State Parks, Heyburn State Park near Chatcolet

A power plant on the Spokane River has created an unusual paddling experience 32 water miles away at the south end of Lake Coeur d'Alene. Construction of

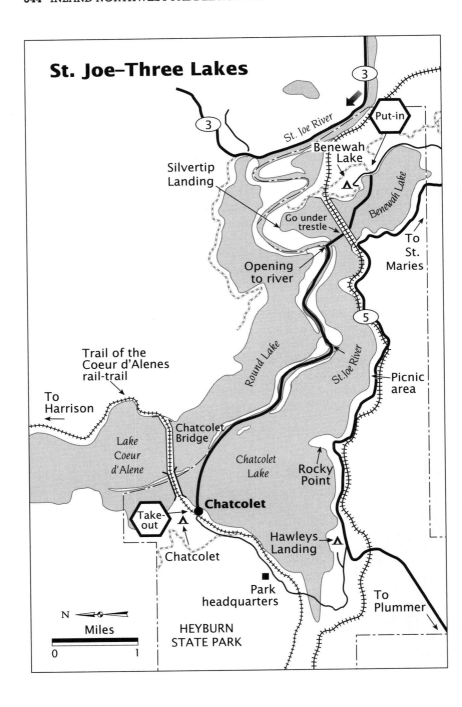

St. Joe–Three Lakes

Post Falls Dam in 1906 backed water through Lake Coeur d'Alene and raised the level of Chatcolet Lake to merge it with Round and Benewah lakes. However, the banks of the St. Joe are high enough to form a natural tree-lined levee that creates a river within the lakes.

Paddlers can enjoy an intimate visit with these final few miles of what is known as the Shadowy St. Joe, because of the shade offered by the cottonwoods lining the river. The entire route is within Heyburn State Park, the first state park to be designated in Idaho. Heyburn, the second largest of Idaho's state parks, totals 7825 acres; 2333 acres are water.

Access. This trip can be done in either direction. To reach the west access from US 95, drive east on SR 5 from Plummer, Idaho, for 6.5 miles and turn north onto the paved road toward Chatcolet. Go north 2.5 miles, passing Hawleys Landing Campground and Heyburn State Park headquarters, to a large boat launch and parking area.

To reach the east access, drive back to SR 5. Continue east 5.3 miles and turn north at a sign toward Benewah Lake Campground. (If coming from St. Maries, the turnoff is between mileposts 11 and 12.) Follow the paved road a mile to the resort, then bear left toward the campground. The boat launch is between the resort and the campground.

Paddle Route. Beginning from Benewah Lake, the route passes wild rice stands and then heads under a railroad trestle. Bear left along the cottonwood-studded banks of the St. Joe River. Look for an opening in the bank that allows

"River within a lake" at St. Joe River mouth

access to the river channel. Beware of powerboats and the occasional tug towing a raft of logs bound for area mills. Follow the channel northwest. Boathouses at Rocky Point make a good landmark. The destination, however, is the next cluster of boathouses farther north at Chatcolet.

The St. Joe, elevation 2125 feet at its mouth, is the world's highest navigable river, according to Idaho State Parks literature. Benewah Lake plus portions of Chatcolet and Round Lakes typically freeze by mid-December. Wild rice grows throughout marsh areas. The harvest is done by airboats starting in early September.

The lakes, marshes, rice, and river attract a variety of songbirds, plus larger-profile birds including herons, waterfowl, ospreys, and wild turkeys. Fish include bass, bluegills, crappies, perch, and squawfish, plus the occasional trout straying down from the cooler mountain waters of the upper St. Joe. Wildflowers are plentiful in spring.

Heyburn State Park is open year-round. Campgrounds, however, close late in November and reopen in April. Cabins are available at Benewah Lake Resort.

93 St. Joe River

Location: Avery Ranger Station to Calder, Idaho
Distance: 17 miles
Paddle time: 6 hours or overnight
Season: Generally June through mid-July
Rating: Class 2 above Marble Creek, Class 1 below
Hazards: Strainers, scattered rapids
Shuttle: 17 miles, mostly pavement
Flow information: USGS Idaho website
River gauge: 12414500 at Calder
Historic flows: Average 2324 cfs; maximum 40,000; minimum 100
Maps: USGS Wallace SE, Wallace SW, Calder SE, Calder SW; St. Joe National Forest map
Information: Idaho Panhandle National Forests, St. Joe River District, Avery office

Anyone who reads national fly-fishing magazines has heard of the St. Joe River. Cars with license plates from around the nation can be spotted at dusty pullouts along the upper river. From those rigs step anglers who search the river for wild westslope cutthroat trout.

While the catch-and-release fishing can be spectacular, it is not the only attraction on the St. Joe. Flowing 134 miles from the Bitterroot crest to Lake Coeur d'Alene, the river offers nearly every style of boating imaginable. Tour boats, ski boats, and tugs ply the slow, broad expanses near the river's mouth, while white-water kayakers ride Class 4 waves near its mountainous source. Between are many miles of river suitable for casual paddlers.

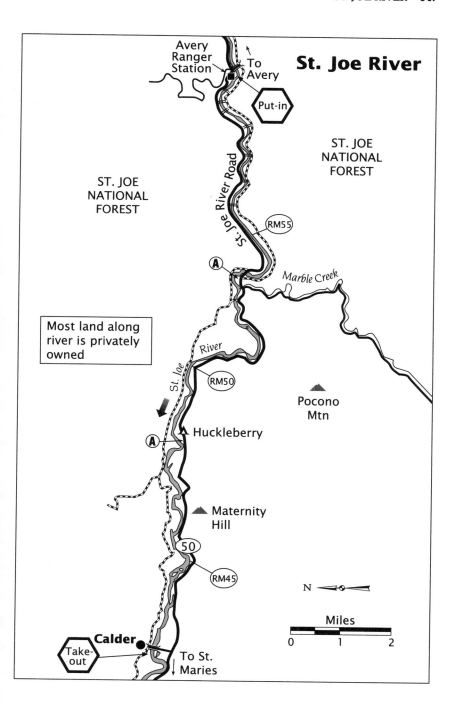

Paddling the St. Joe near Huckleberry Campground

This trip explores 17 miles of water starting at the Avery Ranger Station, about 6 miles downstream from the town of Avery. The trip can be shortened by using either of two alternative accesses. One eliminates most of the whitewater.

Access. Boaters going the entire distance should leave a car in Calder, Idaho. From St. Maries, drive north on SR 3 to the paved St. Joe River Road (FR 50) and turn right (east). After driving 23 miles up the river, turn left on Calder Road, which crosses the river in less than half a mile. The take-out is a rough boat ramp on the north side of the river.

The Avery Ranger Station put-in is 16.5 miles upstream from Calder. Turn right off the St. Joe River Road, then take an immediate left to a bridge across the river. The put-in is a steep and obvious trail just downstream from the bridge, on the north side of the river.

Boaters who want to shorten the trip will find good river access at the Huckleberry Campground, about 4 miles upstream from Calder.

A fourth access is about 9 miles upstream from Calder. Drivers headed east should watch for a dirt road about a half mile past Marble Creek, just before the St. Joe River Road crosses the river. The river is about 200 feet down this rough road.

Paddle Route. Most of the whitewater in this trip is between the ranger station and Marble Creek. Indeed, the upper stretch can be far too violent in spring for all but the most experienced boaters. Rapids are more scattered between Marble Creek and Huckleberry Campground, and are nearly nonexistent between the campground and Calder. The river is too low for canoeing when flows drop below 750 cubic feet per second, usually by August.

Among the common wildlife are ospreys and deer. Moose are less common. Houses and cabins, plus a few restaurants, are scattered along the shoreline.

Boaters who want to experience more of the river will find many other accesses in the 33 miles between Calder and Lake Coeur d'Alene. Powerboats may be encountered anywhere downstream from the town of St. Joe, and become common near St. Maries. The final 5-mile stretch is especially lovely (see Trip 92).

The farther upstream one heads from the Avery Ranger Station, the more severe the whitewater and the fewer the opportunities for casual boaters to enjoy safe paddling. Rapids in Skookum Canyon, a narrow chasm between Packsaddle and Turner Flat Campgrounds, range to Class 4. Tumble Down Falls, near the Conrad Crossing Campground, is a 6-foot drop preceded by several hundred yards of violent rapids.

Wilderness adventurers enjoy a short season on the 17 roadless miles of the St. Joe between Heller Creek and the Spruce Tree Campground. Here, the whitewater ranges to a remote and potentially deadly Class 5. Logjams are common. Spruce Tree Campground to Fly Flat, as well as Bluff Creek at the Road 509 bridge to Turner Flat Campground, are Class 2–3 stretches at 3000 to 4000 cfs in mid-June.

94 St. Maries River (Lower)

Location: St. Maries River Road to St. Maries
Distance: 7 miles
Paddle time: 2 to 3 hours
Season: March through November
Rating: Class 1
Hazards: Strainers, deadheads
Shuttle: 7 miles, pavement, gravel, dirt
Flow information: USGS Idaho website
River gauge: 12414900 near Santa, Idaho
Historic flows: Average 338 cfs; maximum 9120; minimum 25
Maps: USGS St. Maries; St. Joe National Forest map
Information: Idaho Panhandle National Forests, St. Joe River District, St. Maries office

North Idaho has no shortage of great boating water. The Selway, Salmon, Snake, and Moyie are revered by whitewater junkies everywhere. Canoeists ply the St. Joe, Priest, Coeur d'Alene, and Pack rivers. Powerboats cut Vs in the region's three large lakes.

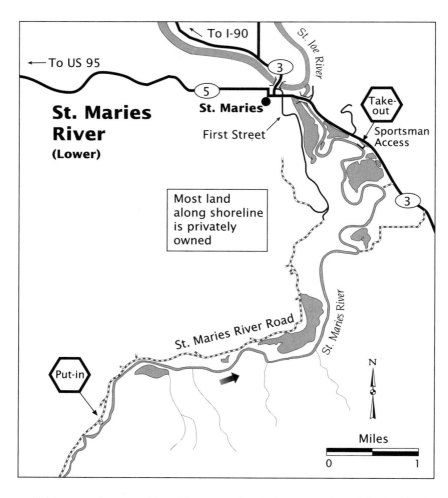

With so much competition, it's no wonder the lower portion of the St. Maries River is often overlooked. The river begins in the Grandmother Mountain area southeast of Clarkia, Idaho, and runs 44 miles before it empties into the St. Joe River at the town of St. Maries.

Sluggish and broad in its final miles, the lower river has nothing to offer whitewater enthusiasts. (But see Whitewater Trip 11 for a St. Maries River float that froth-water junkies will love.) Anglers can find better luck elsewhere. And while some powerboaters use the river, most stick to the larger St. Joe or nearby Lake Coeur d'Alene rather than risk bashing their boats against the deadheads that rise slightly above the surface or lurk just beneath it.

All the better for canoeists and kayakers, for whom the St. Maries offers a lazy drift through scenic bottomland forests and wetlands. Cedar trees shade the shoreline, sharing space with cottonwoods, aspen, and a variety of shrubs that offer brilliant displays in mid-October. The surrounding hills are evergreen forests dotted with western larch that turn yellow in fall. Waterfowl viewing is prime in spring, while rope swings tempt visitors in summer. Moose and beavers might be seen at any time.

Access. To reach the put-in from SR 3 (College Street) in the town of St. Maries, Idaho, drive south on First Street (behind the IGA store). Two miles from the highway, the road turns from pavement to gravel and gets progressively rougher. Drivers should keep track of railroad crossings. The put-in is nearly 6 miles from the highway, just past the fourth crossing. A very rough trail leads over the tracks to the river. Boaters driving anything but a high-clearance vehicle should avoid crossing the tracks and park in the turnout on the opposite side of the road.

The take-out is the St. Maries River Sportsman Access, a mile south of the town of St. Maries, on SR 3.

Paddle Route. High banks keep most of the scattered development hidden from view, but they also hide the herons hunting in the wetlands that line this meandering river. The steep banks limit options for a midtrip break since there are few places to beach a canoe. Most of the forests in the background are within the St. Joe National Forest, but most of the shoreline is privately owned.

Although this portion of the St. Maries is generally placid, it has moments of rebellion. The evidence includes the debris hanging from cedar branches well

Autumn paddling on the lower St. Maries River

above paddlers' heads. U.S. Geological Survey records show that flows peaked in 1995 during a rain-on-snow event on February 20 with flows reaching 4450 cubic feet per second. On March 10, the river was running at 1600 cfs. On May 23, it had dropped to 263 cfs. By the end of August that year, the flow had dwindled to a still floatable 55 cfs.

OREGON

95 Grande Ronde River

Location: Troy to SR 129
Distance: 7 to 19 miles
Paddle time: 5 hours or overnight
Season: Generally March through November
Rating: Class 2
Hazards: Strong eddies; tricky boulder-strewn stretches in low flows; rattlesnakes, poison oak
Shuttle: 17 miles, gravel
Flow information: National Weather Service in Portland
River gauge: 13333000 at Troy
Historic flows: Average 3016 cfs; maximum 35,700; minimum 344
Maps: USGS Troy (Oregon), Saddle Butte (Washington), Mountain View (Washington); Umatilla National Forest map
Information: Umatilla National Forest, Walla Walla Ranger Station in Walla Walla; U.S. Bureau of Land Management river rangers based at Minam; Wallowa Wild & Scenic River System

The Grande Ronde River is fed by water from sources in the region's stunning and pristine backcountry, including the Elkhorn Mountains, the Eagle Cap Wilderness, and the Wenaha–Tucannon Wilderness. The river takes on its own character as it rumbles down from forests, through tortured canyonlands, under towering basalt cliffs, and to the breaks lined with sage and prickly pear cactus.

This trip features the most accessible and least dangerous section within 83 miles of popular floating from the confluence with the Wallowa River downstream to the confluence with the Snake River. The area holds a wide range of notable wildlife, including elk, deer, bighorn sheep, raccoons, and otters, plus golden and bald eagles. Anglers can hook smallmouth bass and rainbow trout as well as steelhead in fall and early spring.

The Grande Ronde below and above the section featured in this trip involves roadless stretches, lengthy car shuttles, and Class 3 and Class 4 rapids. Above

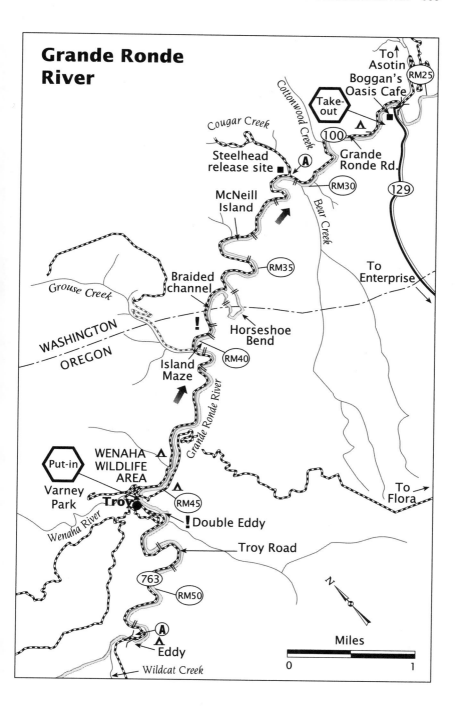

Grande Ronde River

- To Asotin
- Boggan's Oasis Cafe
- RM25
- Take-out
- 100
- Grande Ronde Rd.
- RM30
- 129
- Cougar Creek
- Cottonwood Creek
- Steelhead release site
- McNeill Island
- Bear Creek
- To Enterprise
- RM35
- Grouse Creek
- Braided channel
- Horseshoe Bend
- WASHINGTON
- OREGON
- Island Maze
- RM40
- Grande Ronde River
- WENAHA WILDLIFE AREA
- Put-in
- Varney Park
- Troy
- RM45
- Double Eddy
- Troy Road
- To Flora
- Wenaha River
- 763
- RM50
- Eddy
- Wildcat Creek
- N
- Miles
- 0
- 1

Grande Ronde River near Troy, Oregon

this stretch, the 44 miles of Grande Ronde downstream from Minam, Oregon, was designated "Wild and Scenic" by Congress in 1988. That stretch includes Class 3 rapids and is a popular three-day trip for rafters. From SR 129 to the confluence with the Snake are two sections totaling 26 miles of remote paddling, requiring up to 4 hours of shuttling. That trip includes one Class 4 (with difficult portage) at The Narrows, about 5 miles above the confluence.

The trip described here is within the limits of intermediate paddlers, with play spots that will appeal to advanced paddlers as well. This section is designated a "Recreation River," which provides some restrictions on shoreline development. Private land is scattered within U.S. Bureau of Land Management and state land. Paddlers must stay off private land. Be warned that nothing pushes a rancher's hot button faster than the sight of a campfire in this arid landscape. The safest course is to stay below the high-water mark except in designated public access areas and campsites.

This route can be run as a day trip or a boat-camping trip. Stretches of flatwater are jazzed up with numerous Class 1–2 rapids. Scouting the rapids is easy, since roads parallel the river in this stretch. Car camping also is possible, allowing boaters to travel light.

Access. To reach the take-out from Asotin, Washington, drive south on SR 129 about 33 miles, through Anatone (no services) to the Grande Ronde River. (*Note:* The last 10 miles from Field Springs State Park involve a slow, steep descent down the curvy Rattlesnake Grade.) Cross the bridge over the river. The take-out is at the fishing access upstream of the bridge at Boggan's Oasis Cafe.

To reach the put-in, go to the north side of the SR 129 bridge and head west along the Grande Ronde River on Grande Ronde Road (Asotin County Road 100). Drive 17 dusty miles to Troy, Oregon. Take this opportunity to note several public access sites and primitive camping areas along the road. Troy offers food and camping, but no gas station. Drive through town, crossing the bridge over the Grande Ronde River. Turn left to the put-in at Varney Park.

Paddlers can add 7 miles of floating by continuing on Grande Ronde Road (becomes Troy Road) to an upper put-in. In Troy, instead of crossing the bridge over the Grande Ronde River, bear right and cross the bridge over the Wenaha River. Then follow Troy Road (County Road 763) paralleling the Grande Ronde upstream 7 miles to Wildcat Creek. The undeveloped access has a camping area nearby.

Paddle Route. Ideal paddling conditions for canoeists in this stretch are roughly 2000 to 3000 cfs. At lower flows, exposed boulders can make paddling trickier. Higher flows wash out many of the riffles, but create powerful hydraulics and eddylines. The map in this book highlights rapids in the Class 1+ to Class 2 range. But numerous splashy riffles occur between each notable rapid.

The first hazard for canoeists starting at Wildcat Creek is Double Eddy, a tight Z-curve above Troy that causes strong eddies. The Forest Service rates this Class 3 in high spring flows. The main hazard downstream from Troy is Island Maze, which includes a braided channel and a sizable drop. In flows below 2700 cfs, the only way to get through without pounding rocks is a channel at river right. Stay river right at McNeill Island, the only named island on the river.

Anglers who don't have fishing licenses for both Oregon and Washington should note that the river crosses state lines twice at Horseshoe Bend.

Although the Walla Walla Ranger District has information on this section, the BLM's Grande Ronde river rangers based at Minam may have a better handle on river conditions. Also check at Minam for details on the ever more restrictive rules for human waste and fire pans.

Shuttle services traditionally have been available from Boggan's Oasis. A helpful mile-by-mile river runner's map, Wallowa and Grande Ronde Wild and Scenic Rivers, is available from the Walla Walla Ranger District. It also helps define public and private land.

MONTANA

96 Clark Fork River

Location: St. Regis to Quinns Hot Springs
Distance: 13 to 23 miles
Paddle time: 6 to 8 hours or overnight
Season: Virtually year-round
Rating: Class 1, with some Class 2 to 3
Hazards: Bridge abutments, rocks, rapids
Shuttle: 20 miles, pavement
Flow information: USGS Montana website
River gauge: 12354500 at St. Regis
Historic flows: Average 7188 cfs; maximum 68,100; minimum 800
Maps: USGS St. Regis, Keystone Peak, Quinns Hot Springs; Lolo National Forest map
Information: Quinns Hot Springs Resort near Paradise

Although SR 135 parallels the river for most of this route, the Clark Fork River offers a surprisingly backwoods experience. This stretch of the river skirts through the Lolo National Forest and a puzzle of private landholdings scattered along the shoreline. The trip ends near a commercial hot springs resort.

The Clark Fork can become seriously swollen with snowmelt gathered in the 333 miles from its origin near Anaconda, Montana, to where it empties into Idaho's Lake Pend Oreille. Generally, with the notable exception of the gorge near Alberton, Montana, it offers easy paddling with numerous splashy waves and a few challenges. Most of the river traffic consists of rafts and drift boats with anglers casting for trout. The fishing is best in March and April before the normal runoff, and then again from late June through October. Two campgrounds and several camping areas are available. Forest Service Trail 223 parallels much of the south shore.

Access. To reach the put-in, exit I-90 at St. Regis, Montana, and drive north to the four-way stop at the junction with Mullan Gulch Road (Old Highway 10). (*Note:* Milepost mileage begins here.) Drive north on SR 135 about half a mile. Turn right to the St. Regis fishing access site.

Traveling to the take-out allows you to scout many of the river's features. Continue north on SR 135. Just before milepost 11, pull over to see the first significant rapids. Halfway between mileposts 11 and 12, pass a primitive campground accessible from the road or the river. Other campsites on national forest land are found just downstream from this campground on river left. Halfway between mileposts 12 and 13, pass the optional take-out at the developed Ferry Landing boat launch.

Just before milepost 16, pull over to scout Cascade Rapids (Class 3). Pass developed

Cascade Campground another quarter mile downstream. An optional take-out on public land is at the big bend just past the campground. The recommended take-out is halfway between mileposts 19 and 20, across the highway from Quinns Hot Springs. However, this is private property; permission must be secured at the resort prior to the trip. The junction of SR 135 and SR 200 is 2 miles north of the resort.

Paddle Route. The Clark Fork can be broad and featureless during high spring flows, but it moves quickly with power that must be respected. In summer, flows are mellow; rocks show in the riffles.

The first significant rapids follow a long straight stretch of slow water. The

Canoeists at beach below Cascade Rapids on Clark Fork River

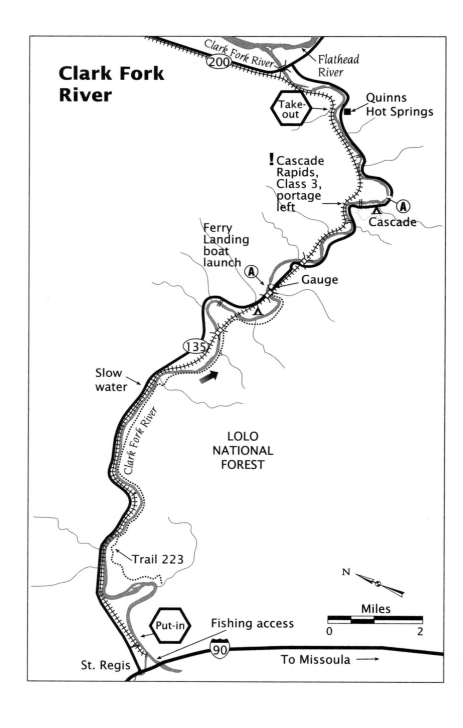

Clark Fork River

Clark Fork River

200

Flathead River

Take-out

Quinns Hot Springs

! Cascade Rapids, Class 3, portage left

Cascade

Ⓐ

Ferry Landing boat launch

Ⓐ

Gauge

135

Slow water

Clark Fork River

LOLO NATIONAL FOREST

Trail 223

N

Miles

0   2

Put-in

Fishing access

90

St. Regis

To Missoula →

river bucks up against the rock rubble below the highway. Paddlers must pick their way through in low flows. Pass under a railroad trestle and note campsites on the bench between the river and the highway. The optional take-out at the Ferry Landing boat launch is on river right just beyond the highway bridge.

Paddle downstream until small rapids on river right warn that Class 3 Cascade Rapids are just ahead around the bend. In low water, paddlers can go to river right before the bend and scout the rapids from the road. In higher water, stay on river left to avoid being sucked into the rapids after rounding the bend. Eddy out on river left and begin scouting or portaging where the railroad tracks depart from the riverbank. When flows are very high, say 20,500 cubic feet per second, paddlers without decked boats or adequate flotation can avoid the rapids by maneuvering through rocks along river left. In typical summer flows, it is possible to sneak through Cascade Rapids without decked boats.

Note the optional take-out at the next big bend in the river. The area is marked by large rocks along the road and a small rocky peninsula that can become an island in high water.

Several waysides along the shuttle route help explain the great Ice Age floods that carved this valley and scoured the downstream landscape all the way to the Pacific Ocean. A short nature trail from Cascade Campground leads up to a good vantage of the Clark Fork valley. The trail follows an old mine road that gave access to the area before the river road was built in 1934.

97 Flathead River

Location: Buffalo Bridge to Perma
Distance: 14 to 54 miles
Paddle time: 3 days
Season: Virtually year-round
Rating: Class 1
Hazards: Wind
Shuttle: 65 miles, pavement and gravel
Flow information: Kerr Dam, or USGS Montana website
River gauge: 12388700 at Perma
Historic flows: Average 11,600 cfs; maximum 47,100; minimum 2670
Maps: USGS Buffalo Bridge, Round Butte, Melton Ranch, Sloan, Dixon, McDonald, Perma; Lake and Sanders County maps
Information: Confederated Salish and Kootenai Tribes at Pablo

Whitewater paddlers know the three forks of the Flathead River. These famous whitewater streams tumble from the spine of the Rocky Mountains near Glacier National Park to feed the largest natural lake in the West.

Lower Flathead River

It is a gentler, though still impressive, river that leaves Flathead Lake and winds 70 miles through the sparsely populated Flathead Indian Reservation. With the exception of the 7-mile canyon of Class 3+ whitewater playground from Kerr Dam downstream to Buffalo Bridge (not included in this trip), the lower Flathead is broad, deep, and friendly. The surrounding hills are cloaked in juniper and bunchgrass, rather than the larch, aspen, and beargrass familiar to visitors to the three forks. In places, the river is hemmed by clay cliffs naturally carved into spires, caves, and bridges.

Visitors to this remote country can expect to see golden and bald eagles, along with a variety of waterfowl and deer, elk, and the occasional moose. Those with sharp eyes or good binoculars may spot herds of grazing bison on the velvety hills of the National Bison Range. Lucky anglers hook toothy northern pike on spoons, 6-inch flies, or dead smelt drifted beneath bobbers.

The tribes prohibit boat motors larger than 15 horsepower. The quietest time to visit the Flathead is between March 15 and June 30, when all internal-combustion engines are banned to protect nesting waterfowl. Typical flows range from an average of 7430 cubic feet per second in August to an average of 19,710 cfs in June.

Permits are required for anyone who is not a Flathead tribal member. Fees are charged for boating and camping, and tribal fishing permits are required for anglers. Permits are available without advance notice at many restaurants and stores on and near the reservation, or at tribal headquarters in Pablo, Montana. Sporting goods stores in Ronan usually sell permits for floating and camping. Groups of twenty or more must get special permission from the tribes.

Access. Road signs are rare in the reservation's backcountry, so reaching the put-in at Buffalo Bridge can be tricky for those unfamiliar with the country. Drivers should keep a good map and compass handy. Virtually any road headed toward the river will eventually come to the put-in, though it may take many twists and turns in the process.

To reach Buffalo Bridge from US 93 in Polson, Montana, turn west onto Main Street, then take a right onto Seventh Avenue East. After 3 miles, turn right onto Kerr Dam Road, which is well marked. The road passes the Kerr Dam turnoff at about 3 miles. It makes a number of turns in the next 3 miles, before coming to an unmarked gravel road where drivers should turn right. Turn right again after driving a little more than a mile, and stay right where the road forms a Y. The bridge is about a half mile beyond the Y.

For three or four days of leisurely river travel, boaters should plan on ending their trip at the Perma Bridge, 54 miles downstream from Buffalo Bridge. Perma is 11 miles east of the junction of SR 135 and SR 200. The bridge is on SR 382 less than a mile north of SR 200.

Alternative access points are Sloan Bridge, about 20 miles downstream from Buffalo Bridge, and the boat launch in Dixon, about 40 miles downstream from Buffalo Bridge.

To reach Sloan Bridge, drive west on SR 211 from Ronan. The paved highway turns sharply south at 10 miles and comes to the graffiti-covered bridge almost 3 miles past the bend.

SR 200 is the main street for tiny Dixon. To reach the boat launch, drive about a quarter mile north from the highway on a gravel road opposite the U.S. Post Office.

Paddle Route. The four accesses mark rough divisions in the geography of the river valley. The most remote stretch and most of the clay cliffs are between Buffalo Bridge and Sloan Bridge. The river gorge broadens into a valley dotted with a few farms as one nears Dixon.

At Dixon, the river turns west, and paddlers no longer view the Mission Mountains, to the east. The shore becomes more wooded downstream from Dixon, and anglers in powerboats are more common.

The only riverside outhouse and picnic tables are at the Dixon boat ramp, where camping is not recommended. But good campsites abound around nearly

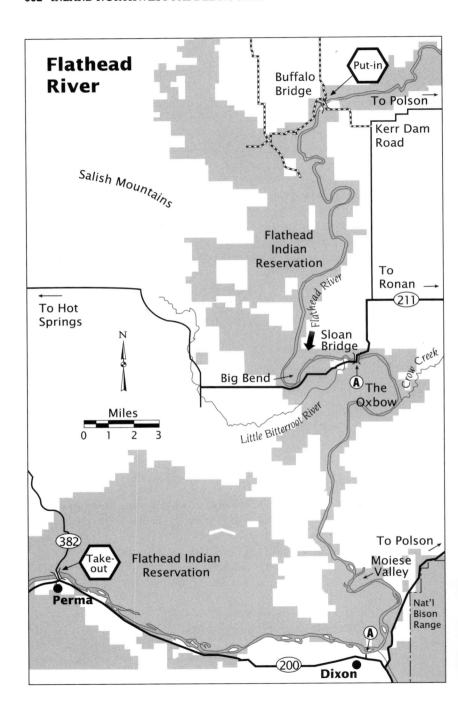

Flathead River

every bend of the river, with lots of room for open-country wandering. Poison ivy is also abundant, so caution is warranted. Visitors should bring their own water, as the Flathead upstream flows through highly developed areas, and its tributaries meander through farm and ranch country. Water refills (along with midtrip treats) are available in the town of Dixon, but it's about a mile walk to town, and gear should not be left unattended at the boat launch.

98 Thompson River

Location: Bend Junction to Clark Memorial Campground
Distance: 30 miles with shorter options
Paddle time: 2 days
Season: Generally May through early June
Rating: Class 2 above Little Thompson River, Class 2+ below
Hazards: Fallen trees, shoreline brush; rapids; one cross-stream cable
Shuttle: 26 miles, gravel
Flow information: USGS Montana website
River gauge: 12389500 near the mouth
Historic flows: Average 445 cfs; maximum 5360; minimum 67
Maps: USGS Bend, Richards Peak, Calico Creek, Priscilla Peak; Lolo National Forest map
Information: Lolo National Forest, Plains Ranger Station

The small and uncrowded Thompson River requires better-than-average paddling skills to maneuver through scattered rapids while avoiding the fallen trees that paddlers likely will find blocking their paths. After high water in spring 1997, the upper 18 miles of this trip were blocked in at least twelve places, each requiring a short portage. Hawthorns with half-inch spines overhang the shoreline in many places, so a wide turn on this narrow river sometimes draws blood. Elsewhere, the river meanders through meadows, the current all but disappears, and paddling is not so much a challenge as a chore.

But few streams are as lovely. The river begins at Thompson Lakes chain and runs 51 miles to its confluence with the Clark Fork River east of Thompson Falls. Streamside cottonwoods fill the air with their cottonlike seedpods. The many clearcuts one sees from roads are mostly invisible from the water. The roads themselves are hidden in the upper 18 miles of river, which is seldom paddled. Cabins sit streamside in places.

Wild roses bloom pink in June, complementing the Indian paintbrush and assorted other wildflowers that poke out of the thick underbrush. Paddlers have a good chance of seeing moose at close range. The Thompson holds good numbers of trout and threatened bull trout (actually a char), which must be carefully released.

Access. To reach the river from Thompson Falls, Montana, drive east about 5 miles on SR 200. Turn north on the Thompson River Road (FR 56) at milepost 56. The Forest Service road runs parallel to the river, as does Plum Creek Road, a private timber company road that usually is open to the public. The two roads sometimes are on opposite sides of the river; occasionally they are separated by only a few feet of brush, and sometimes they cross each other. Mileposts listed below are for the timber company road.

For a long trip of flatwater and rapids, paddling can start near Bend Junction, just beyond milepost 31. Turn right onto FR 56, and drive about a quarter mile to the river. Parking and an informal campsite are nearby.

The trip ends about 30 river miles downstream at Clark Memorial campground, on the west side of the river. The campground is about 5 miles from SR 200, along the Forest Service road.

Four accesses are between the put-in and take-out, giving paddlers options to create trips to fit their skills and time restraints:

(1) Downstream from Bend, at a bridge near milepost 27. (2) At a bridge and campsite near milepost 21. (3) Turn right (east) near milepost 19 at a junction with FR 56. Drive about 1.5 miles to a bridge and meadow. (4) At a bridge near milepost 17 where the Little Thompson River flows into the Thompson.

Paddle Route. While rapids are scattered through the trip, the final 12 miles from the Little Thompson River to Clark Memorial campground have the biggest and most frequent whitewater. This section is the least likely to be blocked by trees. Popular with local kayakers, rafters, and whitewater canoeists, this stretch can be scouted by driving roads along both banks. Intermediate paddlers can run it with proper equipment and skilled companions.

Thompson River below Little Thompson Creek (Tom Eggensperger photo)

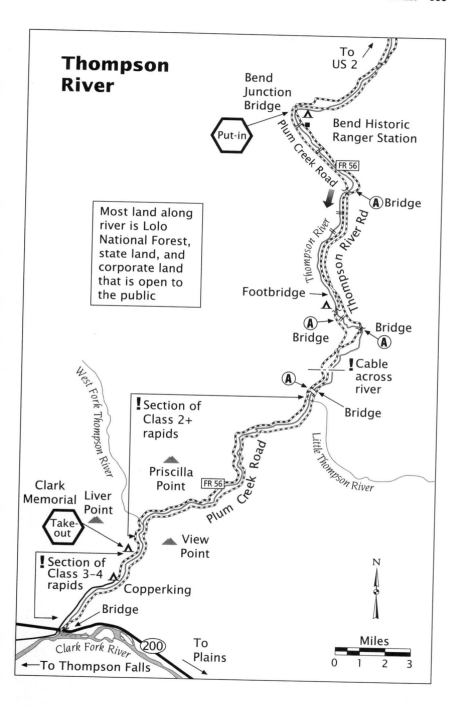

Thompson River

Most land along river is Lolo National Forest, state land, and corporate land that is open to the public

To US 2

Bend Junction Bridge

Put-in

Bend Historic Ranger Station

Plum Creek Road

FR 56

Ⓐ Bridge

Thompson River

Thompson River Rd

Footbridge →

Ⓐ → Bridge

Bridge

Ⓐ

Ⓐ

! Cable across river

Bridge

West Fork Thompson River

Little Thompson River

! Section of Class 2+ rapids

Priscilla Point

Plum Creek Road

FR 56

Clark Memorial

Liver Point

Take-out

View Point

! Section of Class 3-4 rapids

Copperking

Bridge

Clark Fork River

200

To Plains

← To Thompson Falls

N

Miles
0 1 2 3

Below the take-out are rapids that should be attempted only by skilled white-water paddlers. At one point, the river drops over a ledge just as it twists through a slot that can become clogged with logs.

Flows of about 1200 cubic feet per second—higher than the river achieves some years—are ideal for the upper 18 miles of river. Higher flows increase the risk of getting caught in a strainer. The final 12 miles can be run with flows as low as 750 cfs.

While the entire 30 miles could be run in a single day, it would be a long one, with little time for fishing or other fun. Allow about 2 hours of steady paddling between the put-in and first access, and another 2 hours to the bridge at milepost 21. The next two segments require about an hour each. The whitewater section below the Little Thompson River takes about 2.5 hours.

An inch-thick cable strung across the river about 2 miles above the Little Thompson River can catch inattentive boaters by the neck.

Camping is at the Clark Memorial and nearby Copperking campgrounds, or at informal campsites along the river. More campsites are at the river source at the Thompson Lakes chain.

99 Bull River

Location: Near Noxon
Distance: 6 to 14 miles
Paddle time: 5 hours
Season: Virtually year-round
Rating: Class 1 upstream from Bull River Ranger Station; Class 2 downstream
Hazards: Bridge abutments; whitewater; strainers
Shuttle: 11.5 miles, pavement
Flow information: USGS no longer monitors a gauge
Maps: USGS Smeads Bench, Ibex Peak; Kootenai National Forest map
Information: Kootenai National Forest, Cabinet Ranger Station near Trout Creek

The Bull River offers a quiet float in view of Montana's snow-topped Cabinet Mountains, from which the river finds its source. Paddlers who carry binoculars may spot bighorn sheep on either side of the river valley. Some will startle moose and otters.

The trip starts in a soggy meadow dotted with cottonwood trees and beaver ponds. The meadows gradually melt into forests toward the take-out. While the scenery is wonderful, this is not a wilderness trip. Cars on SR 56 are frequently within earshot, and the two-lane highway is visible in places. Most of the land in sight is federally owned, and managed by the Kootenai National Forest. But the

Bull River in western Montana

valley floor itself is mostly private, and dotted with houses. Livestock has over-grazed the riverbank in places.

Access. Because much of this area is private land, access is limited. The trip has three access points, all on SR 56. The highway follows the river north from SR 200, about 5 miles west of Noxon, Montana. All road miles refer to distance from the intersection of the two highways. Access points are not marked, nor particularly obvious. Be sure to check your odometer at the intersection.

The most popular take-out is a wide gravel shoulder 2.5 miles up SR 56. The site is identified by a large eddy and old wooden bridge abutments upstream, although the bridge itself is gone. The take-out is steep and rocky; footing is tricky. River-weary paddlers may be tempted to skid boats up the grassy slope a few feet from the rocks. Don't do it: This is private land! Take care to avoid blocking the landowner's driveway.

The most popular put-in is a small highway turnout 11.5 miles up SR 56. If you come to the second bridge over the river, you've driven a mile too far. A faint trail, often ankle-high with water in spring, leads to the put-in.

Between the take-out and the put-in is a third access, about 7 miles from SR 200, where SR 56 crosses the river.

Paddle Route. The Bull runs 26 miles from its source at Bull Lake to the Clark Fork River at Cabinet Gorge Reservoir. This trip is 14 miles.

From the uppermost put-in to the SR 56 bridge, the river has scarcely a ripple. Oxbows and backwaters beg to be explored. Two private bridges and the highway

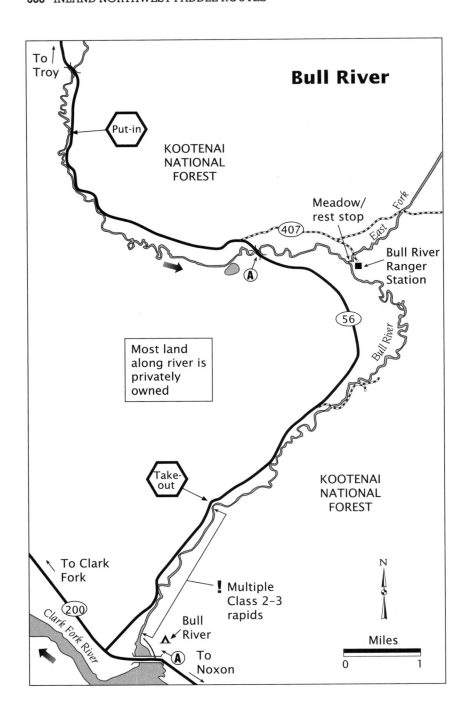

Bull River

To Troy

Put-in

KOOTENAI NATIONAL FOREST

Meadow/ rest stop

East Fork

407

Bull River Ranger Station

56

Bull River

Most land along river is privately owned

Take-out

KOOTENAI NATIONAL FOREST

To Clark Fork

200

Clark Fork River

! Multiple Class 2-3 rapids

Bull River

To Noxon

N

Miles

0   1

bridge are the only hazards. Allow at least 1.5 hours of steady paddling or 2 hours for a more enjoyable trip.

About 2 miles downstream from the highway bridge, just upstream from the East Fork of the Bull River, is a large meadow on the left. Administered by the Forest Service, the meadow is a good rest stop. Paddlers willing to hike a short distance can visit the Bull River Ranger Station, a 1909 structure that has become a state historic site. The cabin is available for rent through the Cabinet Ranger Station, providing paddlers an option to camping.

The valley narrows and becomes more wooded downstream from its confluence with the East Fork. Downed trees are common, particularly on the outside corners of turns. A few rapids may rate Class 2, depending on river flows. Four private bridges cross the river. The stretch may be too rocky to paddle during low water.

The final 2.5-mile stretch of the Bull River (below the final take-out described here) is much swifter than the upper sections, and has more obstacles and rapids that approach Class 3. Only expert paddlers should float it.

100 Kootenai River

Location: Yaak River to Moyie River
Distance: 16 miles
Paddle time: 6 hours or overnight
Season: May through October
Rating: Class 2
Hazards: Wind; scattered rapids
Shuttle: 18 miles, pavement and gravel
Flow information: Libby Dam recording
Historic flows: Average 11,130 cfs; maximum 47,200; minimum 1900
Maps: USGS Kilbrennen Lake, Leonia, Curley Creek, Moyie Springs; Kootenai National Forest map
Information: Kootenai National Forest, Three Rivers Ranger Station in Troy

For most of its length in the United States, the Kootenai River is within sight of roads. This trip, which starts in Montana and ends in Idaho, takes paddlers through a remote and heavily forested canyon, where cars cannot be heard or seen. An occasional house peeks over the horizon and trains screech and grind along riverside tracks, disrupting the solitude about every hour. Otherwise, river travelers likely will have the place to themselves.

Fishing is a big attraction, with healthy populations of pan-sized cutthroat and rainbow trout, along with a few lunkers. In early October, the shoreline becomes a mix of yellows and reds, with the deep green of pine forests in the background.

Access. The trip starts at the Forest Service's Yaak River Campground, about 8 miles northwest of Troy, Montana. The campground has two entrances off US 2; boaters should use the one on the west side of the Yaak River, staying right at all turns in the campground until they come to a rough gravel road. The road leads about a half mile to the Kootenai River.

To reach the take-out, drive about 16 miles northwest from Yaak River Campground on US 2. At Evergreen School is a well-marked road to the privately owned Twin Rivers Campground. (Drivers who miss the turn will come to the Moyie River gorge a mile beyond.) The road to the campground twists downhill for 2 miles, turning from pavement to gravel halfway to the river. The owners charge for overnight parking, camping, and other activities. The campground is open May through October.

Paddle Route. Broad and swift, the river is gentle for long stretches that are separated by rapids. The whitewater should not cause problems for intermediate paddlers. About 5 miles into the trip, the river crosses under an abandoned bridge at the old village of Leonia. Anglers should note the spot carefully, since it also marks the Idaho state line. Those with only Montana fishing licenses must reel in their lines.

About a mile beyond the bridge is a cedar-covered island with rapids at the head. A good, undeveloped campsite is on a high bench at the tail of the island. A second island, 5 miles downstream from the first, also provides good camping. The islands and most of the south shore of the Kootenai are public land, administered by the U.S. Forest Service. The north shore is a mix of public and private land.

Strong headwinds can be a problem the last several miles of the trip.

Kootenai River near Canoe Gulch Ranger Station

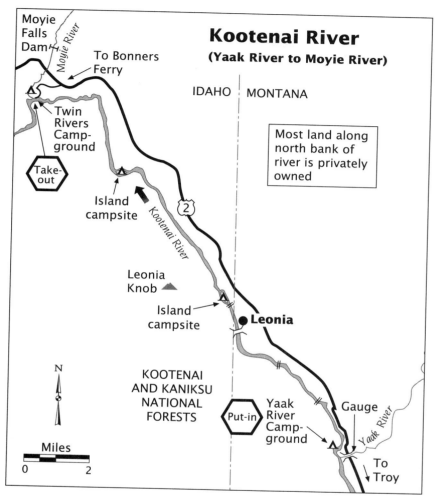

Kootenai River
(Yaak River to Moyie River)

IDAHO | MONTANA

Most land along north bank of river is privately owned

Moyie Falls Dam
Moyie River
To Bonners Ferry
Twin Rivers Camp-ground
Take-out
Island campsite
Kootenai River
Leonia Knob
Island campsite
Leonia
KOOTENAI AND KANIKSU NATIONAL FORESTS
Put-in
Yaak River Camp-ground
Gauge
Yaak River
To Troy
N
Miles
0   2

Libby Dam controls the Kootenai, and flows can range as high as 25,000 cubic feet per second in spring and early summer to 4000 cfs in fall. And it's not just the season of the year that can affect flows—efforts to help endangered fish species also play into the mix. The river may be raised dramatically at times for the sake of local sturgeon or Columbia River salmon, or lowered to help Kootenai River burbot, a species once so populous that it supported a commercial fishery in Bonners Ferry, Idaho. As a result, campers must be cautious where they tie their boats and pitch their tents, since the river can rise several feet overnight, even if there is no change in the weather.

This trip is ideal when the river is at 10,000 cfs, give or take a few thousand.

12 "choice" whitewater runs for paddlers

WHITEWATER

1 Cowlitz River

Location: La Wis Wis to Packwood
Distance: 3 to 8 miles
River time: 2 to 3 hours
Season: July to early August
Rating: Class 2
Hazards: Logs
Elevation: 1255 to 1050 feet—25 feet per mile
Shuttle: 8 miles, pavement
Flow information: USGS Washington website
River gauge: 14226500 at Packwood
Historic flows: Average 1587 cfs; maximum 36,600; minimum 130
Maps: USGS: Packwood, Tatoosh Lakes, Ohanapecosh Hot Springs; Gifford Pinchot National Forest map
Information: Gifford Pinchot National Forest, Cowlitz Valley Ranger Station

The beauty in the first mile and a half of this trip captivates boaters as they pass between towering rock walls and under the branches of virgin evergreens that overhang the channel. The crystalline water collects in deep green pools, then flows into fun, straightforward rapids. Enjoy the early portion of the trip: once the Muddy Fork of the Cowlitz joins the channel, the scenery is much less spectacular.

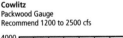

Cowlitz
Packwood Gauge
Recommend 1200 to 2500 cfs

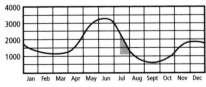

The name Cowlitz comes from an Indian name that had many different spellings but was applied to both the river and the Salish tribe that lived along its banks. Its exact meaning has been lost, but it is roughly translated as "capturing the medicine spirit" since the tribe used a prairie along the river for its young men to commune with the Great Spirit.

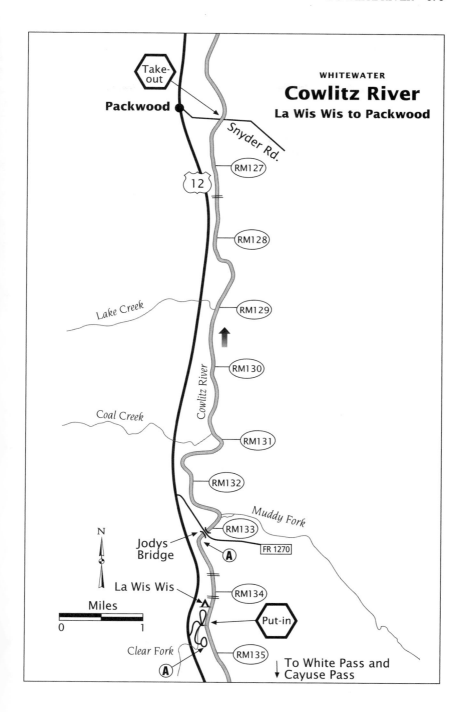

Take-out

Packwood

Snyder Rd.

RM127

12

RM128

Lake Creek

RM129

Cowlitz River

RM130

Coal Creek

RM131

RM132

Muddy Fork

RM133

FR 1270

Jodys Bridge

(A)

La Wis Wis

RM134

N

Miles

0   1

Put-in

Clear Fork

(A)

RM135

To White Pass and Cayuse Pass

WHITEWATER
Cowlitz River
La Wis Wis to Packwood

Skirting a rock slide on Clear Fork of the Cowlitz

Access. From I-5, the trip is nearly 67 miles east near Packwood, Washington,where the Cowlitz flows along US 12. The put-in is south of Mount Rainier at La Wis Wis Campground, mile marker 138 on US 12. The campground is normally open from Memorial Day weekend until November.

For a short, fast, section of the Clear Fork of the Cowlitz above its confluence with the Ohanapecosh, take the first right and proceed to the bridge over the narrow Clear Fork. It's a steep path to the river and no parking is available right near the bridge, but it's a beautiful stretch of river.

The main put-in is at the confluence of the Clear Fork and the Ohanapecosh. Take the second right into the campground's day-use area. The best river access is just downstream of the picnic area at the upper end of the camping area along the river.

You can also put-in or take-out at Jodys Bridge, about a mile from US 12 on FR 1270. The road turns off US 12 about 2 miles south of La Wis Wis Campground and about 4.9 miles north of Packwood. Coming from the north, the road leaves US 12 just beyond a yellow highway sign indicating a road leaving the opposite side of the highway from FR 1270 and going to Lava Creek. The access here is very steep, but possible on the upstream right-hand side of the bridge.

To reach the take-out, turn off US 12 in the middle of Packwood onto Snyder Road. The take-out is on the left bank, just downstream of the bridge over the river.

Paddle Route. The Cowlitz is a good run at 1200 to 2500 cubic feet per second on the Packwood gauge.

The first 1.5 to 2 miles of the trip are breathtaking. Some canoeists may want to run the upper section to Jodys Bridge, then take out and go back up to run the section again. The scenery deteriorates as soon as the Muddy Fork of the Cowlitz joins the channel. It's interesting to watch the water of the Clear Fork mix with the silt-laden Muddy Fork, but within 200 yards, the whole river is gray. The channel becomes braided and winds constantly around many islands and gravel bars. However, from the wider river channel, paddlers have good views of Mount Rainier and the surrounding mountains.

The rapids on this trip are straightforward, and experienced paddlers shouldn't need to scout them except at water levels higher than those recommended. The most difficult maneuvering is required at the two headwalls about a mile into the trip. In the lower part of the run, keep a sharp eye out for logs blocking some of the braided channels, sometimes requiring a short portage. The rapid at about river mile 127.5 provides the largest waves of the trip in a drop that funnels all the river's water through a gap about 35 feet wide.

2 Cispus River

Location: Road 28 Bridge to Iron Creek
Distance: 8 miles
River time: 2 to 3 hours
Season: April to July
Rating: Class 2
Hazards: Logs
Elevation: 1265 to 1085 feet—23 feet per mile
Shuttle: 8 miles, pavement and gravel
Flow information: USGS Washington website
River gauge: 14231900 near Randle
Historic flows: Average 1001 cfs; maximum 24,600; minimum 165
Maps: USGS Tower Rock, Greenhorn Buttes; Gifford Pinchot National Forest map
Information: Gifford Pinchot National Forest, Cowlitz Valley Ranger Station

The Cispus provides a pretty but little-known trip through the Gifford Pinchot National Forest. It has enjoyable Class 2 rapids at moderate water levels and a fairly long season. The Cispus gathers its water on the west sides of Mount Adams and the Goat Rocks Wilderness and drops rapidly to the west toward its

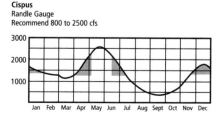

Cispus
Randle Gauge
Recommend 800 to 2500 cfs

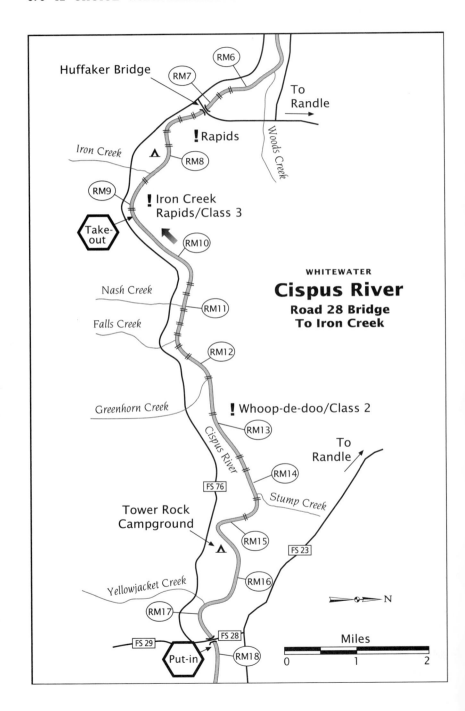

Huffaker Bridge

RM6

RM7

To Randle

Woods Creek

! Rapids

Iron Creek

RM8

RM9

! Iron Creek Rapids/Class 3

Take-out

RM10

WHITEWATER

Cispus River

**Road 28 Bridge
To Iron Creek**

Nash Creek

RM11

Falls Creek

RM12

Greenhorn Creek

! Whoop-de-doo/Class 2

RM13

To Randle

Cispus River

RM14

FS 76

Stump Creek

Tower Rock Campground

RM15

FS 23

RM16

Yellowjacket Creek

RM17

N

Miles

FS 29

FS 28

Put-in

RM18

0   1   2

Playing upstream out of an eddy on the Cispus River

confluence with the Cowlitz. Good rafting and kayaking trips are found on the Cispus both above and below the route described here, but this trip is a scenic run suitable for canoes.

Access. The Cispus is usually approached through the town of Randle, Washington, named for early settlers in the surrounding Big Bottom Valley area. Randle is on US 12 about 54 miles east of I-5. To reach the put-in from Randle, take FR 23 (Cispus Road) south toward Trout Lake. Cross the Cowlitz just after leaving Randle and bear left about 0.5 mile beyond the bridge toward the Cispus Environmental Center and Trout Lake. After driving about 3 miles through private land, the road enters the Gifford Pinchot National Forest. About 9.2 miles from the bridge over the Cowlitz, turn right onto FR 28 toward the Cispus Center and Tower Rock Campground.

The put-in is on the upstream, river-left side of the FR 28 bridge.

To reach the take-out, continue south on FR 28. In about 0.5 mile, the road crosses Yellowjacket Creek; shortly thereafter, bear right on Cispus Road 76. Pass the Cispus Environmental Center and continue downstream on Road 76, which becomes gravel in about 4 miles. About 6.7 miles downstream from the Cispus Environmental Center, cross a small bridge over an unnamed stream coming down the hillside into the river. The take-out is at a turnout just downstream of the bridge. Coming from the other direction (upstream from Iron Creek Campground on Road 25), the take-out is about 0.7 mile above the bridge over Iron Creek.

Paddle Route. This part of the Cispus provides a good canoe trip at 800 to 2500 cfs.

The trip begins with a nice view of Tower Rock, which is the core of an ancient volcano. The former bridge across the river near Tower Rock Campground was destroyed in flooding on the river in the 1990s; the campground provides a nice place to stay if you make a weekend of your paddling on the Cispus. The shoreline for the first 3.5 miles of the trip is dominated by gravel bars with piles of logs and cabins along the left bank.

The remaining 4.5 miles of the trip provide exceptionally beautiful scenery. Evergreen trees reach for the heavens straight up from the banks of the river, creating a cathedral-like effect. The clear water winds through a very rocky channel that alternates between gently flowing pools and fast, easy rapids. Several swift creeks, including Greenhorn and Falls creeks, splash into the river on the left bank.

The bedrock in this area is formed by the western Cascades volcanic rocks, which provide the hard outcroppings that produce the big rapids above and below this run. They consist of hard andesites, mostly lava flows, and mudflow deposits that are simply masses of rubble hardened into rock.

About a dozen Class 2 rapids are encountered between RM 15 and RM 9, with Whoop-de-doo having a little bit bigger waves than the other rapids. While two stretches have many cabins in the first few miles, few signs of civilization are found below RM 14.

The Cispus River should be designated as a "scenic river" in our National Wild and Scenic Rivers System.

3 Elwha River

Location: Altaire Camp to gauging station
Distance: 4 miles
River time: 1.5 to 2 hours
Season: May to August
Rating: Class 2, some Class 3
Hazards: Logs
Elevation: 350 to 220 feet—32 feet per mile
Shuttle: 4 miles, pavement
Flow information: USGS Washington website or NOAA recording
River gauge: 12045500 at McDonald Bridge
Historic flows: Average 1507 cfs; maximum 41,600; minimum 10
Maps: USGS Elwha; Olympic National Forest map
Information: Olympic National Park, Elwha Ranger Station

The Elwha River provides summer boating in a pristine Olympic river valley with fine views of the surrounding mountains. It is easily reached just off US 101 a little west of Port Angeles. Elwha means "elk" in the local Indian tongue, and the valley is an important wintering place for the large Roosevelt elk. Putting in at Altaire

Campground, you will find rapids that are exciting but not very difficult on a gorgeous river.

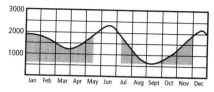

Elwha
McDonald Gauge
Recommend 600 to 1800 cfs

Access. From Port Angeles, Washington, drive west on US 101 about 7 miles. Before crossing the Elwha River, turn south on Olympic Hot Springs Road toward Olympic National Park. About 1 mile from US 101, turn into an unmarked gravel turnout next to a power pole. This is the take-out, just downstream of the river gauge

To reach the put-in, continue up the road on the east bank of the Elwha River into Olympic National Park, which charges a substantial vehicle entry fee. About 1 mile into the park, the road is right along a bend in the river. Here is Fishermans Bend, the most difficult rapid on this part of the river. Stop and scout it during the shuttle.

About 1.5 miles beyond Fishermans Bend, the road crosses the river. Altaire Campground is to your right just beyond the bridge. The boat access area is at the downstream end of the campground.

Paddle Route. The Elwha provides a good canoe trip at flows between 600 and 1800 cubic feet per second. Over 2000 cfs, there are very few eddies and rescue becomes difficult. Best rafting levels are 1200 up to 2600 cfs. The rapids on the trip are all Class 2, except for Fishermans Bend. If you can run Fishermans Bend, you should have a good trip on the Elwha.

Paddling out to swimmers on the Elwha

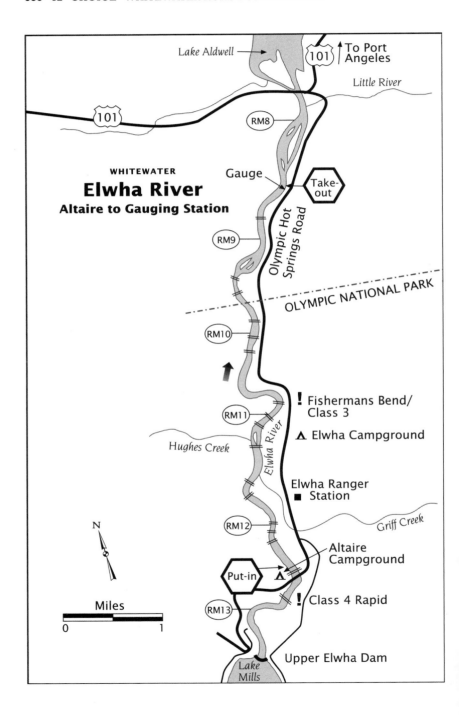

Lake Aldwell

101

To Port Angeles

Little River

101

RM8

WHITEWATER
Elwha River
Altaire to Gauging Station

Gauge

Take-out

Olympic Hot Springs Road

RM9

OLYMPIC NATIONAL PARK

RM10

! Fishermans Bend/ Class 3

RM11

Elwha River

▲ Elwha Campground

Hughes Creek

Elwha Ranger
■ Station

RM12

Griff Creek

N

Altaire Campground

Put-in

▲

! Class 4 Rapid

Miles

RM13

0   1

Upper Elwha Dam

Lake Mills

Logs frequently block portions of the Elwha. In 2006, for example, a large tree and root ball were in the main channel in Fishermans Bend. There was a passage around the left side of the tree, but careful maneuvering was required. The lesson: Scout your route.

The banks of the Elwha are heavily forested with many fine mountain views. The gorge just above the bridge near Altaire Campground is particularly pretty. (*Note:* Gorge Rapids upstream from the put-in for this trip approach Class 5 in some flows, a run that's for experts only.) Deer and elk heavily affect the vegetation in the forest. This is graphically demonstrated on the left bank where a small part of the forest has been secured by a 12-foot-high wire fence as an experiment. In contrast to the knee-high underbrush in most areas, the fenced-off area is choked with dense brush 15 feet high. In most of the forest each year, the deer and elk efficiently "mow" the underbrush.

All of the bedrock in this area is part of the steeply tilted oceanic crust that wraps around the Olympic Peninsula. The Elwha valley was carved by a glacier in the last ice age. The valley is filled with glacial debris, which often impounds bogs and ponds in depressed areas. The landscape is littered with erratic boulders carried down from British Columbia on the great ice sheets. The glacial debris can be unstable and result in landslides. Thousands of years ago, Lake Crescent drained east into the Elwha, but landslides blocked the channel, resulting in Lake Sutherland and in the new outlet to Lake Crescent, the Lyre River.

4 Soleduck River I (Upper)

Location: Riverside to Bear Creek
Distance: 7 miles
River time: 2 to 3 hours
Season: April to June
Rating: Class 2, two Class 3 rapids
Hazards: Logjams
Elevation: 710 to 535 feet—23 feet per mile
Shuttle: 7 miles, pavement
Flow information: USGS Washington website; NOAA recording
River gauge: Refer to 12045560 Elwha at McDonald Bridge
Historic flows: Average 1507 cfs, maximum 41,600; minimum 10
Maps: USGS Pyscht; Olympic National Forest map
Information: Olympic National Forest/National Park Recreation Information Center in Forks

The Upper Soleduck is a step up in difficulty from the lower river, providing interesting rapids on a rain-forest odyssey. The rapids are not difficult at the moderate

Play time on the Soleduck River (Bob Schneider photo)

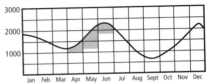

McDonald Briddge Gauge
Upper Soleduck
Recommend 1200 to 2600 cfs (May)

water levels found in spring and summer, but they enliven one of the most beautiful river trips in Washington. There are lush, moss-covered forests, abundant wildlife, and crystalline water in a boulder-studded channel.

Access. From Port Angeles, Washington, drive west on US 101 about 30 miles to where the highway parallels the Soleduck River. The Riverside put-in is simply an easily accessible bank of the river next to a wide asphalt turnout on US 101. The turnout is 0.8 mile west of the bridge over the Soleduck near Klahowya Campground. Or, heading east on US 101, the turnout is 1.6 miles beyond an Olympic National Forest sign and just east of a sign saying "Slow Vehicle Turnout."

The take-out, 7 miles west, is the Washington Department of Fish and Wildlife's Bear Creek boat ramp, at the end of Hilstrom Road, which turns off of US 101 about 0.4 mile east of the turnoff for Bear Creek Road. Go about 0.7 mile down the Hilstrom Road to the boat ramp. A WDFW vehicle access permit is required.

Paddle Route. No gauge provides current reports on the Soleduck, so the water level must be judged by the gauge on the Elwha, the next basin over. The Elwha provides a fairly good indication of the conditions on the Soleduck, but the Elwha has more snow runoff so a higher reading is needed on the Elwha gauge later in the season. Look for somewhat greater-than-average flows in the spring; this usually occurs after a good rain or after a couple of days of hot weather that melts the snow. For trips in April, the author recommends between 1000 and 2200 cubic feet per second on the McDonald Bridge gauge. In May, look for flows of 1200 to 2600 cfs at McDonald. In June, recommended flows range from 1800 to 3600 cfs on the McDonald gauge.

Most of the rapids on this stretch are just Class 2 boulder gardens that require technical maneuvering, but do not present large waves or holes. Two Class 3 rapids

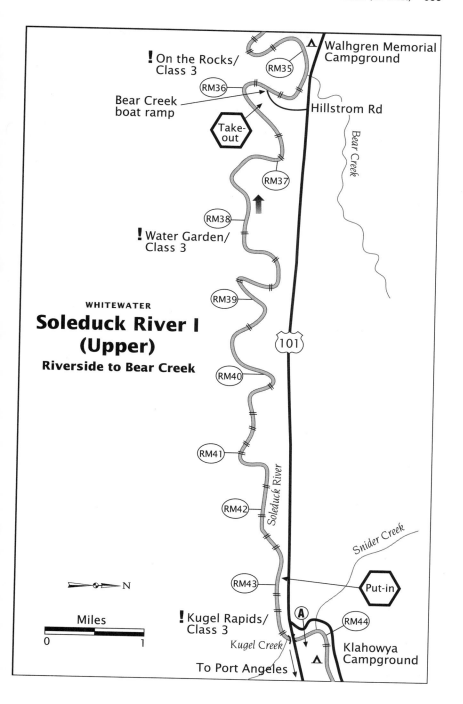

! On the Rocks/
Class 3

Walhgren Memorial
Campground

RM35

RM36

Bear Creek
boat ramp

Hillstrom Rd

Bear Creek

Take-
out

RM37

RM38

! Water Garden/
Class 3

RM39

WHITEWATER
Soleduck River I
(Upper)
Riverside to Bear Creek

101

RM40

RM41

RM42

Soleduck River

Snider Creek

RM43

Put-in

N

Miles

0   1

! Kugel Rapids/
Class 3

A

RM44

Kugel Creek

Klahowya
Campground

To Port Angeles

appear a little over halfway through the trip. The first of these, labeled Water Garden on the map, requires some maneuvering as you go left around an island. The second Class 3 is just a little below Water Garden, and a little easier.

Although paralleled by roads, much of this run seems quite natural. It presents a fantasy of greenery: deep green ferns, luxuriant mosses, and bright new shoots blend into a study of green, accentuated by the brown of the trees and rocks. Between the rapids are many deep, clear pools where the salmon and steelhead can be seen. Bald eagles come to the Soleduck for fish, and the author has seen them consistently on this part of the river.

The hills surrounding the Soleduck show evidence of the westward flow of the glaciers through this valley in the last ice age. The bedrock exposures in the area are of dark greenish black or black pillow basalts, once bedrock of the Pacific Ocean. Jasper has intruded into the rocks and often results in red pebbles in the bed of the Soleduck.

The river has cut its own narrow channel, which lies about 30 feet below the level of the surrounding valley. Its heavily forested slopes screen out most evidence of civilization. A trip on the Soleduck is the best way to see the rain forest, and this part of the Soleduck would make an outstanding addition to the National Wild and Scenic Rivers System.

5 Soleduck River II (Lower)

Location: Fish hatchery to Maxfield Road
Distance: 7 miles
River time: 2 to 3 hours
Season: April to June
Rating: Class 2
Hazards: Waves in Tyee rapids
Elevation: 330 to 260 feet—10 feet per mile
Shuttle: 8 miles, pavement
Flow information: USGS Washington website; NOAA recording
River gauge: Refer to 12045500 Elwha at McDonald Bridge
Historic flows: Average 1507 cfs; maximum 41,600; minimum 10
Maps: USGS Lake Pleasant, West of Pyscht; Olympic National Forest map
Information: Olympic National Forest/Olympic National Park Visitor Information in Forks; Forks Chamber of Commerce

The Soleduck is named after the Sol Duc Hot Springs near its headwaters in Olympic National Park. The Indian spelling, Sol Duc, means "sparkling water." Indians believed that the water had medicinal powers. Whatever the healing powers of the hot springs may be, a trip on the river can be healing to the soul. The clear water, overhung by lush trees festooned with moss, teems with salmon and steelhead and flows through largely untouched banks. The Soleduck has magic.

Access. To reach the take-out from Forks, Washington, drive about 6 miles north on US 101 and turn onto Maxfield Road. The Washington Department of Fish and Wildlife boat ramp is

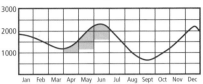

McDonald Bridge Gauge
Lower Soleduck
Recommend 1200 to 2500 cfs (May)

on the right just before the bridge over the river. (A WDFW vehicle access permit is required at the take-out and the put-in.)

The put-in is a total of about 12 miles north of Forks. From US 101, take the turnoff to the Soleduck River Salmon Hatchery near Sappho. (From either direction on US 101, the turn-off is about 0.2 mile after one of the highway bridges over the Soleduck.) Turn south and take an immediate right, following the sign, onto the paved road that leads to the "Fish Hatchery." The road parallels the river downstream about 1.5 miles to the hatchery. The boat ramp is to the right.

Paddle Route. No gauge has current readings for the Soleduck, so the water level must be judged by the gauge at McDonald Bridge on the Elwha, the next basin over. The Elwha gets more snow runoff than the Soleduck, so the reading needed on the McDonald Bridge gauge is higher later in the year. Boaters should look for somewhat greater than average flow in the spring or early summer. It is

Clear water and densely forested banks characterize the Soleduck.

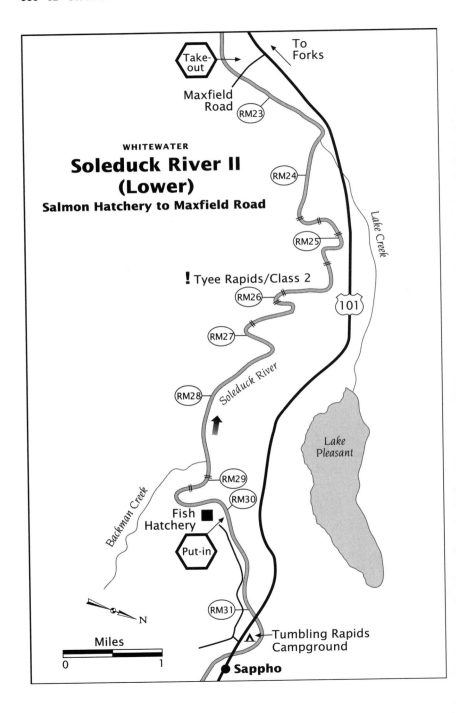

usually present after a good rain or a couple of hot days that melt the snow. The Lower Soleduck should provide a good canoe trip at flows on the McDonald Bridge gauge between 1000 and 2000 cubic feet per second in April, between 1200 and 2500 cfs in May, and between 1600 and 3200 cfs in June.

Good canoeists can negotiate the mild rapids on this trip. They consist mostly of rock gardens, requiring considerable threading through boulders, but they do not have powerful hydraulics. Tyee Rapids provide some waves that can swamp a poorly handled canoe, however.

The Soleduck is a beautiful river with lots of wildlife living in its stream and along its banks. Except for scattered cabins, the thick foliage screens away the sights and sounds of civilization. The author has seen deer, ducks, salmon, and bald eagles while threading through bouldery drops and drifting on crystal-clear pools.

Below this run, the river is almost entirely Class 1, except for three Class 2 rapids in the lower 23 miles of river: Shuwah Rapids, at the mouth of Shuwah Creek, about a mile below Maxfield Road; Double Rapids, a few miles farther down, just below the US 101 bridge near Forks; and a rapid just above the mouth of the river. This lower section also has pleasant scenery, but homes and cabins along the banks are much more common and nearly all the land is privately owned.

6 Upper Middle Fork Snoqualmie River

Location: Taylor River to Granite Creek
Distance: 7 miles
River time: 3 to 4 hours
Season: April through early July
Rating: Class 2, one Class 3 rapid
Hazards: Logjams, Class 3 rapid
Elevation: 1020 to 850 feet—24 feet per mile
Shuttle: 6.5 miles, gravel
Flow information: USGS Washington website; NOAA recording
River gauge: 12141300 near Tanner
Historic flows: Average 1223 cfs; maximum 49,000; minimum 91
Maps: USGS Mount Si, Bandera; Mount Baker–Snoqualmie National Forest map; Middle Fork of the Snoqualmie River Whitewater Recreation Guide from the Forest Service
Information: Mt. Baker–Snoqualmie National Forest, North Bend Ranger Station

The Upper Middle Fork of the Snoqualmie provides a wilderness-like trip within an hour's drive of the Seattle metropolitan area. With stunning mountain views and only one difficult rapid (which can be portaged with some difficulty), the

Paddling the clear waters of the Upper Middle Fork Snoqualmie

Upper Middle allows canoeists to get a feeling for the sort of experience that draws advanced rafters and kayakers to the few difficult several-day whitewater trips in the western United States. The Snoqualmie River takes its name from the Indian tribe from this area; the name derives from the Snoqualmie word for moon, the legendary life source for the tribe.

Access. From I-90, about 34 miles east of Seattle, just east of North Bend, take Exit 34 (Edgewick Road) and turn north. In about 0.2 mile, take a right on SE Middle Fork Road. About a mile farther, the road divides (take either fork) and then rejoins again in 1.2 miles. Within a couple miles of the road rejoining, the pavement ends; about 3 miles farther is the Granite Creek take-out. The take-out, on the left as you drive up the road, is signed and about 50 yards downstream of the bridge over the Middle Fork.

Check the odometer when crossing the bridge over the river. Russian Butte View river access is on the right side of the road about 3 miles above the bridge along a turnout marked by nine or ten large boulders. Riverbend access is another 2.2 miles (5.2 miles from the bridge) up the road (again marked by boulders placed along a pull-out). This access is below Rainy Creek Drop, the one Class 3 rapid of the trip, allowing those who want to avoid Rainy Creek to start their trip here.

The main put-in is at Bridgeview river access 1.1 mile above River Bend (6.3 miles above the bridge) at another pullout marked by boulders, a couple hundred yards below the trail suspension bridge that crosses the Middle Fork just below the mouth of the Taylor River. Due to limited parking at the put-in, it should be used just for unloading boats. Park vehicles at the large turnout just a couple hundred yards down the road.

Paddle Route. The Upper Middle Fork makes for a good canoe trip between 800 and 2500 cubic feet per second. It can be run at higher levels, but becomes quite pushy in places.

Most of the rapids on this stretch

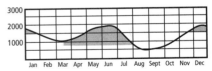

Upper Middle Fork Snoqualmie
Middle Fork Gauge
Recommend 800 to 2500 cfs

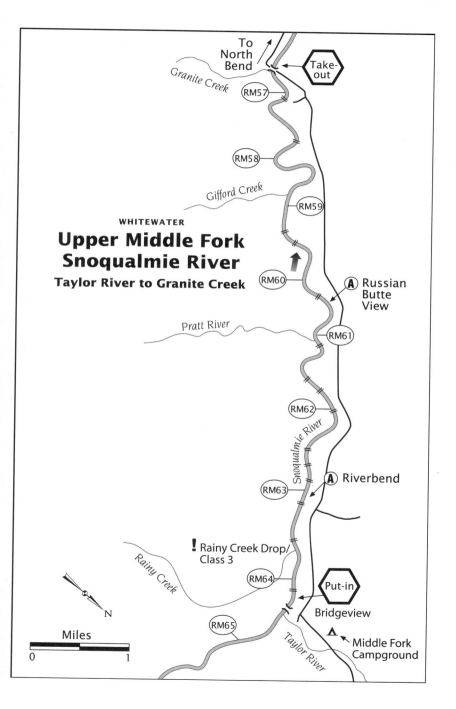

To North Bend

Granite Creek

Take-out

RM57

RM58

Gifford Creek

RM59

WHITEWATER

Upper Middle Fork Snoqualmie River

Taylor River to Granite Creek

RM60

Ⓐ Russian Butte View

Pratt River

RM61

RM62

Snoqualmie River

Ⓐ Riverbend

RM63

! Rainy Creek Drop/ Class 3

Rainy Creek

RM64

Put-in

Bridgeview

N

RM65

Taylor River

▲ Middle Fork Campground

Miles

0   1

are straightforward Class 1 and 2, but Rainy Creek drop is more difficult. It has some good-sized waves and ends in a headwall on the left bank. Watch for the river plunging down out of sight toward the left bank as the sign for this rapid. It can be portaged (with some difficulty) on the right bank, which is steep and rocky, but there is a nice eddy to put into below the drop.

On a clear day, the scenery is outstanding, with breathtaking views of Mount Garfield above the put-in (between the Upper Middle and Taylor rivers). The valleys of both the Middle Fork and the Taylor were carved out by glaciers in the last ice age. Continuing downriver, Preacher Mountain and Russian Butte come into view to the south and Green Mountain to the north. The Pratt River valley is revealed as a dramatic cleft between Preacher Mountain and Russian Butte in the middle of the run. The Upper Middle has natural forested banks and several nice beaches.

Just upstream from the Bridgeview river access is a parking area for the suspension trail bridge over the Middle Fork. It provides access to great hiking trails up the Middle Fork and Pratt River valleys. A Forest Service park pass may be required here. A little farther up the road along the Taylor River is the Forest Service's Middle Fork Campground.

The Middle Fork, Taylor, and Pratt rivers would make fine additions to our National Wild and Scenic Rivers System.

7 Skagit River

Location: Goodell Creek to Copper Creek
Distance: 9 miles
River time: 2 to 3 hours
Season: Year round, best August to October
Rating: Class 3
Hazards: S-bends, rapids
Elevation: 473 to 355 feet—13 feet per mile
Shuttle: 8 miles, pavement
Flow information: USGS Washington website; NOAA recording
River gauge: 12178000 at Newhalem
Historic flows: Average 4395 cfs; maximum 63,500; minimum 54
Maps: USGS Mount Triumph, Big Devil Peak, Marblemount; Skagit River Boating Map and Guide available from North Cascades National Park or Mount Baker–Snoqualmie National Forest
Information: North Cascades National Park at Marblemount

The Skagit River area is full of wonders. Paddle the river in early fall, and you'll see salmon spawning. Paddle it during the winter months, and you'll often be treated to the sight of bald eagles feeding on the spawned salmon. The Skagit takes its name from the local Indian tribe, which made extensive use of the river.

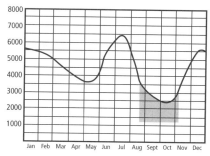

Skagit
Newhalem Gauge
Recommend 1200 to 3500 cfs

Although the Skagit is dam-controlled (by Seattle City Light's Ross, Diablo, and Gorge dams), the river and surrounding area have remained so pristine that they are part of the Ross Lake National Recreation Area attached to North Cascades National Park. The NRA does not prohibit dam construction, however, and this section of the Skagit should be added to the National Wild and Scenic Rivers System (joining the rest of the river below Bacon Creek) to assure that it remains free-flowing.

Prepare to paddle hard for boat control in the Skagit River.

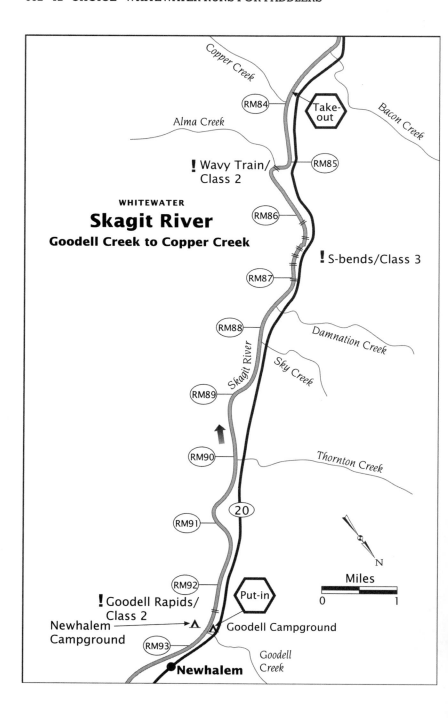

Copper Creek

RM84

Take-out

Bacon Creek

Alma Creek

! Wavy Train/ Class 2

RM85

WHITEWATER
Skagit River
Goodell Creek to Copper Creek

RM86

! S-bends/Class 3

RM87

RM88

Damnation Creek

Skagit River

Sky Creek

RM89

RM90

Thornton Creek

20

RM91

Miles

0   1

N

RM92

Put-in

! Goodell Rapids/ Class 2

Newhalem Campground

Goodell Campground

RM93

Goodell Creek

● Newhalem

Permits for trips on the river are self-issued at the Goodell Creek launch site.

Access. SR 20 east of Sedro Woolley parallels the Skagit River. The put-in is at Goodell Creek Campground, about 60 miles east of Sedro Woolley, Washington, near the Seattle City Light town of Newhalem (a corruption of the Indian word meaning "goat snare").

The take-out, 9 miles downstream, is at the end of a gravel road marked by a very small sign, saying "NP-213." The road leaves the main highway about 0.9 mile upstream of the bridge over Bacon Creek or about 0.1 mile downstream of a sign for Ross Lake National Recreation Area.

Paddle Route. The Skagit is an exciting trip at flows from 1200 to 3500 cubic feet per second. Above 3500 cfs, the S-bends are too big for any but the very best canoeists. Because the Skagit is dam-controlled, its water level fluctuates more in relation to the need for power during the week than it does seasonally, but it tends to be at good levels August to October.

Most of this trip is Class 1 or 2, the notable exception being the S-bends that occur about three-fourths of the way through the route. The S-bends (Shovel Spur or The Portage) are the trip's most difficult part: a series of four to five drops, beginning and ending with Class 2s and having a couple of Class 3s in between.

Scout the S-bends before undertaking this run. To do so, stop at the turnout along SR 20 just upstream of mile marker 114. The first Class 2 rapid is nearly 0.2 mile upstream from here, but the big Class 3s are just downstream of the turnout. When you are on the river, the steep rock bank formed by the highway on river right provides a good view, but you may find landing and scouting easier on river left.

This section of the river is steeper and has more rapids than the part downstream because the rocks underlying this trip are much harder than those downstream. A major fault line in the North Cascades, the Straight Creek Fault, runs roughly north–south and crosses the Skagit a little upstream from Marblemount (named for the marble in the mountains surrounding the town). The fault line is a little downstream from the take-out on this run. The rocks east of the Straight Creek Fault are hard granites and gneisses, while the rocks west of the fault are softer mudstones and muddy sandstones.

The Skagit is a pretty clear-green color and, on this trip, runs between banks unmarked by civilization except for SR 20, which generally doesn't intrude on the paddling experience since it is well above the river. The river is always cold, since the water is held in the deep pool in Ross Lake rather than warming in river shallows. The trip offers nice views of the nearby mountains and wildlife. Ducks, geese, deer, and raccoons are frequently seen along this stretch. Present, but less frequently seen are coyotes, otters, beavers, and bears.

8 Naches River

Location: Sawmill Flat to Tieton River
Distance: 6 to 26 miles
River time: 5 to 7 hours (spring flows)
Season: Late April to late June
Rating: Class 2, some Class 3
Hazards: Class 3 rapids, dams, logs, brush
Elevation: 2485 to 1575 feet—35 feet per mile
Shuttle: 22 miles, pavement
Flow information: U.S. Army Corps of Engineers Yakima Basin website
River gauge: Cliffdell
Historic flows: Not available
Maps: USGS Cliffdell, Manastash Lake, Nile, Milk Canyon, Tieton; Wenatchee National Forest map
Information: Wenatchee–Okanogan National Forest, Naches Ranger Station

The Naches derives its name from an Indian word meaning "plenty of water." While this is dry country, there is usually plenty of water in the Naches during the May and June boating season. The upper part of the river is in the Wenatchee National Forest in a

Naches
Cliffdell Gauge
Recommend 800 to 1800 cfs

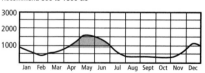

canyon lined with basalt cliffs and pine-forested hillsides. The lower end of the run is in stark desert country, and the rapids become more exciting. The Naches often has sun and warm temperatures in May and June, when the water levels are good.

Access. The Naches is about 19 miles northwest of Yakima, Washington, along SR 410. This run starts in the Wenatchee National Forest at the picnic area of Sawmill Flat Campground. The river can also be accessed at the bridge on Old River Road at river mile 38.8. To reach this put-in, exit the highway at the sign for Lost Creek Village and drive about a half mile to the bridge.

Two other access points are just downstream of the upper Nile bridge on the left bank and just downstream of the lower Nile bridge on the right bank. To run (or avoid) Horseshoe Canyon near the end of the run, you can access the river near Mile Marker 113 on SR 410. The bottom take-out is almost directly under the US 12 bridge over the river. There is no nearby parking, but it is possible to exit the river on the left bank right under the bridge.

Paddle Route. Expect a good canoe trip on the Naches when the water is from

Cabins and foliage are common along the Naches River.

800 to 1800 cubic feet per second on the Cliffdell gauge. The river can be run at flows above 1800 cfs, but there are likely to be few eddies.

The most difficult rapids on the Naches can be seen from the highway, allowing boaters to determine if this run suits their abilities. Carefully study Cottonwood Rapid, about a quarter mile below Cottonwood Campground, and the Horseshoe Bend area before running them. Sticks and Stones Rapid is listed as Class 3 because it's difficult to run some of the channels on the right side between the islands. The large boulders on the right identify it.

Downed trees and brush sometimes block the smaller channels between the islands, particularly in the section of the river around lower Nile bridge. In 2006,

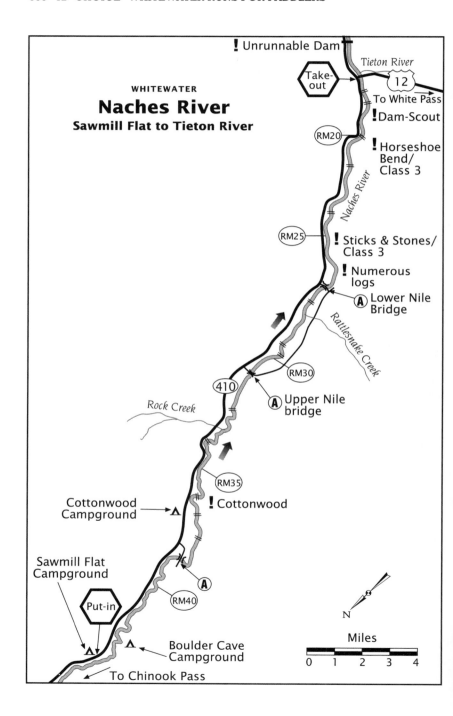

WHITEWATER
Naches River
Sawmill Flat to Tieton River

! Unrunnable Dam

Tieton River

Take-out

12

To White Pass

! Dam-Scout

RM20

! Horseshoe Bend/ Class 3

Naches River

RM25

! Sticks & Stones/ Class 3

! Numerous logs

(A) Lower Nile Bridge

Rattlesnake Creek

RM30

410

(A) Upper Nile bridge

Rock Creek

RM35

! Cottonwood

Cottonwood Campground ▲

Sawmill Flat Campground

(A)

RM40

Put-in

▲▼

▲ Boulder Cave Campground

To Chinook Pass

Miles

0 1 2 3 4

N

for example, a dangerous log blocked most of the river a little above the dam at the end of the trip near highway mile marker 115.

Check out the dams. The one near the end of the trip can be seen from the highway. Scout, line, or run it on the right, but be very cautious since the hydraulics behind even a very low dam can trap and hold anyone swimming in the river. A very dangerous dam is just below the take-out. Boaters must be sure they don't go beyond the US 12 bridge.

In May and June, the area above the upper Nile bridge is often thick with wildflowers, and throughout the boating season, boaters enjoy the beautiful basalt cliffs lining much of the upper portion of the river. Although the area is nearly all national forest land, many private cabins and bridges have been built in this stretch of river.

Spelunkers might want to take a side trip when they reach Boulder Cave picnic area on the right bank of the river, a short way into the trip. A 0.75-mile hike leads up to Boulder Cave, formed by the erosive action of Devil Creek, which runs through it.

Below upper Nile bridge, the pine forests disappear as the land becomes drier. Paddlers leave behind the cliffs as the valley widens. But the trip ends with a bang. A spectacular canyon, narrow and dry, forms the Horseshoe Bend area near the end of the run, where the river has saved the best rapids of the trip for last.

9 Wenatchee River

Location: Peshastin to Cashmere
Distance: 9 miles
River time: 3 to 4 hours
Season: July to August
Rating: Class 3
Hazards: Class 3 rapids, dam
Elevation: 1000 to 740 feet—28 feet per mile
Shuttle: 10 miles, pavement
Flow information: USGS Washington website; NOAA recording
River gauge: 12459000 at Peshastin
Historical flows: Average 3053 cfs; maximum 41,300; minimum 183
Maps: USGS Peshastin, Cashmere; Wenatchee National Forest map
Information: Wenatchee–Okanogan National Forest, Wenatchee River Ranger Station

The Wenatchee is a snow-fed river running off the east side of the North Cascades. It is probably the most popular and frequently run river in Washington. After the winter snowpack has melted and pooled in Lake Wenatchee, the river thunders through Tumwater Canyon and exits near Leavenworth. "Wenatchee" comes from a Native American name for the river, which means "river flowing from canyon."

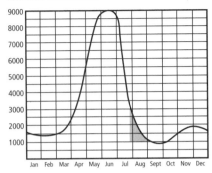

Wenatchee
Peshastin Gauge
Recommend 1000 to 3000 cfs

Access. US 2 runs along this stretch of the Wenatchee River, which is between Wenatchee and Leavenworth, Washington. The put-in is at the Department of Fish and Wildlife access (vehicle access permit required) at the end of School Street in Peshastin, which takes its name from an Indian word meaning "wide bottom canyon." Cross the bridge from US 2

Wenatchee River paddlers buck around on high water in the Rodeo Hole. (Kathy Spencer photo)

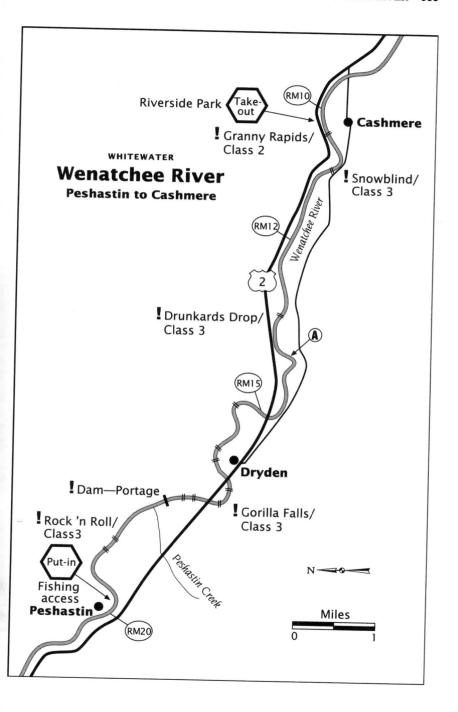

Riverside Park

Take-out

RM10

● **Cashmere**

❗ Granny Rapids/
Class 2

WHITEWATER
Wenatchee River
Peshastin to Cashmere

❗ Snowblind/
Class 3

RM12

Wenatchee River

2

❗ Drunkards Drop/
Class 3

Ⓐ

RM15

● **Dryden**

❗ Dam—Portage

❗ Gorilla Falls/
Class 3

❗ Rock 'n Roll/
Class 3

Put-in

Peshastin Creek

N

Fishing
access
Peshastin ●

RM20

Miles

0   1

to Peshastin and turn right on School Street. Go 0.3 mile to the access on the north side of the river.

The take-out is provided by the City of Cashmere just below the Division Street bridge. Parking, restrooms, and a changing area are available; follow the signs to Riverside Park. Note that to reach the take-out, you have to go to the right of a gravel bar, which is to the right of the center of the river.

Paddle Route. Rafters and kayakers usually run this river at flows of 4000 to 15,000 cubic feet per second. For canoes, the author recommends 1000 to 3000 cfs—flows that virtually assure the crowds will be gone in July or August. Only very good canoeists are likely to avoid swamping an open canoe at levels above 1800 cfs in Rock 'n Roll and Drunkards Drop.

Rock 'n Roll (RM 18.5), the first major rapid on the Wenatchee, is also its longest. High water produces huge waves and holes here. Below 3000 cfs, it is a rock garden with water washing over and rushing through the gaps between the rocks. At flows over 2500 cfs, a hole named Satan's Eyeball forms in the right center of the channel. Scout by landing at the head of a brush-covered island on the left side of the river (watch for a small amount of water that goes off through boulders and brush on the left side of the island). Generally, the best route is a bit left of center.

Shortly after Rock 'n Roll, you will come to the diversion dam, which *must* be portaged on the right bank. It is easy to take out on the right bank upstream of the structure with the metal hoist and carry around on the path cleared for portaging. A wheeled cart may be available to help haul your boat. The dam is a drowning machine; it creates a uniform wave breaking upstream all the way across the river. The water on the surface is moving upstream toward the dam and will trap anyone swimming in the river until they drown.

Below the dam and under the highway bridge is the second major rapid on the river, Gorilla Falls. The best run is near the right pier, away from the rocks on the left.

Drunkards Drop (RM 13.3) is the third significant rapid on the Wenatchee. It involves a 3–4 foot drop, which is at an angle to the flow of the river and creates waves that hit boats at an angle from the right. The rapid occurs right where the river turns along a dirt bluff on the left. Scouting can be done on the gravel bar on the right side.

For smaller boats, the rapid is most difficult at about 2000 cfs because the first wave becomes a back-curler, creating a hole that extends all the way across the river. The back-curler is 2 to 3 feet high and will easily flip a small raft or a poorly handled canoe or kayak. At 2500 cfs, the back-curler becomes a smooth wave, while at 1500 cfs, the back-curler is too small to be a significant obstacle.

The last significant rapid on the river is Snowblind (RM 10.8). The river tumbles over several rocks and ledges, creating waves and holes. Generally it can be run down the center or left by threading around the rocks and holes.

Granny Rapids (RM 10.2) provides some fun, clean waves to end the trip.

10 Methow River

Location: Carlton to McFarland Creek
Distance: 10 miles
River time: 3 to 4 hours
Season: July to August
Rating: Class 2
Hazards: Logs, sunburn
Elevation: 1390 to 1190 feet—21 feet per mile
Shuttle: 8 miles, pavement
Flow information: USGS Washington website, NOAA recording
River gauge: 12449950 near Pateros
Historic flows: Average 1522 cfs; maximum 46,700; minimum 150
Maps: USGS Methow; Okanogan National Forest map
Information: Washington Department of Fish and Wildlife, North Central Office in Ephrata

The Methow (pronounced MET-how) originates high in the North Cascades and runs with melting snow into the lake formed on the Columbia by Wells Dam near Pateros. The Indian name for the river means "salmon falls river." It's a good description. The river has a lot of rapids and runs of salmon and steelhead. The valley through which it flows is surrounded by dry, sagebrush-covered hills that look like the setting for a Hollywood western movie. In fact, Owen Wister wrote *The Virginian* while he was living in Winthrop, where the Chewuch joins the Methow.

Methow
Pateros Gauge
Recommend 1000 to 3000 cfs

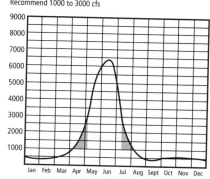

Access. SR 153, which can be reached on either SR 20 near Winthrop, Washington, or on US 97 at Pateros, parallels the Methow.

The put-in is at the Department of Fish and Wildlife's fishing access at Carlton (vehicle access permit required). The access is just upstream of the bridge over the river at Carlton, named after early settler Carl Dillard. The take-out is at the McFarland Creek fishing access (vehicle access permit required). The fishing access is just above the bridge 3 miles upstream from the town of Methow. The trail to the river is steep.

Paddle Route. Flows of 1000 to 3000 cubic feet per second are generally ideal for canoeing the Methow. Plenty of kayakers and rafters float the Methow at high

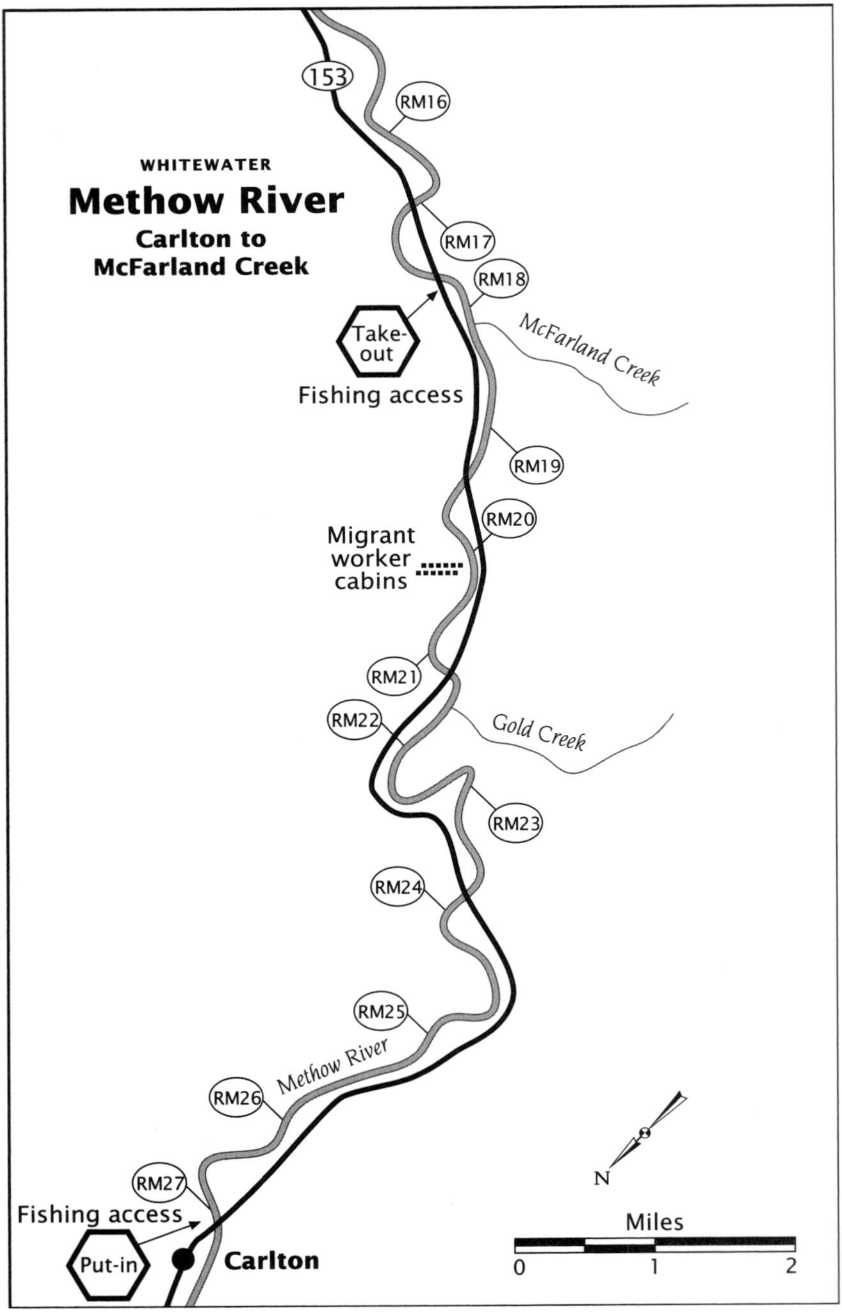

WHITEWATER
Methow River
Carlton to McFarland Creek

153

RM16

RM17

RM18

Take-out

Fishing access

McFarland Creek

RM19

RM20

Migrant worker cabins

RM21

RM22

Gold Creek

RM23

RM24

RM25

Methow River

RM26

RM27

Fishing access

Put-in ● Carlton

N

Miles
0   1   2

flows in May and early June, but the river is pretty quiet in the summer at good canoeing levels.

The river valley narrows appreciably at Carlton, due to the harder metamorphic rocks underlying the lower part of the valley. Where the valley floor above Carlton is often a couple of miles wide with broad orchards and alfalfa fields, below Carlton the valley is rarely more than 300 yards wide with the orchards confined

Wide, rocky stretch on the Methow River

to narrow fields along the river and benches along the highway. The steeper banks along the lower part of the river make boating this stretch seem more like boating through wild country rather than farmland.

The rapids on this run gradually increase from an occasional Class 1 to fairly frequent Class 2 rapids by the end of the trip. The trip provides fine dry-side-of-Washington scenery: open-range hills with pine-filled gullies and apple orchards on the valley floor. The bridges over the river provide the major landmarks along the way. Note that all the land along the river is privately owned, so paddlers must drive away from the river for camping. Campsites are available at Alta Lake State Park just south of the river valley near Pateros and at Forest Service campgrounds at Foggy Dew up the Gold Creek road or at Blackpine Lake up the Libby Creek road, leaving SR 153 a little over a mile south of Carlton.

11 St. Maries River (Upper)

Location: Santa to St. Maries River Road
Distance: 19 miles
River time: 6 to 10 hours
Season: Typically April through May
Rating: Class 2 to 3
Hazards: Drops, rocks, sharp bends, sweepers, strainers
Elevation: 2600 to 2100 feet—26 feet per mile
Shuttle: 22 miles, pavement, gravel
Flow information: USGS Idaho website
River gauge: 12414900 near Santa, Idaho
Historic flows: Average 338 cfs; maximum 12,300; minimum 15
Maps: USGS Lindstrom Peak, Santa; St. Joe National Forest map
Information: Idaho Panhandle National Forests, St. Joe River District, St. Maries office

This trip on the St. Maries starts out deceptively calm. A paddler can enjoy the swallows that nest under the SR 3 bridge and the eagles that have their own nest nearby, at much loftier heights. Campers wave from shore at a speck on the map called Mashburn. Deer splash across the river.

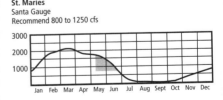

St. Maries
Santa Gauge
Recommend 800 to 1250 cfs

The peace lasts for roughly the first third of the trip, even as the narrow river begins dropping into a heavily wooded canyon. But a close look at a topographical map shows the contour lines coming close upon each other in the middle miles,

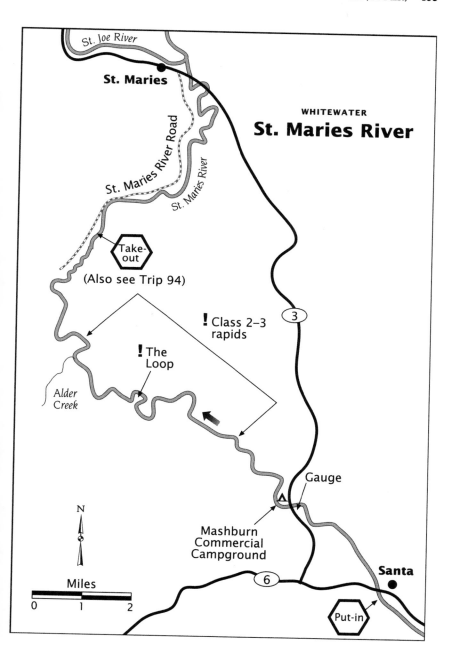

Paddling the Upper St. Maries

where the canyon is especially remote. There, paddlers can do little but pry, draw, and cross-draw—often in quick succession—to keep their boats upright. There are few breaks between rapids, and at low water, even the best of paddlers will simply ricochet from rock to rock.

Then the calm returns, as the St. Maries broadens into the shady, lazy stream that eventually joins the St. Joe River at the town of St. Maries (see Trip 94).

Access. This trip ends where Trip 94 begins. To reach the takeout from SR 3 (College Street) in the town of St. Maries, Idaho, drive south on First Street (behind the IGA store). Two miles from the highway, the road turns from pavement to gravel and gets progressively rougher—though not so bad as to pose a problem for most passenger cars. Drivers should keep track of railroad crossings. The takeout is nearly 6 miles from the highway, just past the fourth crossing. A very rough road leads over the tracks to the river, but it's not necessary to take it; those driving low-clearance vehicles can park in the turnout on the opposite side of the road.

To reach the put-in, follow SR 3 south from the town of St. Maries. The highway crosses the river at 11 miles; keep going another 3, to the junction with SR 6. Turn left and drive about 2 miles to the community of Santa. Turn right onto Davis Road (just after the highway crosses the river), which leads about 100 yards to a grassy river access.

Paddle Route. The canyon stretch of the St. Maries is rarely floated on days when paddlers are wiping sweat from their brows and craving cold beverages. It is spring, not summer, when paddlers will find the ideal flows of about 1200 cubic feet per second. The water will be chilly from rain and snowmelt, and the weather often overcast, if not rainy. Most veterans recommend flows of no less than 800 cfs, and so many rocks are exposed at 500 cfs that paddlers will leave a trail of Dagger green, Mad River red, or Prijon blue.

The waves come steadily, starting about 8 miles into the trip, with most of the Class 3s in a section called The Loop. Visitors will know where The Loop begins because the river passes under a railroad trestle. The other end of The Loop can be viewed by walking through the adjacent railroad tunnel, a distance of only about one-quarter mile by land but over a mile by river.

The rapids become less severe near Alder Creek, after which the canyon gradually broadens and the St. Maries becomes lazy again.

This is logging country, as evidenced by the clearcuts visible from the river. Land ownership is a mix of corporate, Forest Service, and state, with much of the land to the north included in the St. Maries State Wildlife Management Area.

The only decent river access in the canyon is a forest road that leaves SR 3 about 6 miles south of the town of St. Maries. It's clearly marked as "Sportsman's Access" at the highway, but a first-time visitor is likely to become lost in the maze of logging roads before reaching the river (although the primary road was being upgraded as this book was published). There's little reason for a paddler to begin or end the trip at this point; and doing so would greatly complicate an otherwise simple shuttle. There is, however, a rough campsite at the access.

The St. Maries isn't particularly known for its fishing—nothing like the nearby St. Joe, at any rate. Runoff is needed for prime flows for paddling, and that makes the angling tough for trout. The lower river is locally popular for bass and pike.

12 Selway River

Location: Near Lowell
Distance: 9 to 16 miles
River time: 3 hours
Season: Generally mid-June through July
Rating: Class 3 above Getney Creek; Class 2+ below
Hazards: Numerous rapids
Elevation: 1700 to 1540 feet—15 feet per mile
Shuttle: 9 miles, gravel
Flow information: USGS Idaho website
River gauge: 13336500 near Lowell
Historic flows: Average 3695 cfs; maximum 45,300; minimum 150
Maps: USGS Goddard Point, Stillman Point, Selway Falls; Nez Perce National Forest map
Information: Nez Perce National Forest, Fenn Ranger Station near Lowell, River Dance Lodge, and Three Rivers Resort

From its sources at 9000 feet, and for most of its 90-mile journey, the Selway River flows through one of the largest roadless tracts in the lower forty-eight states. Permits for an extended whitewater float through the Selway–Bitterroot Wilderness are among the most coveted in the West, with about thirty applicants for every permit issued in recent years.

The river becomes visible to roads and civilization fewer than 20 miles from its confluence with the bigger whitewater on the Lochsa River. In that short, final stretch, the Selway has enough challenging whitewater and deep, green pools to keep a paddler busy for a weekend, and grinning through the week beyond.

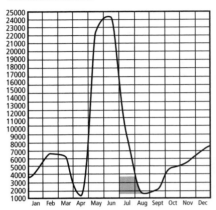

The lower river flows through a narrow canyon, heavily wooded with Douglas-fir, spruce, and pine. Impressive cedars crowd its banks.

Access. To reach the Selway, follow US 12 southeast from Orofino, Idaho, through the towns of Kamiah and Kooskia. About 62 miles from Orofino, the highway comes to the village of Lowell, where the Selway and Lochsa join to form the Middle Fork of the Clearwater River.

From Lowell, FR 223 follows the north bank of the Selway. At 7 miles, FR 661 (O'Hara Creek Road) takes off to the south, following O'Hara Creek. The beach where the two roads meet is an excellent take-out for a half day of boating.

FR 223 turns from rough pavement to even rougher gravel at O'Hara Creek. Eleven miles upstream from O'Hara is Selway Falls, which should not be attempted.

Paddlers skilled in negotiating Class 3 whitewater (and with the proper equipment, including helmets) can launch at Getney Creek, just downstream from the falls. The recommended put-in for intermediate paddlers is a small, unnamed turnout 2 miles downstream from Getney Creek.

Paddle Route. Below Gentry Creek are two major rapids, rated to Class 3, in 1.5 miles. Below that, the river is studded with many rapids—though not as large—and interspersed with lovely pools and riffles. The toughest water in the intermediate stretch is a challenging Class 2+ where the river splits around Rock Island. Boaters should pick the left channel and scout the rapids from shore.

If 9 miles on the Selway isn't enough, paddlers can continue downstream. From the O'Hara take-out, it's another 7 miles to the confluence with the Lochsa. From there, paddlers can continue downstream about 6 miles on the Middle Fork of the Clearwater River to the town of Sylvanite. Both the lower Selway and the upper Clearwater are studded with whitewater, which should be scouted from the road and again from shore.

While the Selway is blessed with a plethora of Forest Service campgrounds,

Opposite: On the Selway River in Idaho

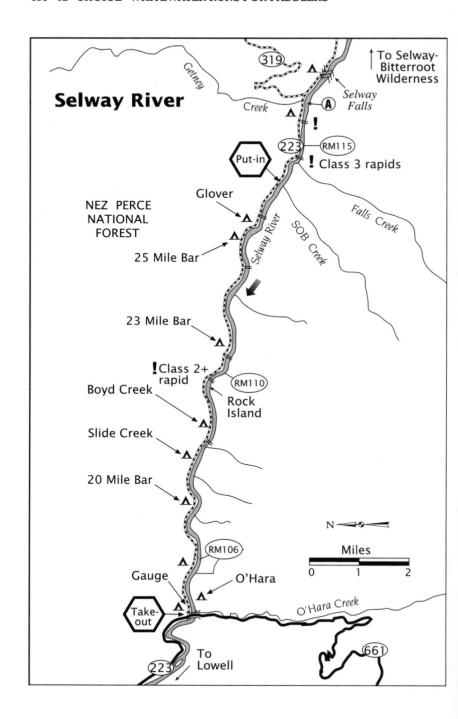

most are small and fill quickly. Those who travel light can load gear into a boat and choose numerous gravel bars on the roadless south side of the river.

Lowell is headquarters for several rafting companies. Three Rivers Resort has a private campground, motel, and cabins, along with a small store and restaurant. The resort is a good source for up-to-date river information.

Because its headwaters are protected, the Selway has not suffered as much from logging as many other Idaho streams. It holds healthy numbers of native cutthroat trout. Special fishing regulations are enforced and anglers are encouraged to gently release their catch.

appendices
appendix a: paddler's equipment list

Paddlers should list the gear they might take on any trip. All of the gear might go on an extended trip, only part of it on day trips. But always refer to the list when packing. Following is a sample list that can be personalized.

A signaling whistle should always be attached to life vests. In backcountry situations, put survival items (sealed in zippered plastic bags) in a fanny pack. Wear it at all times so the matches, knife, firestarter, etc., stay with you should your boat capsize and be lost.

BOAT
Paddles
Extra paddle
Life vests
Grab lines
Lashing cord
Flotation
Bail buckets
Sponge
Cushions
Extra dry bags
Rescue throw rope

CLOTHING
Fleece jacket
Fleece sweater
Long-sleeved shirt
Tee shirt
Socks
Underwear
Long underwear
Shorts
Long pants
Windbreaker
Raingear
Gloves

Brimmed hat for sun
Pile or wool hat for cold
Bandannas
Sandals or booties
Rubber boots
Dry shoes
Wet suit or dry suit

SHELTER
Tarp
Tent and groundcloth
Tent stakes
Sleeping bag and liner
Sleeping pad

FOOD PREPARATION
Stove and fuel
Water bag
Water purifier
Pliers (for handling pots)
Pots, pans
Plastic cup and bowl
Spoon, fork
Large knife
Foil
Pot scrubber

412

Hot drinks
Cold drinks
Snacks
Breakfasts
Lunches
Dinners
Salt, pepper, sugar, spices

PERSONAL
Toilet paper, wisely packaged
Biodegradable soap
Towel
Toothbrush
Floss
Candle
Lip salve
Hand lotion
Headnet

ESSENTIALS
First-aid kit
Map in waterproof case
Compass (GPS)
Knife
Extra food
Flashlight, extra batteries and bulb
Matches in waterproof container
Firestarter
Sun protection, including sunscreen
    and sunglasses with straps
Waterproof dump bag with complete
    clothes change
Plastic garbage bag
Waterproof bags and packs
Signaling devices (whistle, mirror)
Water bottles
Insect repellent
Licenses and permits
Nylon cord
Repair kit for boat and other gear;
    include duct tape

ACCESSORIES
Notepad and pen
Reading material
Field guide to flowers, birds, trees, etc.
Zippered plastic bags
Camera and film
Folding saw
Fire pan
Plastic trowel (for latrines)
Latrine (sometimes required)
Fishing gear
Fillet knife
Collapsible bucket
Binoculars
Day pack
Pepper spray

appendix b: information sources from trip summaries

Following are the contact references for information sources mentioned in the summaries at the beginning of each trip in this book. Use them as a quick or Internet reference for specific trips. They are listed alphabetically according to the region in which the trip occurs.

WESTERN WASHINGTON

AquaTrek, 360-403-1681; *www.seakayak-aquatrek.com*

Bay Center Marina in Port of Willapa, 360-942-3422

Blake's Skagit Resort and Marina, 360-445-6533; *www.blakesrvpark.com*

Cedar River Trail Park, 206-296-8687; *www.metrokc.gov/parks/trails/cedarriver .html*

Cowlitz County Tourism in Kelso, 360-577-3137; *www.co.cowlitz.wa.us*

Dungeness Kayaking, 360-681-4190; *www.dungenesskayaking.com*

Dungeness National Wildlife Refuge, 360-457-8451; *www.dungeness.com/refuge*

Everett Chamber of Commerce, 425-257-3222; *www.everettchamber.com*

Everybody's Store in Van Zandt, 360- 592-2297; *www.everybodys.com*

Forks Chamber of Commerce, 800-443-6757; *www.forkswa.com*

Grays Harbor Chamber of Commerce, 360-532-1924, toll-free 800-321-1924; *www.graysharbor.org*

Grays Harbor County Visitor's Center, 800-621-9625; *www.tourismgraysharbor .com*

Kent Parks and Recreation Department, 253-856-5100; *www.ci.kent.wa.us/parks*

King County Parks and Recreation Division, 206-296-8687; *www.metrokc.gov/parks*

King County Department of Natural Resources, 206-296-6500; *http://dnr .metrokc.gov/wlr/watersheds/cedrLKWA/cedar-river-public-access.htm*

Kroll Map Co., Seattle, 206-448-6277; *www.krollmap.com*

La Push Marina (Quillayute Reservation), 360-374-4338 or 360-374-5392

Lewis County Tourism, toll-free 800-525-3323; *www.tourlewiscounty.com*

Lummi Indian Tribal Council, 2616 Kwina Road, Bellingham, WA 98226-9298; 360-384-1489; *www.lummi-nsn.org*. Weather: 360-384-2365

Marysville Parks and Recreation Department, 360-363-8400; *www.ci.marysville .wa.us*

Monroe Chamber of Commerce, 318-323-3461; toll-free 888-531-9535; *www.monroe.org*

Mount Baker–Snoqualmie National Forest, 425-783-6000; toll-free 800-627-0062 *www.fs.fed.us/r6/mbs;*
  Darrington Ranger Station, 360-436-1155; *www.fs.fed.us/r6/mbs/about/drd;*
  Mount Baker Ranger Station, 360-856-5700; *www.fs.fed.us/r6/mbs*
  North Bend Office, 425-888-1421; *www.fs.fed.us/r6/mbs*

Nisqually National Wildlife Refuge, 360-753-9467; *www.fws.gov/nisqually*

Nisqually Reach Nature Center, 360-459-0387; *www.nisquallyestuary.org*

North Cascades National Park Visitor Information, 360-873-4500 or 360-854-7200; *www.nps.gov/noca*

North Olympic Peninsula Visitors Center in Port Angeles, toll-free 800-942-4042 or 360-452-8552; *www.olympicpeninsula.org*

Northwest Source; *www.nwsource.com*

Olympic National Forest, 360-956-2402; *www.fs.fed.us/r6/olympic*

Olympic National Park, 360-565-3130; *www.nps.gov/olym*
  Pacific District North, 360-374-6522
  Pacific District South, 360-288-2525

Port Angeles Boat Haven Marina, 360-457-4505; *www.portofpa.com/marinas*

Port Angeles Chamber of Commerce, 360-452-2363; *www.portangeles.org*

Port of Seattle Public Affairs, 206-728-3000; *www.portseattle.org/seaport /waterfront*

Port of Willapa, 360-942-3422; *www.portofwillapaharbor.com*

Port Townsend Chamber of Commerce, toll-free 888-365-6978 or 360-385-2722; *www.ptchamber.org*

PT Outdoors in Port Townsend, 888-754-8598; *www.ptoutdoors.com*

Rainforest Paddlers, Inc., 866-457-8398; *www.rainforestpaddlers.com*

Redmond Recreation and Arts, 425-556-2300; *www.ci.redmond.wa.us /recreationarts/recreation_arts.asp*

REI/Outdoor Recreation Information Center, 206-470-4060; *www.nps.gov /ccso/oric.htm*

Ride Store in Lynnwood, 425-348-2350

Semiahmoo Park, 360-733-2900; *www.co.whatcom.wa.us/parks/parklist.jsp*

Sequim-Dungeness Valley Chamber of Commerce, toll-free 800-737-8462 or 360-683-6197; *www.cityofsequim.com*

Skagit River Bald Eagle Interpretive Center in Rockport, 360-853-7626; *www.skagiteagle.org*

Skagit-Snoqualmie Wildlife Area, 360-445-4441; *http://wdfw.wa.gov/reg /region4.htm*

Snohomish Chamber of Commerce, 360-568-2526; *www.cityofsnohomish.com*

Snohomish County PUD, 360-563-2200; *www.snopud.com*

Snohomish County Tourism Bureau, 425-348-5802 or toll free 888-338-0976; *www.snohomish.org*

Snoqualmie Valley Chamber of Commerce, 425-888-4440; *www.snovalley.org*

Sound Bikes & Kayaks, 360-457-1240; *www.soundbikeskayaks.com*

Tacoma Public Utilities, 888-502-8690; *www.ci.tacoma.wa.us/power*

Town Graphics, 425-486-2067; *www.nwplaces.com*

USGS Washington Web site, *http://wa.water.usgs.gov;*
Real-time streamflows; *http://waterdata.usgs.gov/wa/nwis/rt*
National streamflow site, *http://waterdata.usgs.gov/nwis/rt*

Verlot Public Service Center, 360-691-7791

Wahkiakum County Visitor Information, 360-795-9996; *www.wahkiakumchamber.com*

Washington Coast Chamber of Commerce, 800-289-4552; *http://washingtoncoastchamber.org*

Washington Department of Fish and Wildlife website for Wildlife Areas and Access Points, *http://wdfw.wa.gov/lands/wildarea.htm*

Washington Department of Parks and Recreation, *www.parks.wa.gov*
Flaming Geyser State Park, 253-931-3930
Sequim Bay State Park, 360-683-4235

Washington Department of Natural Resources, 800-527-3305; *www.dnr.wa.gov.*
Castle Rock Office, 360-577-2025
Forks Office 360-374-6131

Washington State Travel Information, toll-free 800-544-1800; *www.experiencewashington.com*

Washington Water Trails Association in Seattle, 206-545-9161; *www.wwta.org*

Whatcom County Parks and Recreation Department, 360-733-2900; *www.co.whatcom.wa.us/parks*

NORTHERN CASCADES

North Cascades National Park, 360-854-7200; *www.nps.gov/noca*

Okanogan–Wenatchee National Forest Visitor Center in Winthrop, 509-996-4000; *www.fs.fed.us/r6/okanogan*

Ross Lake National Recreation Area, Wilderness Information Center in Marblemount, 360-873-4590 ext. 39, or off-season, 360-856-5700; *www.nps.gov/lach*

Ross Lake Resort, 206-386-4437; *www.rosslakeresort.com*

Seattle City Light, current lake levels recording, 206-684-3030; *www.seattle.gov/light*

Washington Department of Fish and Wildlife, Ephrata Regional Office, 509-754-4624; *www.wdfw.wa.gov/reg/region2.htm*

Wenatchee–Okanogan National Forest, Lake Wenatchee Ranger Station, 509-763-3103 or 509-664-2708 (toll-free from Wenatchee); *www.fs.fed.us/r6/wenatchee*

Wenatchee Valley Chamber of Commerce, 509-662-2116 or 800-572-7753; *www.wenatchee.org*

INLAND NORTHWEST
Eastern Washington

Avista Utilities, 208-769-1357; *www.avistautilities.com*

Beaver Lodge Resort at Lake Gillette, 509-684-5657

Boundary Dam Powerhouse north of Metaline, 509-446-3083; *www.seattle .gov/light/tours/boundary*

Chelan County Public Utility District in Wenatchee, 509-661-8000; *www.chelanpud.org/river-flows.html*

Colville Confederated Tribes Parks and Recreation, 509-633-9265; *www.colvilletribes.com/fishing.htm*

Fishtrap Lake Resort, 509-235-2284

Grand Coulee Dam Chamber of Commerce, 509-632-5043; *www.grandcouleedam.org*

Hanford Reach National Monument, 509-371-1801; *www.fws.gov/hanfordreach*

Lake Roosevelt National Recreation Area, *www.nps.gov/laro;*
   Headquarters in Coulee Dam, 509-633-9441
   Kettle Falls Ranger Station, 509-738-6266

Lyons Ferry Park near Starbuck, 509-399-8020

Mar Don Resort at Potholes Reservoir, 509-346-2651; *www.mardonresort.com*

McNary Dam (Umatilla, Oregon), 541-922-2268

National Resources Conservation Service in Colfax, 509-397-4636, ext. 3

Okanogan–Wenatchee National Forest, *www.fs.fed.us/r6/okanogan*
   Visitor Center in Winthrop, 509-996-4000 or 509-996-4004

River View Campground and Red's Fly Shop, north of Yakima, 509-929-1802; *www.redsflyshop.com*

Soap Lake Chamber of Commerce, 509-246-1821; *www.soaplakecoc.org*

Spokane County Sheriff marine deputies, 509-477-2204; *http://spokanesheriff .org/structure/patrol/default.aspx*

U.S. Army Corps of Engineers in Walla Walla, 509-527-7132; *www.nww.usace .army.mil/CorpsOutdoors*

U.S. Bureau of Land Management in Spokane, 509-536-1200; *www.blm.gov/or /districts/spokane*

U.S. Bureau of Reclamation in Ephrata, 509-754-0215; *www.usbr.gov*

U.S. Fish and Wildlife Service in Othello, 509-488-2668; *www.fws.gov/pacific/ columbiarefuge*

USGS Washington website, *http://wa.water.usgs.gov*
   Real-time streamflows, *http://waterdata.usgs.gov/wa/nwis/rt*
   USGS Water Resources in Pasco, 509-547-2571
   USGS Water Resources in Spokane, 509-353-2633

Washington Department of Fish and Wildlife, *www.wdfw.wa.gov*
  Ephrata Regional Office, 509-754-4624
  Spokane Regional Office, 509-892-1001
Washington Department of Parks and Recreation, *www.parks.wa.gov*
  Lake Wenatchee State Park, 509-763-3101; reservations, 888-226-7688
  Potholes State Park near Othello, 509-346-2759
  Riverside State Park in Spokane, 509-465-5064
  Sun Lakes State Park near Coulee City, 509-632-5583
Wenatchee-Okanogan National Forest, *www.fs.fed.us/r6/wenatchee*
Wenatchee River County Park near Monitor, 509-667-7503; *www.co.chelan
  .wa.us/wrp/wrp_main.htm*
Wenatchee Valley Chamber of Commerce, 509-662-2116 or 800-572-7753;
  www.wenatchee.org

British Columbia

Backroad Mapbook: Kootenays, by Russell and Wesley Mussio (Mussio Ventures),
  check booksellers or Amazon.com
British Columbia Parks in Cranbrook, 250-489-8523; *www.env.gov.bc.ca/bcparks*
Creston Chamber of Commerce, 250-428-4342; *www.crestonbc.com/chamber*
Creston Valley Wildlife Interpretive Centre, 250-402-6908; *www.crestonwildlife.ca*
Fernie Chamber of Commerce, 250-423-6868; *www.ferniechamber.com*
FortisBC (formerly West Kootenay Power Company) Kelowna, 866-436-7847;
  www.fortisbc.com
Kettle River Provincial Park contracted to Kaloya Contracting Ltd., 250-548-
  0076; *www.env.gov.bc.ca/bcparks*
Lemon Creek Lodge south of Slocan, 250-355-2403; *www.lemoncreeklodge.com*
Slocan District Chamber of Commerce, 250-358-2415; *www.slocanlake.com*
Valhalla Provincial Park, contracted to Kaloya Contracting Ltd., 250-548-0076;
  www.env.gov.bc.ca/bcparks
Water Survey Canada, *www.wsc.ec.gc.ca*
  Cranbrook, 250-426-4718; *http://scitech.pyr.ec.gc.ca/waterweb*
  Penticton, 250-770-4451; *http://scitech.pyr.ec.gc.ca/waterweb*
Wildways Adventure Sports and Tours in Christina Lake, 250-447-6561;
  www.wildways.com

Northern Idaho

Avista Utilities, 208-769-1357; *www.avistautilities.com*
Cabinet Gorge Dam, 208-266-1531
Clearwater National Forest, *www.fs.fed.us/r1/clearwater*
  Lochsa Ranger Station in Kooskia, 208-926-4274
Enaville Resort at Enaville, 208-682-3453
Friends of Coeur d'Alene Trails, *http://friendsofcdatrails.org*

Idaho Fish and Game Department in Coeur d'Alene, 208-769-1414;
 http://fishandgame.idaho.gov
Idaho Panhandle National Forests, *www.fs.fed.us/ipnf*
 Headquarters in Coeur d'Alene, 208-765-7223
 Bonners Ferry Ranger Station, 208-267-5561
 Coeur d'Alene River Ranger District, Fernan office, 208-769-3000
 Priest Lake Ranger Station, 208-443-2512
 St. Joe River Ranger District, Avery office, 208-245-4517
 St. Joe River District, St. Maries office, 208-245-2531
Idaho State Parks, *www.idahoparks.org/parks*
 Heyburn State Park near Chatcolet, 208-686-1308
 Old Mission State Park near Cataldo, 208-682-3814
 Priest Lake State Park near Coolin, 208-443-2200
Pack River General Store northeast of Sandpoint, 208-263-2409
Priest Lake Chamber of Commerce, 208-443-3191; *www.priestlake.org*
Sandpoint Chamber of Commerce, 208-263-0887; *http://sandpointchamber.org*
Three Rivers Resort in Lowell, 208-926-4430; *www.threeriversresort.com*
Twin Rivers Canyon Resort campground near Moyie Springs, 208-267-5932;
 www.twinriversresort.com
U.S. Bureau of Land Management in Coeur d'Alene, 208-769-5000; *www.blm*
 .gov/id/st/en.html
USGS Idaho website, *http://id.water.usgs.gov*
 Real-time streamflows, *http://waterdata.usgs.gov/id/nwis/current?type=flow*
USGS Water Resources:
 Sandpoint, 208-263-4123
 Moyie, 208-267-4377

Oregon
National Weather Service in Portland, 503-261-9246; *www.wrh.noaa.gov/pqr.*
Umatilla National Forest, *www.fs.fed.us/r6/uma*
 Walla Walla (Washington) Ranger Station, 509-522-6290
U.S. Bureau of Land Management river station in Minam, 541-437-5580

Montana
Confederated Salish and Kootenai Tribes in Pablo, 406-675-2700, ext. 4;
 www.cskt.org
Kerr Dam near Polson, 406-883-4450; *www.pplmontana.com/producing+power*
 /power+plants/Kerr+Dam.htm
Kootenai National Forest, *www.fs.fed.us/r1/kootenai*
 Headquarters in Libby, 406-293-6211
 Cabinet Ranger Station near Trout Creek, 406-827-3533
 Canoe Gulch Ranger Station near Libby, 406-293-7773

Three Rivers Ranger Station in Troy, 406-295-4693
Libby Dam recording, 406-293-3421 or 406-293-7751
Lolo National Forest, *www.fs.fed/us/r1/lolo*
    Plains Ranger Station, 406-826-3821
Quinns Hot Springs Resort near Paradise, 406-826-3150; *www.quinnshotsprings.com*
USGS Montana website, *http://mt.water.usgs.gov*
    Real-time streamflows, *http://waterdata.usgs.gov/mt/nwis/current?type=flow.*
USGS Water Resources in Kalispell, 406-755-6686

WHITEWATER TRIPS

Forks Chamber of Commerce, 800-443-6757; *www.forkswa.com.*
Gifford Pinchot National Forest, *www.fs.fed.us/gpnf*
    Cowlitz Valley Ranger Station in Randle, 360-497-1100; *www.fs.fed.us/gpnf.*
Idaho Panhandle National Forests, *www.fs.fed.us/ipnf*;
    St. Joe River District, St. Maries office, 208-245-2531
Mt. Baker–Snoqualmie National Forest, *www.fs.fed.us/r6/mbs*
    Snoqualmie Ranger Station in North Bend, 425-888-1421; *www.fs.fed.us/r6/
    mbs/about/snrd*
Nez Perce National Forest, *www.fs.fed/r1/nezperce*; 208-983-4099
    Fenn Ranger Station near Lowell, 208-926-4258
NOAA river level recording, 206-526-3195 or 206-526-8530
North Cascades National Park at Marblemount, 360-873-4590 or
    360-856-5700 ext. 515; *www.nps.gov/noca*
Olympic National Forest/Olympic National Park Visitor Information in Forks,
    360-374-7566 or 360-565-3130
Olympic National Forest/Olympic National Park Visitor Information in Port
    Angeles, 360-565-3130; *www.nps.gov/olym*
Olympic National Park, *www.nps.gov/olym*
    Elwha Ranger Station (seasonal), 360-452-9191
U.S. Army Corps of Engineers Yakima Basin, *www.nwd-wc.usace.army
    .mil/nws/hh/basins/yakima.html*
River Dance Lodge, 208-926-4300
USGS Washington, *http://wa.water.usgs.gov*
    Real-time streamflows, *http://waterdata.usgs.gov/wa/nwis/current?type=flow*
    Also see *http://wa.water.usgs.gov/realtime/rt_latest_map.html*
    National streamflow site, *http://waterdata.usgs.gov/nwis/rt*
Washington Department of Fish and Wildlife North Central Office in Ephrata,
    509-754-4624; *http://wdfw.wa.gov/reg/region2.htm*
Wenatchee–Okanogan National Forest, *www.fs.fed.us/r6/wenatchee*
    Methow Valley Ranger Station, 509-996-4003; *ww.fs.fed/us/r6/wenatchee*
    Naches Ranger Station, 509-653-1400; *www.fs.fed.us/r6/wenatchee*
    Wenatchee River Ranger Station, 509-548-6977; *www.fs.fed.us/r6/wenatchee*

appendix c: administration/ information sources

National Parks/National Forests

Olympic National Park/Olympic National Forest
Recreation Information Center
551 S Forks Avenue
Forks, WA 98331
360-374-7566

Olympic National Park Visitor Center
3002 Mount Angeles Road
Port Angeles, WA 98362
360-565-3130
www.nps.gov/olym

North Cascades National Park
810 State Route 20
Sedro Woolley, WA 98284
360-854-7200
www.nps.gov/noca

National Forest Headquarters

Clearwater National Forest
12730 Highway 12
Orofino, ID 83544
208-476-4541
www.fs.fed.us/r1/clearwater

Colville National Forest
765 S Main, Federal Building
Colville, WA 99114
509-684-7000
www.fs.fed.us/r6/colville

Gifford Pinchot National Forest
10600 NE 51st Circle
Vancouver, WA 98682
360-891-5000
www.fs.fed.us/gpnf

Idaho Panhandle National Forests
(headquarters for Coeur d'Alene, Kaniksu, and St. Joe National Forests)
3815 Schreiber Way
Coeur d'Alene, ID 83815-8363
208-765-7223
www.fs.fed.us/ipnf

Kootenai National Forest
1101 US Highway 2 W
Libby, MT 59923
406-293-6211
www.fs.fed.us/r1/kootenai

Mt. Baker–Snoqualmie National Forest
2930 Wetmore Avenue, Suite 3A
Everett, WA 98021
425-783-6000; 800-627-0062
www.fs.fed.us/r6/mbs

Nez Perce National Forest
1005 Highway 13
Grangeville, ID 83530
208-983-1950
www.fs.fed.us/r1/nezperce

Umatilla National Forest
2517 SW Hailey
Pendleton, OR 97801
541-278-3716
www.fs.fed.us/r6/uma

Wenatchee Okanogan National Forests
215 Melody Lane
Wenatchee, WA 98801
509-664-9200
www.fs.fed.us/r6/wenatchee

U.S. Army Corps of Engineers
Seattle District
4735 E Marginal Way S
Seattle WA 98134-2385
206-764-6183
www.nwd-wc.usace.army.mil/nws/hh
/basins

Walla Walla District
201 N Third Avenue
Walla Walla, WA 99362
509-527-7020
www.nww.usace.army.mil/CorpsOutdoors

U.S. Bureau of Land Management
Spokane District
1103 N Fancher Road
Spokane, WA 99212
509-536-1200
www.blm.gov/or/districts/spokane

Coeur d'Alene Office
3815 Schreiber Way
Coeur d'Alene, ID 83815
208-769-5000
www.blm.gov

Vale District
100 Oregon Street
Vale, OR 97918
541-473-3144
www.blm.gov/or/districts/vale

U.S. Bureau of Reclamation
Upper Columbia Area Office
1917 Marsh Road
Yakima, WA 98901-2058
509-575-5848

Grand Coulee Dam
P.O. Box 620
Grand Coulee, WA 99133-0620
509-633-9501
www.usbr.gov/pn/grandcoulee

U.S. Geological Survey
USGS Water Science Center
934 Broadway, Suite 300
Tacoma, WA 98402
253-552-1600
http://wa.water.usgs.gov

Pasco Field Office
403 W Lewis
Box 1344
Pasco, WA 99301
509-547-2571

Sedro Woolley Field Office
810 State Route 20
Sedro Woolley, WA 98284
360-856-5700

Spokane Field Office
920 W Riverside Avenue, Room 694
U.S. Court House
Spokane, WA 99201
509-353-2633

National Weather Service
www.weather.gov/ahps

State and Provincial Parks
Idaho State Parks and Recreation
5657 Warm Springs Avenue
P.O. Box 83720
Boise, ID 83720-0065
208-334-4199
www.idahoparks.org

Washington State Parks and Recreation
7150 Cleanwater Lane
P.O. Box 42650
Olympia, WA 98504-2650
360-902-8500
www.parks.wa.gov

British Columbia Parks
www.env.gov.bc.ca/bcparks

Fish and Wildlife Agencies
Idaho Fish and Game Department
P.O. Box 25
600 S. Walnut
Boise, ID 83707
208-334-3700
http://fishandgame.idaho.gov

Montana Fish, Wildlife, and Parks
1420 E 6th Avenue
P.O. Box 200701
Helena, MT 59620-0701
406-444-2535
http://fwp.mt.gov/contact

Oregon Fish and Wildlife
3406 Cherry Avenue NE
Salem, OR 97303
503-947-6000
www.dfw.state.or.us

Washington Fish and Wildlife
600 Capitol Way N
Olympia, WA 98501-1091
360-902-2200
http://wdfw.wa.gov

British Columbia Ministry of Water,
    Land and Air Protection
Fish and Wildlife Division
www.env.gov.bc.ca/fw

Other Information Sources
Lake Chelan Chamber of Commerce
102 East Johnson Avenue
Chelan, WA 98816
800-424-3526
www.lakechelan.com

Western Washington Outdoor
    Recreation Information Center
Seattle REI Building
222 Yale Avenue N
Seattle, WA 98109-5429
206-470-4060
www.nps.gov/ccso/oric.htm.

Washington Water Trails Association
4649 Sunnyside Avenue N #305
Seattle, WA 98103
206-545-9161
www.wwta.org

Streamflow Websites
British Columbia, *www.wsc.ec.gc.ca*
Idaho, *http://id.water.usgs.gov*
Montana, *http://mt.water.usgs.gov*
Oregon, *http://or.water.usgs.gov*
Washington, *http://wa.water.usgs.gov*

appendix d: sources for maps

Maps of the Northwest and Canada

Northwest Map and Travel Book Center
525 W Sprague Avenue
Spokane, WA 99201
509-455-6981
www.nwmaps.com

Topographical Maps

U.S. Geological Survey Map Sales
345 Middlefield Road
Mailstop 532
Menlo Park, CA 94025
888-275-8747
www.usgs.gov/pubprod

Specialty Maps

Kroll Map Co.
2700 Third Avenue
Seattle, WA 98121
206-448-6277
www.krollmap.com

Online and Digital Maps

www.topozone.com
www.mytopo.com
www.DeLorme.com
www.mapquest.com
www.maptech.com
http://earth.google.com

appendix e: paddling groups

American Whitewater
P.O. Box 1540
Cullowhee, NC 28723
800-262-8429
www.americanwhitewater.org

Borderline Boaters
1925 Highway 3
Christina Lake, B.C.
V0H 1E2, Canada
www.borderlineboaters.com

Desert Kayak and Canoe Club
Tri-Cities, WA
www.dkcc.org

The Mountaineers
300 3rd Avenue W
Seattle, WA 98119
www.mountaineers.org

Paddle Trails Canoe Club
P.O. Box 24932
Seattle, WA 98124
206-444-4313
www.paddletrails.org

Seattle Canoe and Kayak Club
5900 W Green Lake Way N
Seattle, WA 98103
208-684-4074
www.scn.org/rec/sckc

South Sound Area Kayakers
www.ssak.hctc.com

Spokane Canoe & Kayak Club
P.O. Box 819
Spokane, WA 99210
www.sckc.ws

Washington Kayak Club
P.O. Box 24264
Seattle, WA 98124
www.washingtonkayakclub.org

Washington Recreational River
    Runners
http://groups.yahoo.com/group/wrrr

appendix f: river and lake conservation organizations

American Rivers
1101 14th Street NW, Suite 1400
Washington, DC 20005
202-347-7550
www.americanrivers.org

American Rivers
Northwest Region Office
4005 20th Avenue W, Suite 221
Seattle, WA 98199
206-213-0330

Idaho Rivers United
P.O. Box 633
Boise, ID 83701
208-343-7481
www.idahorivers.org

National Organization for Rivers
212 W Cheyenne Mountain Boulevard
Colorado Springs, CO 80906
719-579-8759
www.nationalrivers.org

appendix g: glossary of selected paddling terms

Backpaddle To paddle backward to slow a canoe or to stop it.

Bail To remove water from a canoe with a bucket or sponge.

Bow The front end of a watercraft; opposite of stern.

Bowman The paddler in the bow of a tandem canoe.

Brace A paddle stroke used to stabilize a canoe. In a high brace, the grip hand is held high, the paddle at an angle in the water, the lower hand applying pressure against the water. In a low brace, the paddle is almost horizontal, the flat of the blade applying a downward pressure against the water.

Capsize To overturn.

Cfs Cubic feet per second, a measurement for streamflows.

Class A rating applied to a stream or section of current describing its navigability.

Confluence The point where two or more streams join.

Deadhead A piling or log, anchored below and afloat at the other end, lurking just above or just below the water surface.

Draw stroke A paddle stroke in which the flat of the blade is drawn directly toward the canoe to pull the craft to one side.

Drop A sudden pitch or unusually sharp dip in a section of rapids.

Dry suit Waterproof coveralls with snug-fitting collars for neck, arms, and ankles to prevent water from seeping in to soak insulating garments. For paddling in cold water.

Eddy Section of a current, downstream of an irregularity in the shore or a major obstruction, where the water flows upstream; often used as a rest stop.

Eddy out A 180-degree turn in direction from the main current into an eddy.

Eddyline The line between a swift downstream current and the circulating or upstream current within the eddy.

Even keel Properly trimmed to float in a level position; also describes spouse who isn't shaken by partner's poor paddling communication skills.

Falls Free-falling water over an obstruction. Heavy rapids also are called falls.

Ferry Angling the canoe so the current, striking the canoe's upstream side, drives the craft toward shore while paddling or backpaddling against the flow.

Flatwater Lake water or river section where no rapids exist. Sometimes a misnomer, since wind can create large waves on so-called flatwater.

Flotation Foam blocks or airbags used in canoes or kayaks to displace water and keep the boats afloat when capsized.

Forward stroke The basic or cruising stroke for propelling a canoe ahead.

Gauging station Streamside device that automatically measures water flow.

Grab line A rope at least 10 feet long attached to each end of a canoe for use in case of upset.

Gradient The average rate of drop in a river, generally expressed in feet per mile.

Gunwale (pronounced "gunnel") Strip along the top of a canoe's sides, extending from bow to stern, providing longitudinal rigidity.

Hull The main body of a canoe, kayak, or other water craft.

Hydraulics A term applied to the movements and forces of moving water.

Hypothermia The lowering of the body's inner core temperature as a result of exposure to cold water or air.

J stroke A stroke in which the paddle blade is thrust away from the canoe at the completion of a forward stroke, used to keep a canoe on course.

Keel Strip of molded or added material along the bottom center of a boat, running from stem to stern, designed to reinforce the hull bottom and to minimize drift and help the canoe track straight during lake paddling. A detriment in whitewater, since it interferes with maneuverability.

Lead canoe A trip leader's canoe, leading a group and selecting passages.

Lee Section of a waterway protected from the wind.

Lining Guiding a canoe downstream through rapids or shallows by means of a rope or line; opposite of tracking.

Mouth The end of a river where it enters a larger body of water. Not to be confused with "mouthy," a term bowmen often use to describe their canoe partner in the stern.

Peeling out Exiting from an eddy.

PFD Personal flotation device; a life vest.

Pivot To turn a canoe within its own length.

Poling Propelling a canoe, usually in a standing position, with a pole, either upstream or down.

Portage To carry a boat around a section of unnavigable water or between two sections of water.

Pry A paddle stroke that uses the gunwale as a fulcrum to thrust the canoe to one side.

Rapids Swiftly flowing water, tumbling among obstructions, creating considerable turbulence.

Riffles Swift, shallow water running over sand or gravel bottom, creating small waves. Could be termed gentle rapids.

River left The left side of the river as you face downstream.

River mile River length measurements starting with zero at the river's mouth and progressing upstream.

River right The right side of the river as you face downstream.

Rocker The curved bottom of kayak or canoe; rocker has opposite function of keel, making a boat more maneuverable—a consideration in choosing the right boat for the type of water.

Rock garden Navigable rock-strewn set of rapids requiring precise maneuvering.

Scout Examine a section of river or set of rapids to determine difficulty and best possible passage.

Slacker Term used to describe "the other person" in a tandem canoe when paddling into a headwind.

Slackwater Slowly flowing or still water without rapids.

Stern Rear section of a watercraft; opposite of bow.

Strainer Fallen tree or other debris with water flowing through it; potentially hazardous because it could hang up a canoe or swimmer.

Surfing In whitewater, riding the upstream side of a type of wave that breaks upstream. The hydraulics will hold or "surf" a boat in a stationary position while facing upstream. In flatwater paddling, riding downwind on the crests of large waves.

Swamp When a boat fills with water without capsizing.

Sweep boat The last canoe in a group, usually paddled by experts ready to assist those in front.

Sweep stroke A wide, shallow stroke, the blade barely submerged, used to pivot the canoe.

Thigh straps Straps attached to the side of the canoe and to the center of the bottom. When in use, they bind across a kneeling paddler's thighs, affording better control.

Throw line Length of rope used in rescue efforts.

Thwart Cross braces running from gunwale to gunwale.

Tongue A smooth V of swift water at the head of a drop or between two obstructions.

Track To paddle in a straight line.

Tracking Towing a canoe upstream with a rope; opposite of lining.

Trim The manner in which a canoe rides on the water: being level.

Tumblehome The inward curving of the sides of a canoe from a point at or slightly above the waterline to the gunwales.

Wet suit A close-fitting garment of foam sandwiched in nylon that provides insulation against cold water; allows water to seep in next to skin.

Whitewater A set of rapids.

index

Verne Huser

Doug North

Dan Hansen

Rich Landers

about the authors

Verne Huser, a professional river guide for half a century, has run more than 120 different rivers in twenty-six states (including forty-five rivers in western Washington) and three Canadian provinces. Called "the dean of river writers," Huser has written hundreds of articles and eight books about rivers including how-to and where-to books such as *Paddle Routes of Western Washington*, published by The Mountaineers Books. He also has edited an anthology of river literature, *River Reflections*. A former National Park Service ranger/naturalist, an environmental mediator, and a teacher of English, history and science, he is retired and lives in New Mexico.

Doug North, a Washington native, has been canoeing and rafting the state's rivers for more than twenty-five years. He previously published *Washington Whitewater* with The Mountaineers Books, a guide to thirty-four whitewater river trips. North lives in Seattle with his wife, Lorrie, and children, Allison and Peter. He also hikes, climbs, and cross-country skis, as well as being active in river conservation.

Dan Hansen grew up fishing for salmon in Puget Sound and hiking in the foothills of the Washington Cascades. Since 1987, he has worked for *The Spokesman-Review* newspaper, currently as an editor. Dan previously reported on natural resource issues, and is remembered by many newspaper readers for exploring 420 miles of the Columbia River in a 13-foot inflatable boat. Dan is co-author of *Paddle Routes of the Inland Northwest*, published by The Mountaineers Books. His work has also appeared in *Canoe & Kayak* magazine. He and his wife, Pam, live near Spokane in Millwood, with their children, Kelly and Kyle.

Rich Landers, a native Montanan and the Outdoors editor for *The Spokesman-Review* in Spokane since 1977, has paddled waters from Baja to the Arctic National Wildlife Refuge and from Maine to the estuaries of Puget Sound. He is the co-author of *Paddle Routes of the Inland Northwest* and a contributing writer for *Field & Stream* magazine. His job and various interests have taken him climbing up Mount McKinley, bicycling across the United States, and researching and authoring *100 Hikes in the Inland Northwest*, also published by The Mountaineers Books. He lives in Spokane with his wife, Meredith, and their daughters, Brook and Hillary.

THE MOUNTAINEERS, founded in 1906, is a nonprofit outdoor activity and conservation club, whose mission is "to explore, study, preserve, and enjoy the natural beauty of the outdoors. . . . " Based in Seattle, Washington, the club is now the third-largest such organization in the United States, with seven branches throughout Washington State.

The Mountaineers sponsors both classes and year-round outdoor activities in the Pacific Northwest, which include hiking, mountain climbing, ski-touring, snowshoeing, bicycling, camping, kayaking, nature study, sailing, and adventure travel. The club's conservation division supports environmental causes through educational activities, sponsoring legislation, and presenting informational programs.

All club activities are led by skilled, experienced instructors, who are dedicated to promoting safe and responsible enjoyment and preservation of the outdoors.

If you would like to participate in these organized outdoor activities or the club's programs, consider a membership in The Mountaineers. For information and an application, write or call The Mountaineers, Club Headquarters, 300 Third Avenue West, Seattle, WA 98119; 206-284-6310. You can also visit the club's website at www.mountaineers.org or contact The Mountaineers via email at clubmail@mountaineers.org.

The Mountaineers Books, an active, nonprofit publishing program of the club, produces guidebooks, instructional texts, historical works, natural history guides, and works on environmental conservation. All books produced by The Mountaineers Books fulfill the club's mission.

Send or call for our catalog of more than 500 outdoor titles:

The Mountaineers Books
1001 SW Klickitat Way, Suite 201
Seattle, WA 98134
800-553-4453
mbooks@mountaineersbooks.org
www.mountaineersbooks.org

The Mountaineers Books is proud to be a corporate sponsor of The Leave No Trace Center for Outdoor Ethics, whose mission is to promote and inspire responsible outdoor recreation through education, research, and partnerships. The Leave No Trace program is focused specifically on human-powered (nonmotorized) recreation.

Leave No Trace strives to educate visitors about the nature of their recreational impacts, as well as offer techniques to prevent and minimize such impacts. Leave No Trace is best understood as an educational and ethical program, not as a set of rules and regulations.

For more information, visit *www.LNT.org,* or call 800-332-4100.

OTHER TITLES YOU MIGHT ENJOY FROM THE MOUNTAINEERS BOOKS

Soggy Sneakers: A guide to Oregon Rivers, 4th ed.
Willamette Kayak & Canoe Club
The go-to guide for canoeing, kayaking, and rafting in Oregon

Digital Photography Outdoors, 2nd ed.
James Martin
"A great all-in-one reference"
—*Digital Photography* magazine

Afoot and Afloat: Seattle's Lakes, Bays and Waterways
Marge and Ted Mueller
Urban boat travel in the Emerald City!

The Outdoor Knots Book
Clyde Soles
" . . . not to be missed if you're an outdoors person"
—Los Angeles Daily News

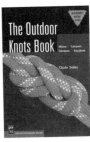

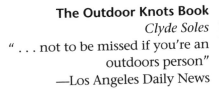

Birdsongs of the Pacific Northwest: A field guide and audio CD
Stewart, Whitney & Briars
Become a Northwest bird expert—by sight and sound!

Spirited Waters: Soloing South Through the Inside Passage
Jennifer Hahn
Unforgettable story of a solo kayaking adventure